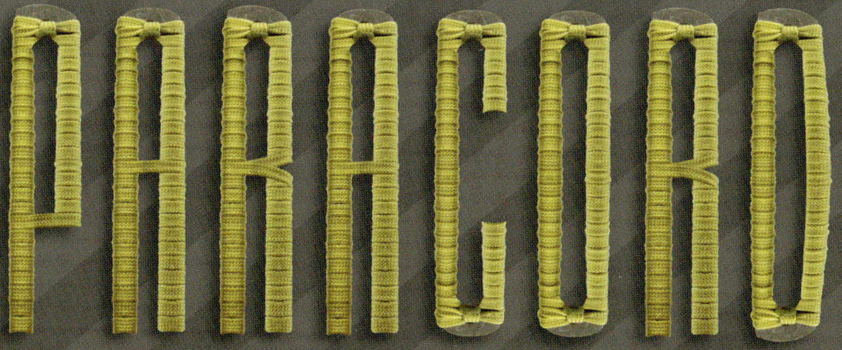

KNIFE HANDLE WRAPS

THE COMPLETE GUIDE from Tactical to Asi

JAN DOX

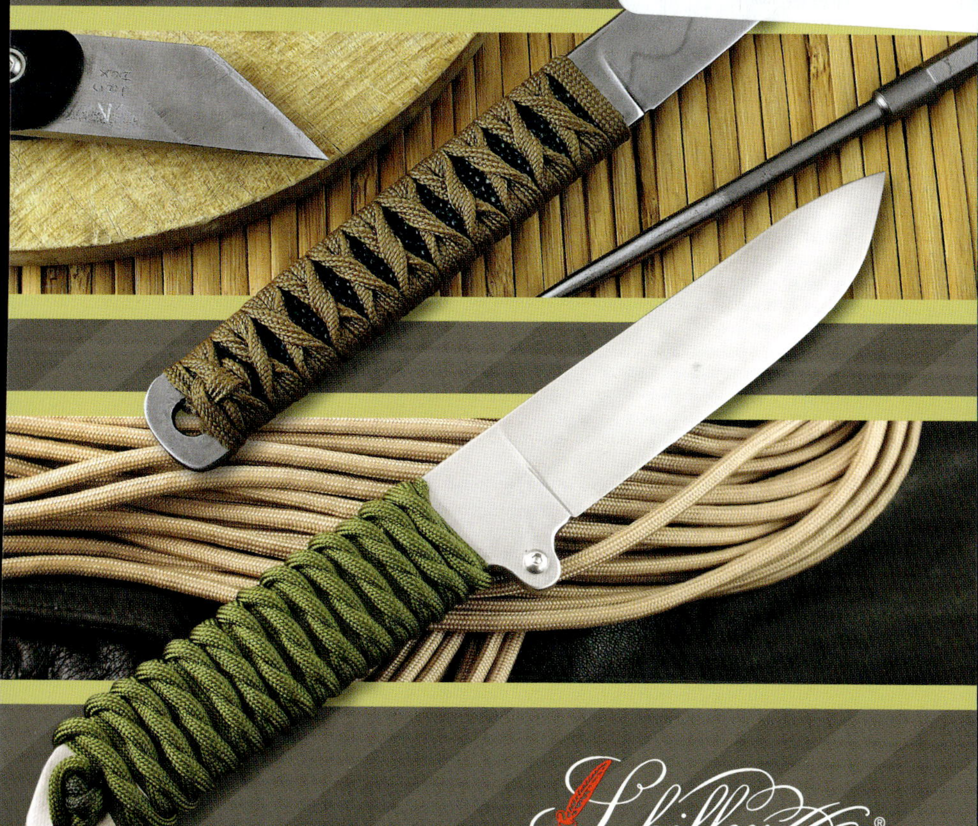

Schiffer Publishing Ltd
4880 Lower Valley Road • Atglen, PA 19310

CONTENTS

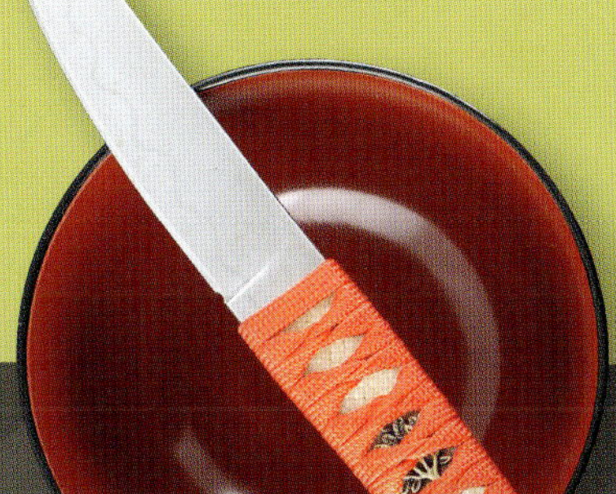

A FEW WORDS UP FRONT

Knife handle paracord wraps are especially poular with survival knives because of their practical advantages: these handles rest comfortably in the hand, they are slip-proof, and are not sensitive to moisture and temperature fluctuations. In case of emergency, the wrap can also be taken off and used as a rope for many purposes.

To a large extent the techniques used for such handle wraps have their origins in Japan and China, but in Europe in the Middle Ages most daggers and swords also had handles wrapped with leather or wire, so this concept is time tested. Today, modern paracord has replaced classic materials such as cotton, silk, or leather.

Not only handmade knives can be provided with paracord handle wraps; many knives manufactured in series can also be retrofitted with such a handle and thus be "pimped." This opens up a new scope for knife enthusiasts who do not want to make an entirely new knife from scratch, but only want to optimize an existing one, so a handle wrap of paracord can be an easy entry into the hobby of knifemaking.

The author of this book is one of few designated handle wrap experts in Europe. Jan Dox has dealt with this topic for more than thirty years and has collected a large treasure of knowledge and even more practical experience. Part of this knowledge he now transfers to you.

This series of books assembles a multitude of themes around knifemaking in such a way to enable you not only to follow each step, but to do it yourself. We especially emphasize the usability of all the volumes in workshop practice.

Thus, all the volumes are provided with a wire binding. This way the book stays open when you put it down. Also, we took care that the size of images and fonts is large enough to still be recognizable and readable when the book is lying next to you during work.

We have tried to explain every work step in the most comprehensive way, but before you pick up your tools, you nevertheless ought to completely read all the descriptions and explanations in this book. This way, you will know what to expect and will not be confronted with unpleasant surprises later. By means of the materials and tools lists you can put together what you need in advance.

I wish you much fun and success with your work.

Hans Joachim Wieland
Chief Editor
MESSER MAGAZIN

PREFACE

During my youth I started to work with knives and ropes. In various youth groups—similar to the Boy Scouts—I enjoyed this work outdoors together with others. We used a lot of hemp ropes and our knives to build our camps. In those days almost nobody knew anything about knives whose handles were wrapped with paracord. From 1984–1985, while serving in the Belgian paratrooper command, we did not have parachute cords (paracords) at our disposal, instead using 3 mm-thick black and olive green nylon cords.

Parachute cords might not be the strongest cords when comparing strength to diameter with other ropes on the market, but their resilience, combined with their structure and elasticity, make them enormously versatile, as well as popular. Paracord has been available in a multitude of colors for a few years and many hobbyists have discovered this material. Some books have already been written about knots, bars, woven cords (called sennits, or sometimes sinnets), and fusion ties, but only a few about wrapping knife handles.

Japanese style knives are one of my favorite knifemaking topics. *Tsukamaki*, the art of wrapping sword handles, is a very interesting area. I will show you some of the *tsukamaki* techniques for use with modern paracord.

Wrapping knife handles is no strict science. I try to introduce you to this wonderful world by means of this book. Be creative! I hope you will enjoy this book as much as I have enjoyed writing it.

Jan Dox

CREDITS

My knowledge and experience with ropes and knives was gained during several decades of trial and error, talks, tests, and practical use. I have discovered that knowledge is shared generously in the world of knifemakers. There are a number of knifemakers whom I want to thank for all their help throughout the years:

- my friends and knifemaker comrades for the tips, commentaries, and encouragement they gave me: Achim Wirtz, Alessio Salsi, Bart Weys, Christophe Verstappen, Filip De Leeuw, Gert van den Elsen, Jacques Delfosse, Pavel and Katharina Rihacek, Rémy B., Tim Wagendorp, and many more.

- Geert Willaert of the International Guild of Knot Tyers (IGKT)

- Don Fogg, a former knife- and swordsmith, who has shared a huge mountain of knowledge about *tsukamaki* and forging techniques on his website, in forums, and seminars.

- Vince and Grace Evans, who helped me more than a decade ago with traditional Chinese wrappings (www.picturetrail.com/evans).

- Nigel Coffi of paracord.nl for convincing me to start working on this book and for his support.

- my customers for their resonance to my work.

- my wife Marie-Claire and my children for the patience they had while I was working on this project.

SAFETY TIPS

In this book we will deal with various techniques used for wrapping knife handles with paracord. Please take into account that blades have sharp cutting edges and tips. While wrapping a knife handle we have to hold the knife more often at its cutting edge than we would prefer. Always protect the blade with tape or a combination of paper, cloth, and tape! Most times I use masking tape. For delicate blades with hamon or hardening line I use a combination of paper tissue and masking tape.

We will also use superglue (cyanoacrylate), epoxy, and other resins. Always use protective goggles and gloves! Cyanoacrylate can glue your fingers or eyelids together in a matter of seconds. If one drop of epoxy gets in your eye it is almost impossible to remove it again. It is a very bad idea to rinse your eye with acetone! Epoxy can cause allergic reactions; some react instantaneously, while others develop an epoxy allergy only after years of use. A well-vented workroom is a necessity.

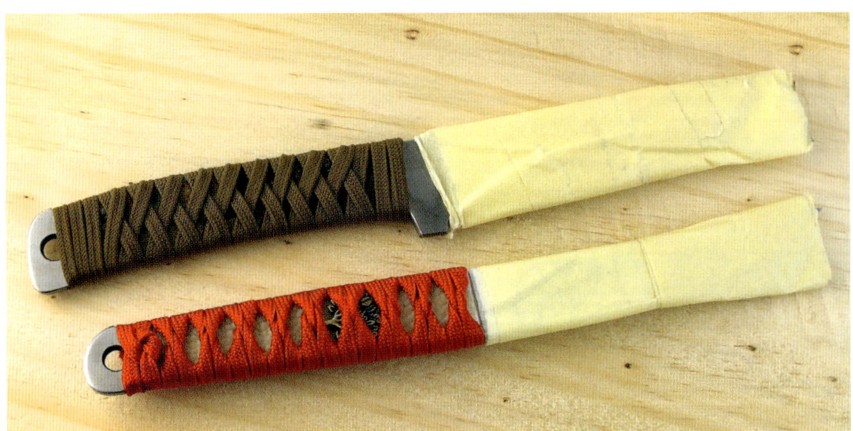

Two knives with a paper and masking tape blade protector.

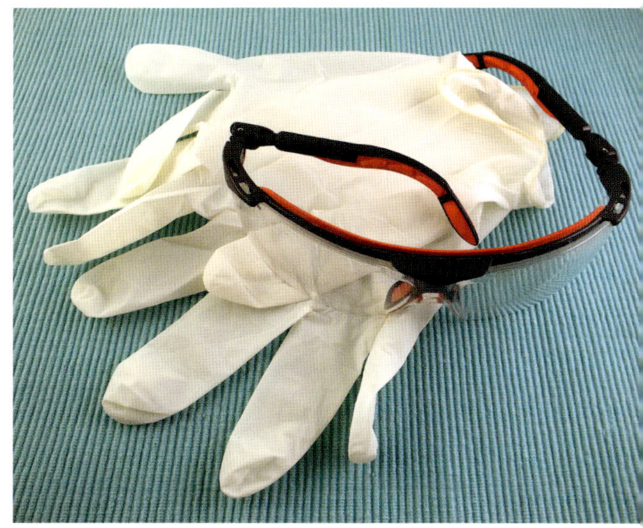

Disposable vinyl gloves (or better butylene or nitrile) and protective goggles are mandatory for work with synthetic resin.

Vinyl gloves can't be used, but disposable latex gloves offer just enough resistance to epoxy and other resins for working comfortably, and they last a while. Resistance to acetone is usually less, so be careful in case you use acetone to clean your tools; a stable container or glass jar is recommended.

Sometimes I use more than one pair of gloves while working on a knife handle. Since contact with resin is limited when you impregnate a handle, latex is sufficient if you replace the gloves regularly. If you have really intense contact with epoxy and acetone during work, gloves of a higher protective material such as butylene or nitrile gloves of sufficient thickness, are necessary.

PARACORD

1.1 What Is Paracord?

Paracord is a nylon cord consisting of a core with several strings made from two to three strands each and an outer woven sleeve that protects the cord from rubbing through. This kind of cord has been used intensively by the military since World War II. Paracord is used to connect the harness with the parachute canopy. After landing, soldiers often cut the connecting lines and used the cords for almost everything.

Military standard Mil-C-5040H describes the specifications of different paracord types for military use. The choice of colors is limited. Because of paracord's success during the last few decades, manufacturers have started production of commercial paracord of the same lengths and thicknesses as military types but without the expensive tests and regulations. Commercial paracord is often made of nylon cord which is not pre-shrunk, as is the yarn for military paracord.

The following paracord types are available in more than eighty different colors in military and commercial versions. Type III is the most often used and also the most well-known of these types.

- 750 paracord type IV (5 mm) with a breaking strength of at least 750 lbs. (American pounds, 1 lb. = 0.454 kg.). The core inside the sleeve consists of eleven strings with three strands each.

- 550 paracord type III (3.5 to 4 mm): minimum breaking strength 550 lbs. The core consists of seven strings with three strands each. Some manufacturers produce it with seven to nine strings with two strands each.

QUALITIES ACCORDING TO MILITARY AND COMMERCIAL STANDARDS

	type I	type IA	type II	type IIA	commercial type III	military type III	type IV
name used by suppliers	100	100	400	225	550	550	750
breaking strength, minimum in pounds (lbs)	95	100	400	225	550	550	750
breaking strength, minimum in kilograms (kg)	43	45	181	102	249	249	340
elongation (%), minimum	30	30	30	30	30	30	30
length per pound of cord in feet (ft), minimum	950	1050	265	495	225	225	165
length per pound of cord in meters (m), minimum	290	320	81	151	69	69	50
core strings	4–7	none	4–7	none	7–9	7 (rarely 8–9)	11
number of strands per string	2 or 3	—	2 or 3	—	2 or 3	3	3

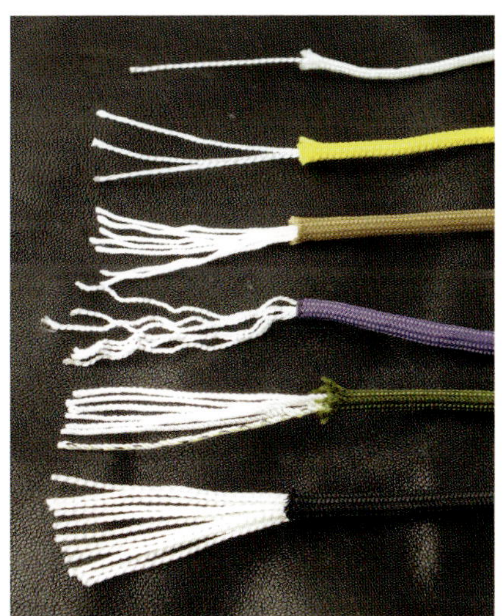

From bottom to top: black paracord type IV, green according to military standard type III, purple and coyote brown commercial type III, yellow type II, and silver type I.

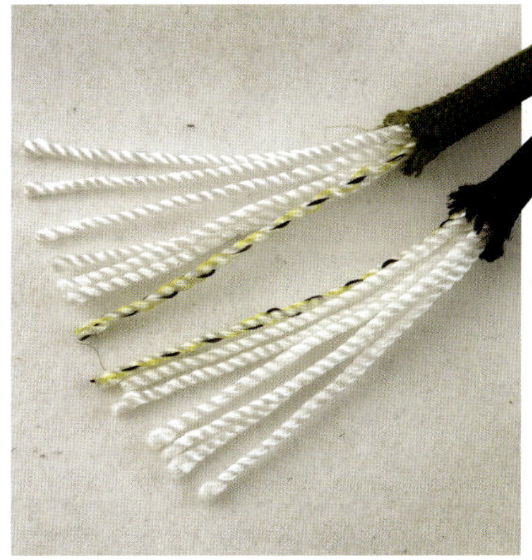

Two different colors produced by the same manufacturer according to military standard. Both have the same core fiber.

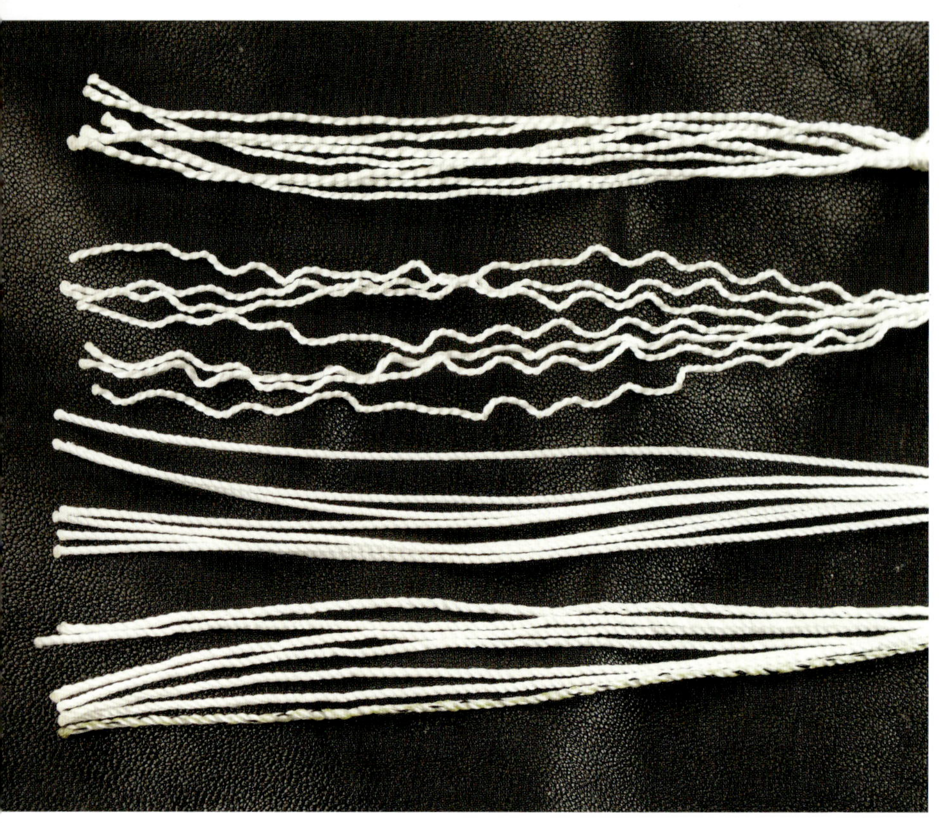

The strings in the core can be very different. From top to bottom: three sets of commercial strings and one set of strings according to military standard.

IMPORTANT PARACORD MEASUREMENTS

	type I	type IA	type II	type IIA	commercial type III	military type III	type IV
diameter of full cord, mm	1.9	n/a	3	n/a	3.5	3.9	3.5
width of empty sleeve (flatline), mm	2.2	n/a	3	n/a	4	4.5	4
thickness full cord on handle, mm	1.7	n/a	2.2	n/a	2.6	2.4	2.6
thickness flatline on handle, mm	0.9	n/a	1.1 to 1.2	n/a	1	1	1

- Mil-C-5040H type III (3.5 mm): minimum breaking strength 550 lbs. Core of seven strings with three strands each. One of the seven strings has one or more different colors than the others. This is specific for each manufacturer and enables tracing the manufacturer. According to my experience, paracord manufactured according to military standards is often stronger, more beautiful, and more roundly shaped than commercial paracord.

- 400 paracord type II (approx. 3 mm) has a breaking strength of at least 400 lbs. (181 kg) with a core of four to six strings. Some suppliers offer paracord similar to type II which they call 425 or 450.

- 100 paracord type I (approx. 2 mm) with a breaking strength of at least 100 lbs. (45 kg) and a single string as core.

There are more types of paracord available, such as 650 paracord. This parachute cord has a diameter of 4.76 mm (³⁄₁₆ inch) with four strings on the inside and a breaking strength of at least 400 lbs. (181 kg). It is broader and flatter than cords of types II and III and has no counterpart in the military. It is well suited for a number of weaving tasks. Caution: some suppliers sell the outer sleeve of 650 paracord with a breaking strength of only 325 lbs. If in doubt ask to make sure that the parachute cord has the desired qualities.

I will show you the use of different paracord types as full cord as well as "flatline," referring to the empty sleeve. The manufacturers of commercial paracord make the sleeves wider or more slim. Some weave them tighter than others. Generally, the sleeves of type IV are the widest at 5 mm. Then follows type III (4 or 4.5 mm), type II (3 mm), and type I (2.2 mm). The thickness of the empty sleeve ranges between 0.9 and 1.2 mm depending on the manufacturer.

1.2 Measuring the Cord

To measure the width of paracord, it is easiest to make ten turns around a broomstick and to measure the result in centimeters. This gives almost exactly the measurements of full cord or empty sleeve in millimeters.

To determine the thickness of the wrapped cord, we wind it around a broomstick and measure the diameter of the cord on its outside. Subtract the broomstick's diameter and you get the thickness of a single paracord layer. Half this value is the thickness of one cord or an empty sleeve under tension.

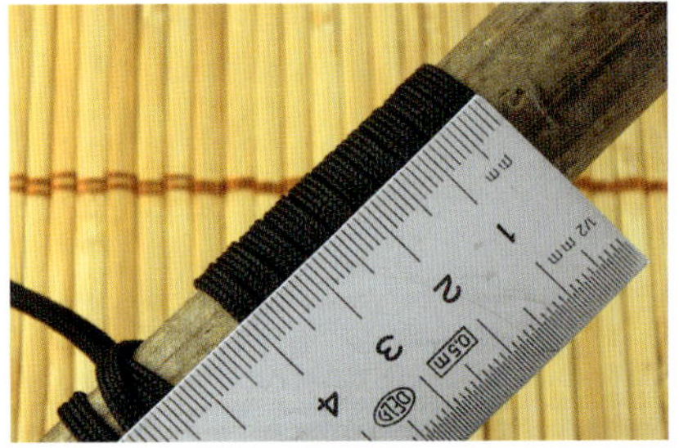

We measure the length of ten turns around the broomstick.

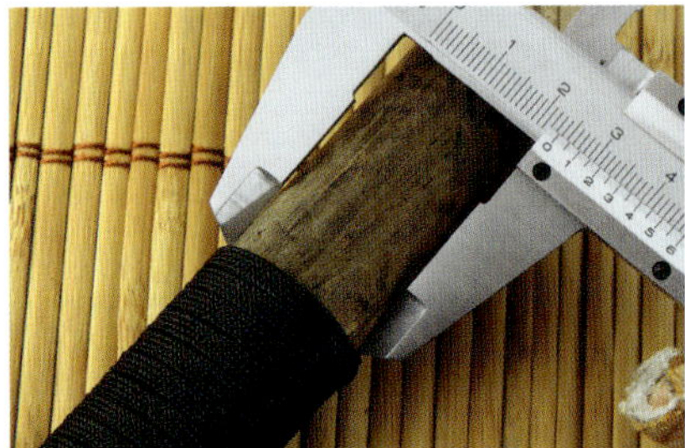

Measuring the cord: measure the diameter of the broomstick.

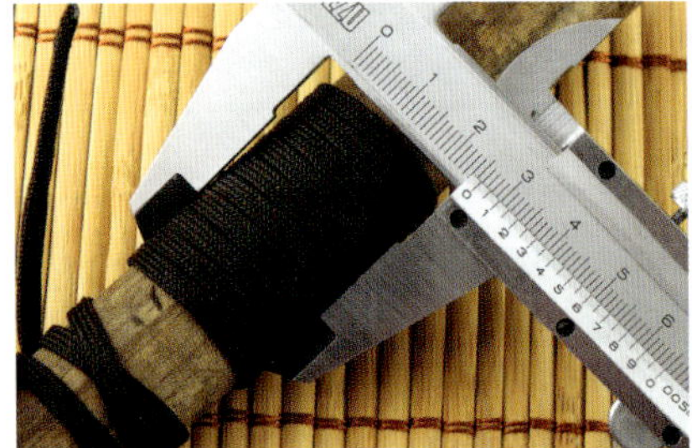

Measuring the thickness of the cord: subtract the diameter of the stick and divide the result by two to get the thickness of the paracord wrap.

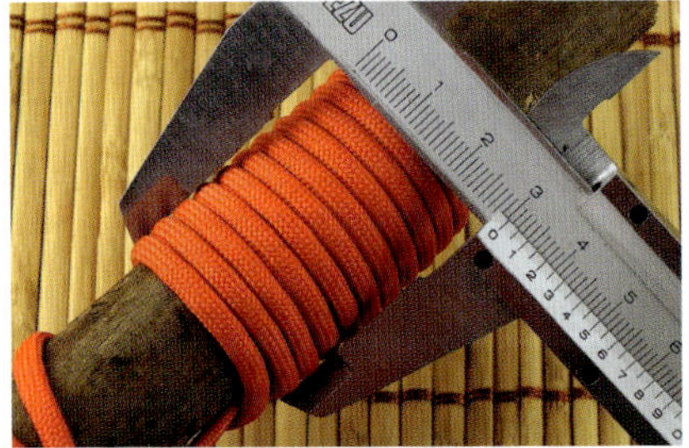

Measuring the thickness of full paracord.

In my test I achieved the following results for full paracord on a broomstick:

    type IV: thickness 3.25 mm
    type III: thickness 2.6 mm
    type II: thickness 2.2 mm
    type I: thickness 1.7 mm

1.3 Shrinking Factor of Paracord

Paracord is made of nylon fibers and shrinks when it is wet. The shrinking factor of commercial paracord is about ten to twenty percent. Military paracord has to be woven from pre-shrunk nylon yarn. The core yarns have to be shrunk in wet conditions for at least sixty minutes at a temperature of 199.4°F (93°C) (+/- 3°C). After this time span they have to be dried at a temperature no higher than 93°C prior to manufacturing the core.

Sleeve yarns have to be shrunk wet at a temperature of 159.8°F (71°C) (+/- 37.4°F [3°C]) for at least thirty minutes. After this period they have to be dried at a temperature which is not to exceed 159.8°F (71°C).

For bracelets, belts, and a number of other things made of paracord, size is important. A bracelet that inhibits blood circulation after a swim is definitely not a good thing, and a braided band which looks warped or crooked after a swim is not much better.

For knife handles, where tighter is often better, subsequent shrinking may even be advantageous. Nevertheless, be careful if you use different paracord types at the same time, because the different shrinking factors may influence the look of the wrap!

Shrinking of the empty sleeve with a wrap in Japanese style can lead to the cord's shrinking at the handle edges and cause openings between the parts of the cord. To avoid these openings it is important to push the turns close enough to each other.

I tested different cords made according to military specs as well as commercial paracord of various suppliers. A number of test pieces were cut to a length of 19 $^{11}/_{16}$ in. (50 cm). A shrinking factor of ten percent with this length of cord means shrinking by 1 $^{31}/_{32}$ in. (five centimeters).

The first test was to put the pieces of cord into a pot containing hot water (approximately 203°F [95°C]). I left the cords in the cooling water for about twenty minutes. The dyed commercial cords shrank between eight and twelve percent during this process; most of the values were between nine and ten percent (average value 9.8 percent). The military cords shrank a good deal less than the commercial cords: a khaki military cord only shrank by 1.6 percent, while a white commercial one shrank by 3.5 percent.

In a second shrinkage test I tested full cord as well as empty sleeves and cords according to military specifications as well as commercial cords. For a brutal shrinkage test the cords were boiled for ten minutes. The military cords shrank much less than the commercial cords. The military cord of one manufacturer only shrank by 1.6 percent, the empty sleeve by about 2.5 percent. The commercial paracord shrank by an astonishing sixteen percent.

The difference between full cord and their empty sleeves was about one percent. Camouflage cord has a tendency to warp because dark colors shrink distinctly more than lighter ones.

Some suppliers suggest boiling the cord for ten to fifteen seconds and taking it out of the water afterward to dry between the folds of a towel or in a garment bag in a dryer.

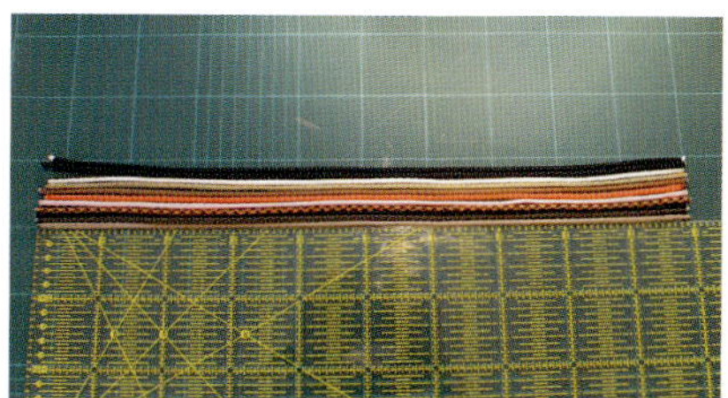

For the test, different cords were shortened to a length of 19 ¹¹⁄₁₆ in. (50 cm) (samples were provided by paracord.de).

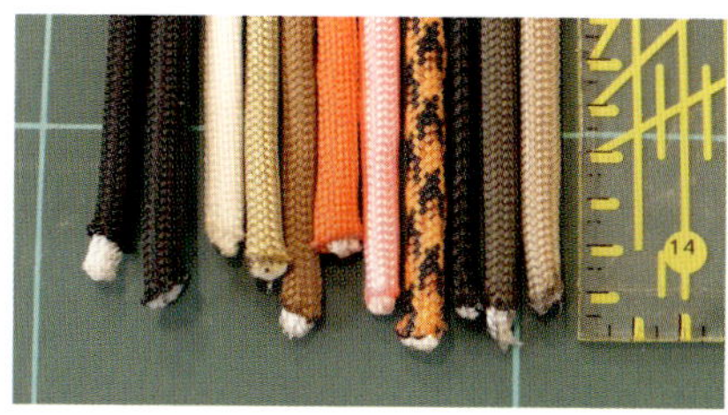

The cord pieces are slightly different in length. The differences are noted.

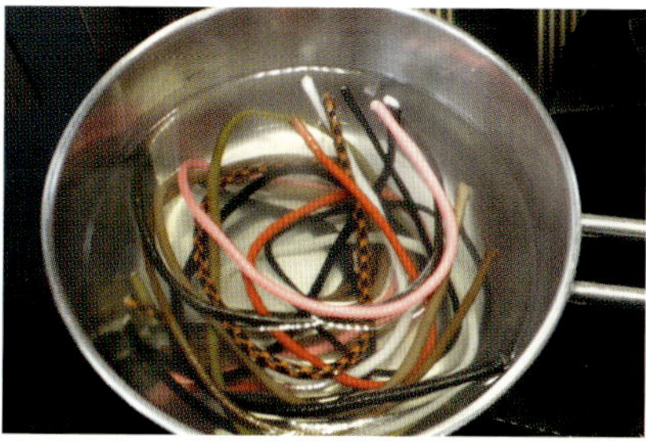

The cords lie in hot water for twenty minutes.

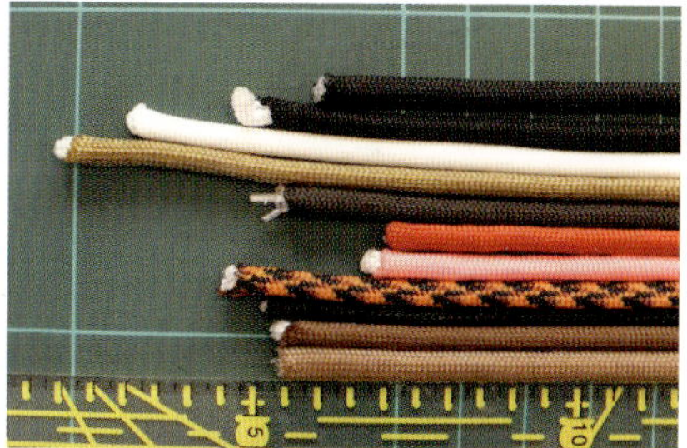

After the shrinking test the cord pieces show distinct differences in length.

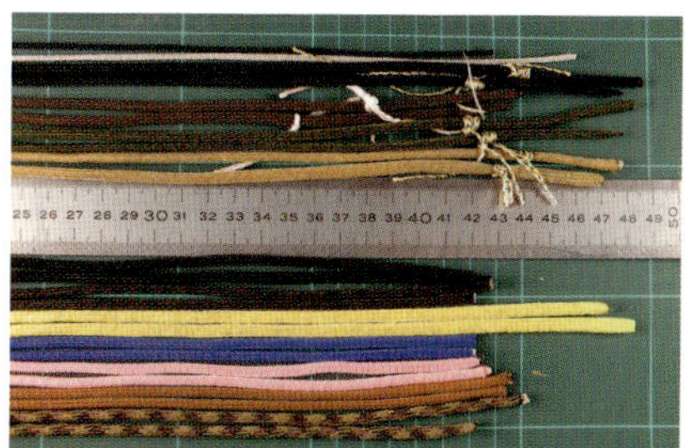

Brutal shrinking test: the result after ten minutes in boiling water. For military cords the identifying core strings are attached on the outside.

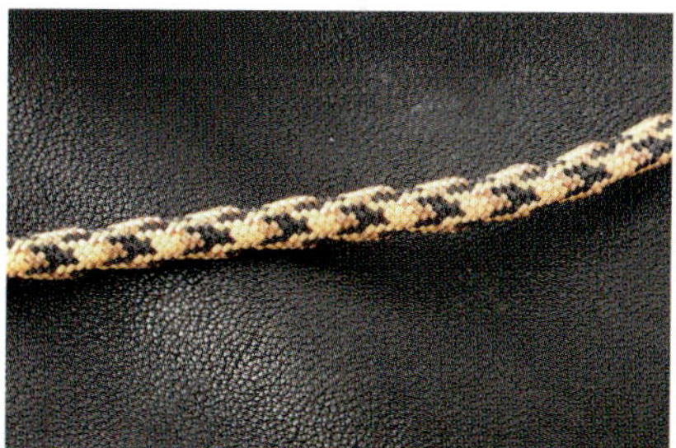

This camouflage colored cord was warping after the test. The black yarn shrank to a distinctly larger extent than the brighter colors.

In any case, if you make things for which exact size is important, do a shrinkage test with full cord as well as empty sleeve before you measure the paracord and cut the required length.

COLOR TEST

As a test, I soaked some samples in two-component epoxy resin. This is a slightly amber colored resin mixture which can darken a bit over time. In the first case dark blue changed to almost black. Neon colors stayed light, but lost their "neon" factor. White became semi-translucent and yellow became somewhat more bright.

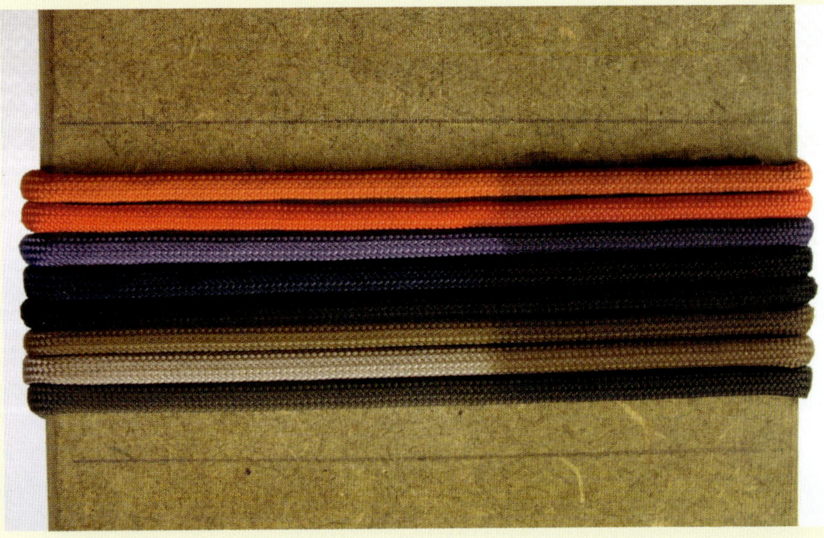

A color test reveals the darkening of the impregnated cord. From top to bottom: orange, red, purple, midnight blue, black, coyote brown, desert tan, and dark olive green.

1.4 Color Change When Impregnating with Resin

For a number of uses we will seal a wrapped handle either completely or partially with resin. The resin makes the colors darker and can drastically change "neon" properties. With black paracord the changes are minimal, medium dark colors such as purple can become almost black, and light colors can either be enhanced or change so much that the completed product looks totally different.

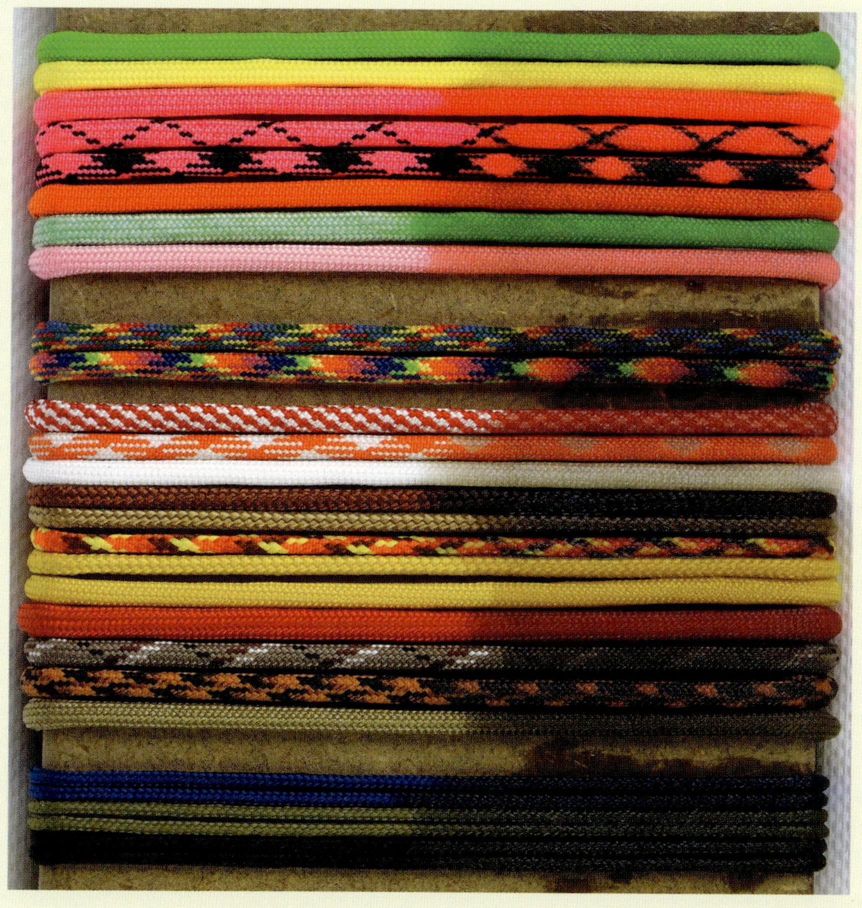

BASICS

To show the different techniques, I made a number of handle dummies. They are made of steel and have the dimensions 4 x 20 and 4 x 25 millimeters. The length is eleven centimeters, measured from the pommel to the end of the hole, the place where the guard would be on a real knife. The holes have a diameter of six millimeters – large enough for at least one empty sleeve and two full parachute cords to be led through without difficulties.

A wrapped handle feels pleasant and provides a comfortable grip for your hand. Depending on the kind of wrap, the paracord can be taken off the handle easily in order to use it in an emergency.

Older or damaged knives can be brought to new life, if the old handle is replaced by a wrap. In case you change the profile of the tang, it may be easier to accommodate the wrap. In many cases the handle contour can be ground down or filed down in order to make room for a wrap. Sometimes it is sufficient to completely saw off the handle and to remove the first ten to twelve centimeters of the cutting edge on the blade by means of a grinding machine in order to create a tang suitable for a cord wrap. The first knife I reanimated in this

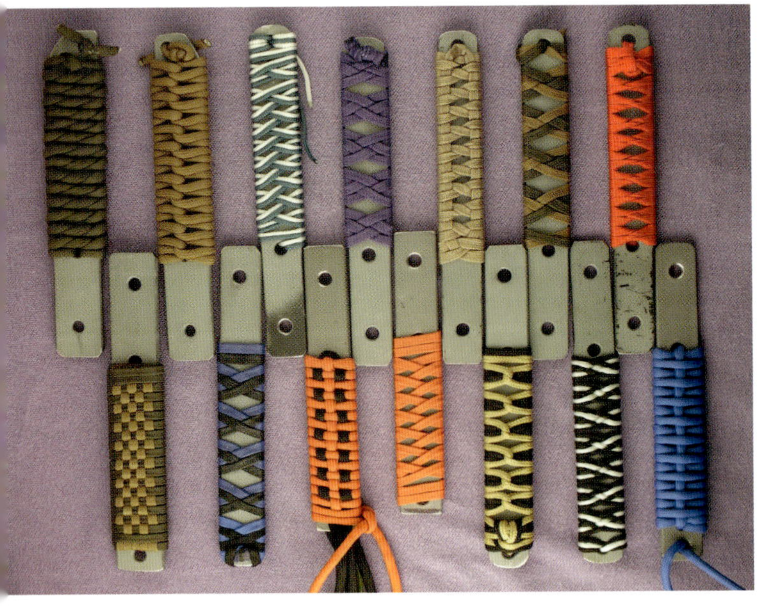

Made especially for the examples in this book: flat steel handle dummies four millimeters thick.

way was an old bread knife which I reground into a Scottish sgian dubh. I wrapped the handle with black cotton cord over red cotton cord. Then I soaked it in polyester resin from a car repair set in order to impregnate it. This was 1986. The inspiration for this came from an article about late knifemaker Phill Hartsfield.

When planning a paracord handle the following things have to be taken into account:

- Is the wrapped handle supposed to be full-size, which means considerable forces can be applied?

- Do we need a basic layer of cord to enhance the volume of the handle?

- Should a decorative basic layer be visible through the gaps of the handle wrap?

- Should the cord be available in case of an emergency?

- Is the knife going to get dirty? How high are the chances it will get soaked with gasoline? In this case, would it be possible to remove the dirty cord and rewrap the handle?

- Is the knife used to gut or prepare animals? Is it used for cooking?

- Is the knife used in maritime surroundings? Is it stainless? If the handle wrap becomes wet will the knife rust underneath?

- Is the knife carried around the neck or hidden somewhere on the body? Excessive amounts of sweat can cause a lot of corrosion.

- Are holes drilled into the handle to save weight or to pull the cord through them?

If a knife tang ought to be wrapped it is necessary to adapt existing holes to the planned wrapping or to drill new holes. It is important that the holes are of proper diameter so that the desired number of cord pieces can be pulled through properly. At the same time, the holes should not be too large so no knots can be pulled through and the wrap looks as

THE QUESTION OF HOLE SIZE

The following list shows what fits through a drill hole of a particular diameter taking **paracord type III** as an example.

hole diameter ⅛ in. (3.5 mm):
- one complete cord or
- one loop of the empty sleeve (pulled through by means of one string out of the cord's core)

hole diameter 0.1654 in. (4.2 mm):
- 2 × an empty sleeve (flatline) with the end of each cord formed to a tip by melting and pulled through with a string
- one loop of the complete paracord pulled through using a string and pliers
- one complete cord with melted tip (moves through the hole easily)

hole diameter 0.187 in. (4.75 mm):
- 3 × an empty sleeve
- loop of one complete paracord pulled through using a string and pliers
- 1 complete paracord plus a second one with pointed end pulled through with pliers (the core is removed for the last inch; the sleeve is melted and formed to a thin tip)

neat as possible. The most important holes are usually the one next to the blade, where we start the winding, and the one at the pommel, where we end the winding. It is very frustrating to realize at the end of the work that the holes are either too small or too large. Generally the holes ought to be between 0.217 and 0.244 in. (5.5 and 6.2 mm) in diameter.

hole diameter 0.1969 in. (5.0 mm):
- 3 × an empty sleeve
- one loop of complete paracord pulled through using a string without pliers
- empty sleeve + full paracord + full paracord with pointed end (difficult)

hole diameter 0.2047 in. (5.2 mm):
- if a complete cord is already in the hole, an additional sleeve (with pointed end) can be pulled through the hole with pliers or a long nail

hole diameter 0.2165 in. (5.5 mm):
- two complete cords with pointed ends are no problem if the sides of the hole are beveled or rounded like the rivets of a kydex sheath

hole diameter 0.2362 in. (6.0 mm):
- two complete cords plus one additional cord with a pointed end can be squeezed through the hole using a nail or pliers
- two complete cords with pointed ends can be led easily and without problems through the hole using your hand

hole diameter 0.244 in. (6.2 mm):
- two complete and pointed paracords plus a third full paracord with pointed end are possible with the help of a long nail and pliers
- this diameter has the advantage that mosaic pins up to 0.236 in. (6 mm) in diameter can be used for decoration

With drill holes having diameters of 6.0 mm, 6.1 mm, 6.2 mm, 6.3 mm (¼ in.) or 6.5 mm, we can make a thin wrap as a basic layer and pull an empty sleeve and the two full paracord ends through the hole to make the final knots. This is done with handle wraps in military style.

If paracord 425 with a 3 mm diameter is used, a loop can be pulled through a 4.25 mm diameter drill hole using a core string. If a 3 mm paracord is already in the hole, a second full paracord can be pulled through with needle-nosed pliers or a long nail. This also works for other 3 mm (⅛ in.) nylon cords with "firm" inside and sleeve.

For Japanese handle wraps, I often use large 9.5 mm diameter drill holes at the pommel, depending on the kind of end knot and wrap. For traditional Japanese end knots a 4 mm hole can be sufficient, because only two sleeves have to go through the hole. If you shape the hole slightly oval then you can also push the sleeves through flat, which makes things easier. In this case the drill hole looks like a traditional hole through the *kashira* (the pommel cap).

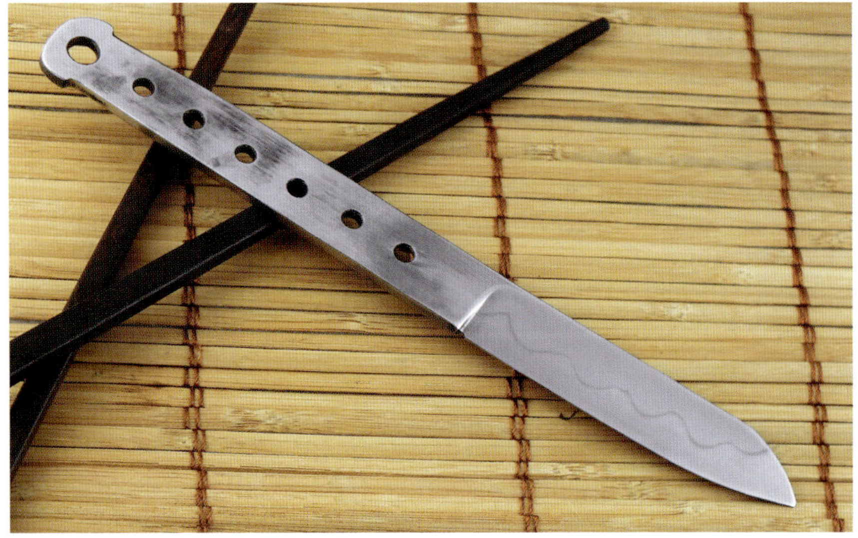

Blade for a *tsukamaki* with *hamon* (hardening line). The pommel is shaped in such a way that it imitates a *kashira*.

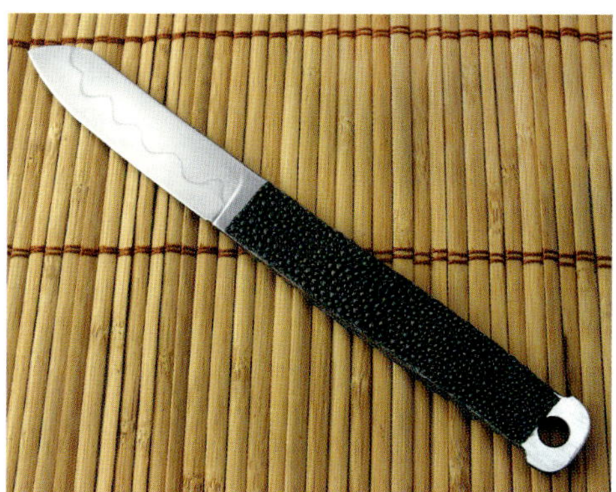

The ray skin was glued to the tang by means of double-sided industrial adhesive tape.

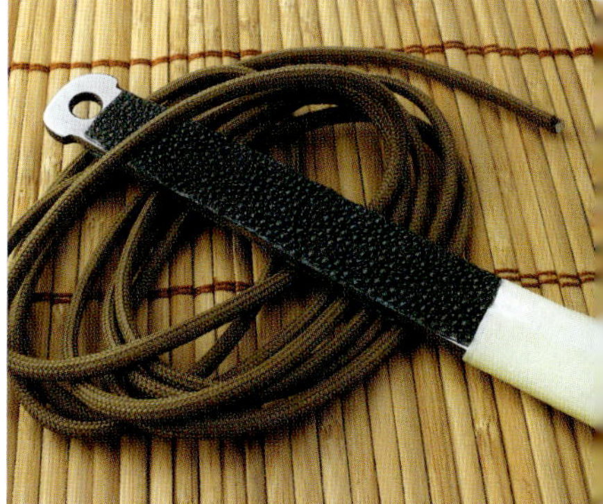

The blade is covered with paper tissue and adhesive tape. The cord is cut to the proper length and can now be "gutted."

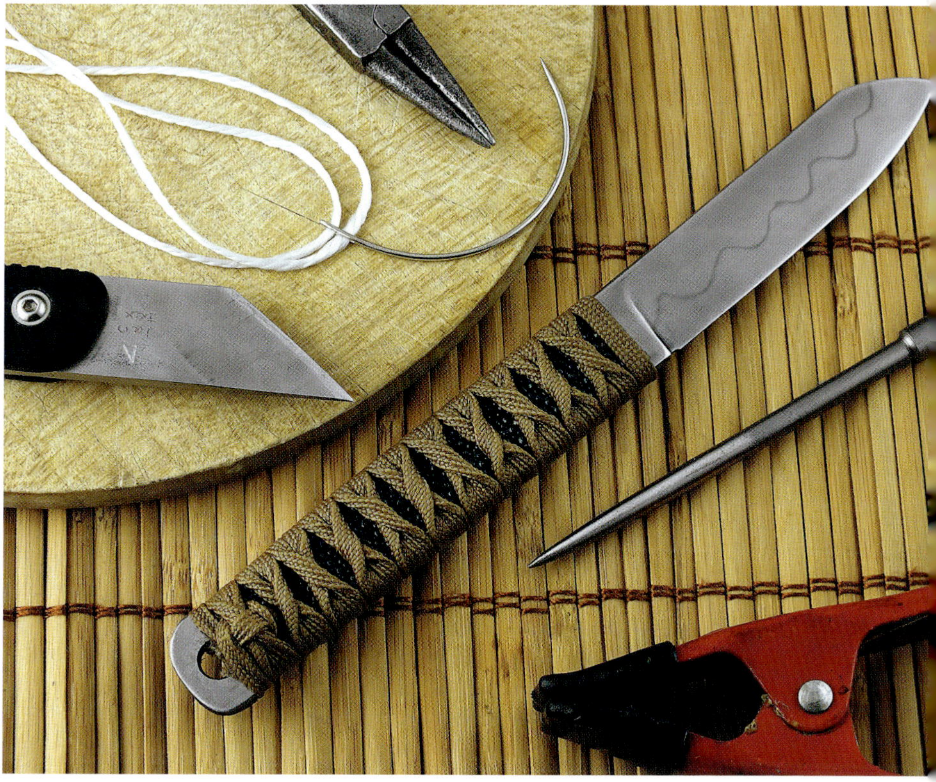

A finished Japanese utility knife: the tools used for its production are lying next to it.

While the handle is being wrapped it can be difficult to prevent the paracord from slipping forward or backward off the handle. Different ways exist for keeping the paracord in position using small file work at the sides of the handle:

- The side of the tang can be filed or ground in such a way to create a ridge over which the cord can't slide. Make sure this ridge is not higher than the thickness of the paracord because it may cut your hand.

- A number of round notches of suitable diameter can be made with a file—either next to each other or evenly spaced, similar to "thumb notches." The file should be between 3.2 mm and 4.8 mm diameter. The depth of the notches and the distance between them are chosen in accordance with the file's diameter to optimize the distance between turns of the wrap.

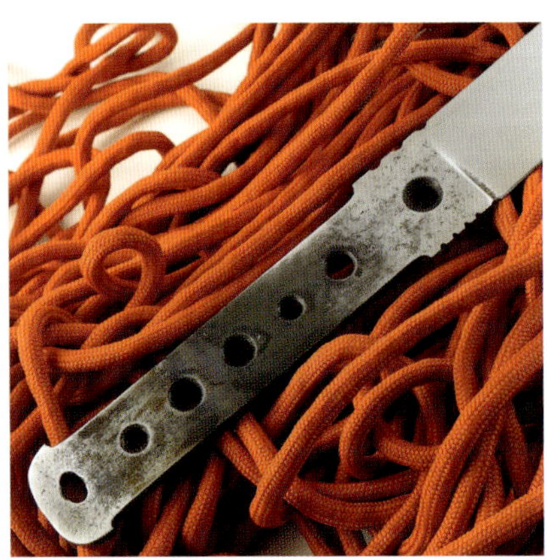

You can create a ridge at the front and rear ends of the handle. This way the paracord can't slip from the handle.

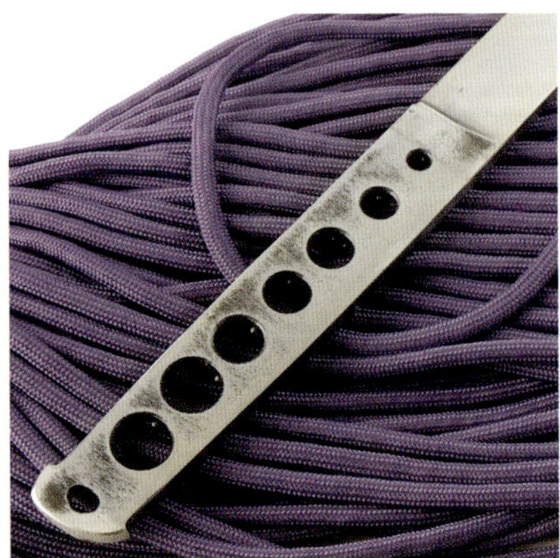

If you make the handle slimmer and leave a ridge, the ridge will hold the cord in place on the handle.

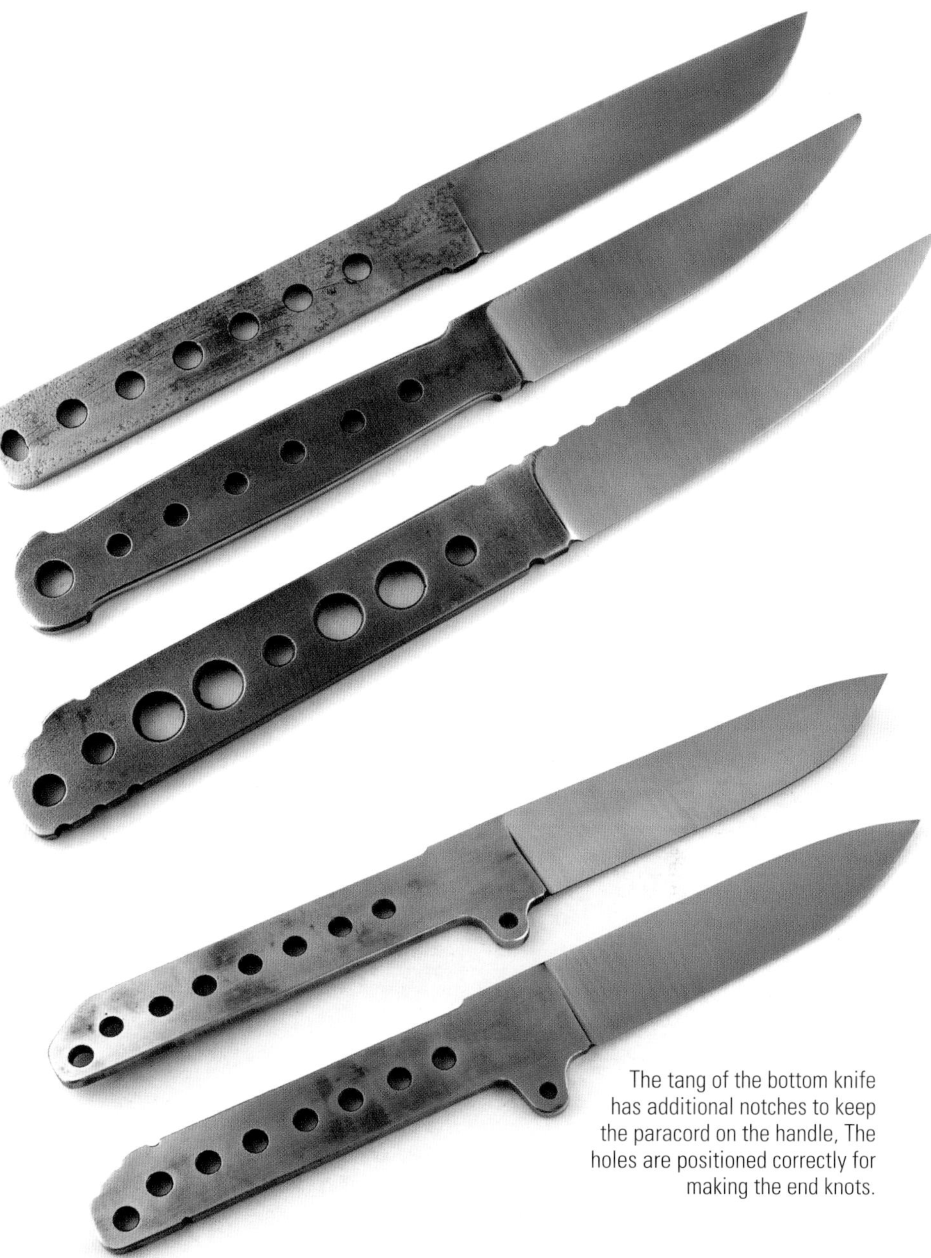

The tang of the bottom knife has additional notches to keep the paracord on the handle, The holes are positioned correctly for making the end knots.

If a knife gets dirty on a regular basis a tight wrap can be a good solution. In this case the wrap should additionally be completely impregnated with epoxy resin. This way a closed structure is created that can be washed. If the epoxy resin wears off and the paracord is revealed, a new protective resin coat can be applied to restore protection.

In case the knife is not stainless and gets wet or is used in maritime surroundings, the tang can also be provided with a special protective paint or a "baked on" protective layer prior to wrapping it. There are different variants of "bake on" products available which are also used for firearms. The epoxy resin we use for impregnating can also be used as a varnish.

For carbon steel tactical knives I prefer to make a basic layer of flatline and impregnate it with epoxy or polyurethane. This protects the knife steel from corrosion. In addition, the knife still retains a simple handle in case the paracord wrapping is used for something else in an emergency.

The wrapping technique has to fit the tang of the knife. Some wraps need a wider handle than others. The "West Country Whipping" needs more width than a looped wrap. The overhand knots of the West Country need enough space for putting the cord correctly. If the tang is too slim the cord slips over the knot and does not stay in position. With wraps done in Japanese style the appearance between crossings and the tightness of the twists change with the handle's width.

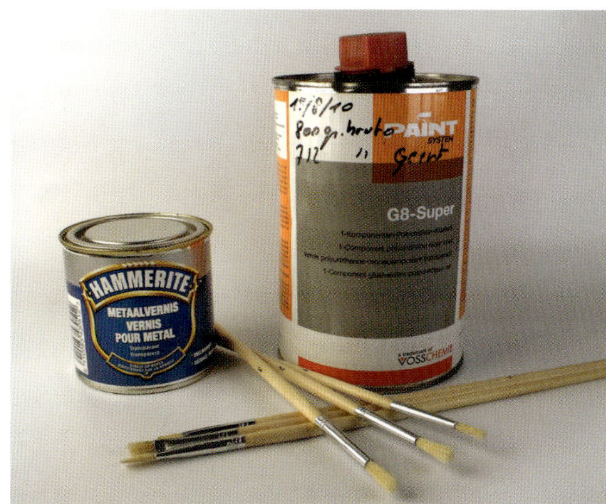

To protect the tang underneath the wrap from corrosion use clear one-component polyurethane varnish or a special metal varnish.

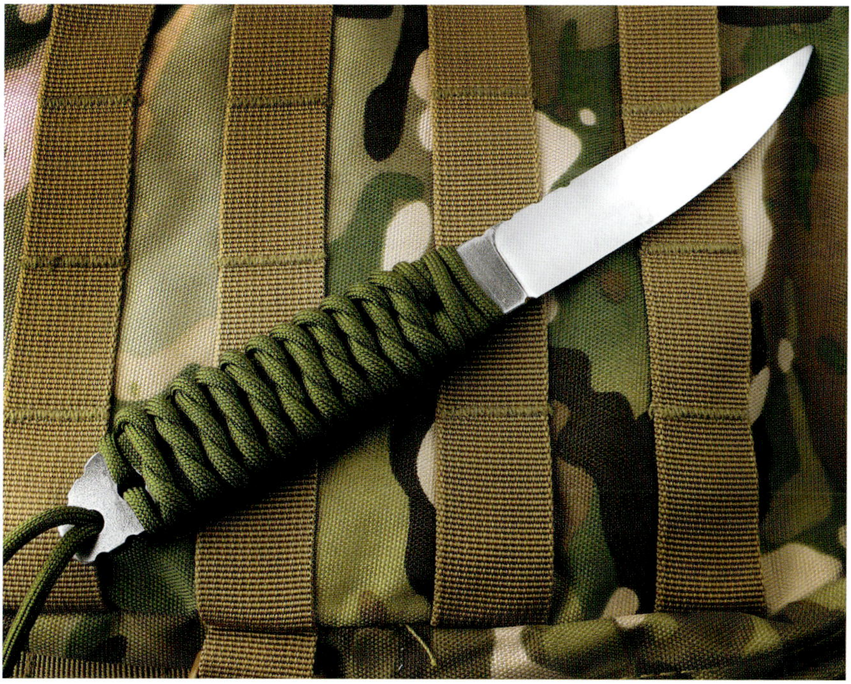

A simple wrap ideal for tactical knives with a relatively wide angle: the West Country Whipping (explained starting on p 42).

WRAPS FOR UNDERLAYS

Sometimes we have to cover the tang of a knife to make it look nicer, or to give more volume to the handle. The tang may be ugly, have a strange pattern of holes, or be so shiny that it can be seen through the holes in the wrap. The thin wrap shown here is often used as a layer underneath a thicker, structured wrap applied above it.

NECESSARY TOOLS

- sharp knife and cutting board (cutting on a wooden board leads to cleaner cuts than cutting with scissors)
- lighter (indispensable to achieve clean paracord ends by melting)
- scissors (to cut off the cord ends)
- smooth, pointed round pliers (for prying, pulling the cords tight, and as a marlin spike)
- super glue (cyanoacrylate)
- masking tape (for protecting the blade and hands)
- acetone (for removing glue residues after the tape has been taken off)
- wire of different diameters
- needle with thread
- clamp
- an additional marlin spike is always useful

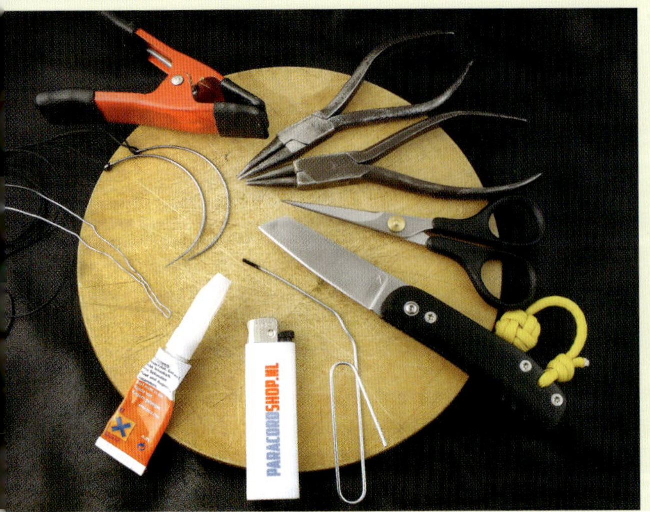

Necessary tools (clockwise): sharp and blunt needle-nosed pliers, fine scissors, heavy wire, cigarette lighter, super glue, bent wire, and needles with string for the end knots, and a clamp.

The techniques employed here are two variations of the plain whipping used by sailors. The same technique can be used with full paracord as an alternative to the simple, even wrapping shown later, but with full paracord small gaps between the individual turns become visible.

3.1 Flat Whipping, Even on Both Sides

This flat wrap is based on a technique used in the nautical realm to prevent thick, heavy ropes from unraveling. This winding provides a well-structured base for most kinds of handle wraps and is quite flat.

For knives without holes, the paracord is folded along the tang and then the wrap made on top of the folded end. Having proper holes in the knife tang makes life easier.

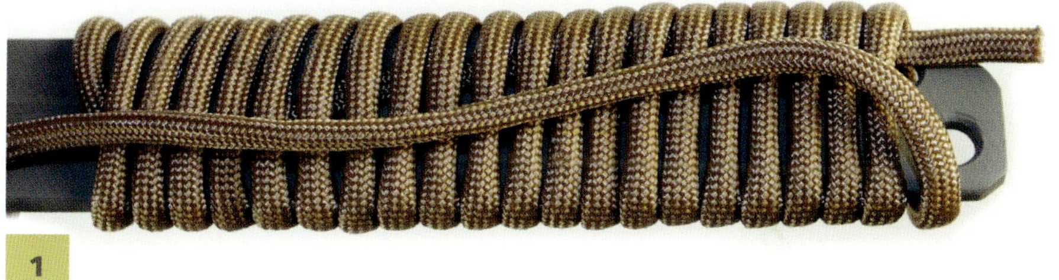

1

Wrapping the handle to determine the needed cord length. Add a bit over two times the handle length for the beginning and end of the wrap. Cut the cord from the spool or hank.

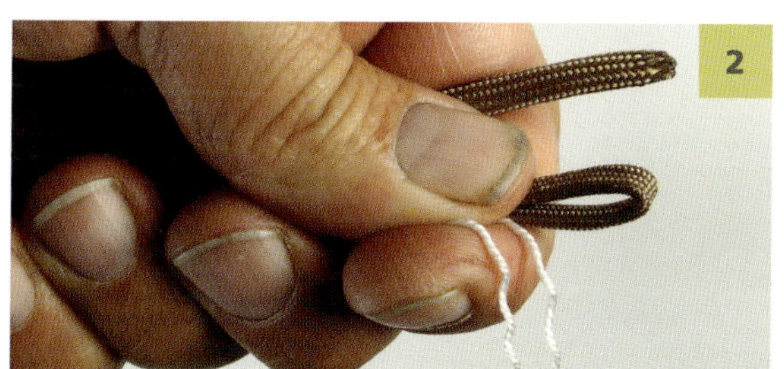

2

Remove the core and melt the ends slightly—just enough to prevent unraveling. Keep one of the core strings to pull the working end underneath the wrap.

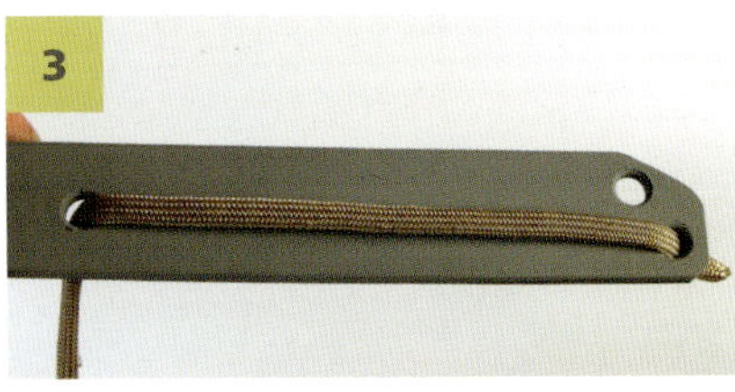

Pull the working end of the cord through the holes as shown.

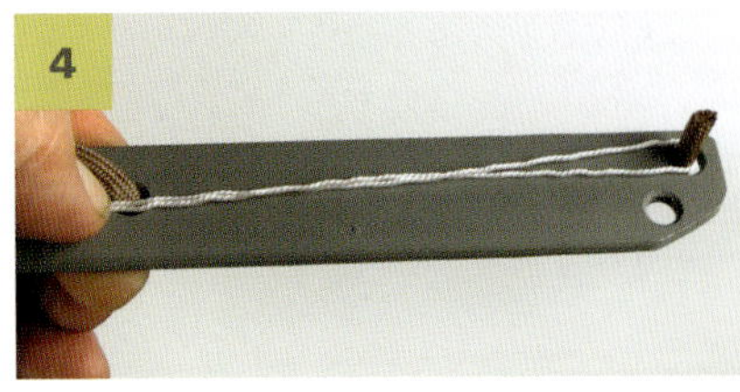

Put the pulling string (from the paracord's core) alongside the other side of the handle.

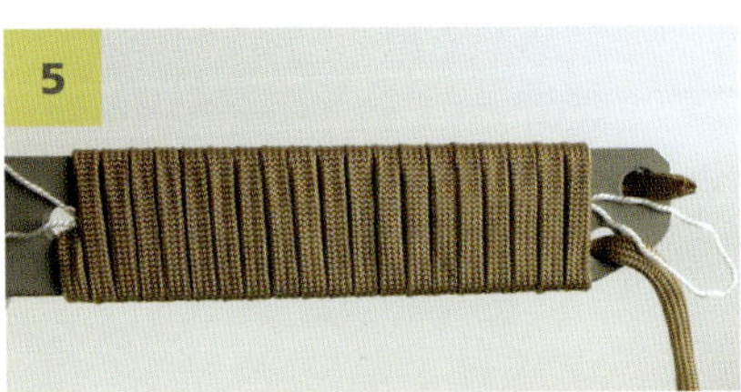

Wrap the tang evenly. The end is guided through the second hole at the pommel to the side of the pulling string.

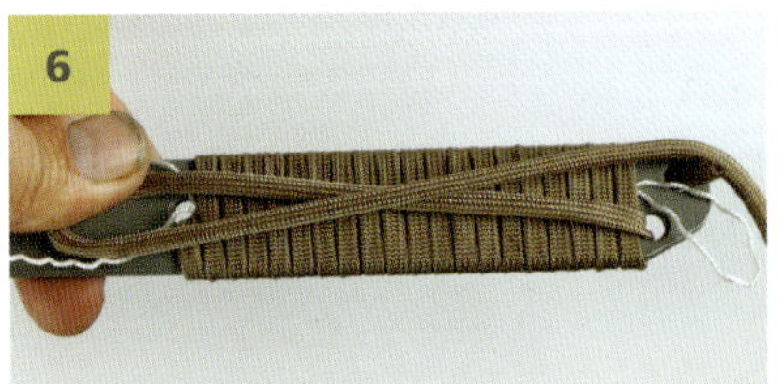

Judge the length that has to be pulled through and pull the cord through the loop of the pulling string.

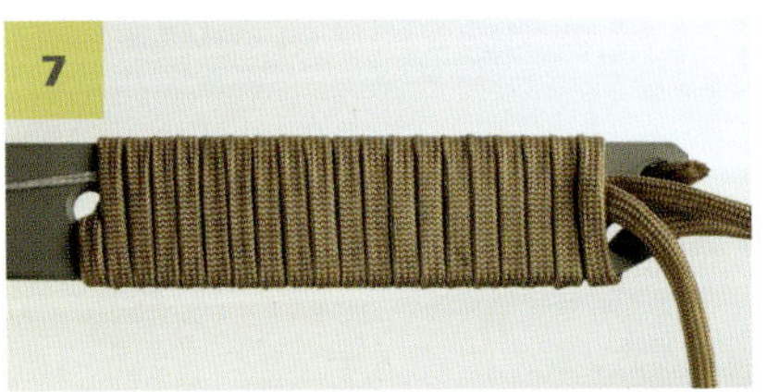

Start with pulling the working end through. Assure that no unwanted twists remain.

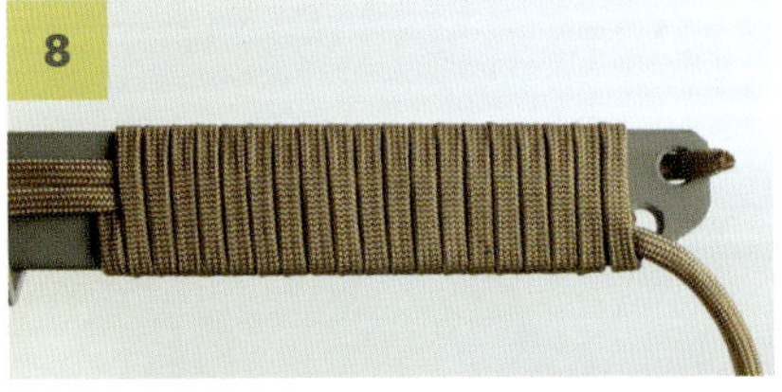

Here the working end is already pulled through.

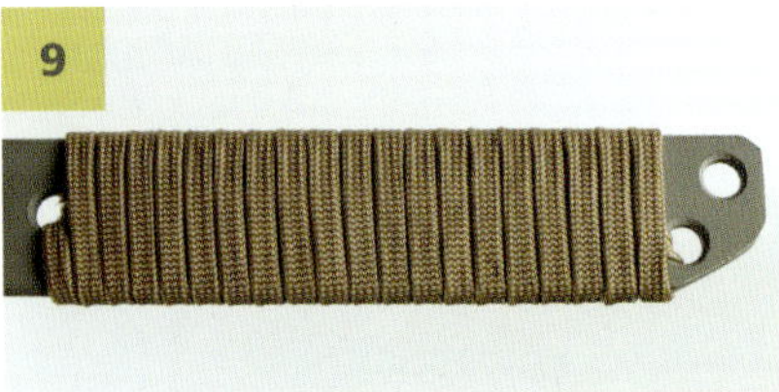

Trim the ends of the cord and melt them.

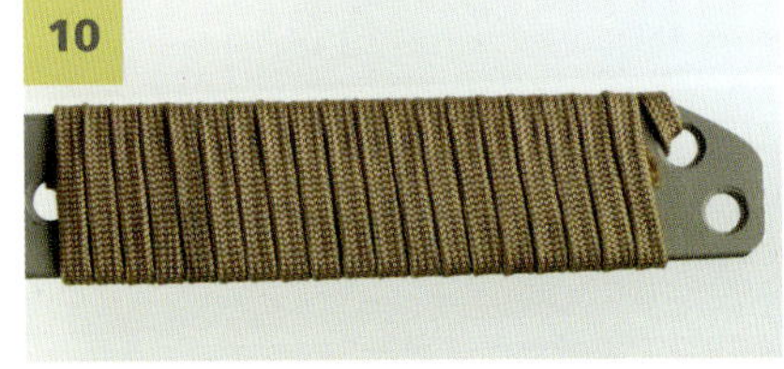

The end on the other side has to be trimmed as well.

When you look at both sides of the handle, you can see that the wrap is neat and flat. It will not disturb the look of the next wrap we will put on top of it. This is advantageous in case we put a wrap in Japanese style on top.

3.2 Flat Whipping with Ends Pulled in Halfway

This whipping is absolutely flat on one side. On the other side the starting and working ends are pulled underneath. This variant can be used for handles with holes or without holes. In this example we did not use the holes of the knife tang.

This is the whipping technique done without an additional string for pulling through. This whipping works very well with thin rope such as paracord type I. To determine the required length, put one length along the handle, wrap the handle, and add two more handle lengths. Pull out the core strings and seal the ends.

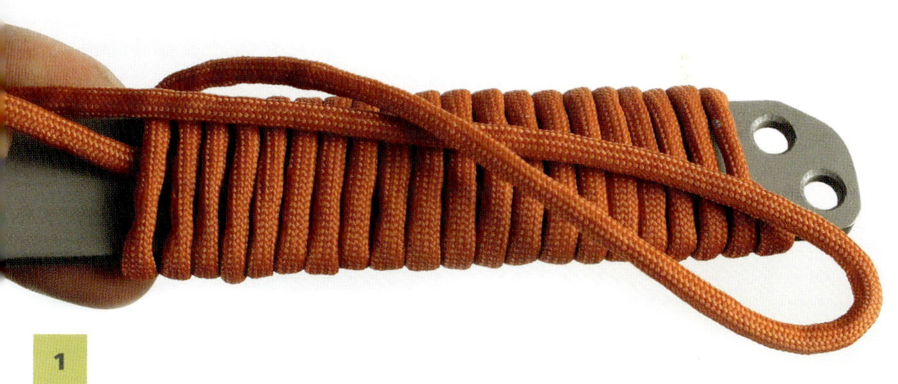

1

Determine the needed cord length by wrapping the handle and adding three times the handle length. If the wrap is done with full paracord of type III or thinner cord such as type II or I, the cord can remain on the spool and only has to be cut off after finishing the wrap.

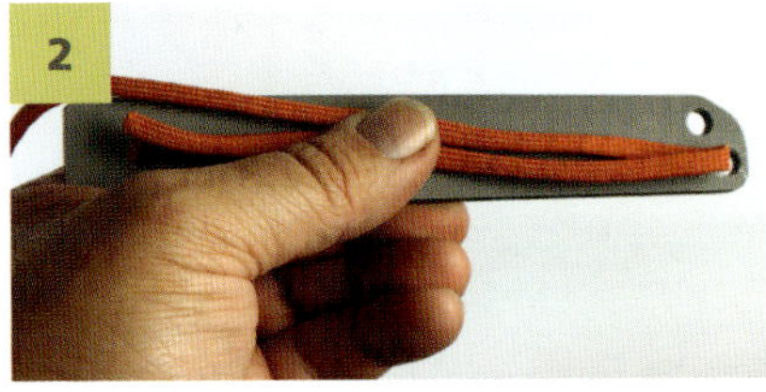

Start with a loop along the knife handle.

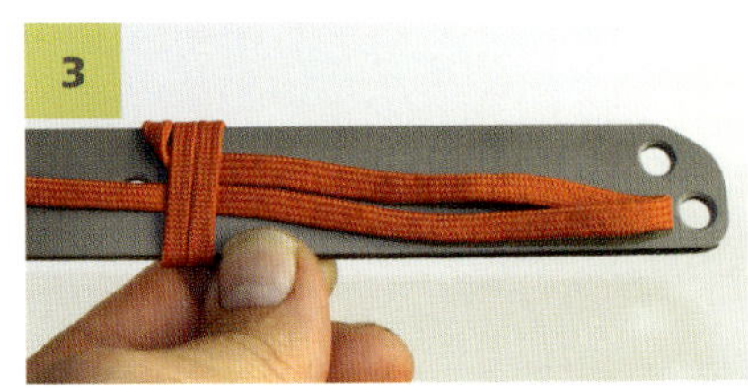

The wrap is started by guiding the cord upward and around the tang.

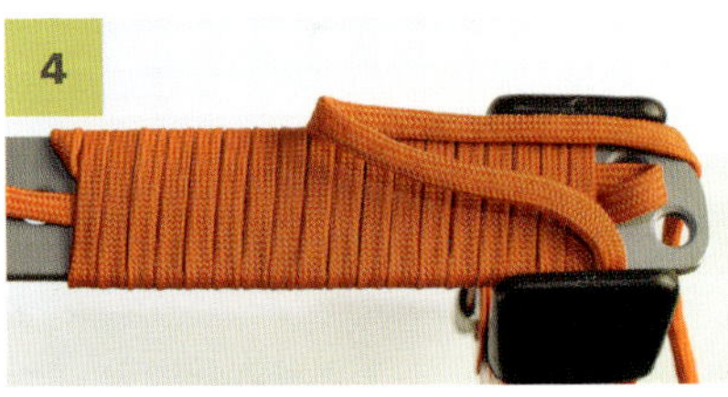

This way the entire tang is wrapped up to the first hole on the side of the pommel.

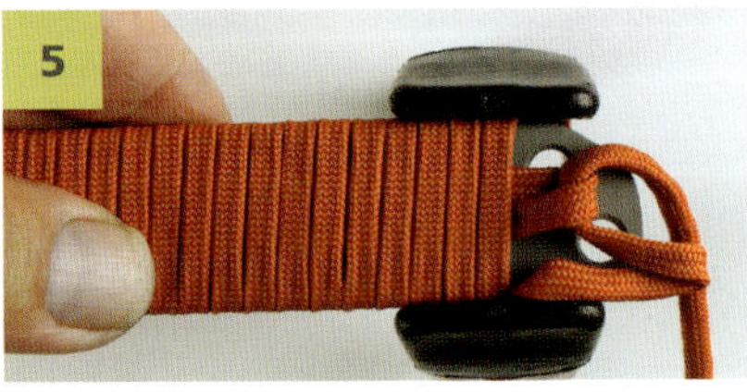

The working end is pulled through the hole from below and then once again through itself.

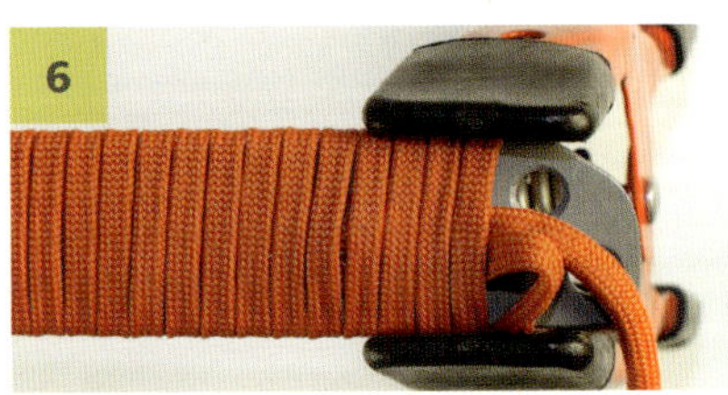

Then the working end is pulled underneath the wrap to the center of the handle.

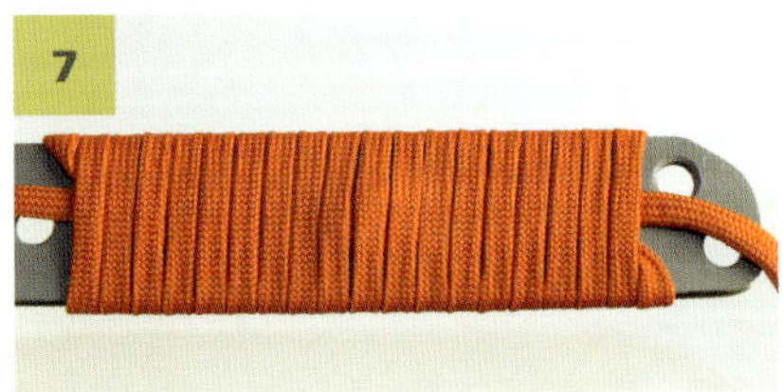

It has arrived in the center. The ends are pulled tight.

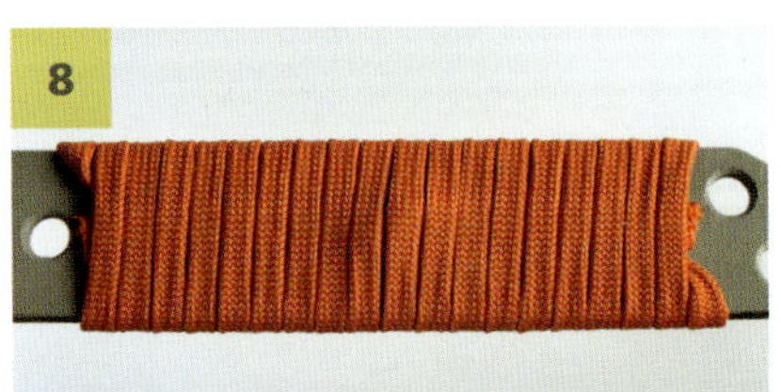

Both cord ends are cut off and singed with a heated steel wire or paper clip. The little bulge is visible in the handle's center.

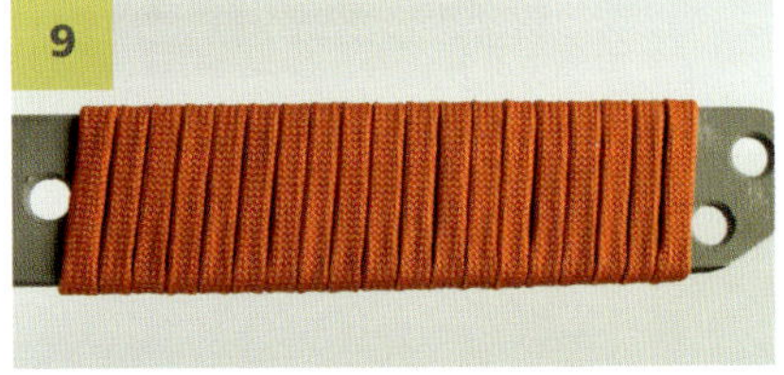

In contrast, the handle's backside is absolutely flat.

3.3 Flat Wrap with Glued Ends

This underlay is often done in Japanese style to decoratively hide the tang. The underlay is visible underneath the diamond shaped gaps in the handle wrap. This wrap is even a bit flatter than the first flat wrap.

Determine the needed length of cord by wrapping the handle once and add some more cord. Cut the cord and remove the strings inside. Melt the ends slightly with a lighter and press them as square and flat as possible with your fingers. Take care not to burn your fingers! A bit of saliva or water is a big help, because the molten plastic will stick less to your fingers.

The wrap can be impregnated with epoxy resin to fix it in place. This will enhance the colors, but also makes them darker, while at the same time providing protection against corrosion for the tang.

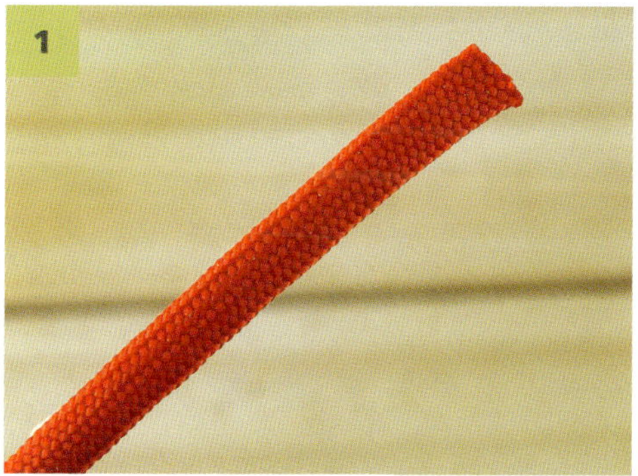

Glued flat wrap: cut the cord at right angles on a cutting board using a knife or scissors. Melt it just enough to shape the ends flat and rectangular.

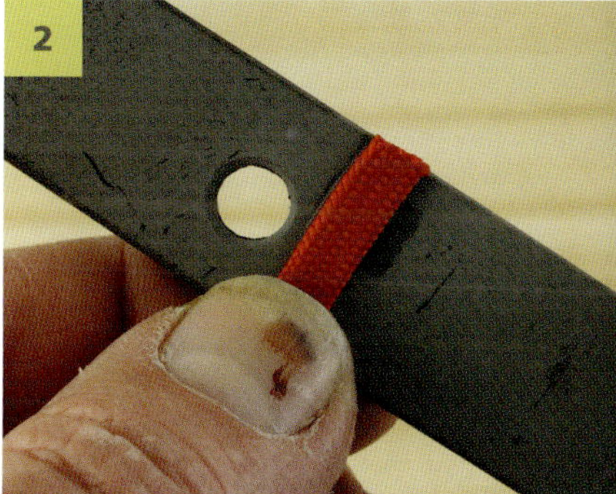

Glue the first end on to the tang. Put it flush to the knife back or the front edge. Lift it and spread a drop of glue. Press forcefully, but take care not to push the end toward the blade, as this would ruin the front edge of the handle.

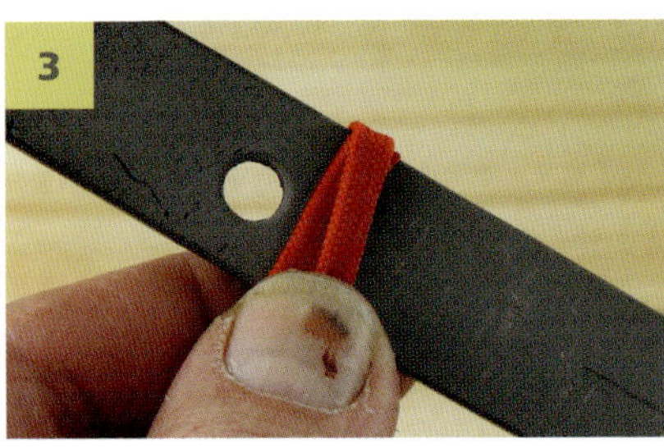

The first turn goes over the glued cord end before it is guided toward the pommel. Start wrapping.

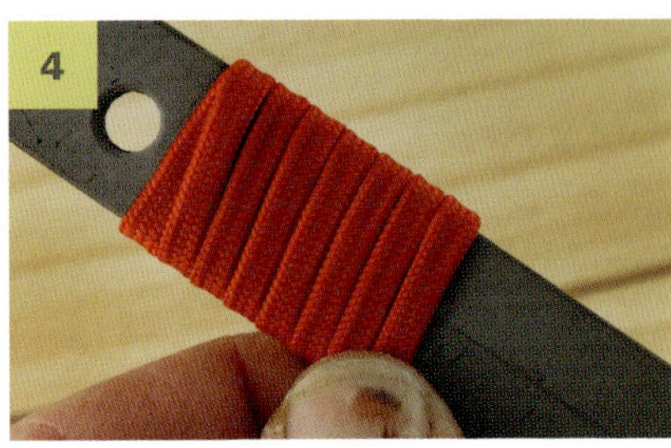

Wrap evenly and tightly!

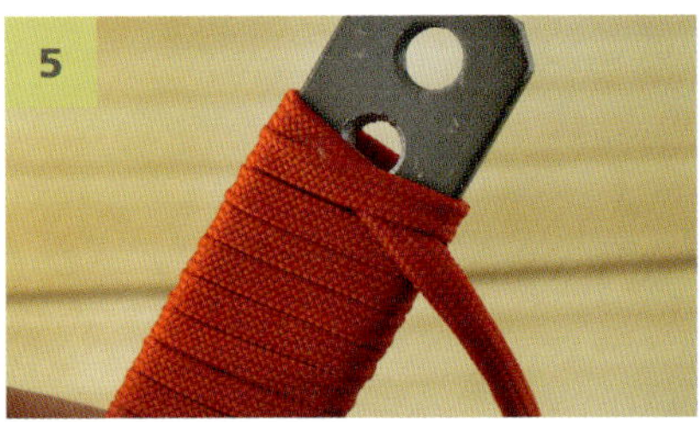

A half hitch and adding a drop of glue ends the work. Cut off the working end between the last turn and the last-but-one.

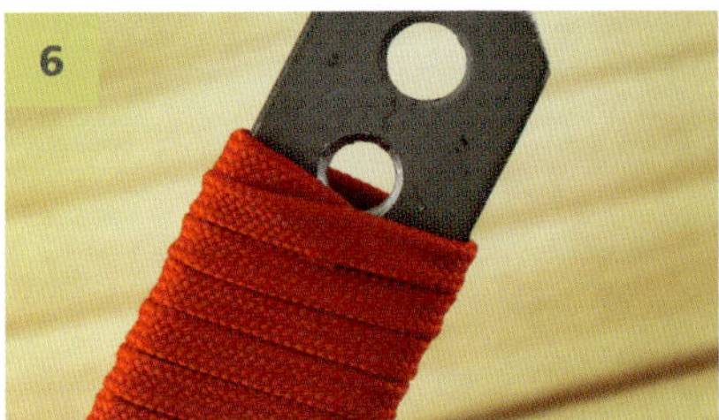

The finished wrap: it can be impregnated with resin to fix it.

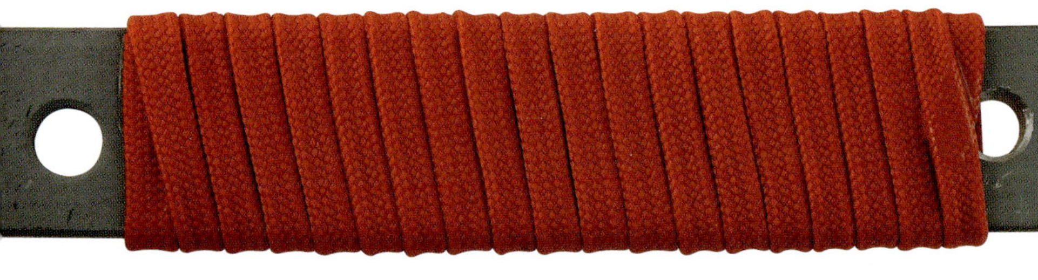

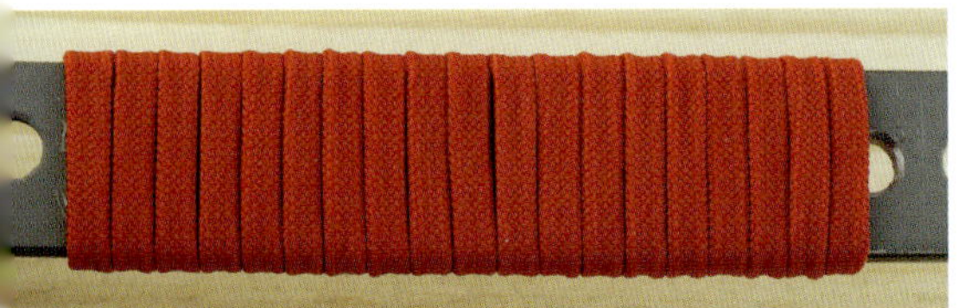

Full view of the handle's backside.

The front side of the knife handle.

3.4 Flat Simple Wrap

A flat, simple wrap can also be used as a plain handle wrap without any other layers on top of it. The following technique provides a wrap that can easily be removed in an emergency; in addition, you will have a wrist thong if desired. Measure the needed cord length by wrapping the handle once and add 19 $^{11}/_{16}$ to 23 $^5/_8$ in. (fifty to sixty cm) for the wrist thong. In case you later need the cord in an emergency you can rip the glued knot apart and unwind the cord.

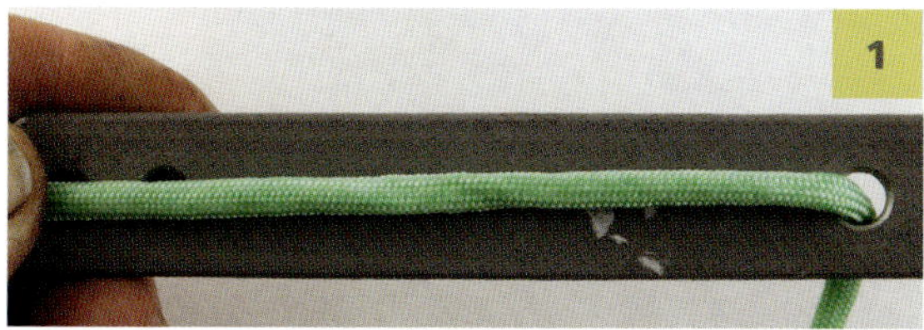

Put the cord end through the hole next to the guard (at right). Guide the cord along the tang and put it through the inner hole at the pommel. Leave at least 9.8425 in. (25 cm) for the wrist thong. Start wrapping at the guard.

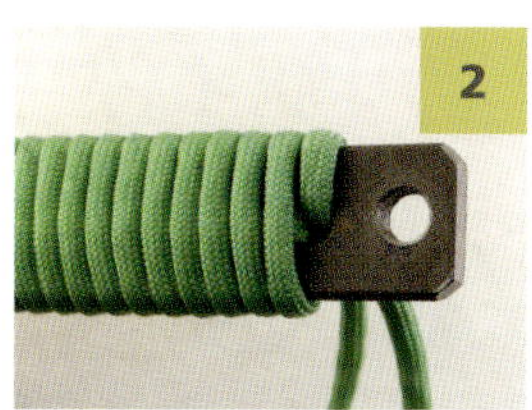

When half of the inner hole is covered by the wrap, guide the working end through the hole next to the other cord end.

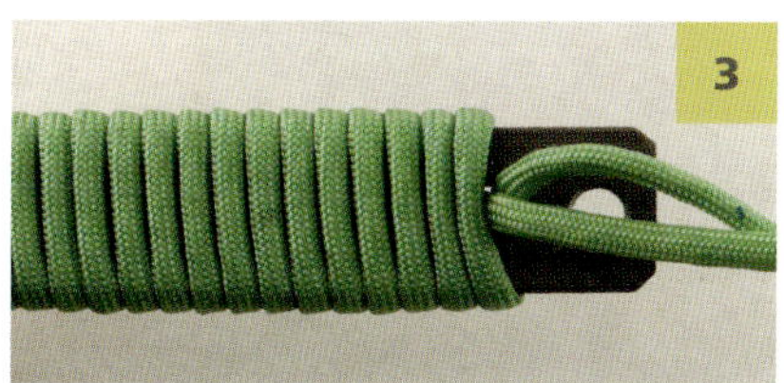

The handle is turned around and both cord ends are pulled tight.

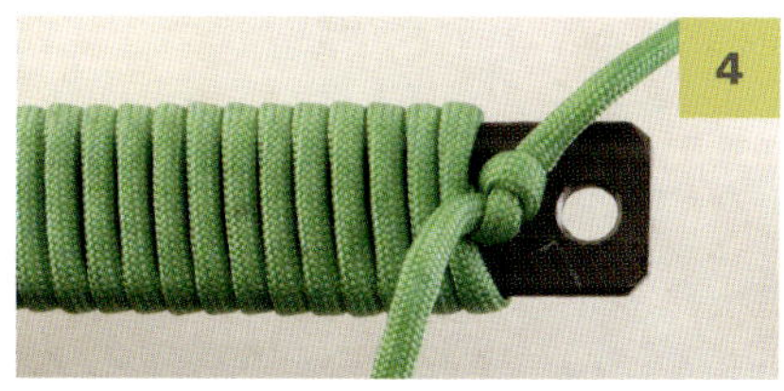

Make an overhand knot (half knot) and pull it tight.

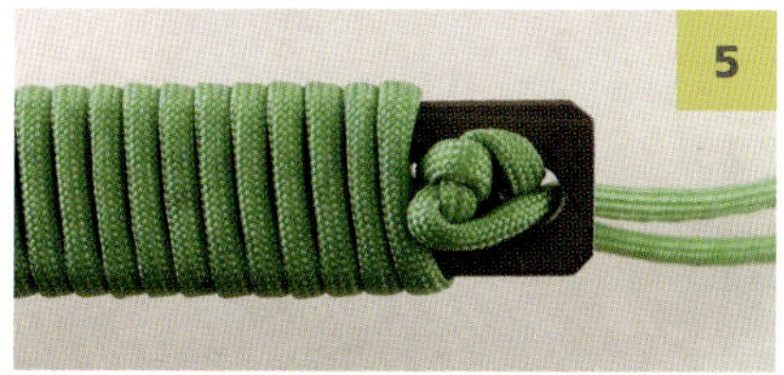

Pull both cord ends through the last hole to shape the wrist thong. The knot can be secured with a drop of glue.

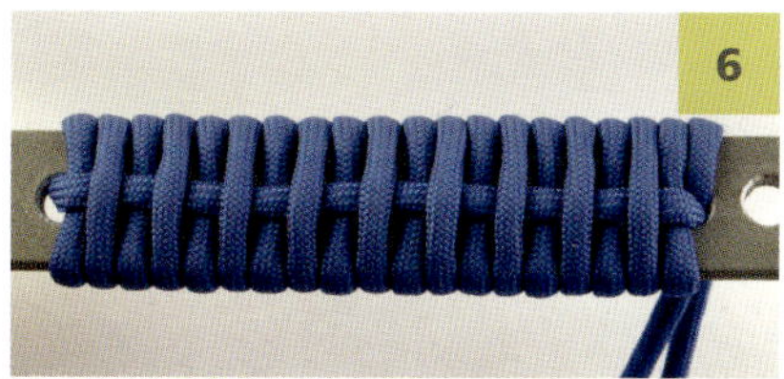

As an alternative, the standing end can also be woven into the wrap on the handle's front side. The details for this are described later.

TACTICAL HANDLE WRAPS

4.1 Flat, Single Layer Wrap

If the flat, single layer wrap of previous section 3.4 is done over a flat basic underlay we already get a full, tactical handle wrap.

Some knives only have a small diameter hole at the pommel. In this case a single cord end can be used to get through the hole and create a lanyard. The wrap starts with the standing end at the pommel. The paracord is put flat along the handle up to the blade, where we start wrapping on top of it in the direction of the pommel.

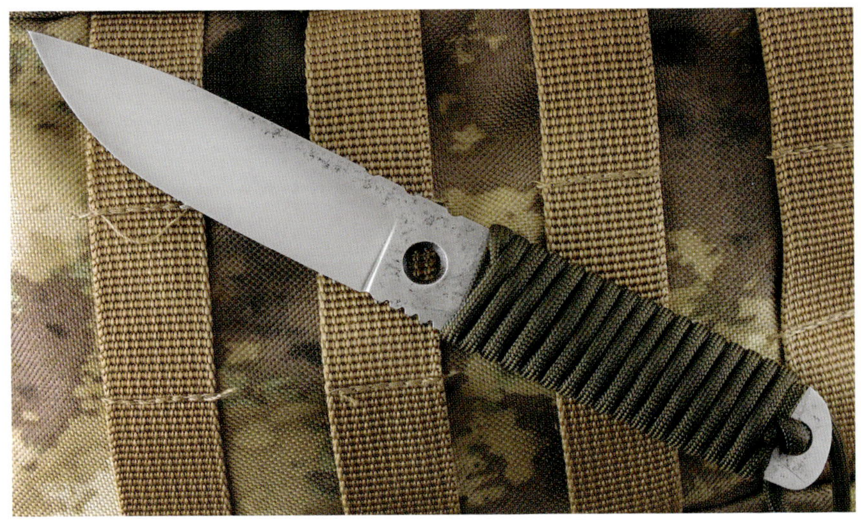

The single layer wrap on top of a flat basic wrap is already a perfect tactical handle wrap.

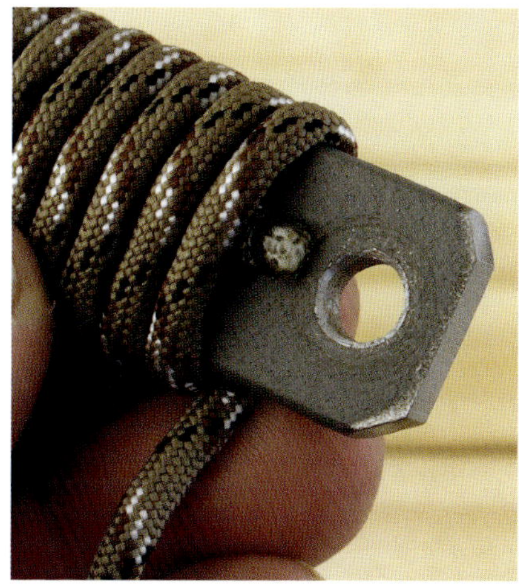

If there is only a small hole at the end of the pommel, the standing end ought to end here; you only work with the other end until you reach the hole.

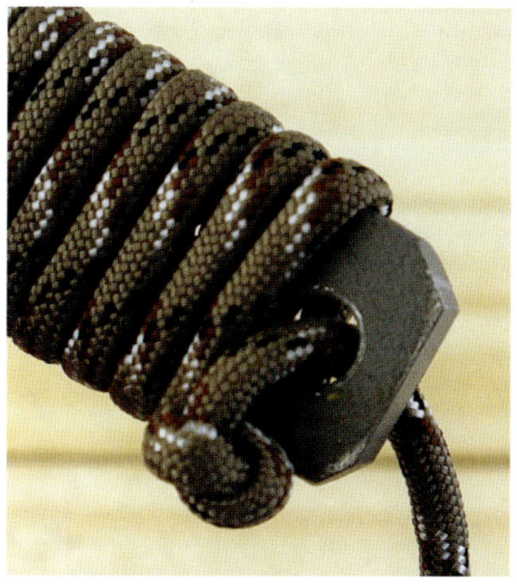

Make an overhand knot at the working end. When pulling the cord through the hole in the tang, the knot presses against the tang.

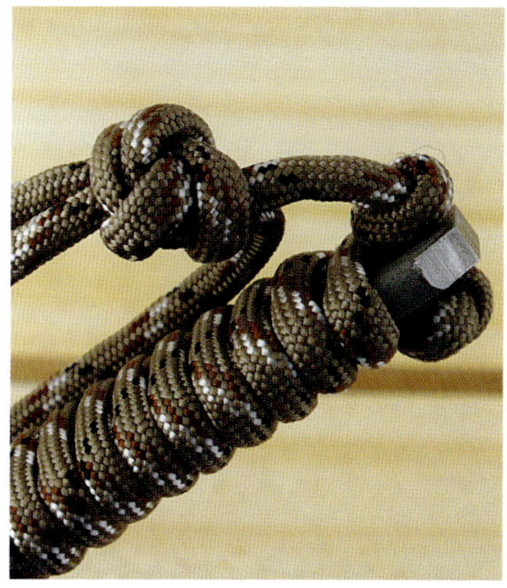

On the other side you make another knot to form the wrist thong.

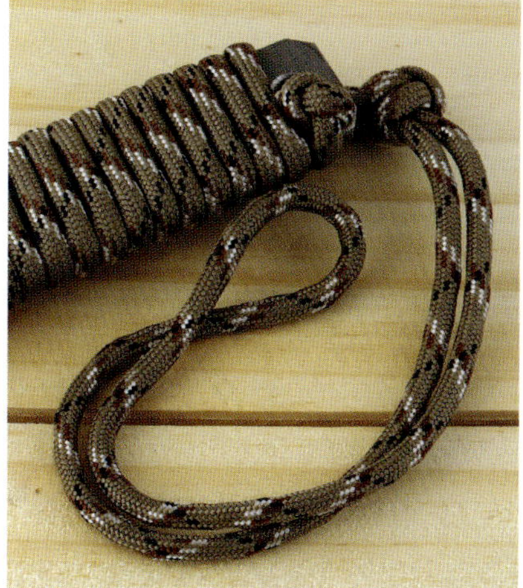

The finished handle wrap.

4.2 Flat, Double Layer Wrap

This handle wrap is a variation on the cord-wrapped handles of John Ek knives after World War II. The way shown for ending the handle wrap and the lanyard differs from the original handle wrap made by the John Ek Company. There the lanyard is made from a single cord end.

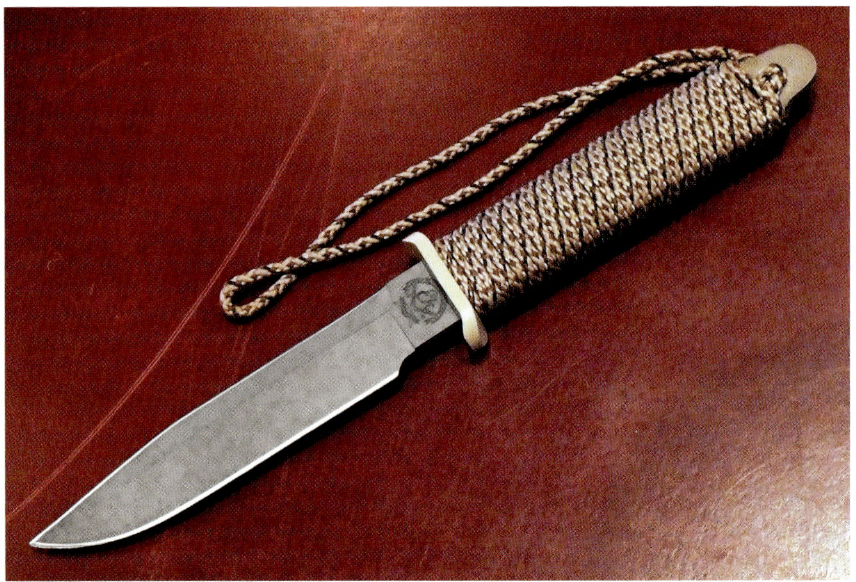

Typical example of a tactical handle wrap: John Ek knife.

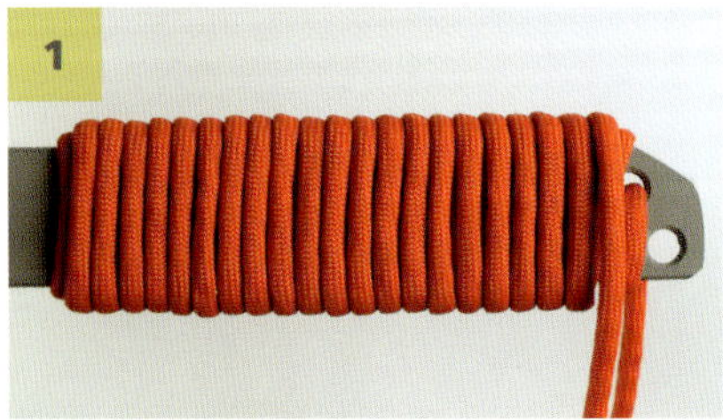

Determine the necessary cord length by wrapping the knife handle two times and adding 23 5⁄8 in. (60 cm).

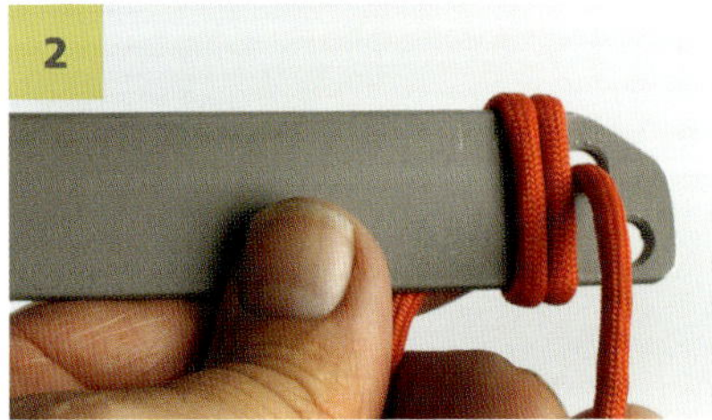

Put 9.8425 in. (25 cm) of the cord through the inner pommel hole and start with the handle wrap.

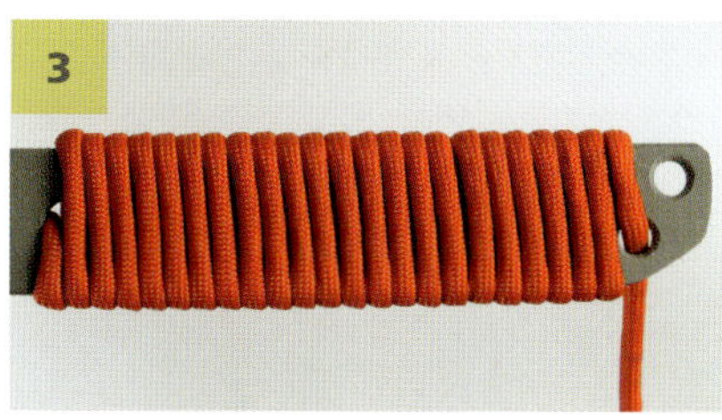

Wrap the handle completely once up to the tang hole next to the blade (at left).

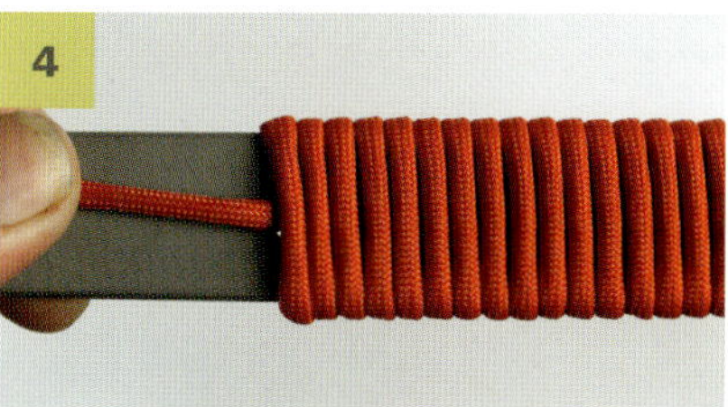

Put the working end through the hole. In the photo it emerges on the other side.

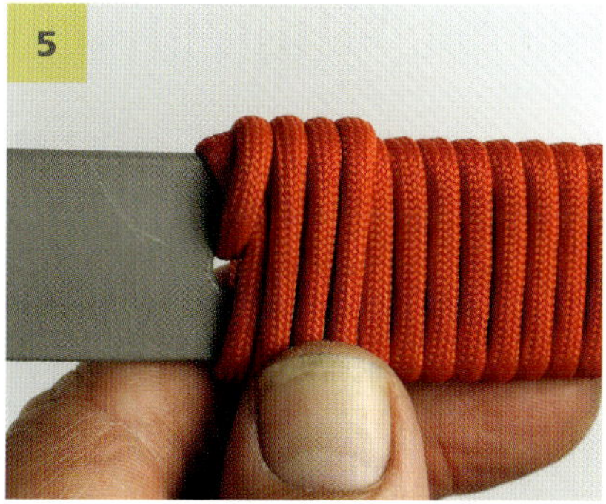

Now start to wrap it back in the direction of the pommel.

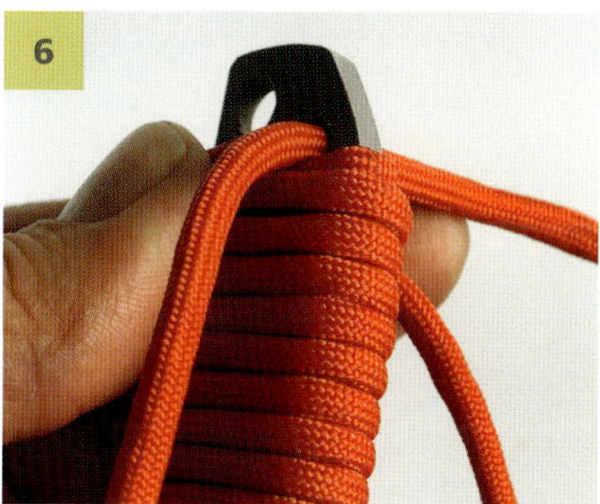

At the pommel end, the cord is put through the inner hole next to the first cord end.

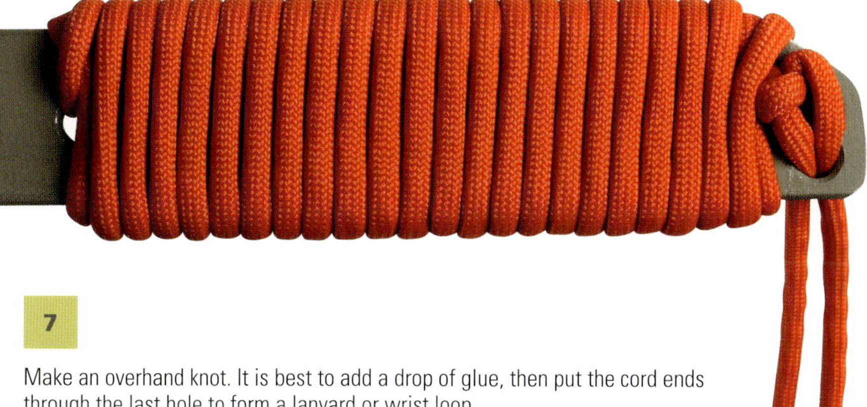

Make an overhand knot. It is best to add a drop of glue, then put the cord ends through the last hole to form a lanyard or wrist loop.

4.3 West Country Whipping

On ships, the West Country Whipping is used to prevent the fraying of heavy ropes. To do it on a knife handle we need about nine feet (2.7 m) of cord.

This is a handle wrap which is seventy-five percent covered by a second wrap. For this we need the length of a single layer plus seventy-five percent, plus 19 $^{11}\!/_{16}$– 23 $^5\!/_8$ in. (50–60 cm) for the wrist loop. Start by folding the cord once to determine the center. If the knife has a hole where the guard would be located it can be used to prevent the handle wrap sliding forward.

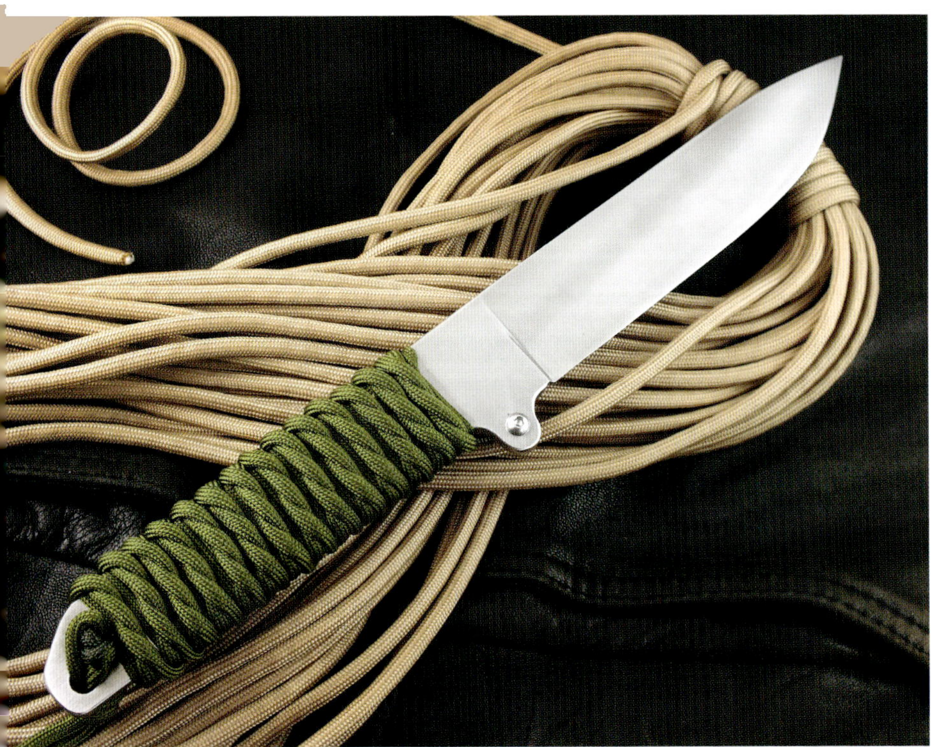

This combat and utility knife of differentially hardened 52100 ball bearing steel has a West Country handle wrap in military green on top of a flat basic wrap. The screw heads in the guard help keep the knife inside the kydex sheath.

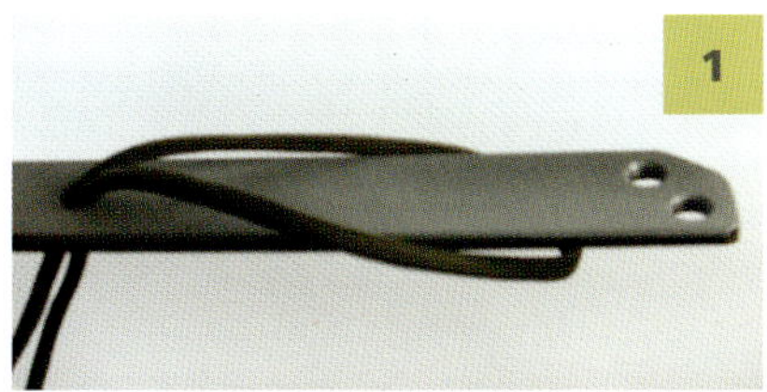

We make a loop and pull both cord ends through the hole next to the blade. The cord ends are the same length.

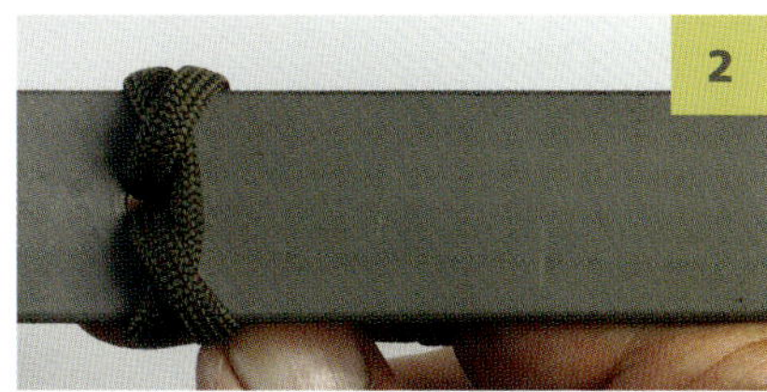

The ends are pulled tight and returned to the opposite side.

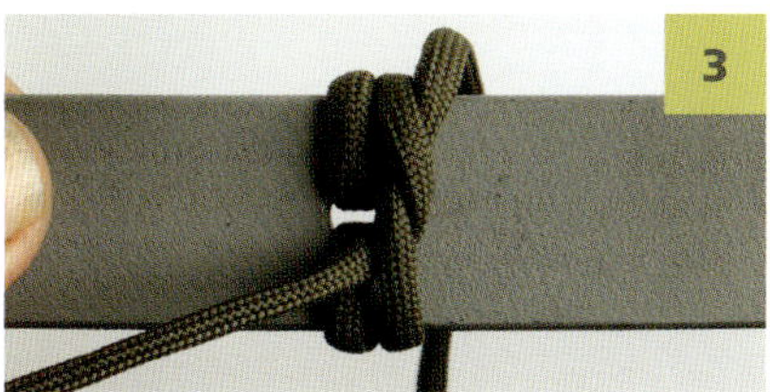

On this side you make a knot and pull it tight.

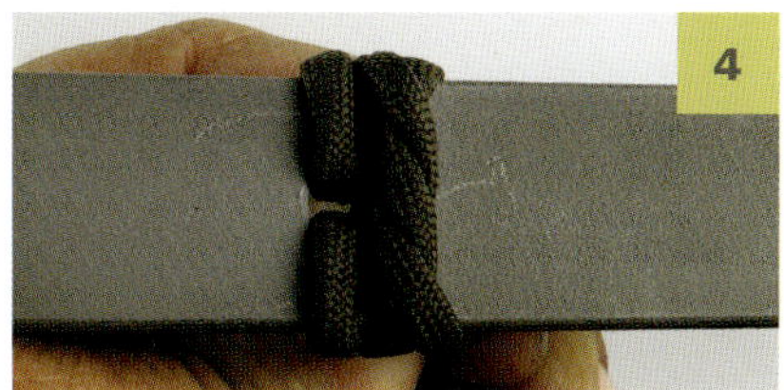

The working end is put over the knot from the left side.

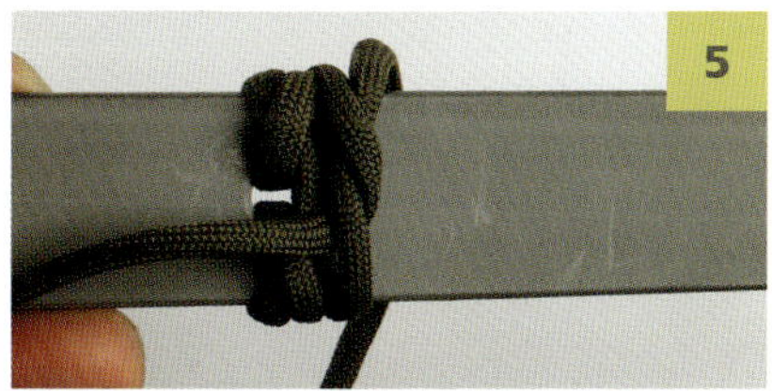

The tang is turned around and the next knot is made.

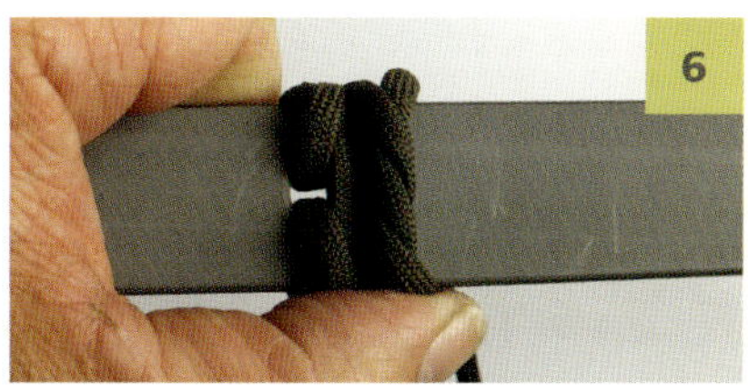

Put the working end to the right and hold it tightly with your thumb.

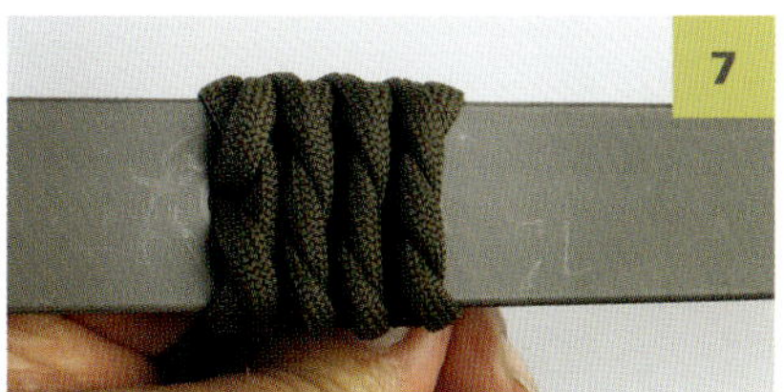

After three knots per side you check whether all the knots look uniform and stay tight; then you continue.

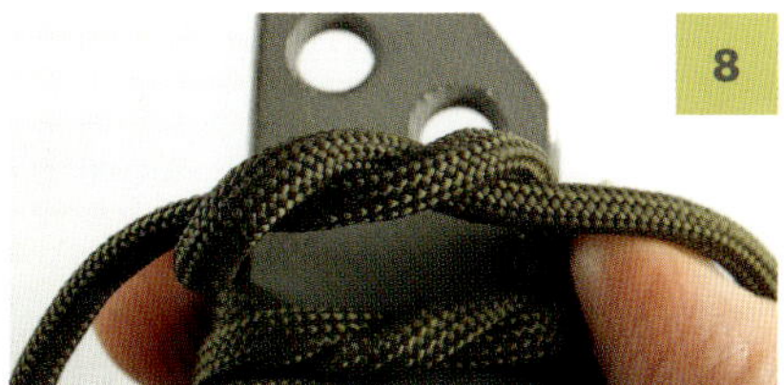

One of the last knots in "slow motion." The overhand knots are always made in the same direction.

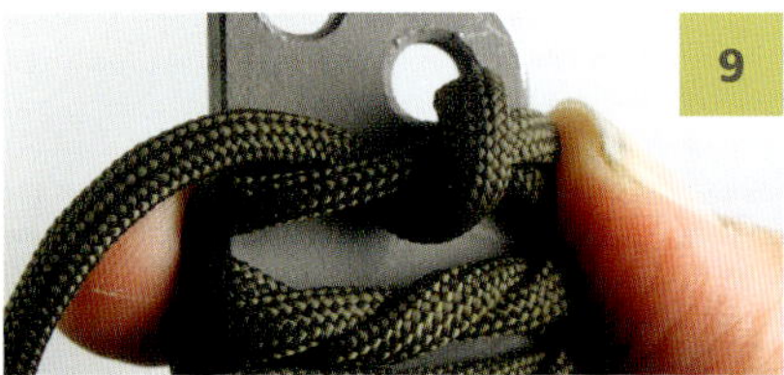

The working end is pulled tight toward the right while the other end is slacked.

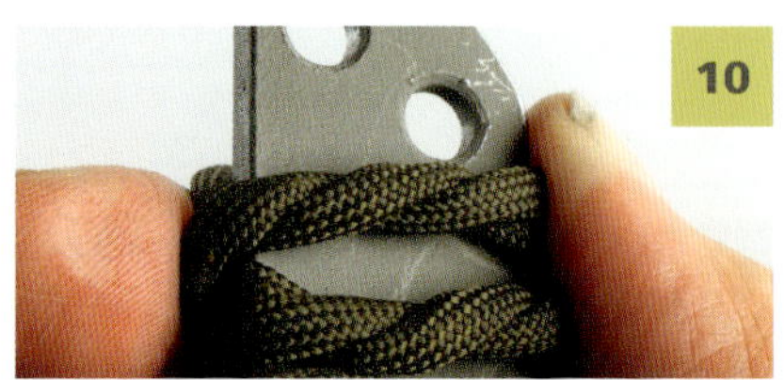

The left working end is pulled tight and pressed against the previous knot.

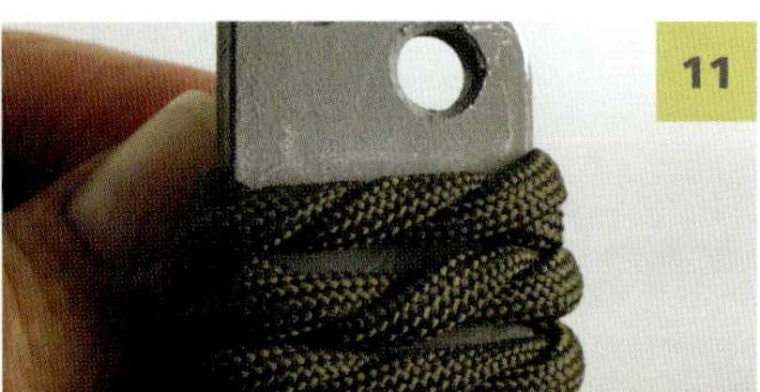

The right working end is put exactly over the knot and pressed tight against the handle side. This is crucial for getting a perfect West Country handle wrap.

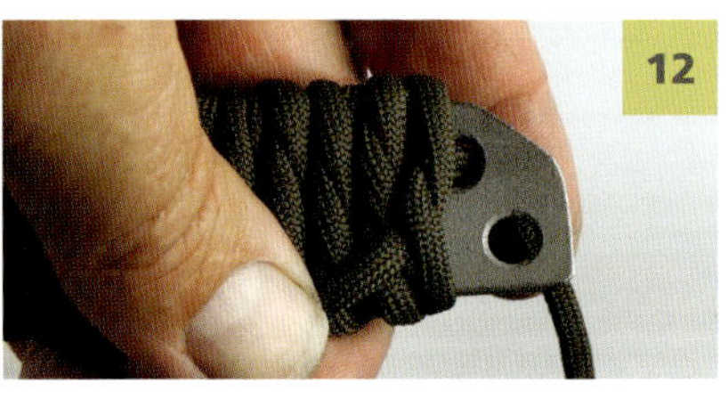

When the inner hole is reached we make the last knot.

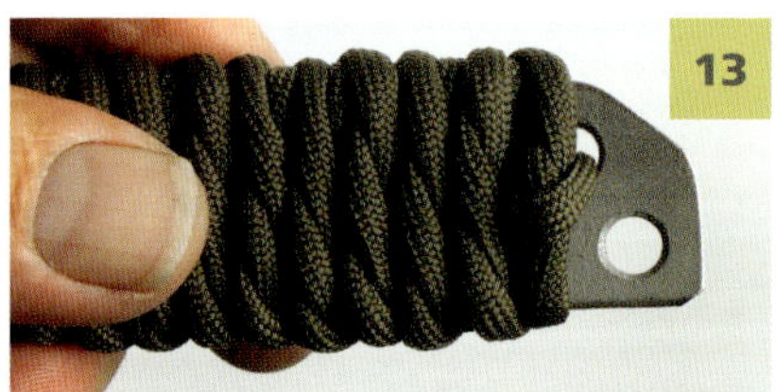

Both cord ends are guided through the inner hole.

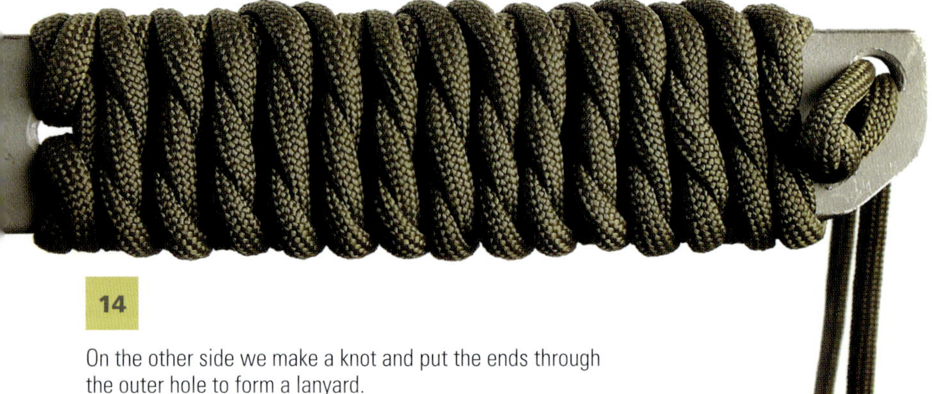

On the other side we make a knot and put the ends through the outer hole to form a lanyard.

A decisive difference between the West Country handle wrap and the looped wrap is the West Country Whipping is flatter and firmer. It is more difficult to execute this wrap correctly and needs more force on the cords. There are gaps between the overhand knots on the handle side.

4.4 Standard Military or Looped Wrap

This handle wrap is one of the easiest and can be done relatively quickly. Strider Knives is one of the most well-known companies using this wrap for their knives. It provides the handle with good volume with or without an underlay. The wrap has an open structure and is best done with a flat, underlying wrap. Strider wraps its handles this way, too.

The handle wrap needs only a relatively small number of holes in the tang. Drill holes with a 5.5–6.3 mm diameter are ideal. A hole at the starting point of the wrap and two holes near the pommel round off the image. The drill holes are important to prevent the wrap from moving forward or backward. If the handle wrap rests against a guard no hole is needed at the front. Additional drill holes can be useful for the basic wrap or for balancing the knife. The following photos show the execution of the loops on a bare knife (without underlay). Thereafter, I will show a few examples of knives with looped wraps.

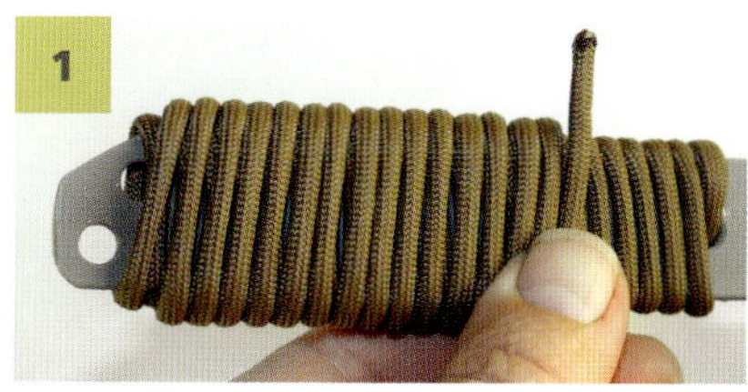

Wrap the handle one and a half times before cutting the cord of the reel.

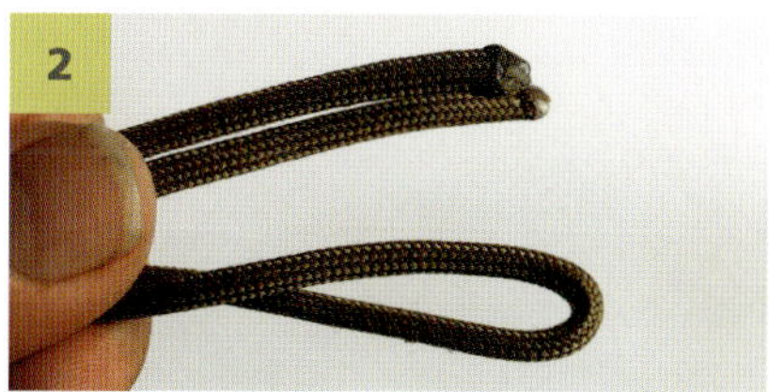

Fold the cord to determine its center and melt and fuse the ends to prevent fraying.

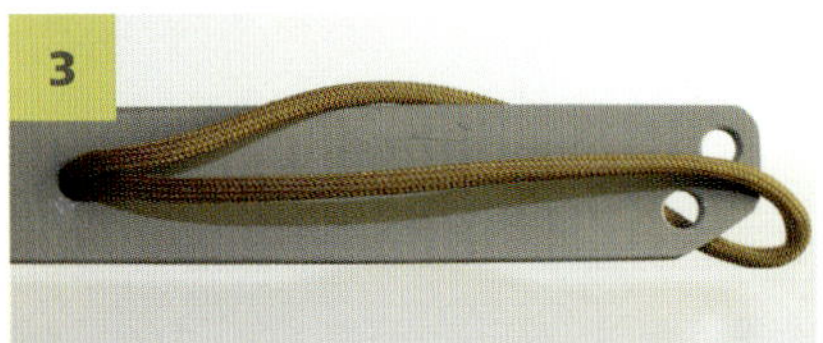

Make a loop with ends of the same length and pull both ends through the tang hole next to the blade.

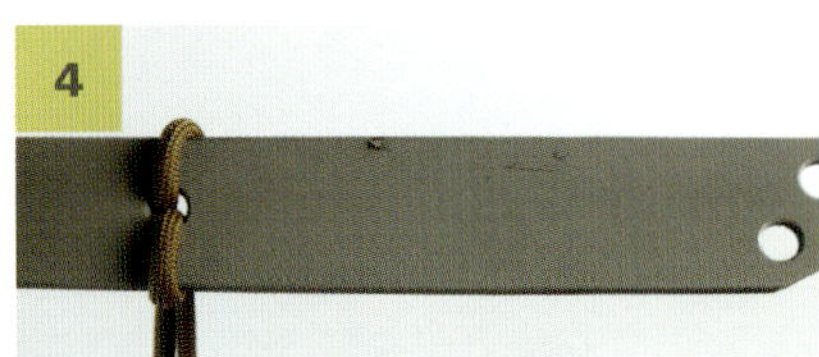

Pull the cord tight.

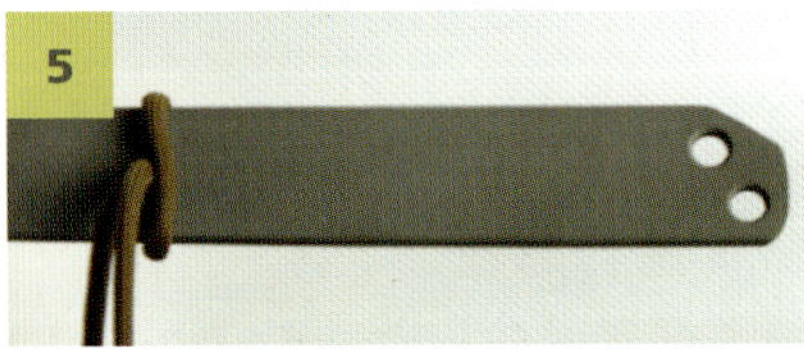

Check the position of the cord on the backside of the tang; it ought to be straight and not twisted.

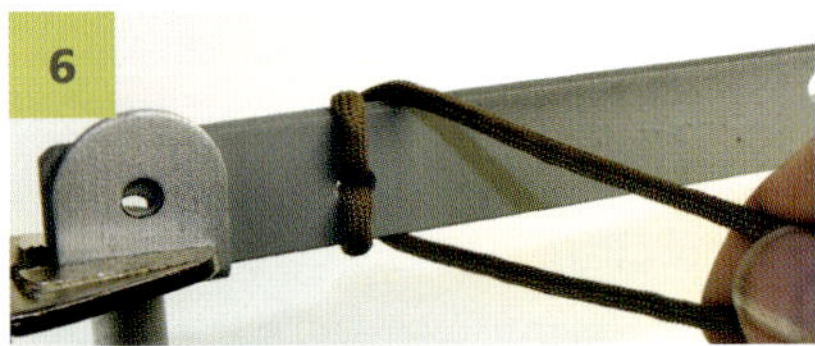

Bring both working ends back to the other side. Pull hard so the cord rests tight!

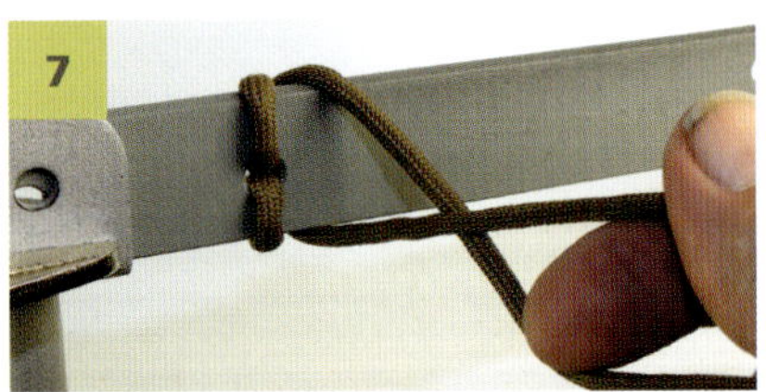

Cross the cord ends as a first step of the twist.

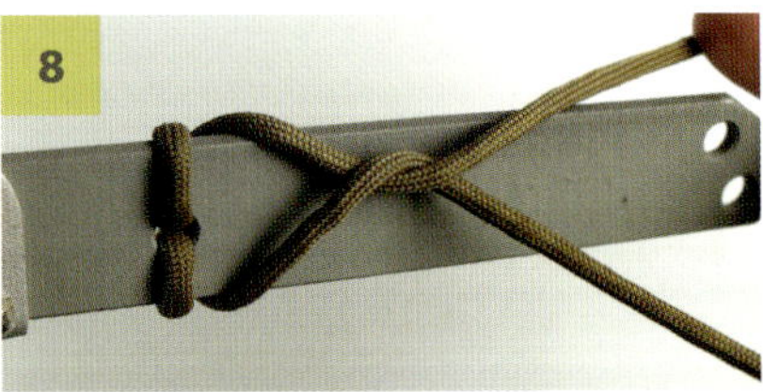

Continue turning the cord ends to complete the twist.

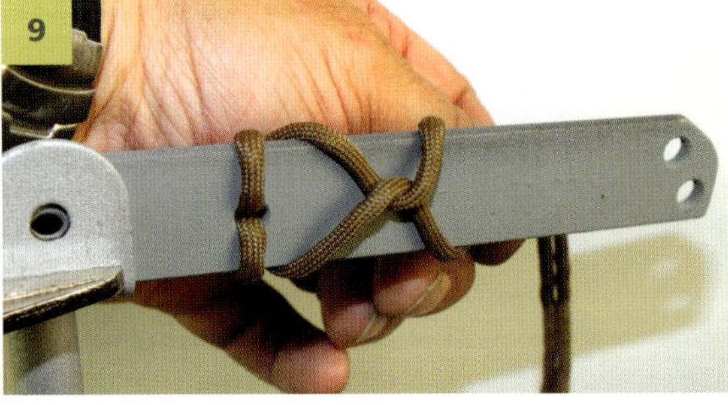

Put the cord ends on the other side and pull the loops close together.

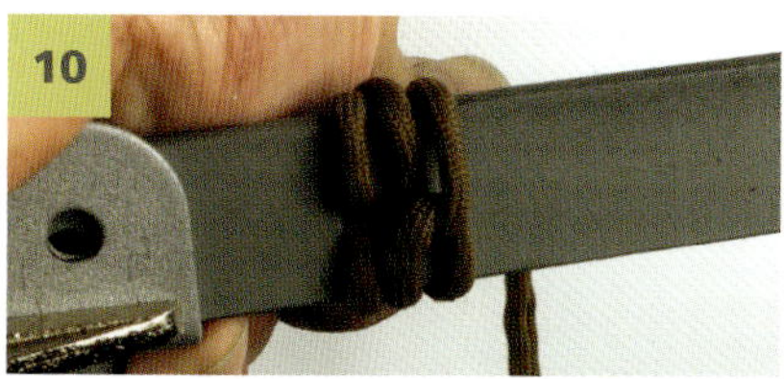

Pull the cord ends tight (again) and check whether the loops are positioned in the handle's center.

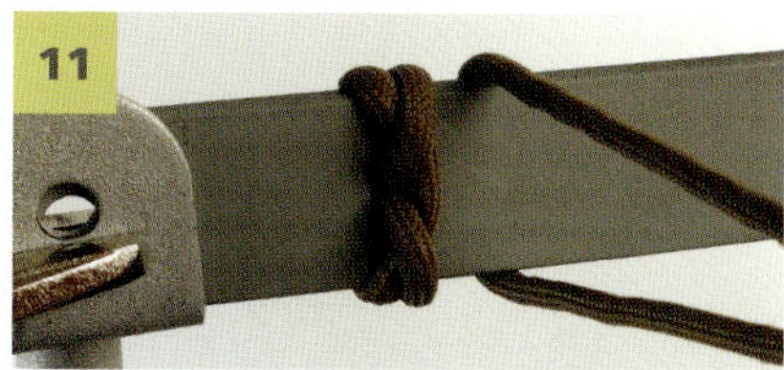

Turn the knife around while keeping tension on the cord.

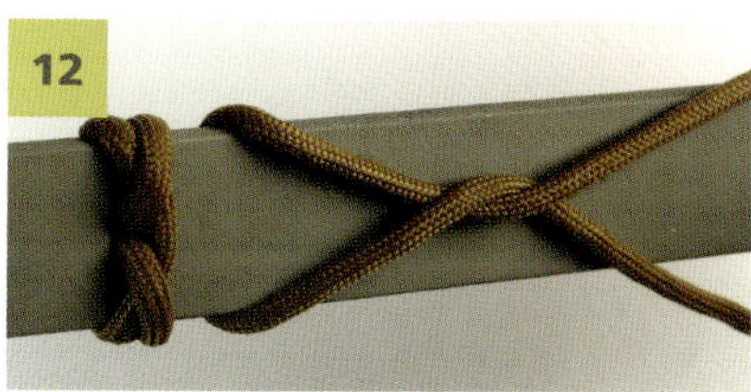

Turn the cord ends in the same direction as the first twist.

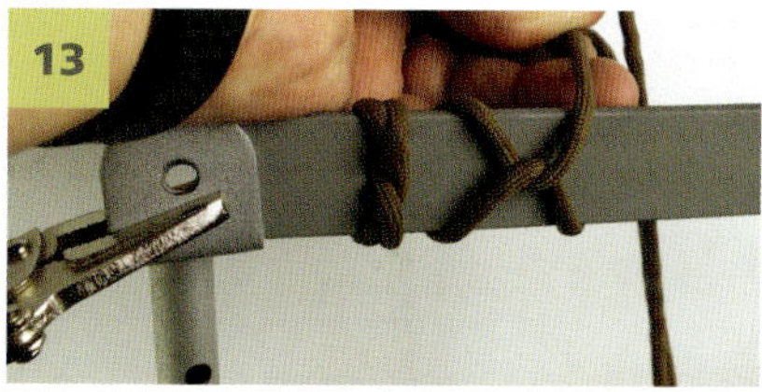

Return the cord ends to the backside of the handle.

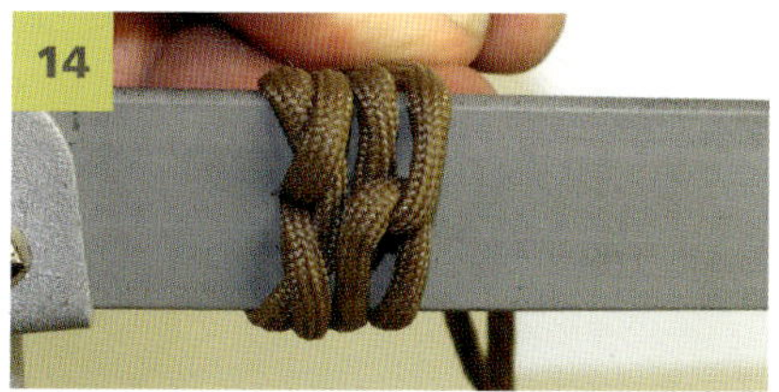

Here both loops rest next to each other.

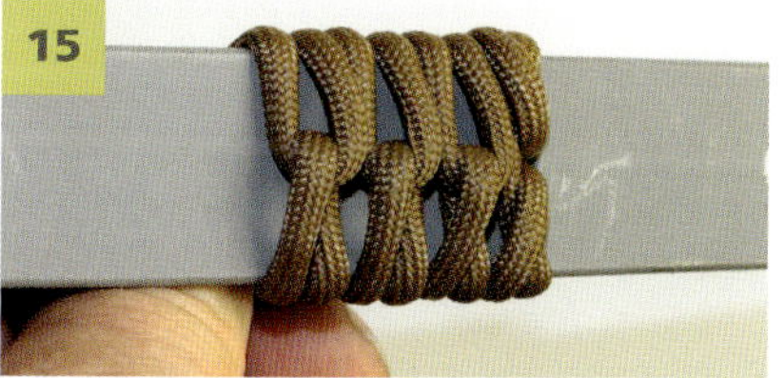

Continue in the same way until you reach the inner pommel hole.

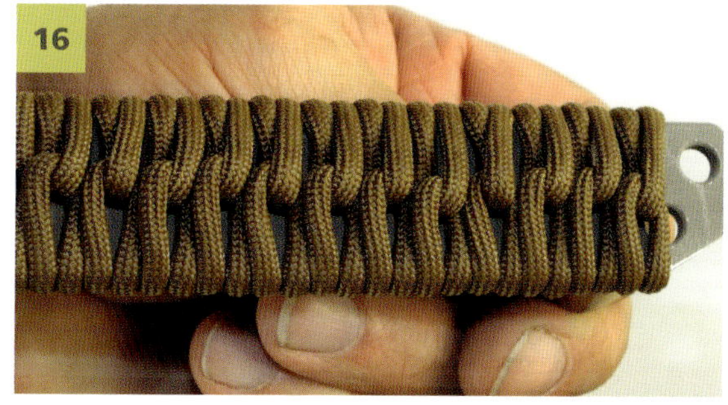

As soon as the inner handle hole is partially covered press the loops close together once more. If enough space is left, make another loop before turning the knife around.

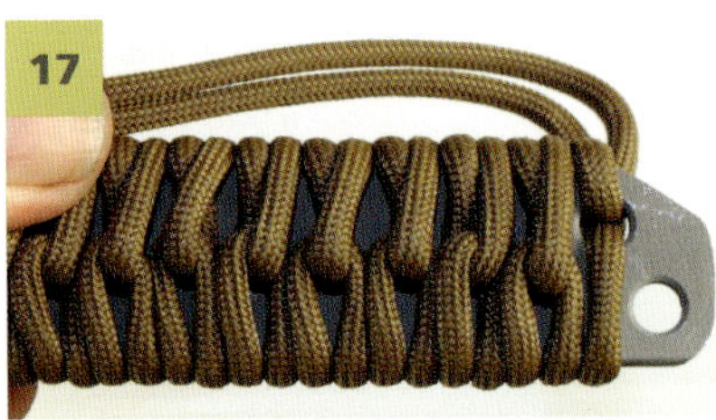

Keep the tension by clamping the working ends to the handle sides and pull both ends through the inner hole.

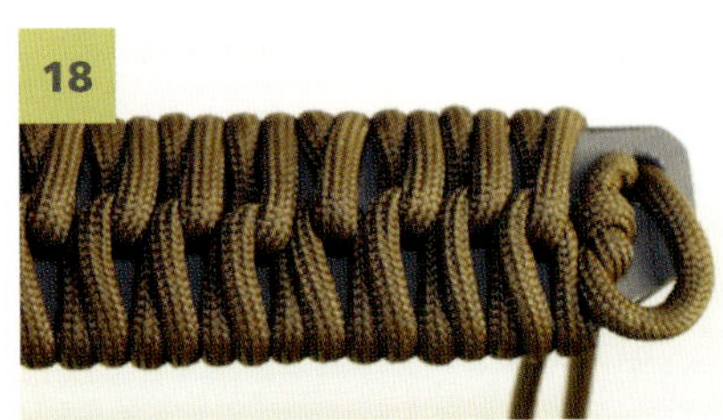

Make an overhand knot and guide both working ends through the last hole.

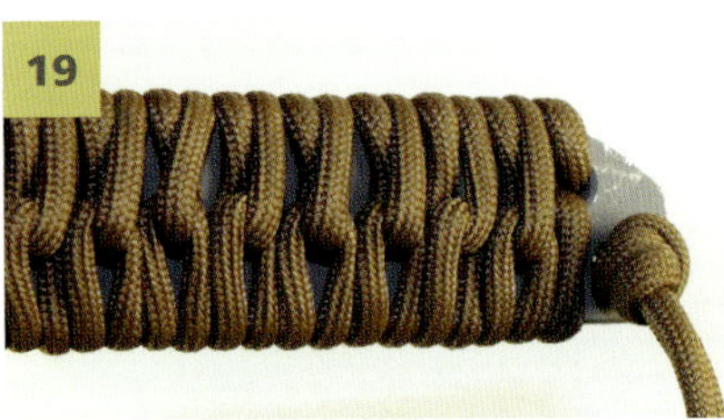

Put both ends together and make an overhand knot you press against the tang. You can form a lanyard with both working ends.

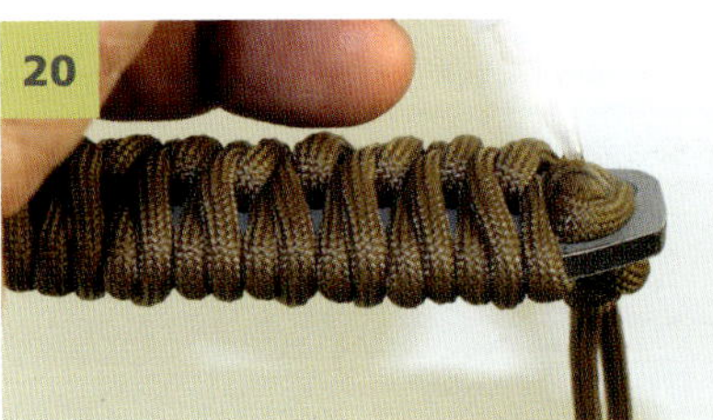

Seal the first knot with a drop of glue to fix it.

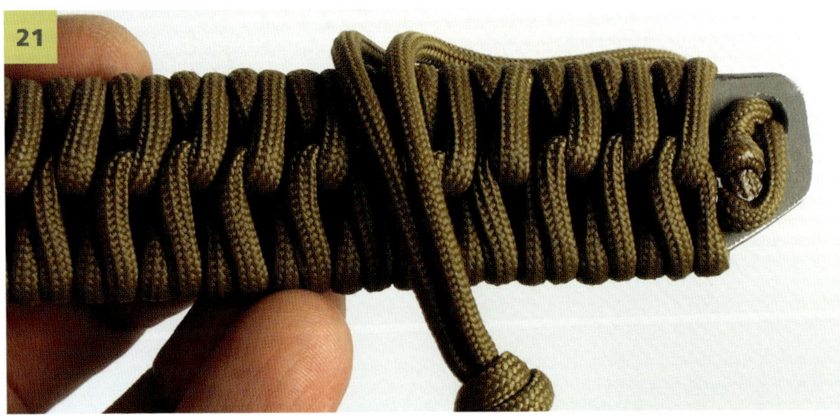

The looped wrap and lanyard are finished.

PARACORD——TSUKAMAKI

5.1 What Is *Tsukamaki?*

Tsukamaki is the art of wrapping a *tsuka*, the Japanese sword handle. Over hundreds of years Japanese sword masters have brought the system of sword handles to perfection. The handles can be removed from the blade by pushing out the *mekugi* (bamboo pin). This way the maintenance of the sword tang, which is necessary in the moist climate of Japan, can be performed. The complete system withstands the forces applied to it during battle.

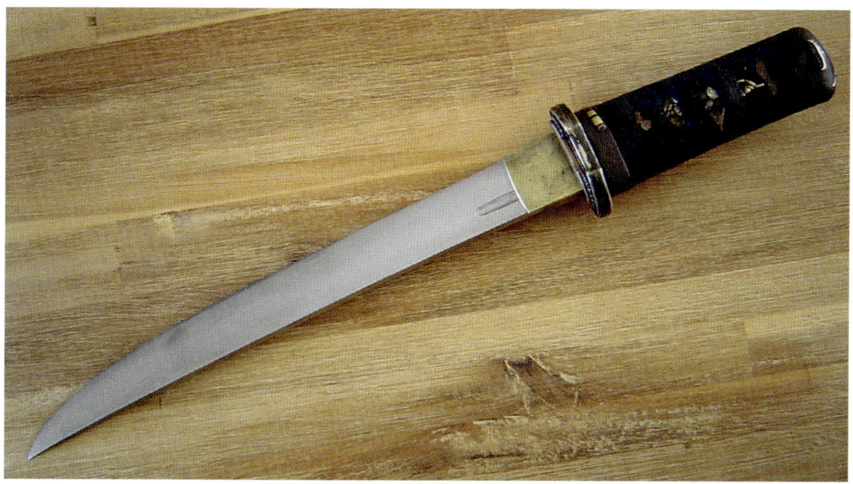

A historical tanto displays the traditional handle structure. Courtesy of Alessio Salsi

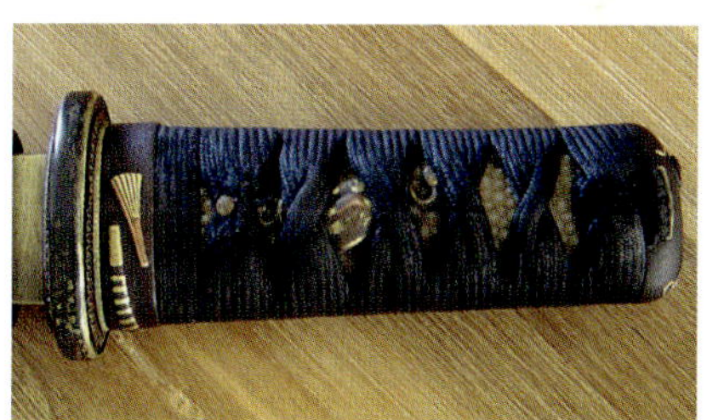

Here you can see the different parts of the handle.

The wrap traditionally is made with *ito*, a flat, woven band of silk or cotton. Different kinds of leather, paper, or woven/braided hemp were used as well. A special type of *ito* is *jabara-ito*: strings of one and 1.5 mm diameter silk. Often two strings of *jabara-ito* were sewn together to make wrapping the handle easier and to make the *ito* more stable.

PARTS OF A JAPANESE SWORD HANDLE

habaki	ferrule in front of the guard providing a friction fit to keep the sword and sheath together. Mostly of copper alloys, but also made of silver and gold.
seppa	spacer (of copper or brass); the spacers between *habaki* and guard and between guard and fushi hold the wooden handle *(tsuka)* under tension after the mekugi has been inserted. They eliminate any play within the construction.
tsuba	guard, mostly made of iron and very often richly decorated. *Tsuba* have become collector's items.
seppa	spacer (second set; sometimes more than one seppa is necessary to eliminate play in the handle).
fushi	metal ferrule around the wooden handle directly behind the guard; helps to prevent the handle splitting.
tsuka	the wooden core of the handle.
same	stingray skin. It is visible beneath the handle wrap or covers the entire tsuka without a handle wrap.
ito	flat, woven band of silk or cotton, leather, or paper. In case of the latter, the handle wrap was often strongly lacquered.
menuki	lucky charm on the handle, sometimes of gold or gilded. Depending on the handle length there is either one (with tantos) or two lucky charms (with katanas).
mekugi	bamboo pin to keep the *tsuka* on the *nakago* (sword tang).
mekugi ana	the hole through the handle and tang for the *mekugi*.
kashira	pommel cover, often with a hole from the *omote* (front side) to the *ura* (back side). Here the ito runs through between the end knots of the wrap. Gunto mountings do not have a kashira with holes.
shito dome	sleeve in the hole through the *kashira*. Decorative, while at the same time protecting the *ito*, which runs through the hole.

An important part of *tsukamaki* is the *hishi-gami*: folded paper wedges pushed under the *ito* to keep the shape of the *ito*'s crossings perfect and to prevent the wrap from shifting or deforming. This art is on a higher level than this book can provide, but if you are inspired to dig deeper into this topic, one of the best sources for this is listed at the end of this book.

The silk- or cotton-*ito* is available in several widths. The longer the handle, the wider the used *ito*. Here is some advice for the best known handle wraps with twisted and flat crossing:

- *katana* handles are 23 cm long. For them 10 mm wide *ito* are used.

- *wakizashi* handles are about 15 cm long and are wrapped with 8 mm wide *ito*.

- For *tanto* and *aikuchi* with 10 cm long handles 4–6 mm wide *ito* are used.

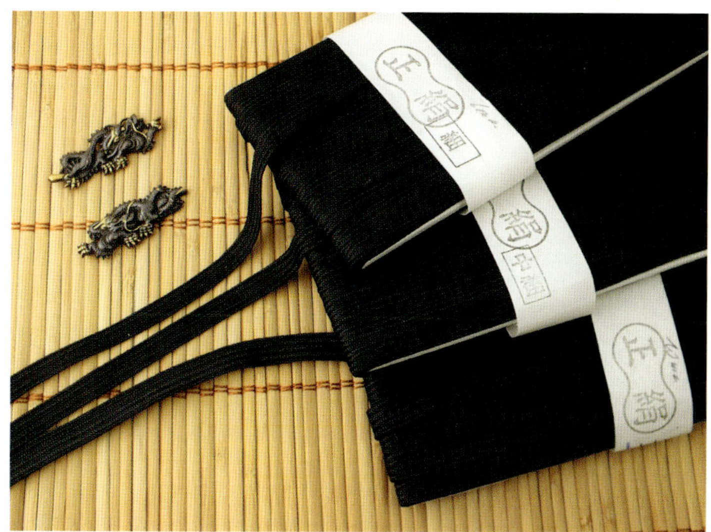

Original Japanese silk *ito* 6 mm, 8 mm, and 10 mm. Two dragon *menuki* in black and gold.

Four millimeter wide *ito* are also used for complicated *tsukamaki* patterns. Here the versatile paracord comes into play; the empty sleeve of paracord is quite close to the dimensions of the small *ito* types used for sword and knife handles. The sleeve of type IV paracord comes closest to the six millimeter wide *ito* and leads to the best results with respect to the classical, twisted handle wrap.

Handles wrapped in the Japanese style can be divided into three categories:

- traditional handles with all decorations.

- flat, modern variants. Usually the flat tang is covered on both sides with *same* (stingray skin) or other exotic kinds of leather. The wrap is either done with shoe laces, true cotton- or silk-*ito*, or with paracord.

- the third category, between the two others. Here the tang receives more volume with wood or another material before the *same* is put on and the handle is wrapped. Wooden handles with fine grain structures are wrapped in such a way that the grain structure remains visible underneath the open structure of the wrap.

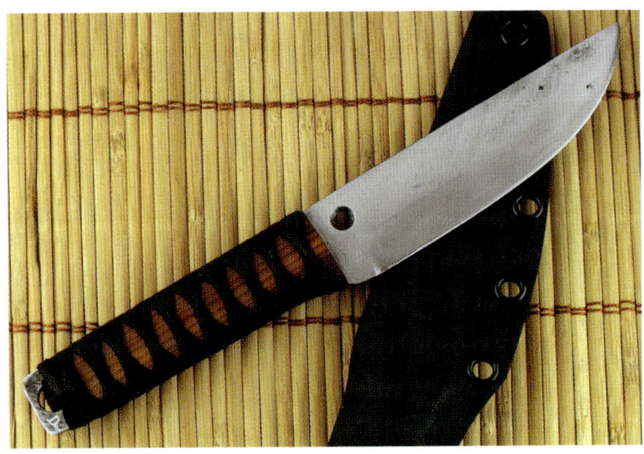

Twisted *maki* on top of yew wood.

An important difference between real *ito* and flatline is that flatline is a hollow sleeve, while *ito* is a flat, woven band. Flatline has the tendency to slip or roll, therefore, it is much more difficult to make perfect twists and folds with it.

While preparing the handle, measure the width of the flatline and the length of the handle. Divide the handle length by the width of the flatline. Round this number upward and mark the number of wraps on the handle's sides. In an ideal case we should have an odd number on both sides (the edges) of the handle. If necessary, you can either choose another width of flatline or you push the cord on the handle a bit closer together (this is advisable to prevent gaps between the turns in case the cord shrinks later on).

It is important that the finishing end knot (*omote* knot) rests on the front side of the handle. *Tsukamaki* artisans glue paper strips on the front- and backsides of the handle to mark the *ito*'s width. This way they have the chance to follow the width of the *ito* and to adjust it, if needed, while working their way forward along the handle.

If we make a basic layer of flatline, we can adjust the width of the flatline in such a way that we achieve the needed odd number of turns. This is no absolute necessity, but it lifts our wrapped handle to a higher level. Japanese *tsukamaki* experts use a contraption to work on a sword handle. Often they also use a sword dummy with a short "blade" and *nakago* (tang) to which the handle (*tsuka*) is fixed during work. This way they avoid ruining a very valuable blade.

5.2 Handle Wraps

5.2.1 Classic Twisted Diamond Handle Wrap
Menpu Maki (Thomas Buck)

Some knifemakers call this wrap samurai wrap or diamond wrap (because during the wrap the gaps take on the shape of diamonds). For this we choose the widest paracord flatline we can get to create the most beautiful pattern.

The flatline is twisted inward while we change from one side of the handle to the other. This way the crossings are raised in the center and thus the feel of grip of the wrapped handle is enhanced.

We start by covering the blade with tape and tissue. As with most Japanese handle wraps, we wrap the handle one and a half times before cutting the cord to the appropriate length.

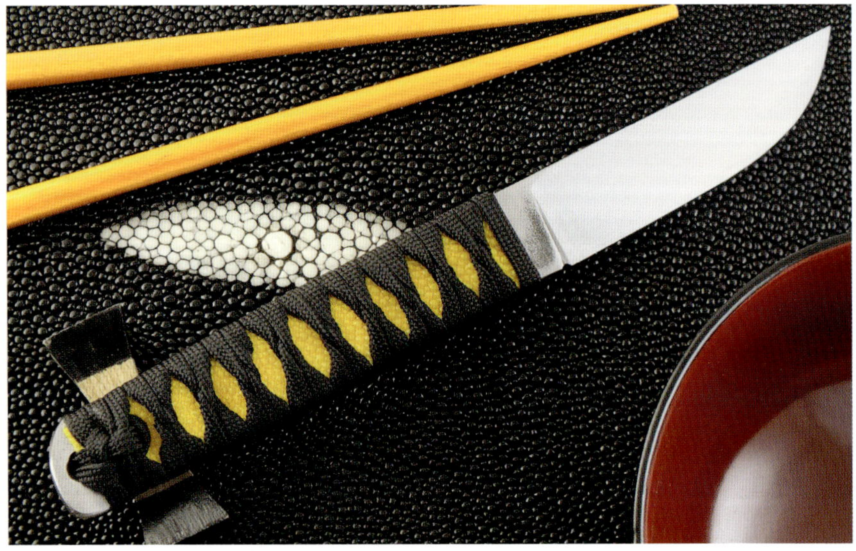

Kaiken of A2 steel with traditional twisted wrap done with flatline of type IV over yellow ray skin.

Empty the sleeve by removing all inner strings, then melt and mold the ends into a slim, flat shape. This prevents the cord unraveling. When everything is tight enough, it makes sense to cut off the hard edge of the melted plastic to prevent it from getting snagged under the two last crossings when it is pulled through underneath.

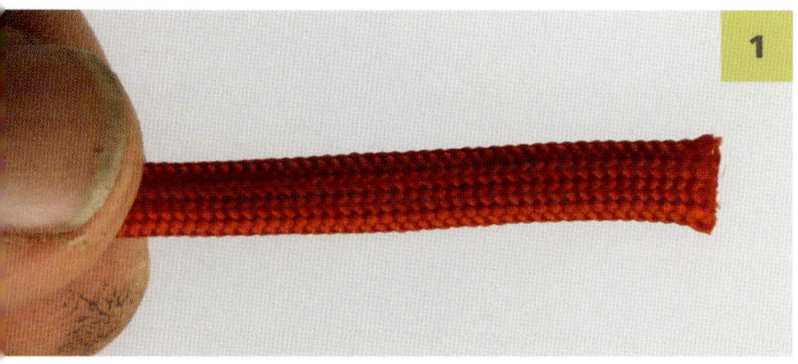

Cut the ends off neatly and at right angles.

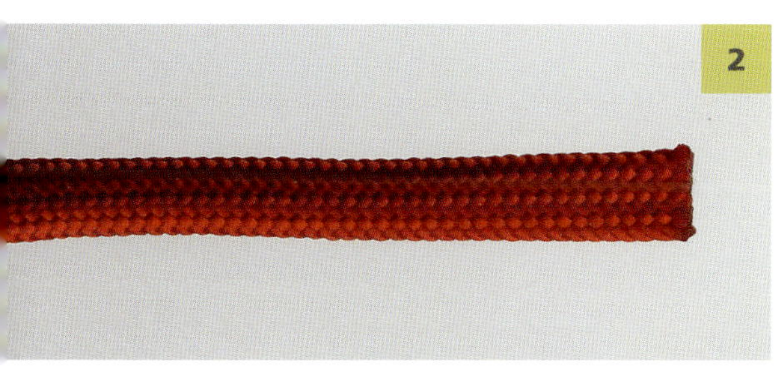

Melt the ends slightly and press them flat.

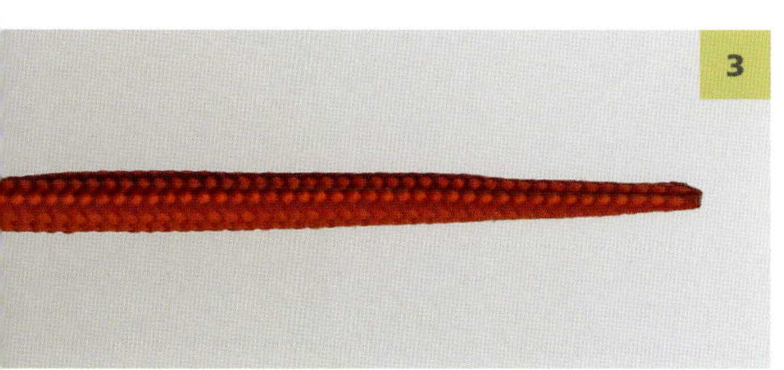

Sometimes it is better to cut such a hard end off before beginning the traditional end knots to prevent the cord getting caught while pulling it through the end knots.

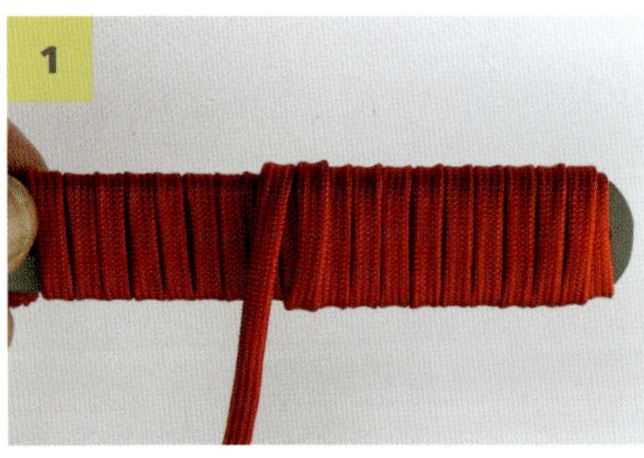

Determine the cord length by wrapping the handle one and a half times. Cut the cord off, remove the core strings, and melt and shape the ends.

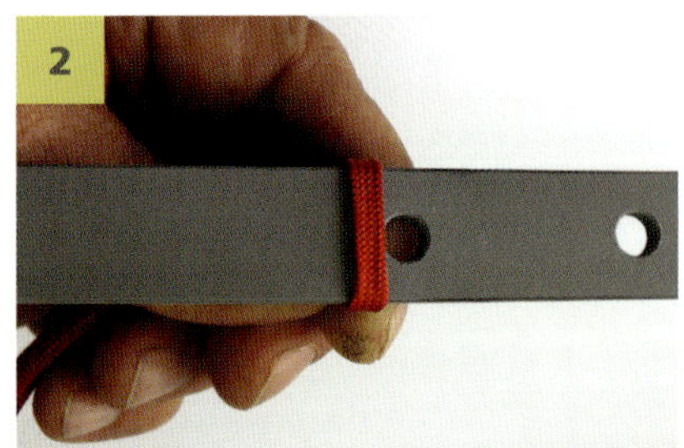

Put the center of the cord on the handle's front end (toward the blade) on the *omote-*side. This is the side visible when the knife is carried in its sheath.

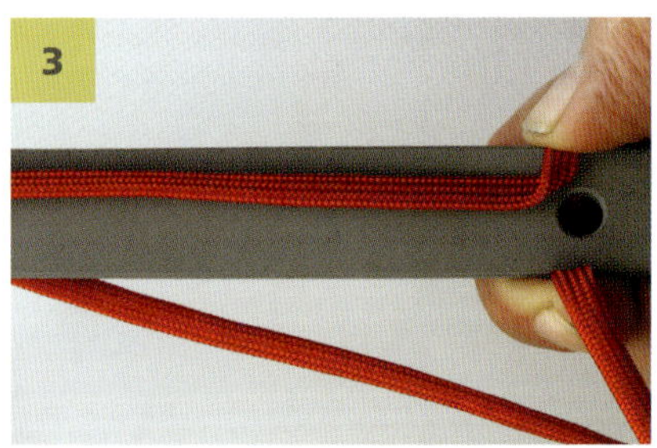

We turn the knife around and twist the upper end (we call it "right cord" to make it simple) inward and put the end alongside the tang.

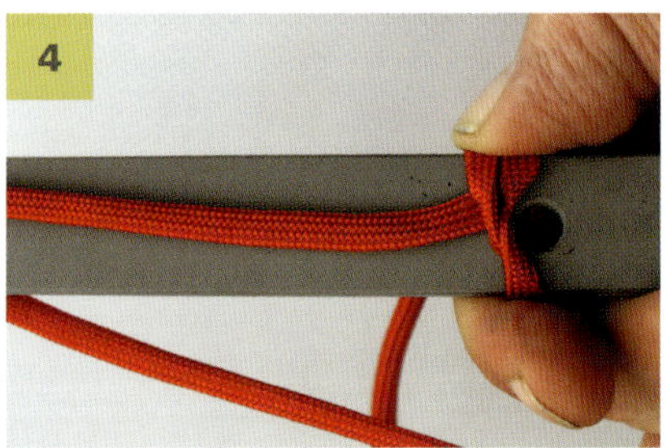

Twist the left cord (the cord end beneath) two times, guide it upward, and hold it tight with your thumb.

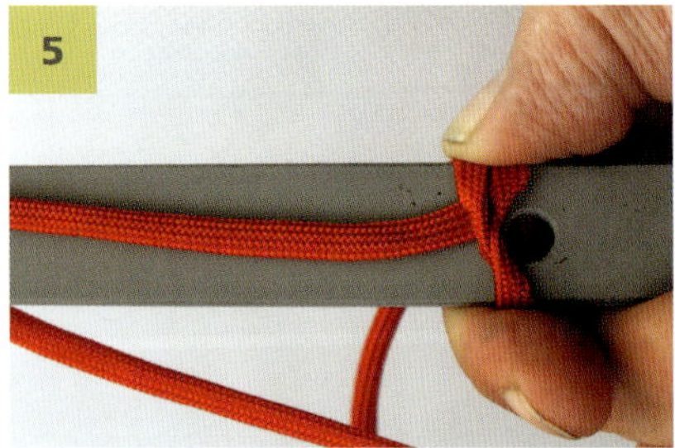

The left cord has to rest behind the right one, meaning toward the pommel (left side of the photo).

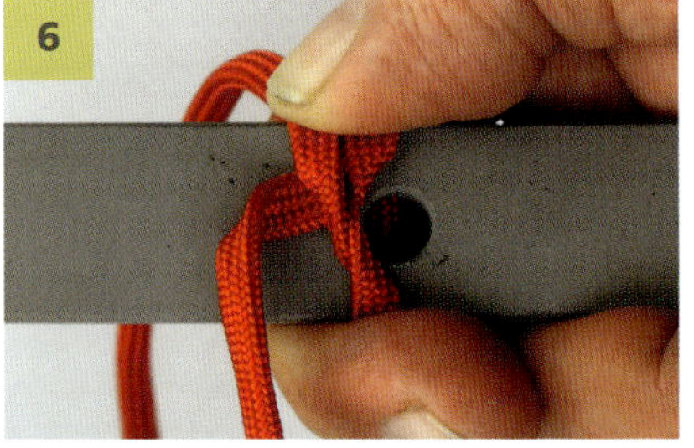

Now twist the right side (through 90° downward) and guide it downward around the tang.

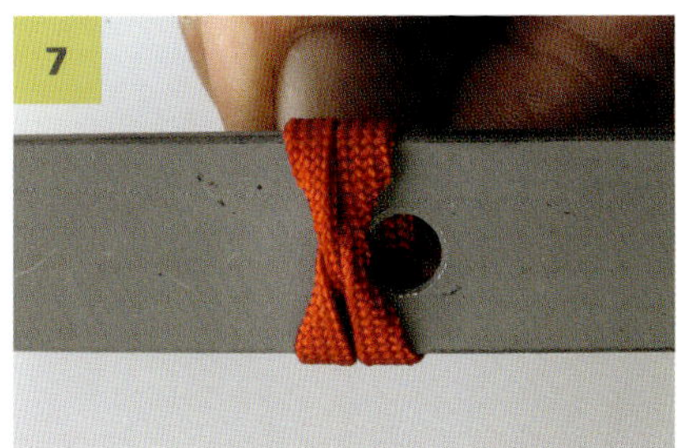

Pull both cords tight and correct the position and the "folds," if needed, by means of a marlin spike or pin.

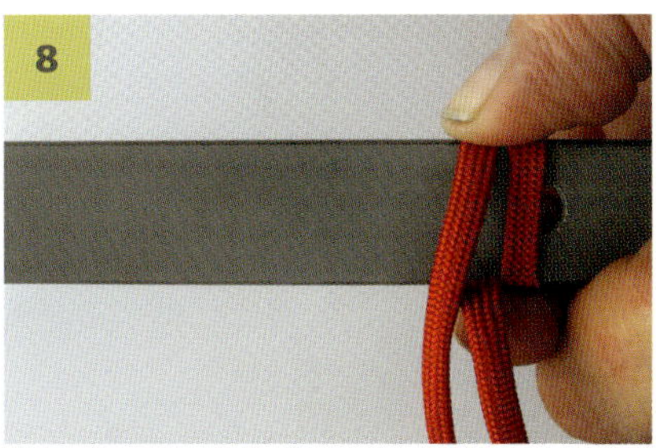

Turn the handle around, but hold everything tight. Pinch both cord ends tight against the edges of the tang with your thumb and forefinger.

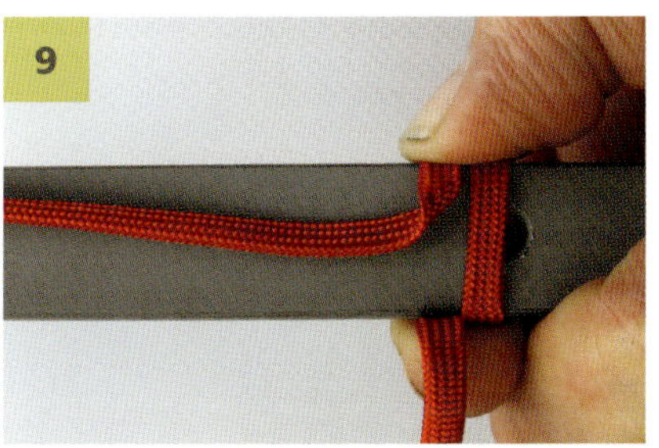

Twist the upper cord inward again by 90° and put the working end alongside the tang.

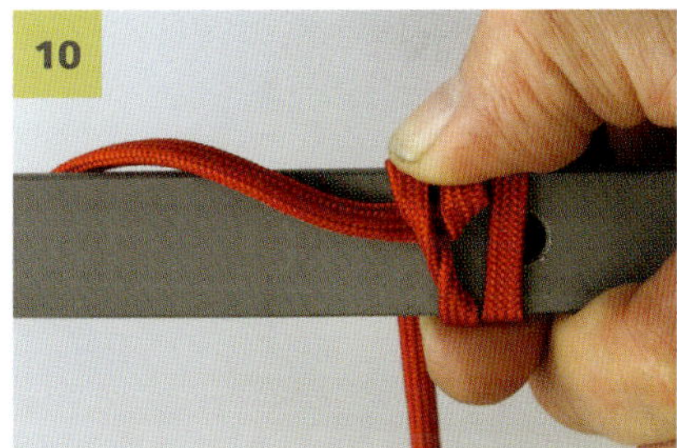

Twist the lower cord twice (these are a full 360°) and put it over the other end.

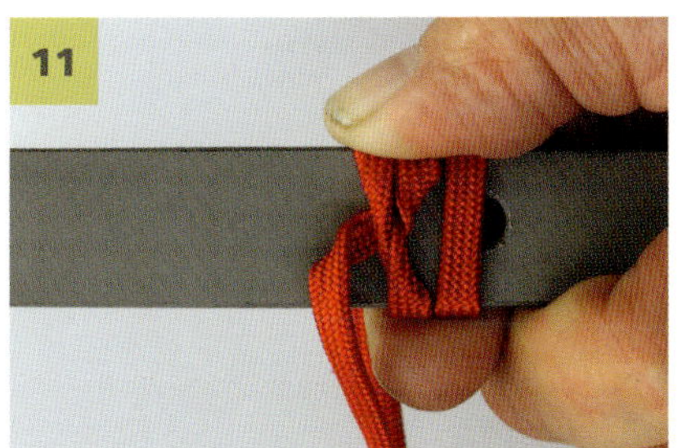

Twist the right end through 90° and guide it downward to complete the move.

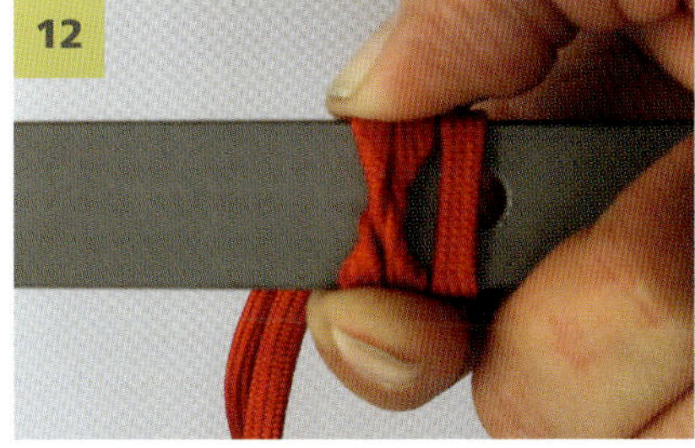

Pull both ends tight, correct the position, if necessary, and turn the handle around.

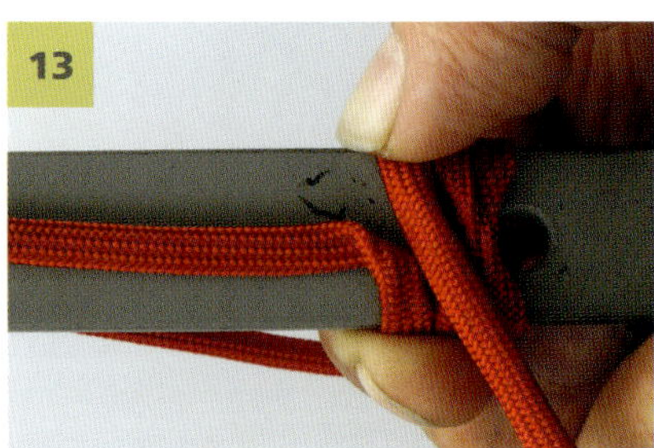

Start the next crossing with the end of the left side (this is now the cord end below).

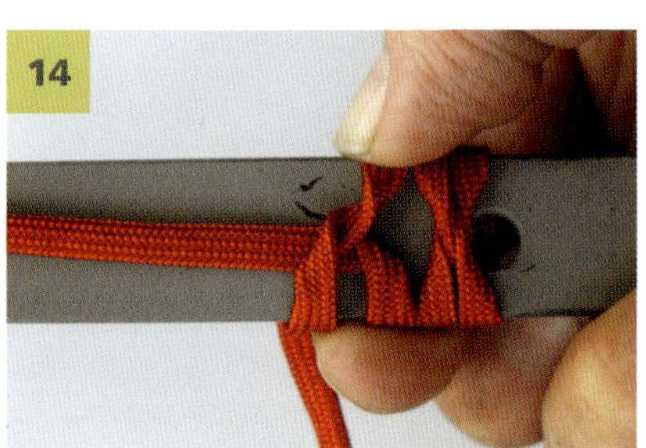

Twist the upper end through 360° and put it downward over the other end.

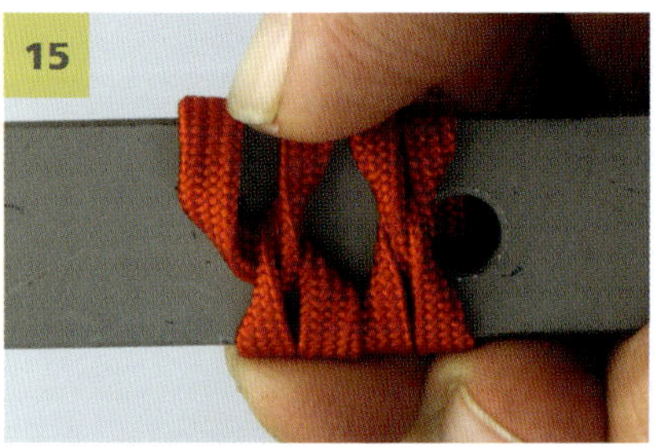

Fold the left (lower) end a second time through 90° and guide it upward to finish the crossing.

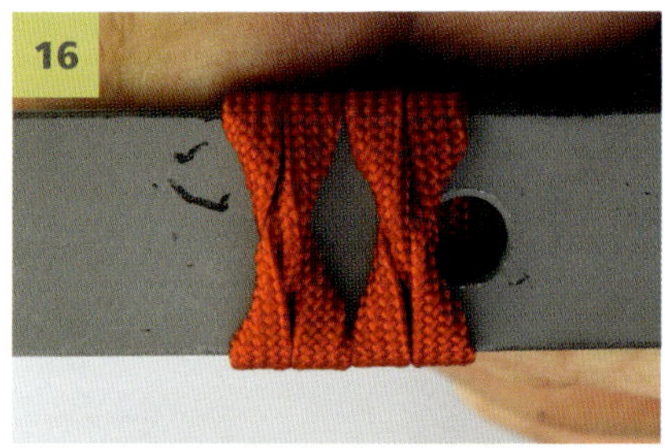

Pull both ends to the backside. Correct the position of the knot. Check whether all folds are alright and the cords rest close to each other on the sides of the handle.

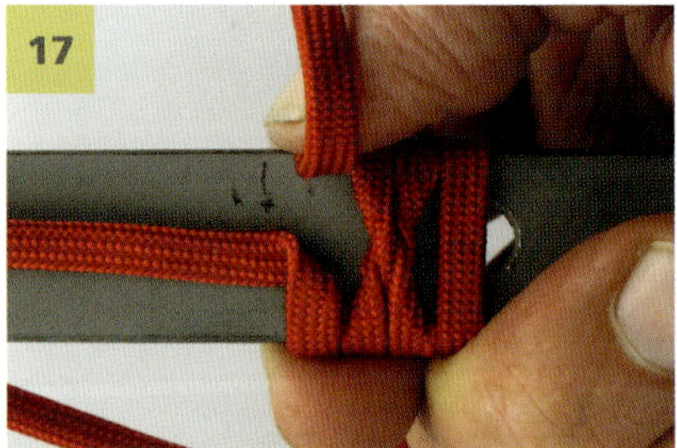

On the other side (*omote*) the crossing this time starts with the left (lower) end, too.

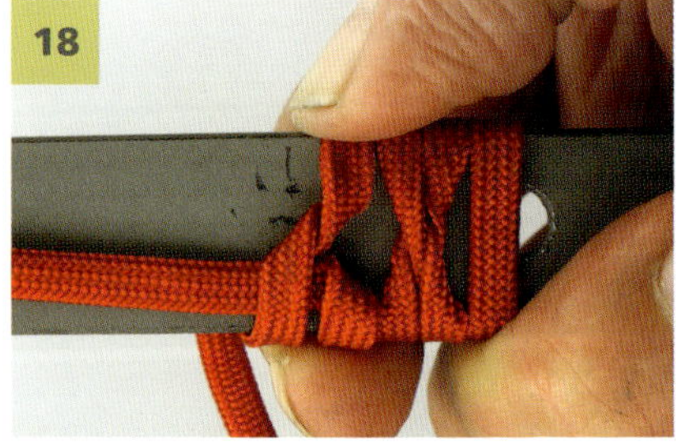

The right end is turned through 360° (we are already used to this) and is guided downward over the other end.

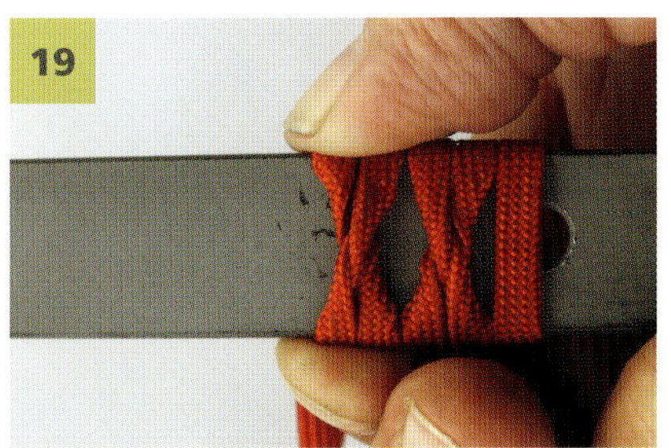

When the other end is twisted through 90° once more and put upward, the crossing is done.

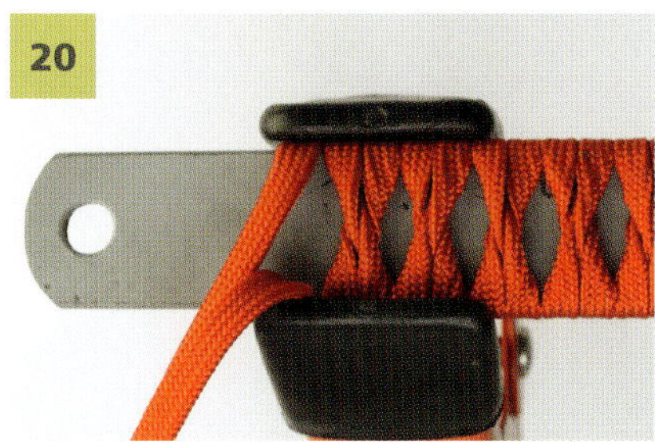

If you need a break you best use a clamp.

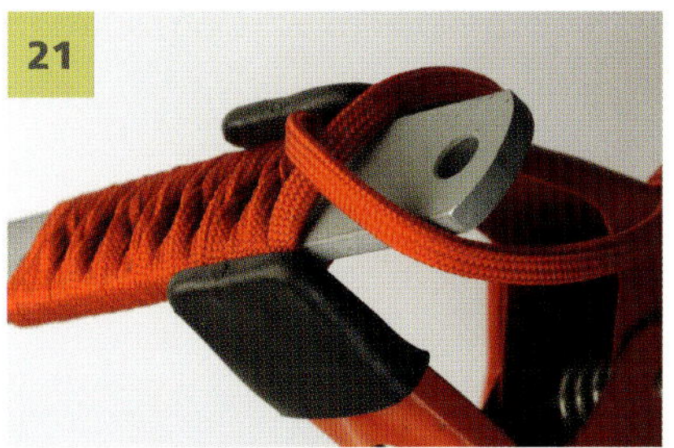

The view of the clamp from the other side. It is important that it holds both cord ends securely in position.

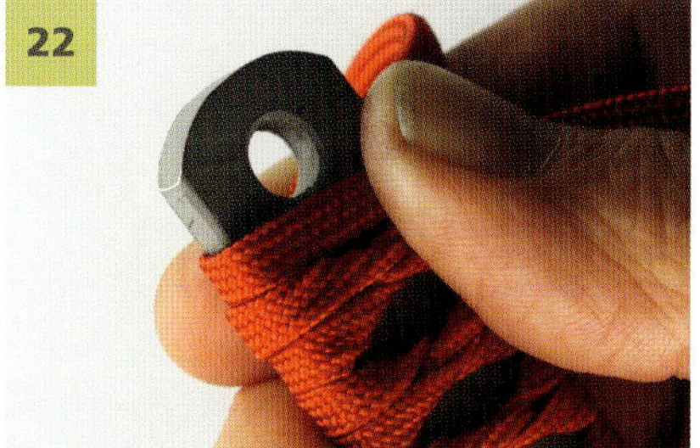

When you have reached the handle's end you can put a drop of glue under the cord to fix the wrap.

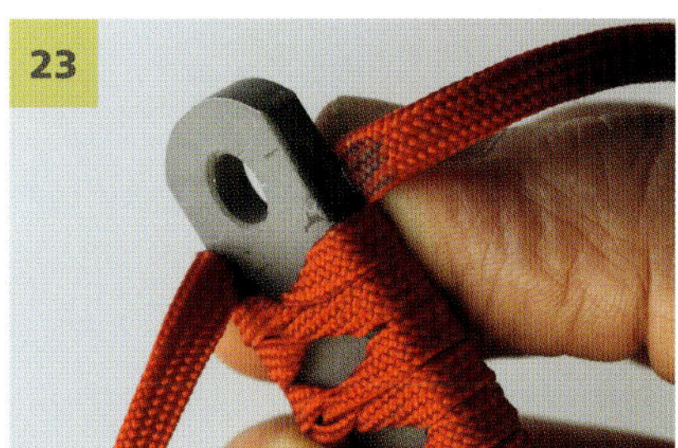

The other end is glued as well.

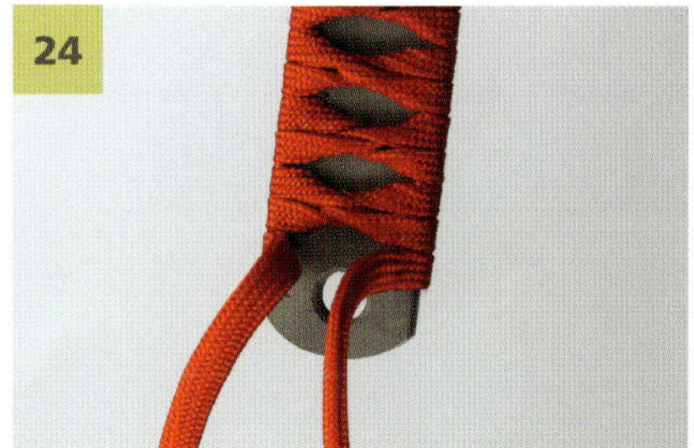

The glue allows us to relax. A clamp is no longer necessary, making creating the end knot easier.

There are two basic types of end knots. The traditional knots are typical for the *ura-* and *omote*-sides of the handle. With classic *tsukamaki*, the last crossing is at the pommel on the *omote*-side of the handle. We will soon deal with the end knots in more detail.

Please notice that I made the first turn of the end on the right side in two steps instead of making everything at once. If this twist is done in a single step and the tension on the cord is applied beyond the edge of the handle it is difficult to "cage" the twist of the second end between the folds of the first one. Quite often we see wraps where the second end of the cord lies on top of the first one and slips forward and backward. Making the crossing in two steps looks better and is also more stable.

It is hard work to keep the tension on the flatline with thumb and forefinger, but tension is very important if you want to make a well-wrapped handle. If you need a break you can attach a clamp at the sides of the handle to prevent the handle wrap from slipping.

If we want to put a *menuki* underneath the wrap, it is best to place it on the *omote*-side and—when using a wider *ito*—after the second or third crossing. But since we use a relatively small flatline material we can choose to place it closer to the handle's center because the total number of shaped diamonds will be higher.

5.2.2 End Knots

End knots are no exact science. Some factors, such as the handle width, the thickness of one or several cords, the type of handle wrap, and the size of the pommel hole (in case there is one) can influence how the knot is done. Sometimes an alternative can be found which leads to a pretty result—a knot which looks really good at the handle end of your knife.

We use a special technique with two needles and a thread taken from the core of your cord (or trout yarn, which is often used for sewing leather sheaths) to pull the cord underneath the quite tight crossings. This works best in case the wrap is done on a hard base or on *same* (stingray skin).

With the "one needle technique" the string is led through the needle's eyes with several loops. Compared to the technique with two needles you need a heavier needle with a larger eye.

Instead of using needle and thread you can also use a bent steel wire to guide the flatline under the last crossing. This is easier if the underlay is made of soft material, such as flatline. With needles you often get stuck in the soft substrate. The wire has to be pushed under the crossings with pliers if the wrap was made pretty tight. The wire will bend and twist under the applied force, but it is a good alternative to the needle technique.

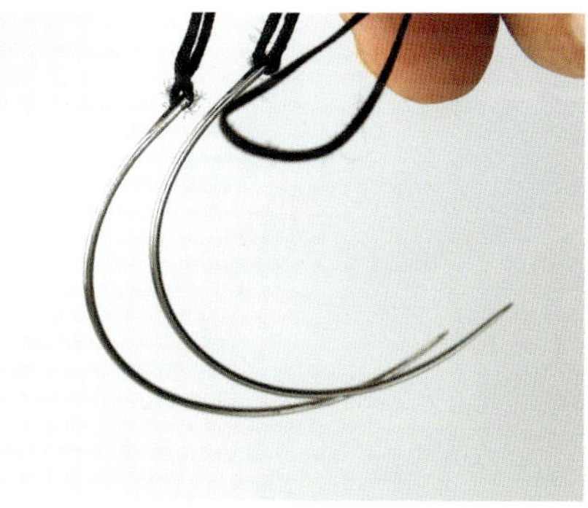

A piece of trout yarn and two curved needles are the best-suited tools for pulling the cord underneath the crossings.

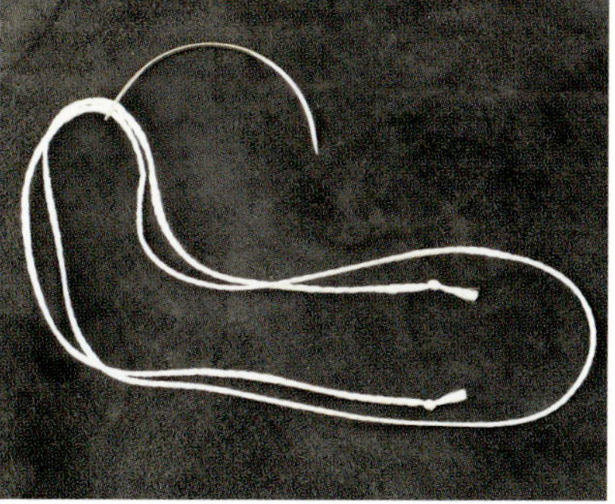

The technique with one needle and yarn: the yarn is guided two times through the needle's eye. The loop is just long enough to guide the *ito* underneath the crossings.

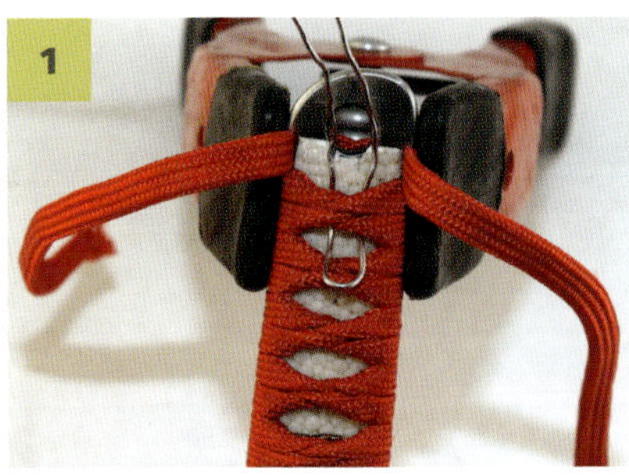

Technique with bent wire: the wire is guided underneath the last crossing to begin an *ura* knot which completes a handle wrap in gunto style.

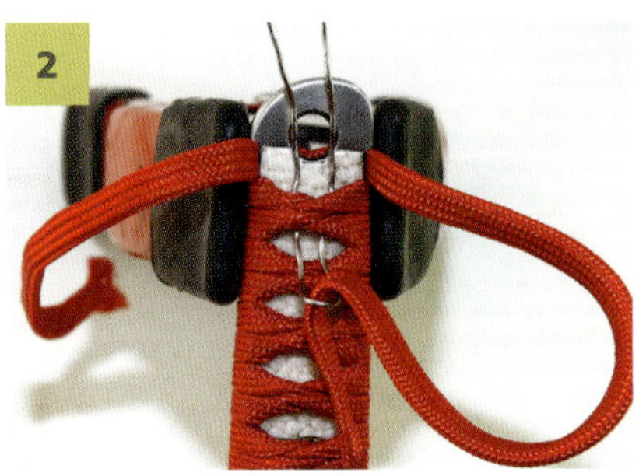

The right cord end is put inside the loop and is ready to be pulled underneath the crossing.

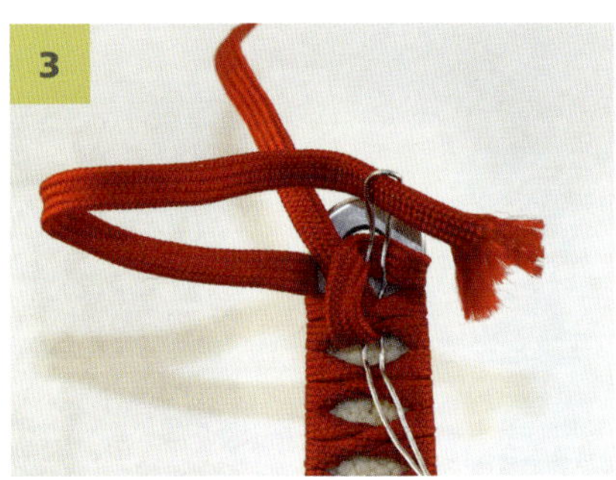

The wire is guided right in the direction of the pommel. The left cord end is in position to be pulled through.

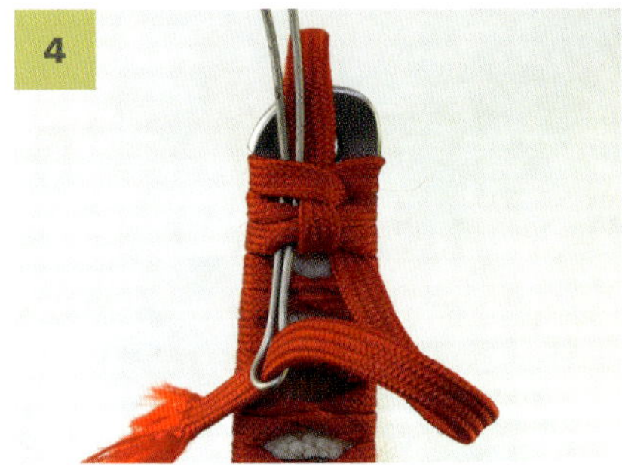

The cord ends are pulled tight. The lower cord end is pulled underneath the last crossing on the left side.

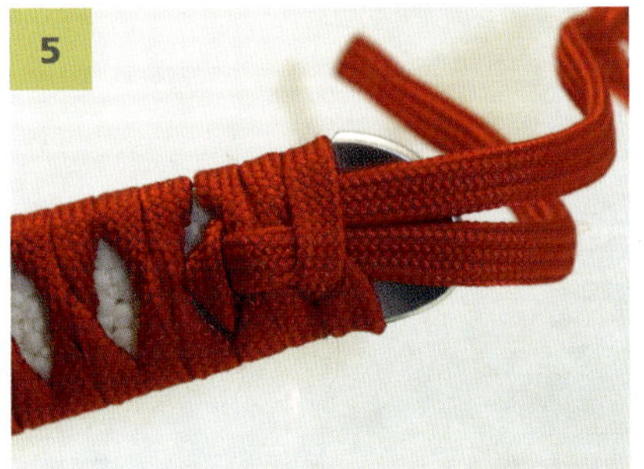

Both cord ends are tight. Here you can see how nicely the curve of the cord fits underneath the knot. Both cord ends are cut off and kept in position with a drop of glue.

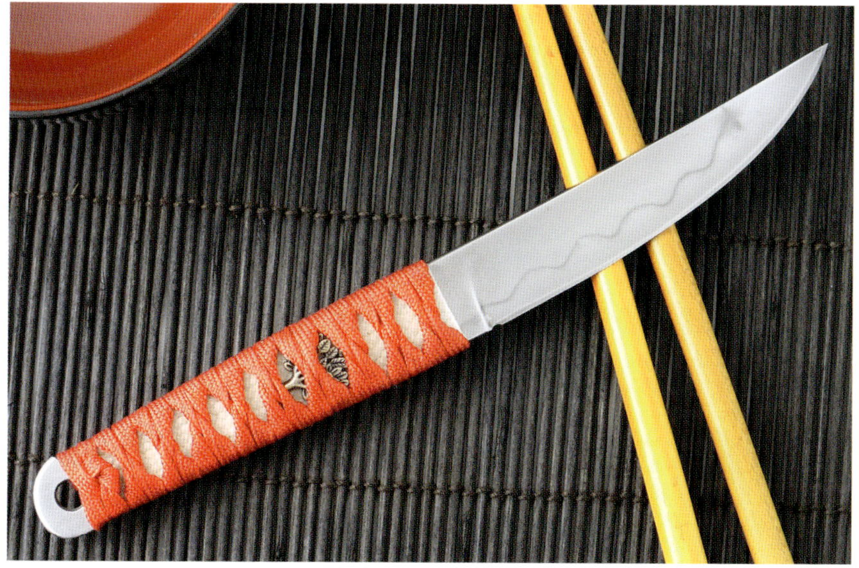

The backside of the finished knife.

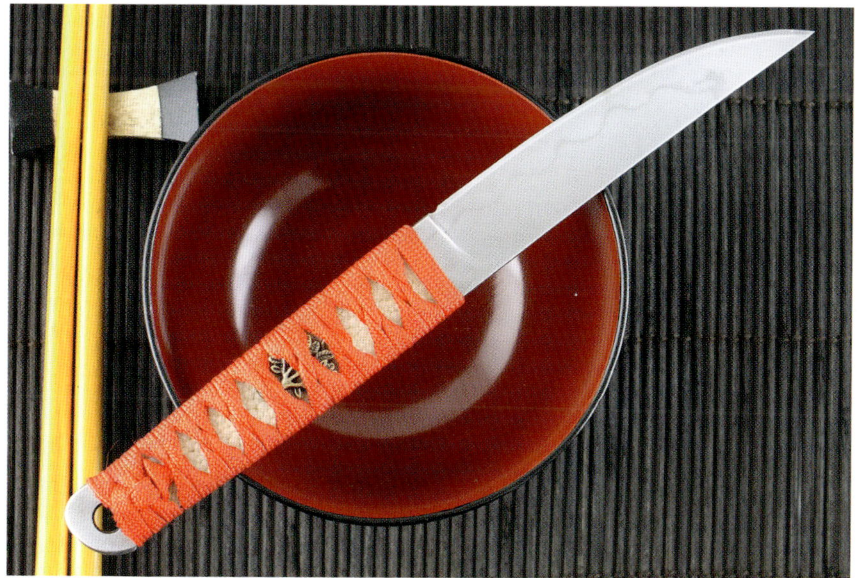

The *omote* side of the *kaiken*.

If the number of turns is correct, we end up at the *ura*-side and can make the knots the right way. We hold the knife with the pommel facing upward.

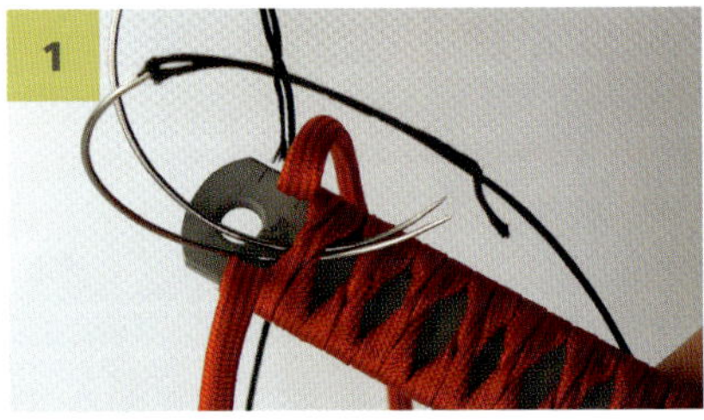

Guide the needles underneath the last crossing.

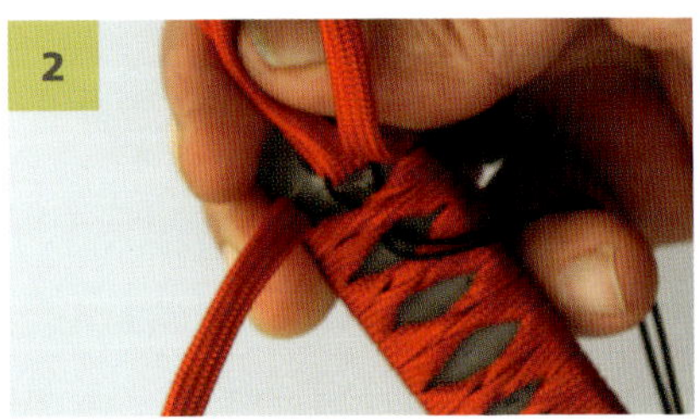

Pull the right cord end underneath the crossing.

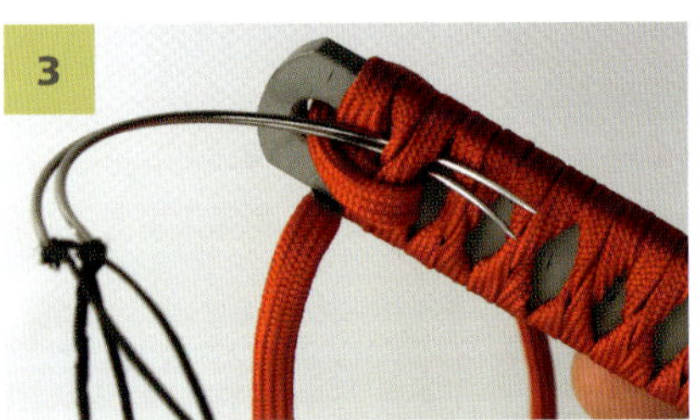

Park the right end on top by leading it through the hole in the pommel. Guide the needles on the right side underneath the last crossing.

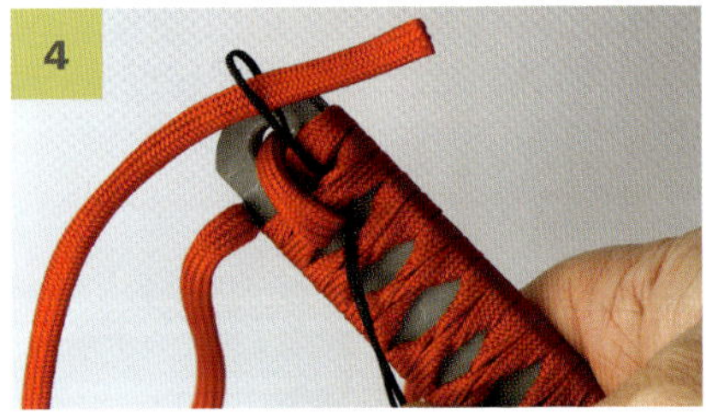

Guide the left working end into the string's loop and pull the string tight. The cord is now positioned at the crossing.

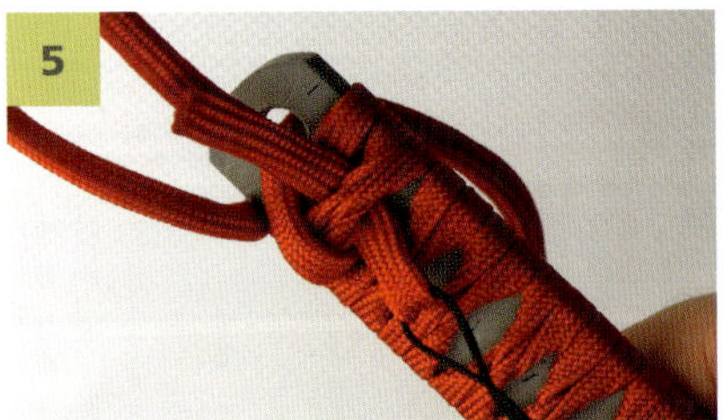

Pull the left end underneath the crossing.

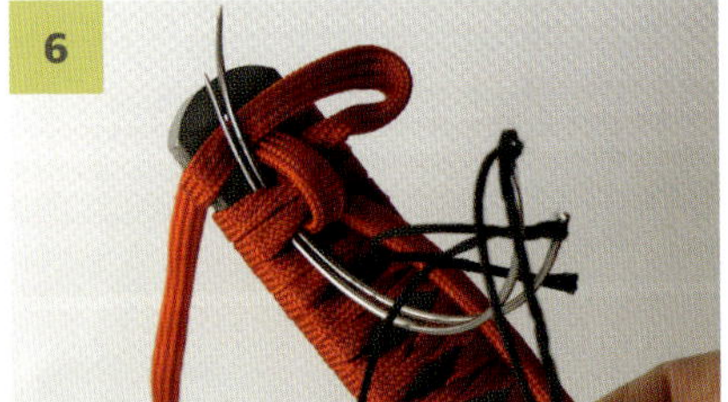

Here the needles are inserted pointing upward on the left side of the knot underneath the crossing.

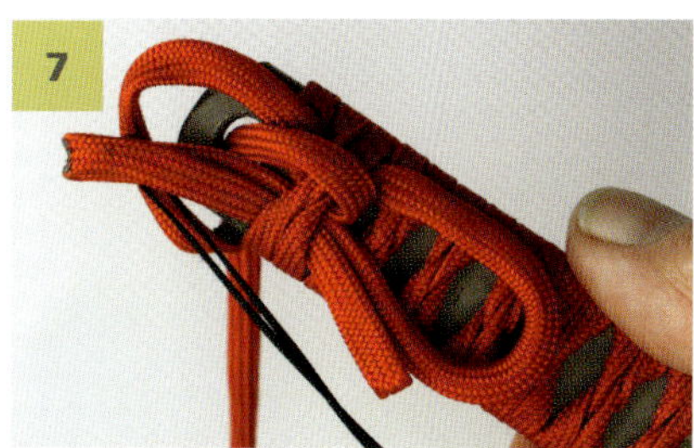

Pull the cord upward. The working end goes under the last crossing. Make sure the cord is not twisted. This way the curve will rest perfectly against the bottom of the knot.

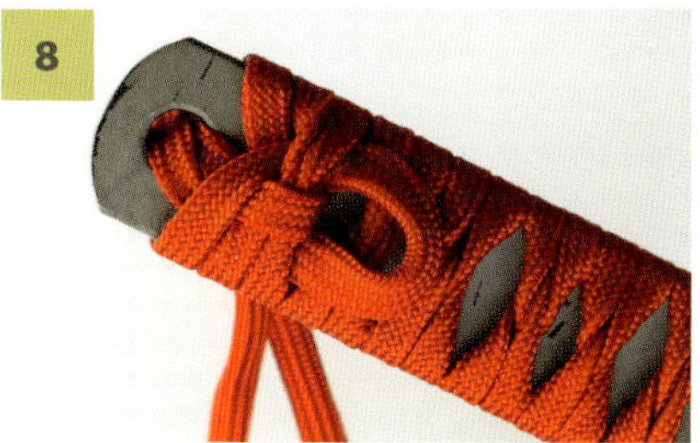

The cord is pulled through completely. The end is brought through the pommel hole to the other side.

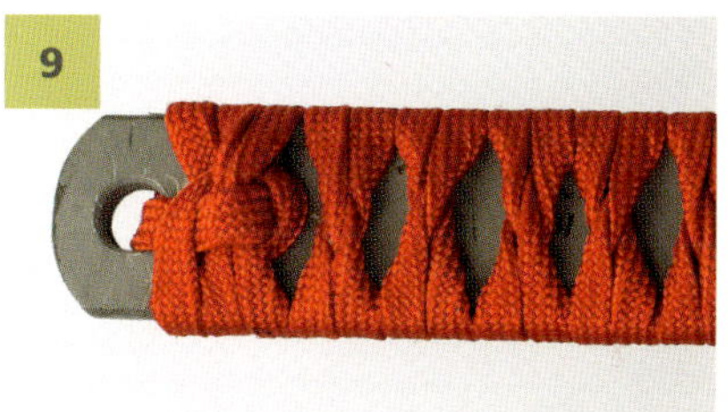

Correct the knot. If the cord is twisted, it can still be corrected so the knot will look neat.

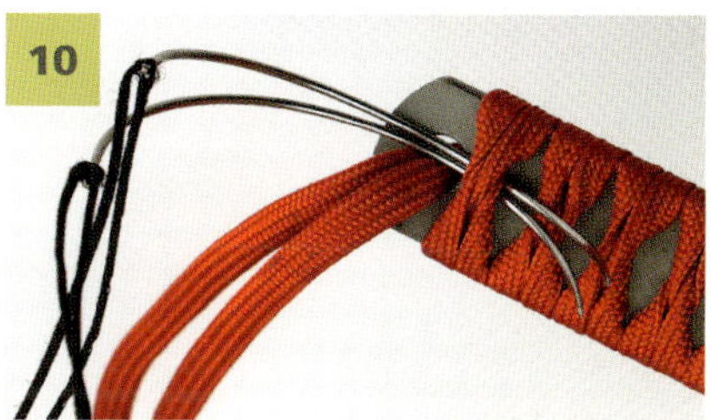

Turn the handle around. Insert the needles underneath the last crossing.

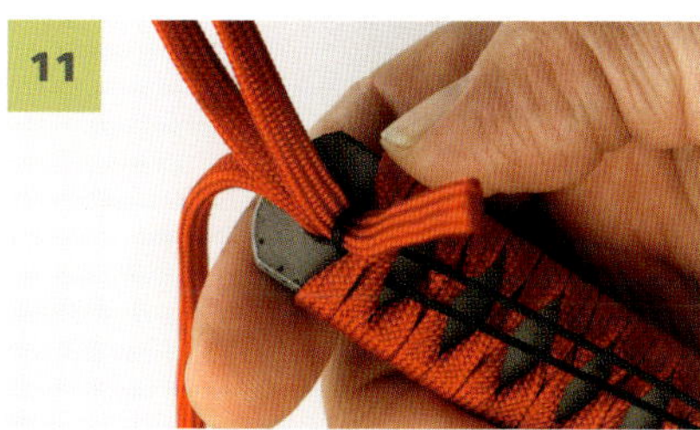

Pull the first end under the last crossing and go upward again through the pommel hole.

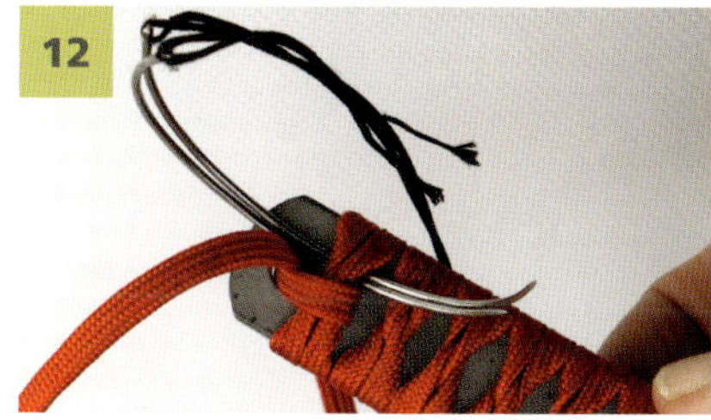

Guide the needles pointing downward on the right side of the knot underneath the crossing.

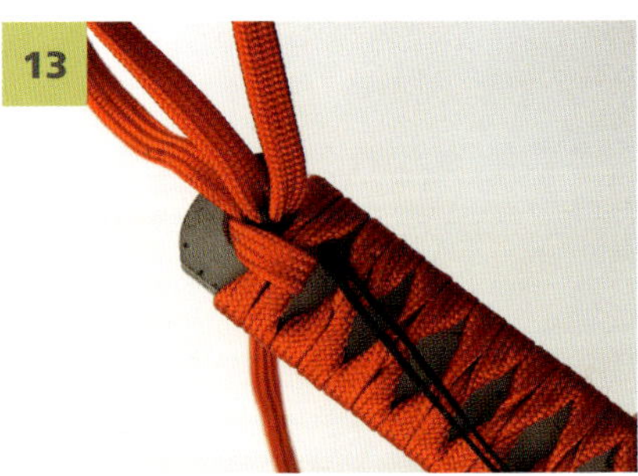

Use a string to pull the cord end through.

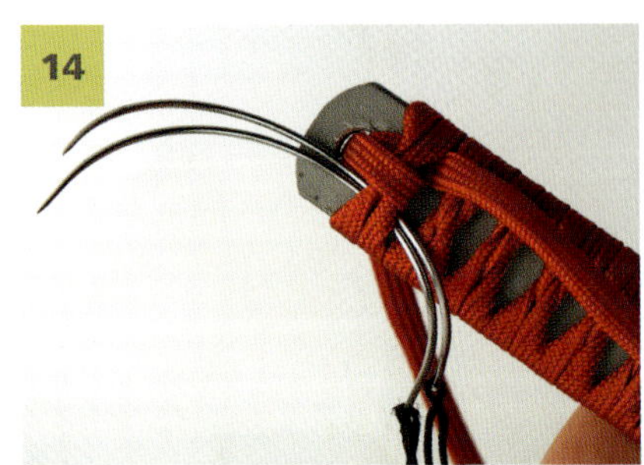

Insert the needles on the left side pointing upward.

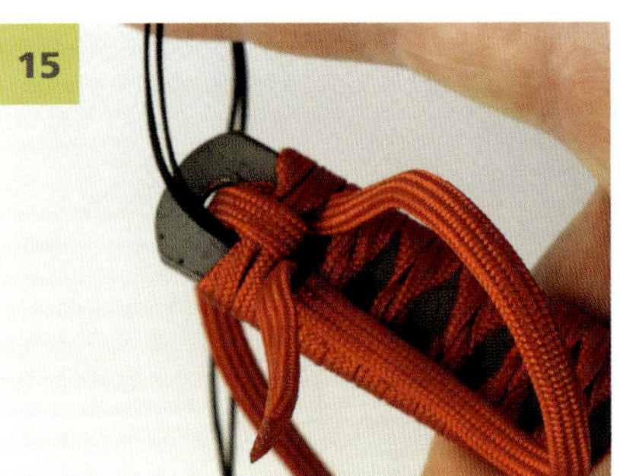

The cord is pulled under the crossing.

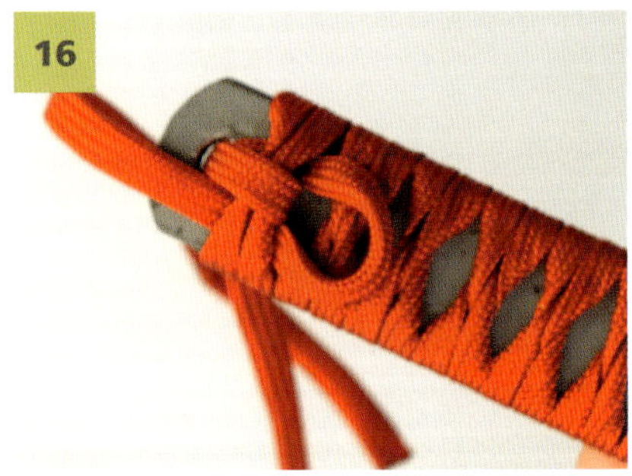

The loop under the knot is adjusted. Remove all twists before pulling the loop tight.

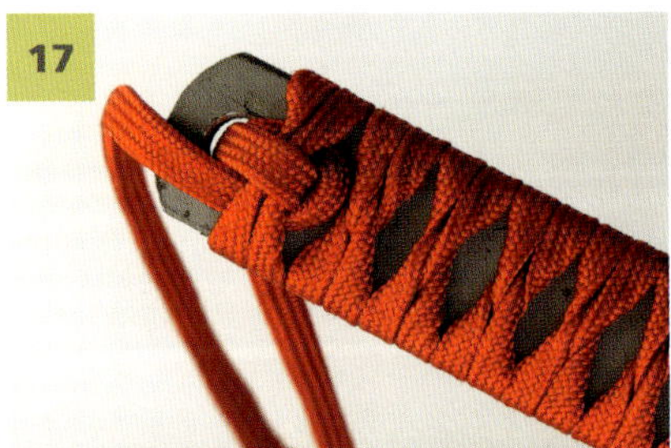

The knot is ready to be completed.

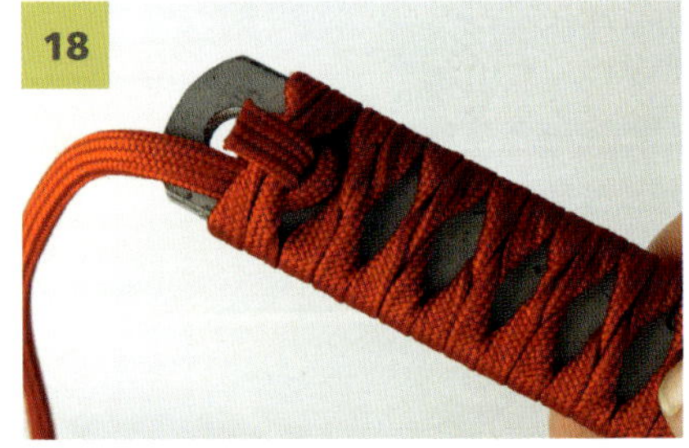

Cut the first end off that you already pulled through the pommel hole. Apply a bit of glue and tuck the end underneath the crossing.

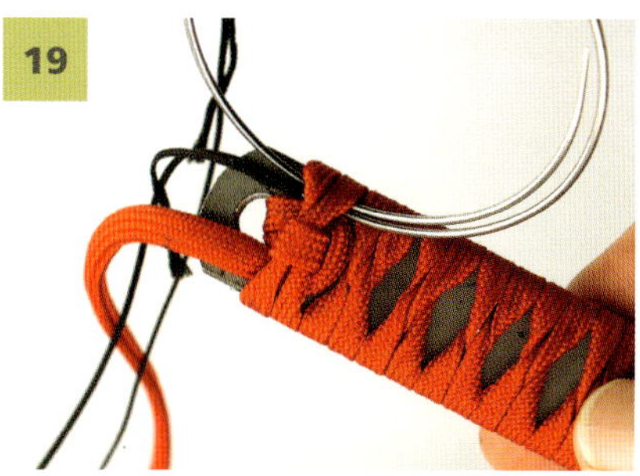

To complete the knot, the needles are inserted for the last time on the right side of the knot pointing downward.

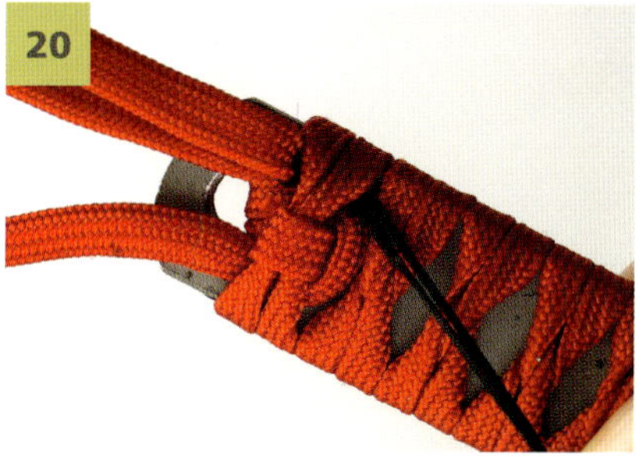

Make sure that all twists of the cord are removed before pulling it through.

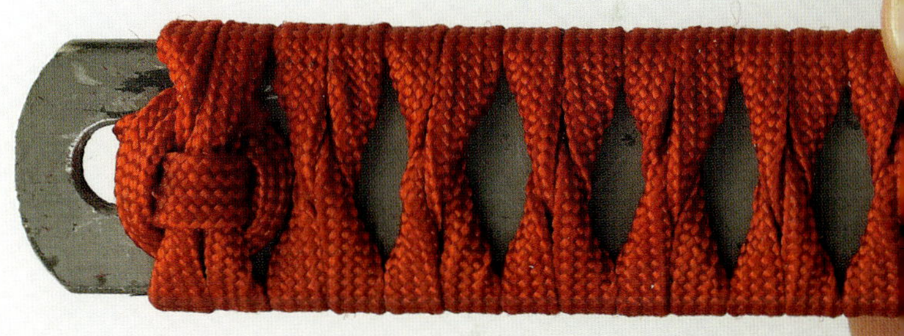

Adjust the last loop. Cut the end off close to the bottom of the knot and apply glue. Now the handle wrap on the *omote* side is finished.

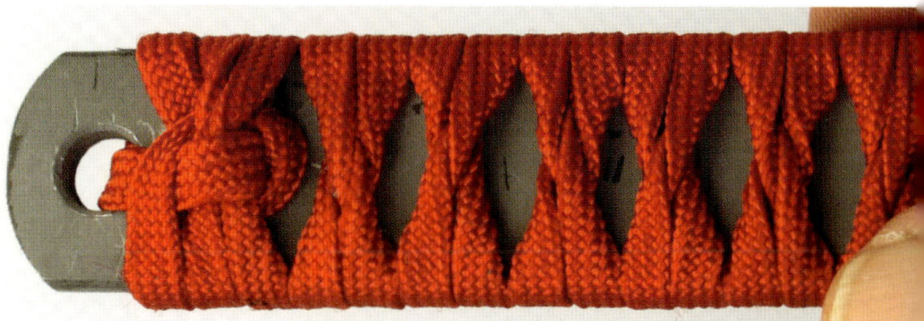

View of the finished *ura* side of the handle wrap.

5.2.3 The Twisted Bastard Wrap

I call this wrap the Twisted Bastard wrap because of how it is twisted. It displays a pretty structure, but is less stable than the twisted standard wrap (*menpu maki*). I have never seen this wrap on any traditional Japanese sword or knife, but I have seen this wrap several times on handmade and serially manufactured knives in "modern" Japanese style.

The wrap is relatively easy to make: the twist of the *ito* is also a double one, but it is done toward the outside, not the inside as with the *menpu maki*. The *ito* is twisted through a full 360°. Sometimes you also see knives which display a twist through only 180° with the *ito*.

With bands that are too thin for a *menpu maki* this technique can lead to acceptable results. If the wrap is impregnated it becomes stable and can be used effectively.

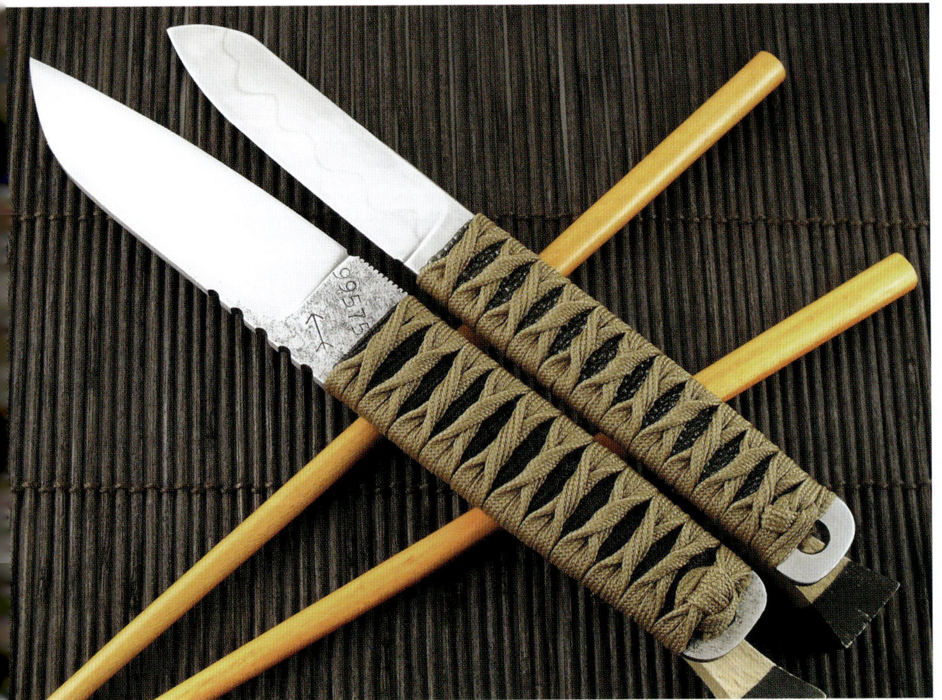

Two similar wraps: the wider one has a basic wrap of black paracord, while the slimmer one has dark green ray skin under the wrap in coyote brown.

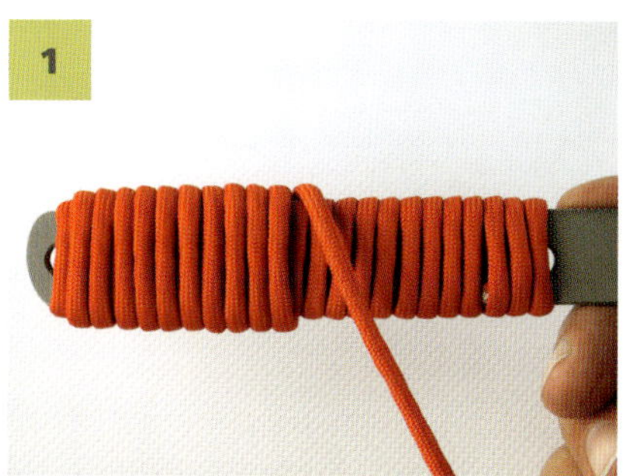

If you wrap the cord one and a half times around the handle you have the perfect working length for the paracord.

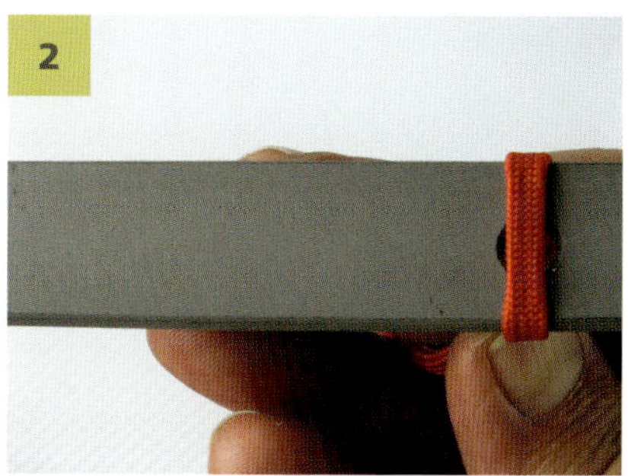

After gutting the paracord, fold it in the middle and begin with the center on the *omote* side of the handle.

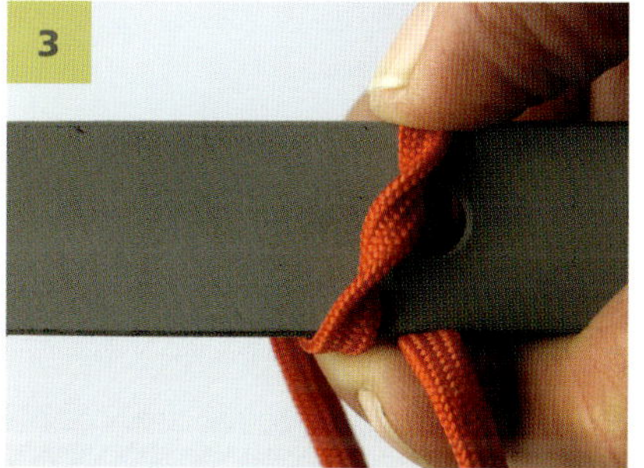

Twist the flat band twice counterclockwise (through 360°) and hold it tight.

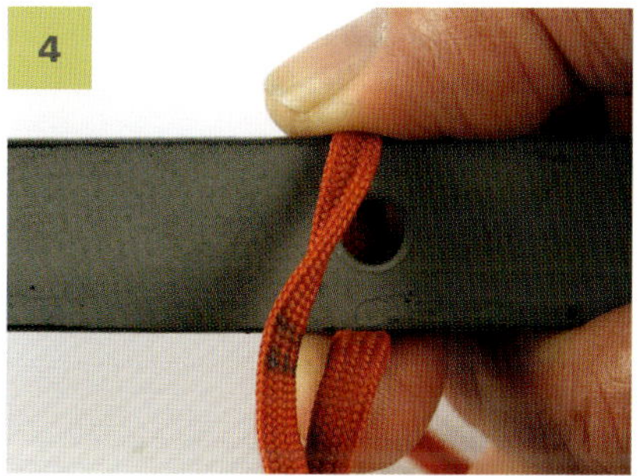

Turn the knife around and twist the upper end the same way.

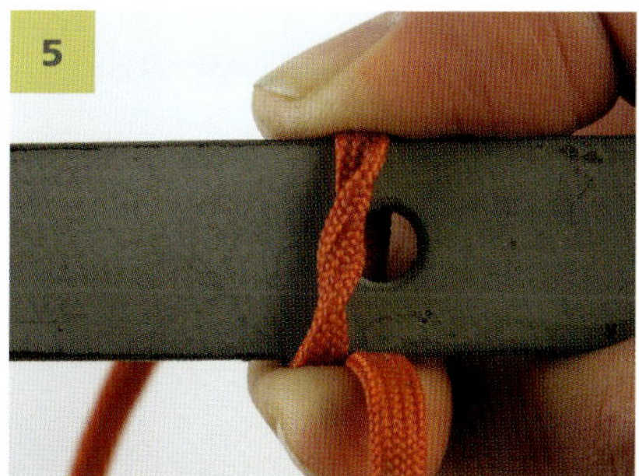

Continue twisting until 360° is completed and pull the wrap tight.

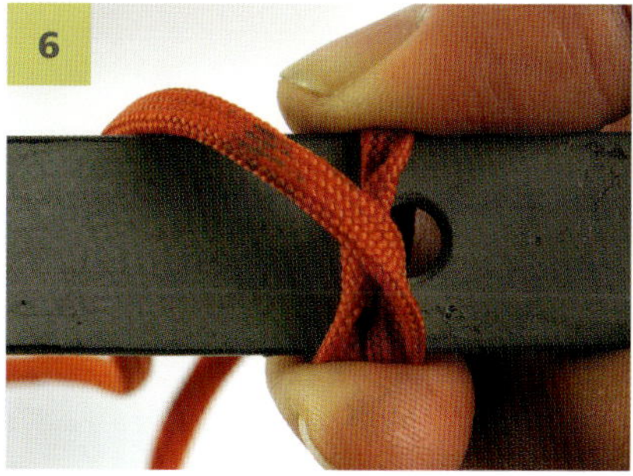

Fold the second end over the first twist.

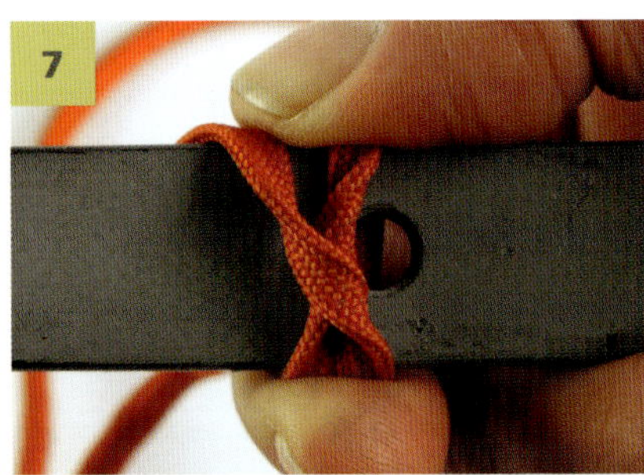

Twist the working end once more (through 360° clockwise). Put it over the edge and hold it tight.

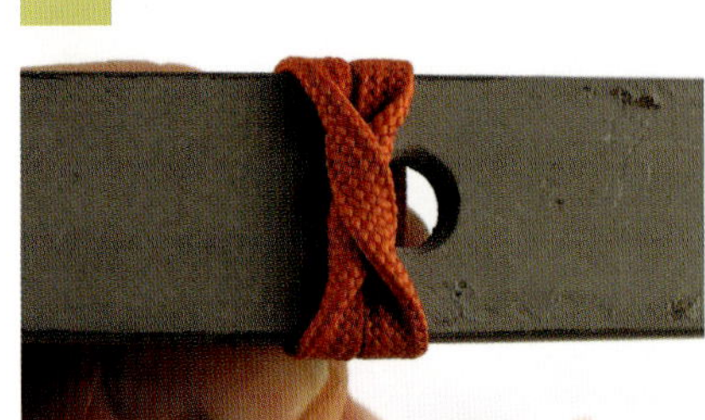

Pull the working end firmly and hold it tight. The first crossing is now complete.

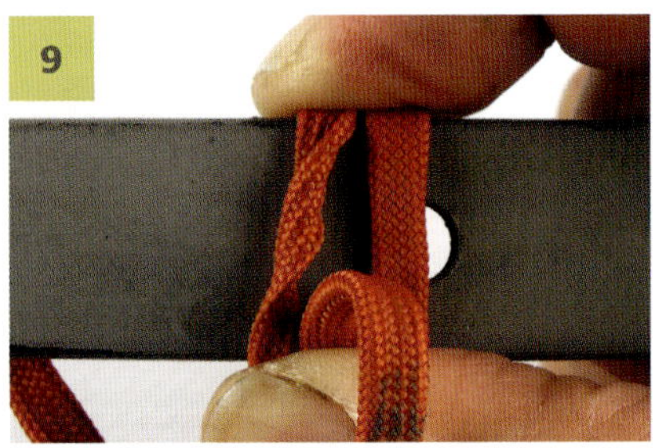

Turn the knife around, twist the first end, and pull it tight. Hold it with your thumb.

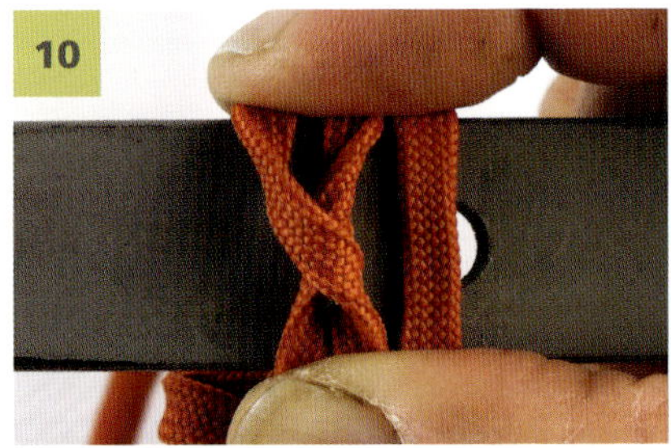

Put the second end twisted over the first one.

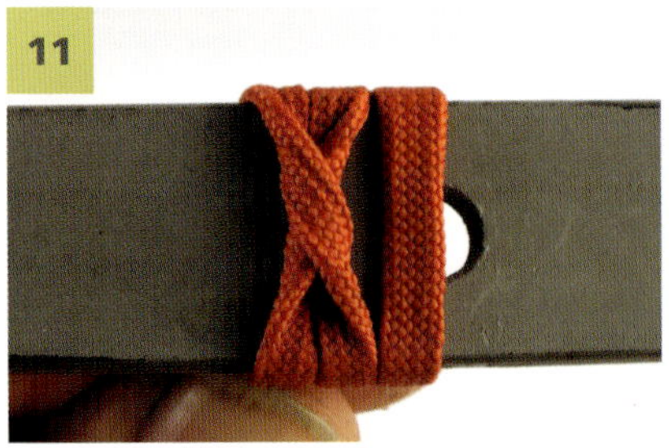

The first crossing on the *omote* side is now finished as well.

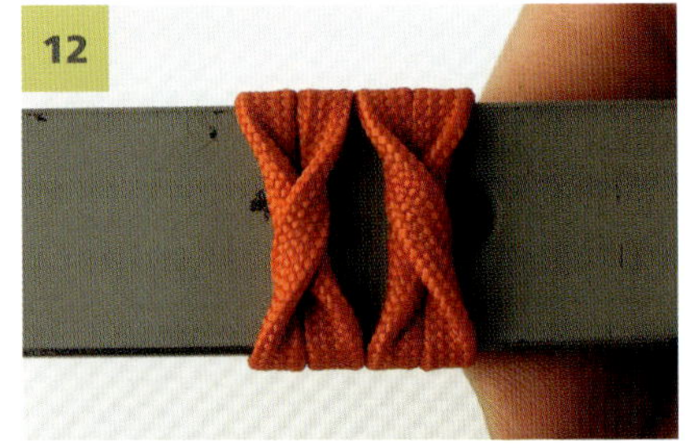

The direction of crossings has to be alternated. Here is the *ura* side.

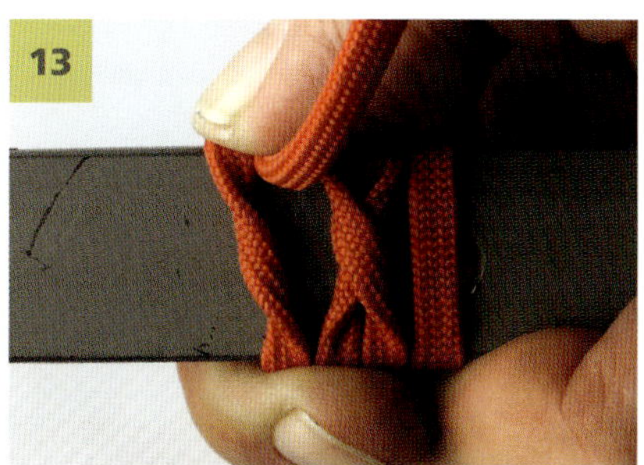

The second crossing on the *omote* side.

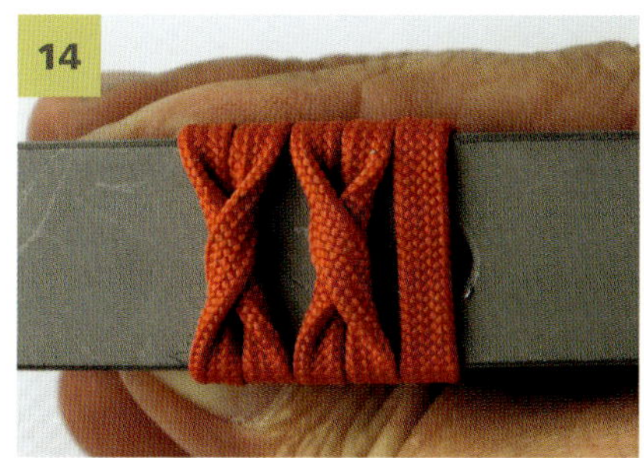

Continuously check the folds and direction of the crossings.

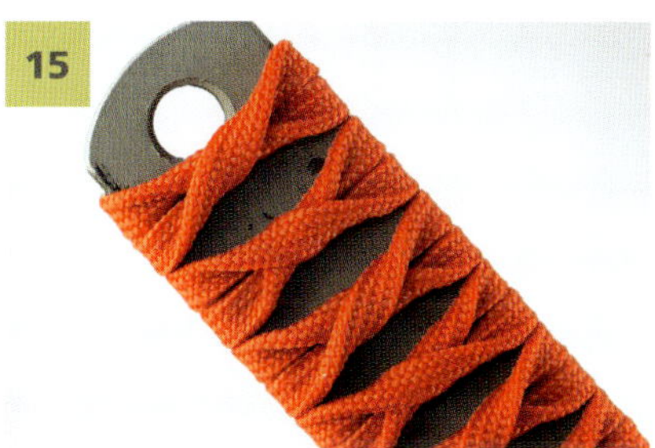

The pommel is reached on the *omote* side.

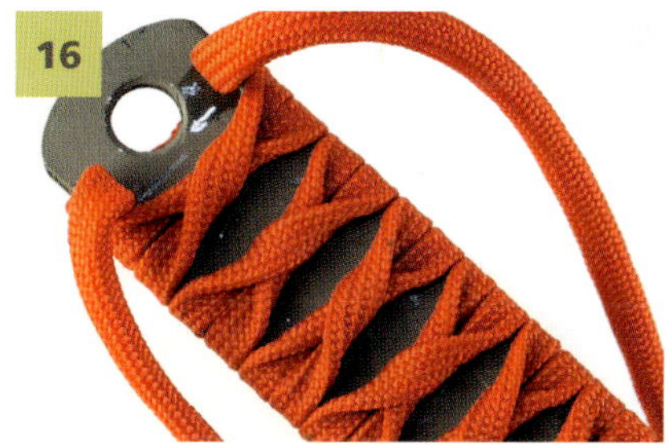

On the *ura* side both working ends are glued in place. No clamp is necessary to keep everything in position.

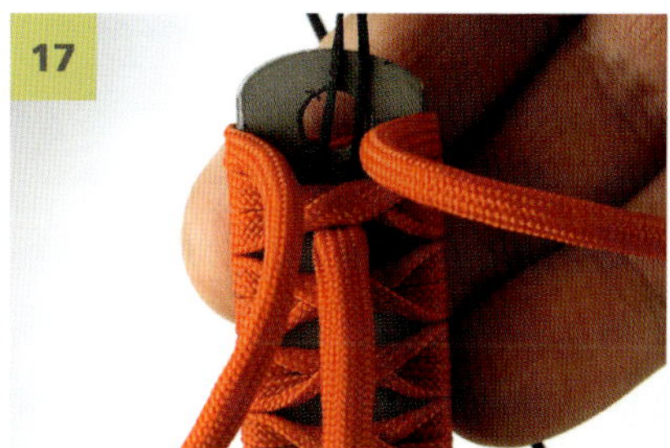

The right working end is pulled underneath the last crossing using needle and thread.

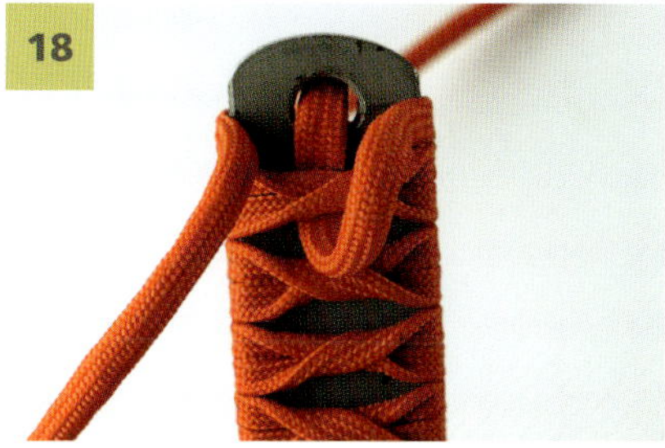

It is pulled tight and led away through the pommel hole.

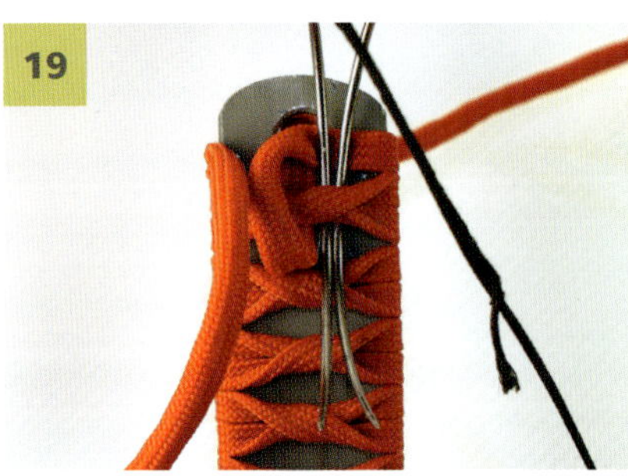

The needles are led underneath the last crossing to the right of the right cord end. Then the left end is pulled underneath the crossing.

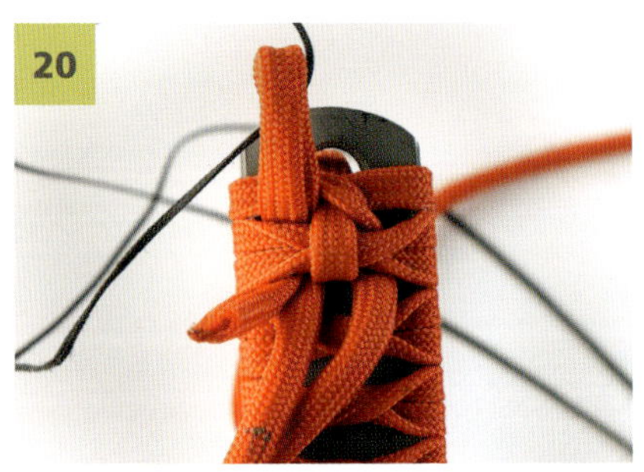

The left end is pulled tight and goes down on the right side and back up again on the left.

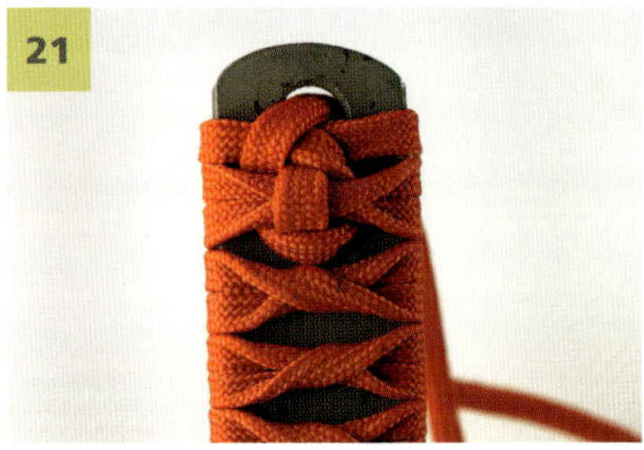

The *ura* knot is completed.

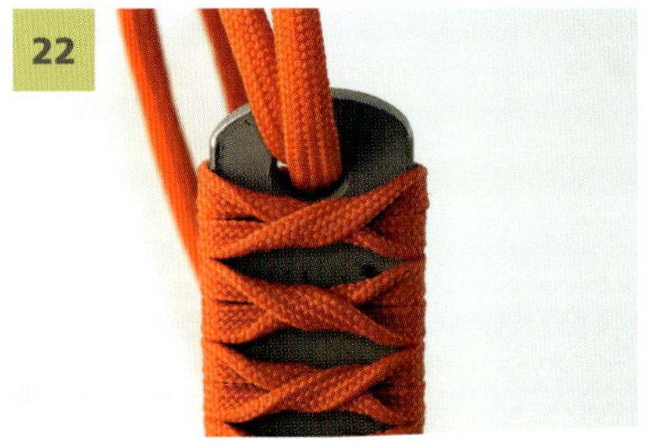

The two ends emerge on the *omote* side.

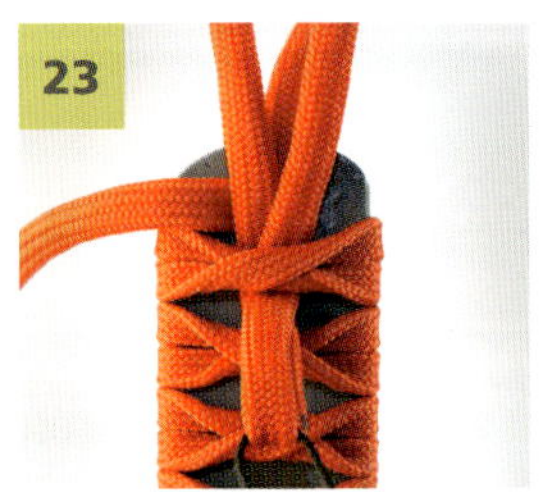

One end is pulled straight down underneath the crossing.

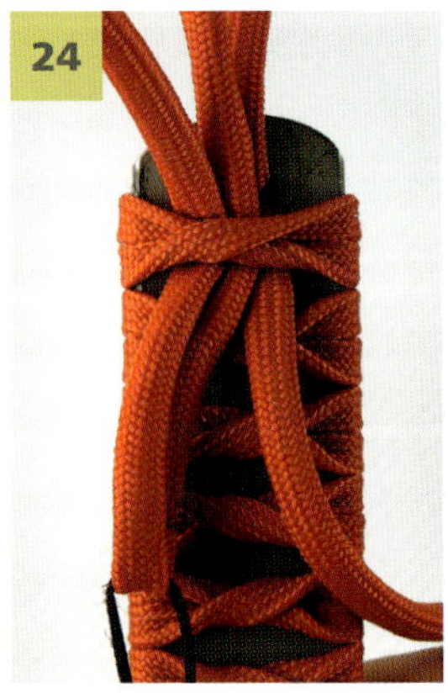

The second end is pulled down next to the first one. The first end is guided on top of the last crossing through the hole in the tang.

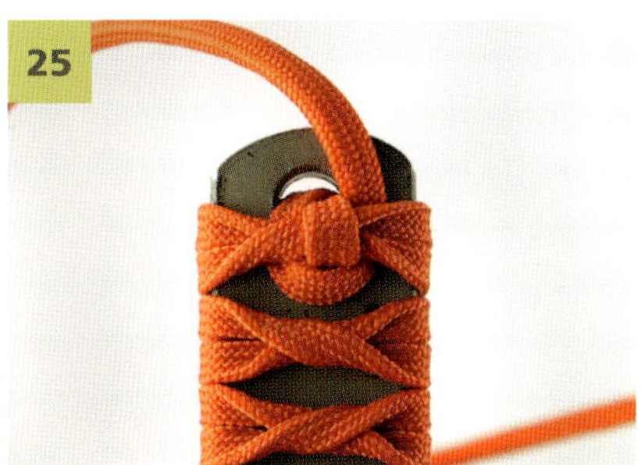

The second working end is brought up on the right side under the crossing. The other end is cut off and glued to the handle's *ura* side.

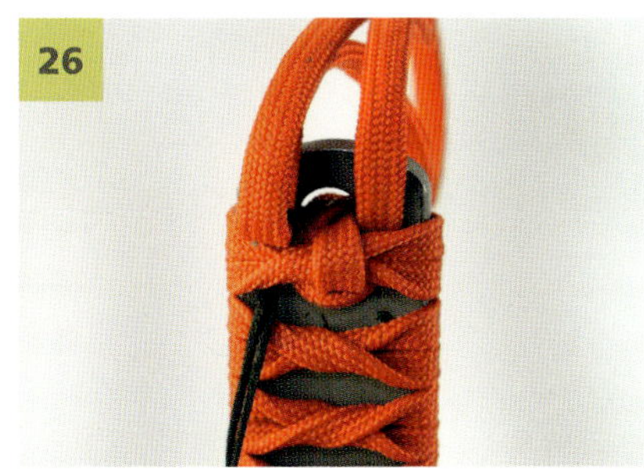

The long working end is pulled underneath the crossing for a last time.

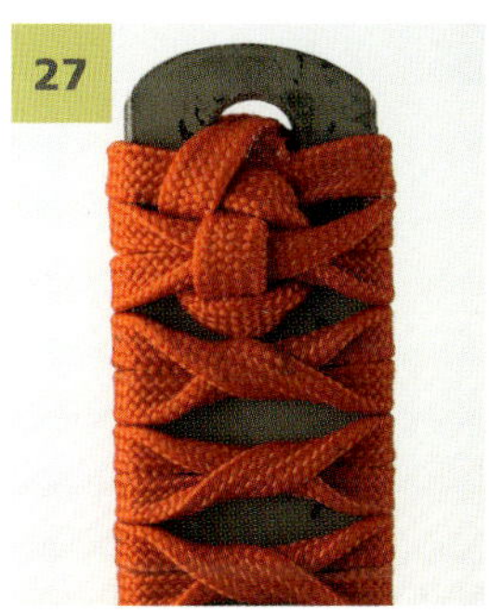

The cut-off end is visible on the ura side underneath the piece of cord on top.

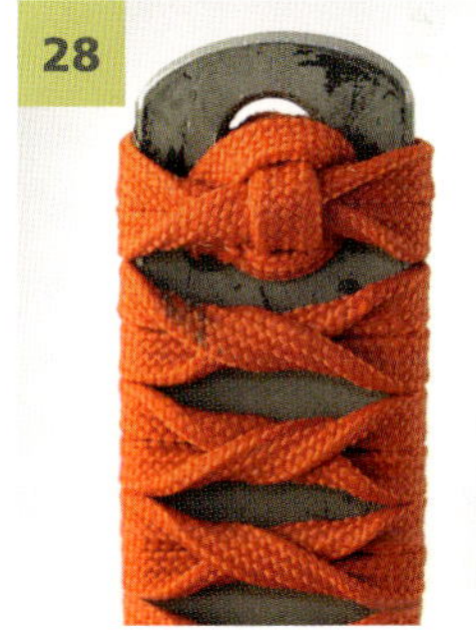

The end is pulled tight and cut off. A drop of glue is applied to keep it in position.

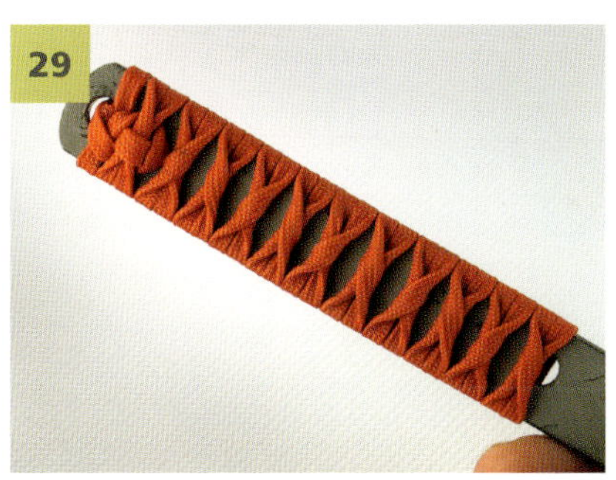

The finished *ura* side.

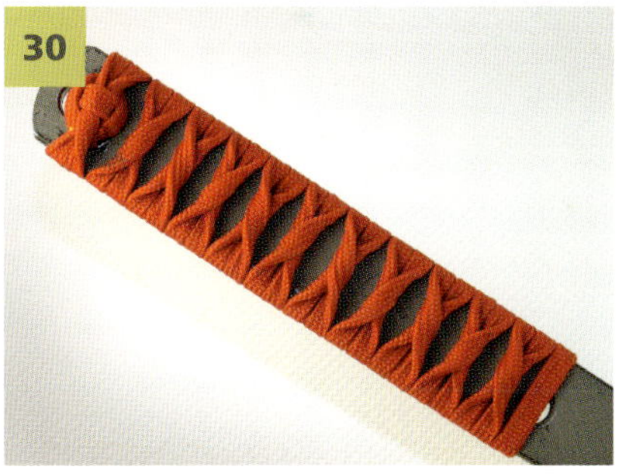

The *omote* side is finished. The wrap can now be impregnated with resin.

5.2.4 *Hira Maki,* the Flat Wrap

Hira maki is the easiest of the so-called diamond wraps. The name stems from a figure between the turns of the *ito* or, in this case, the flatline. In the *hira maki*, the band ends cross each other flat, without any twist. Thus, the width of the flat band is less important, and sleeves of paracord type III and IV are equally suited for the task. *Hira maki* is the flattest of all handle wraps in Japanese style. We also just call it the "flat wrap." Traditional *tsukamaki* artisans also mix the different crossing styles, especially where the *menuki* (handle charm) is put underneath the wrap.

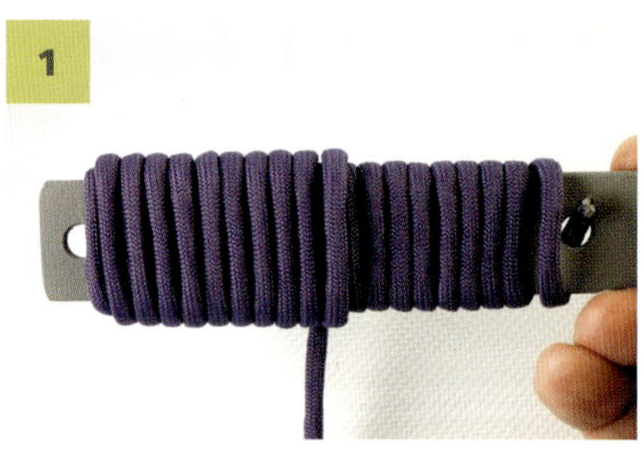

Flatline wrapped around the handle one and a half times results in a good working length and minimizes waste. This works for all kinds of handles, from flat and narrow up to full sized sword handles.

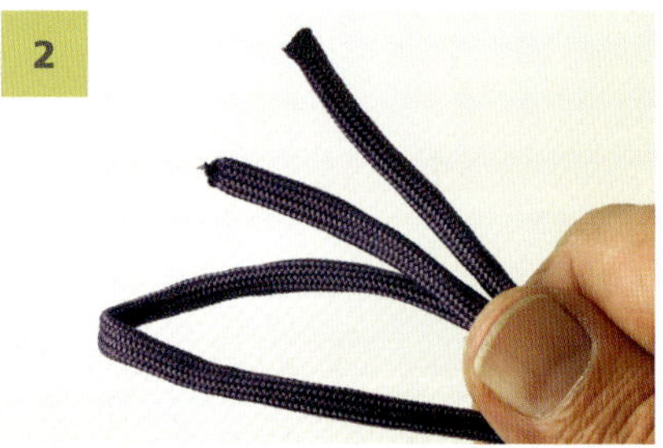

We cut off the cord, remove the core, melt the ends, and squeeze them flat. The cord is folded to determine the center.

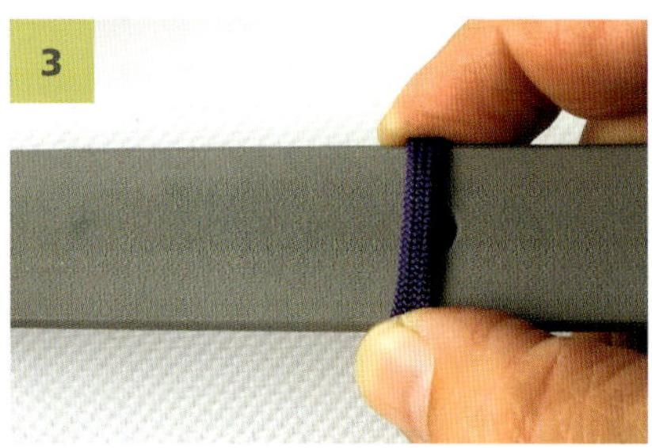

Put the cord's center on the *omote* side of the tang next to the blade.

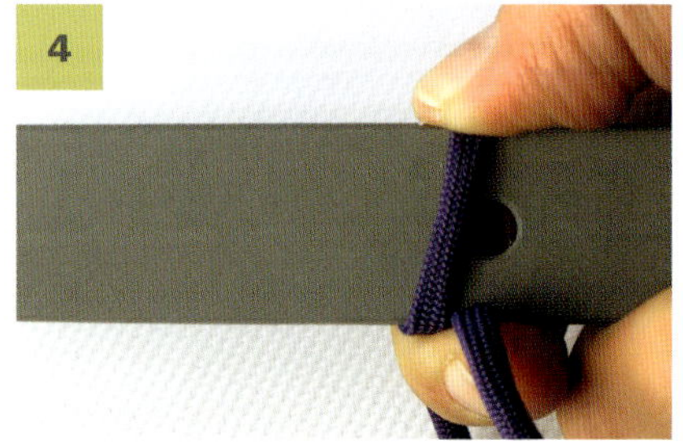

Turn the knife around and make the first crossing.

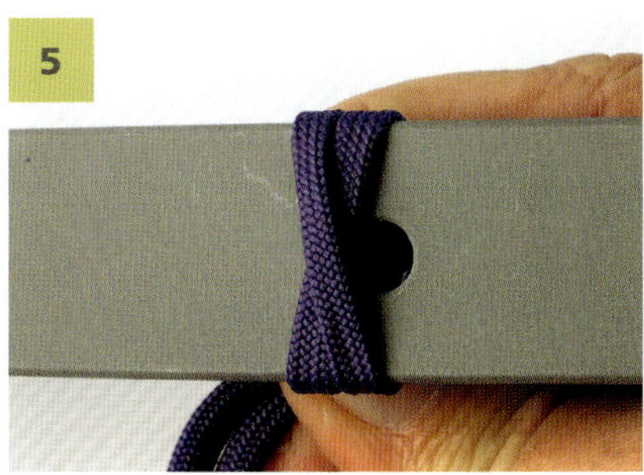

Put the other working end over the first one and pull it tight.

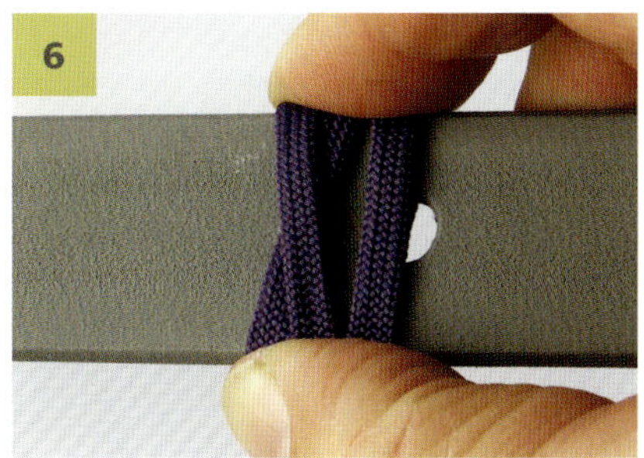

Do the same on the other side.

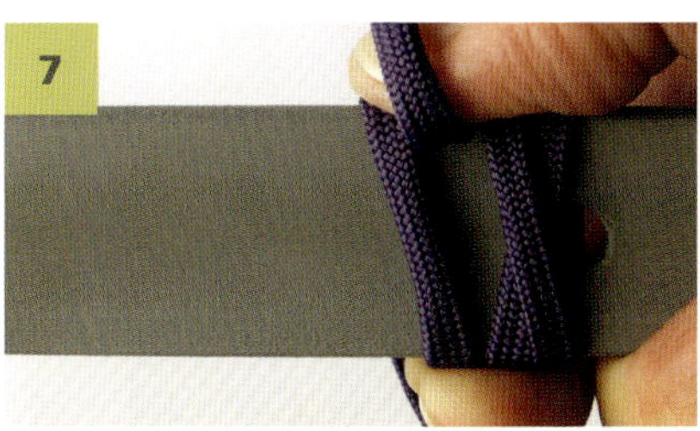

Back on the *ura* side we start with the other end first.

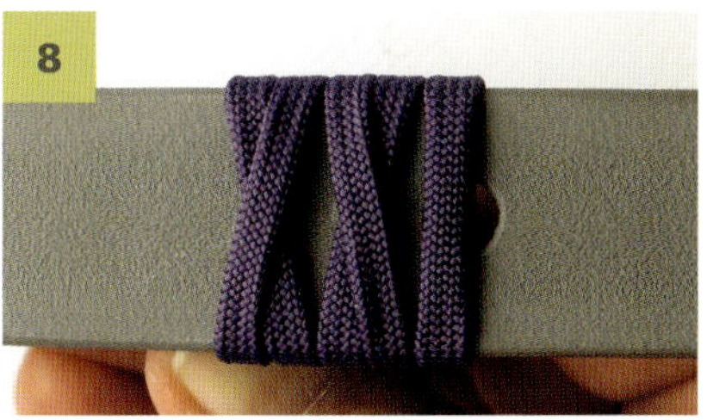

Back on the *omote* side the alternating direction of the crossings becomes clear. We repeat the moves until we reach the handle's end at the pommel hole.

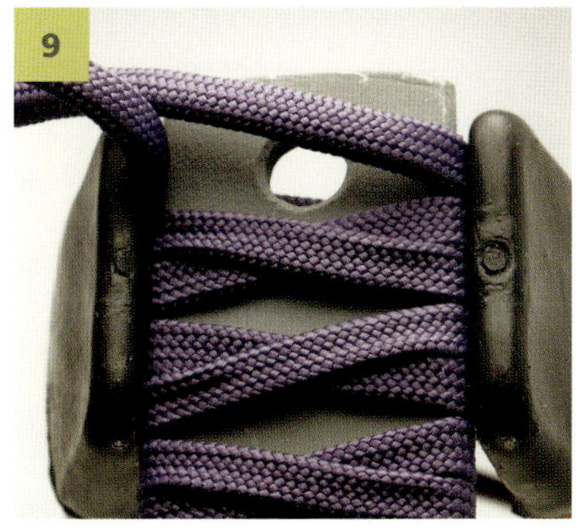

The end of the handle is reached.

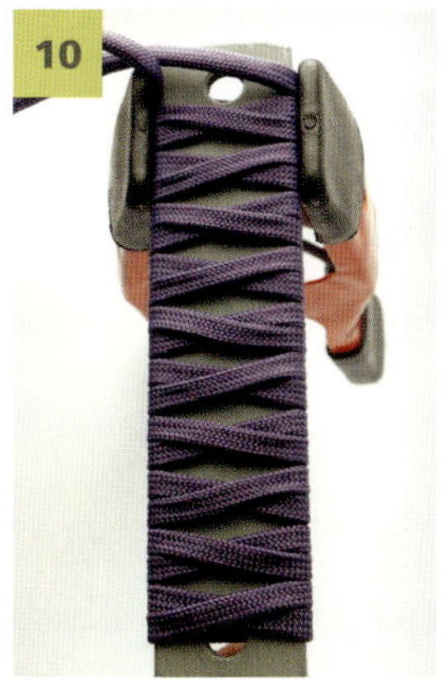

The entire handle on the *ura* side.

A small trick to facilitate making the end knots is to fix the working ends with a small drop of superglue. Do not think you are cheating: Japanese *tsukamaki* artisans use rice glue to help them with a great deal of their work. Be especially careful in case you use a clamp: if the clamp fails you will have to redo the last couple crossings.

Why is the direction of crossings alternated? Not only for aesthetics, but also for functional reasons. In case the upper *ito* or the flatline of one of the crossings ruptures or is cut by the slash of an opponent, the entire handle wrap will not loosen immediately. If I were a samurai I would appreciate this very much, because it could save my life in a sword fight.

An important variant of the end knots existed on Japanese military swords during the World War II era (*shingunto*). With these swords the pommel (*kashira*) did not have an elongated hole for the *ito*. For this type you need just enough space for a last crossing of the flatline on the right and left handle sides in front of the *kashira*.

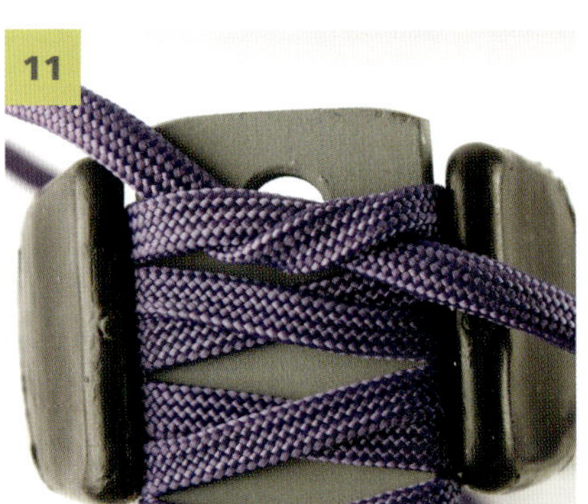

The end knot starts with an overhand knot. Make the knot right over left.

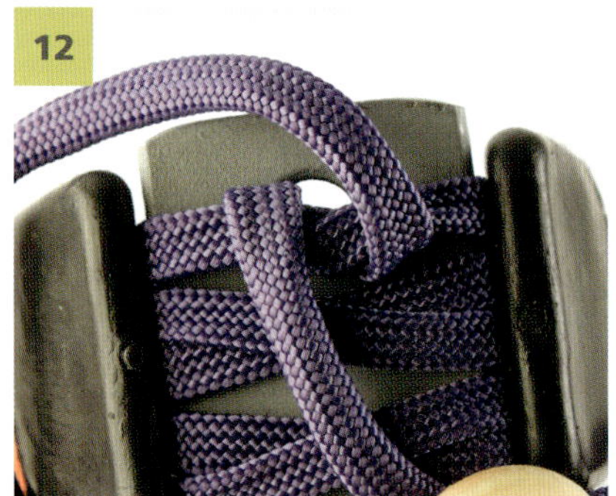

Take the right end to the left and the left end to the right over the other one and back around the handle.

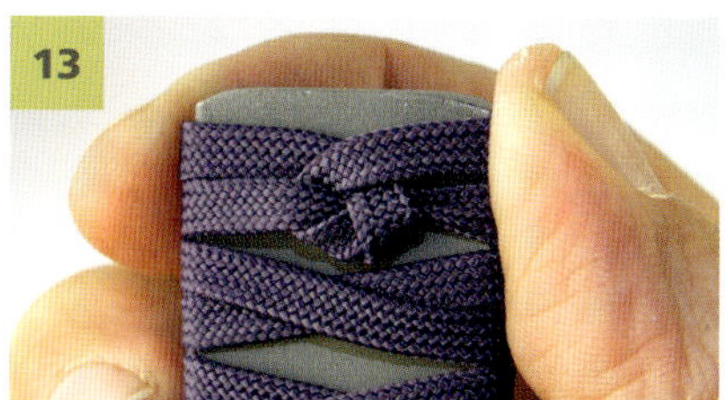

The ends are pulled to the backside. Check the position and hold the flatline tight. Use a clamp and turn the handle around with the other side facing up. You can use a drop of superglue to keep the flatline in position.

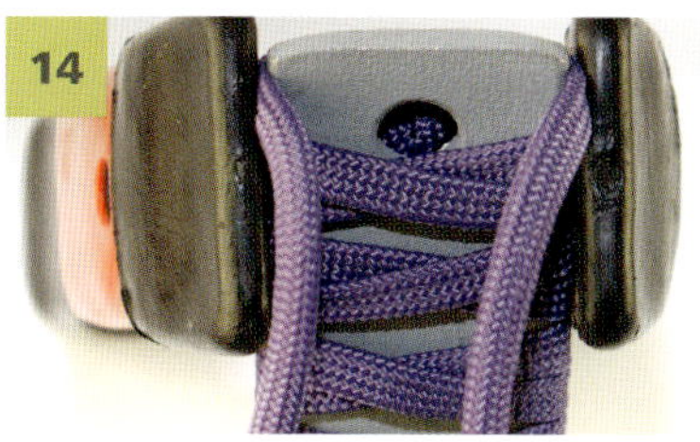

You are now ready to make a hybrid between a ura knot and an omote knot as shown at the end of the twisted wrap. The working ends come from the sides, as with the *ura* knot of the first type.

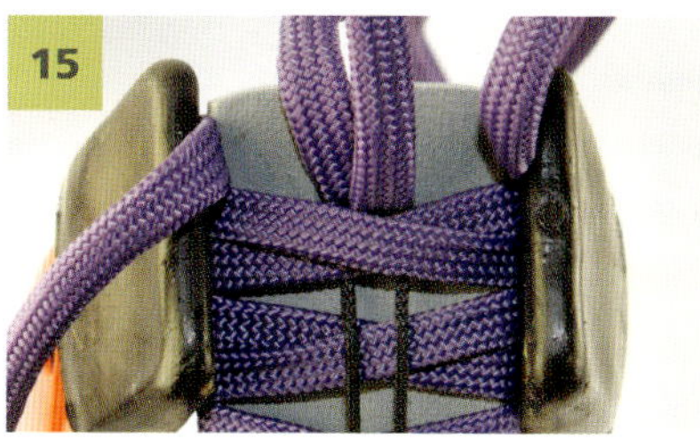

With the curved needles and thread the right end is pulled underneath the last crossing.

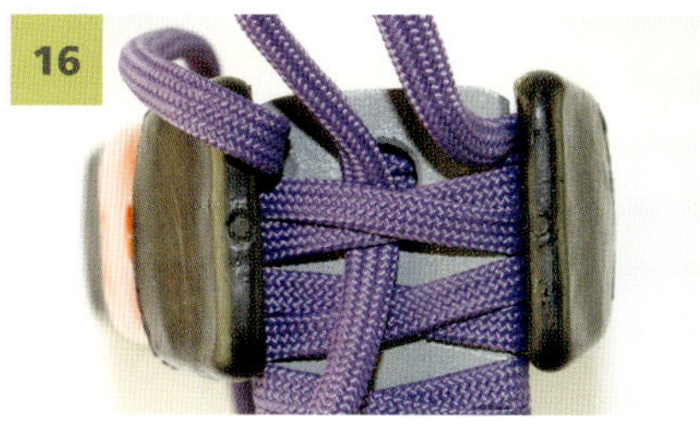

The right cord end is pulled underneath the last crossing almost completely.

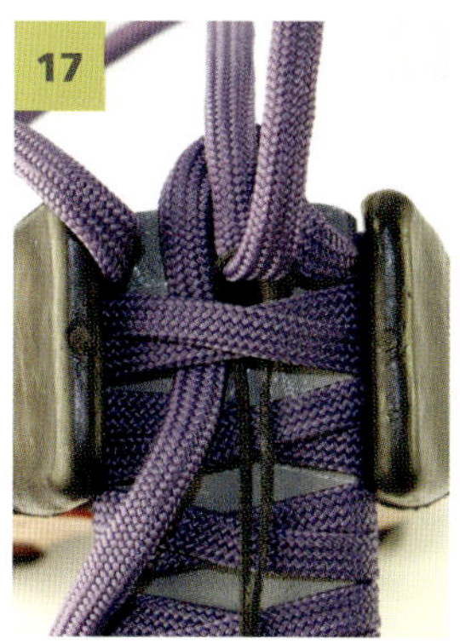

Take the left working end over the right and pull it under the last crossing, but do not pull it tight yet!

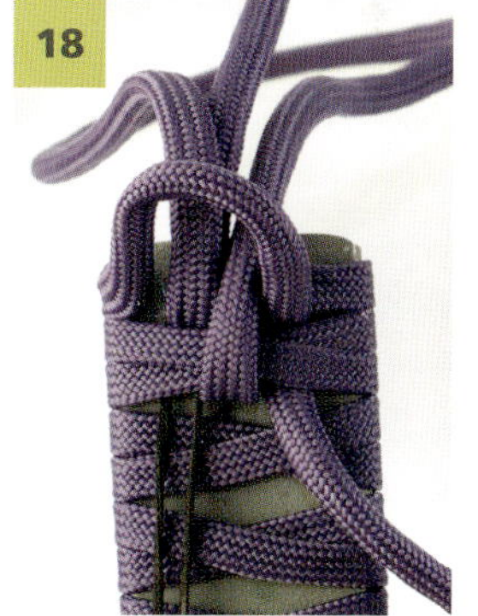

Bring the first working end to the top and pull it down again behind the last crossing.

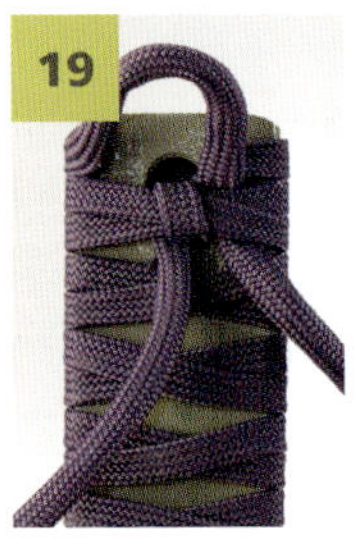

The main difference to the traditional wrap is that here the ends are cut off and tucked away instead of pulling them through the tang hole.

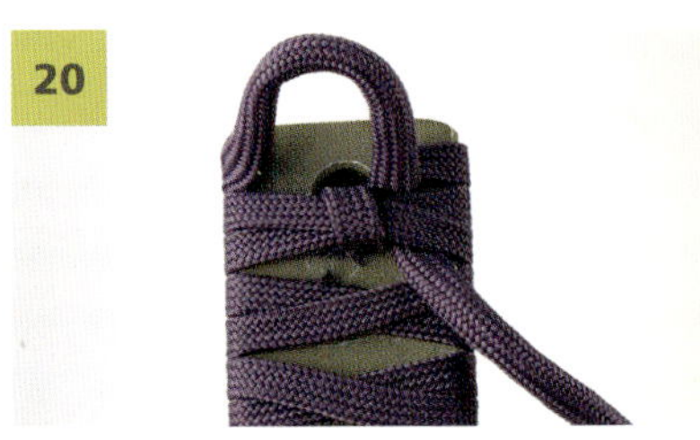

We cut off the end and apply a drop of glue.

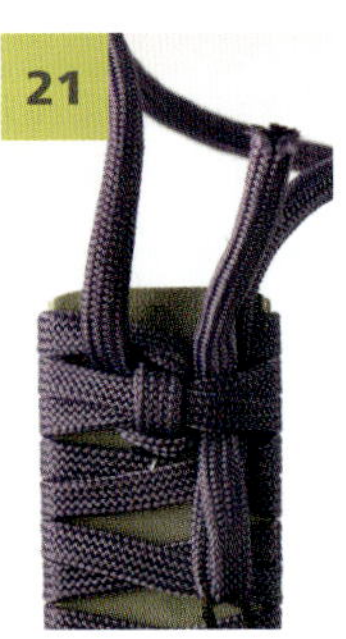

The right end is firmly pulled downward. Then bring it up again under the left side of the crossing, then back down again on the right side.

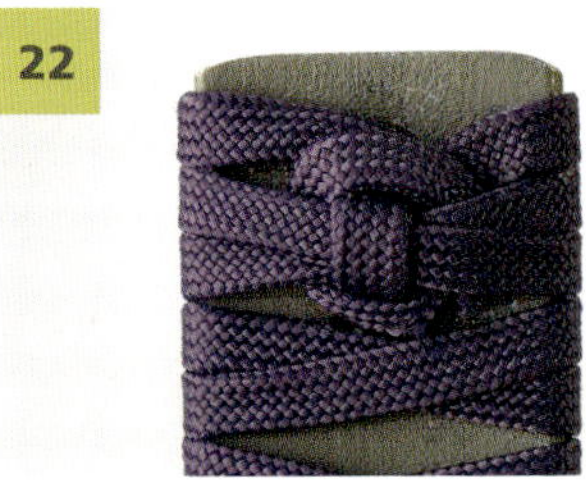

Pull the end completely downward and cut it off. Apply glue here as well.

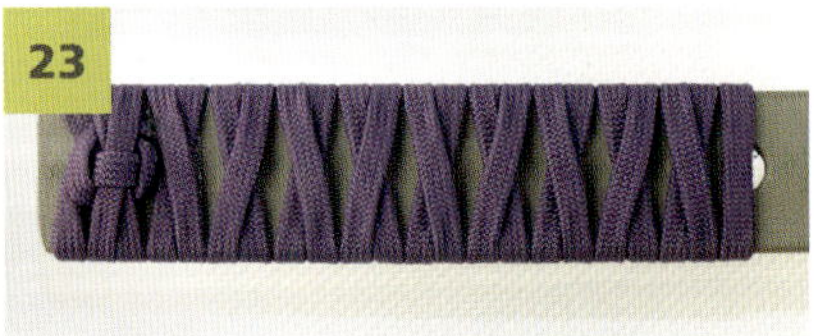

The handle with the finished *omote* side.

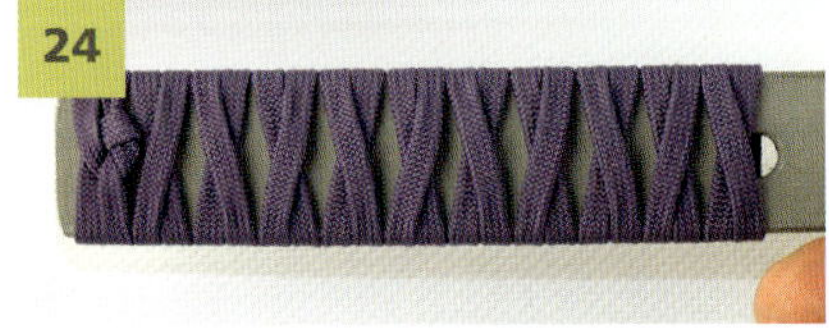

The finished *ura* side with the adjusted overhand knot.

Note: this variant of the knot starts with the cord behind the last crossing. It gives the knot a pretty, round appearance while at the same time preventing the volume of the knot from becoming too large. The knot starts at the sides like the *ura* knot and ends with the cord wrapped around as with the *omote* knot. Often the end knot for a handle wrap with an end of the *gunto* type is the pure *ura* knot, as shown in the example with the bent wire.

5.2.5 *Tsukaito* with Three Woven Strips

Christian influence by Portuguese Jesuits (and others) was important in Japan during the late fifteenth and early sixteenth centuries. It even reached the forging of swords: an example is the *gyu kawa kumiage maki*. The three stripes of *ito* woven into the *tsuka* represent the holy trinity of the father, son, and the holy spirit.

The basis for this wrapping technique is a flat wrap. Flat, winding wraps are always done with the *ito* nicely vertical on the *omote*-side. The *ura*-side is tilted in the direction of the wrap. For swords, the wrap with the weaving pattern was traditionally done on both sides. Because of the direction of weaving on the backside, the weaving pattern is slightly tilted on the *ura*-side.

This technique requires the use of glue. My preferred solution is to stabilize the wrap with resin after finishing.

If you wrap the handle one and a half times it results in enough cord for the basic wrap. Add six pieces of cord or one handle length each for the weaving work (three pieces for each side).

Cut the cord and remove the strings inside the core. Slightly melt the ends to prevent the paracord from unraveling and press the ends flat and square. Prepare all six cord ends the same way.

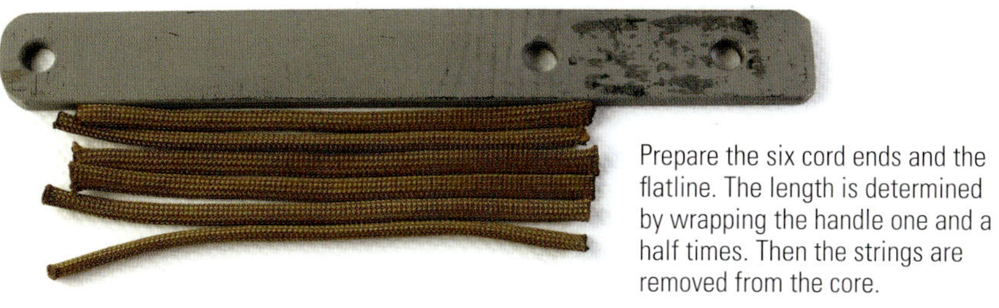

Prepare the six cord ends and the flatline. The length is determined by wrapping the handle one and a half times. Then the strings are removed from the core.

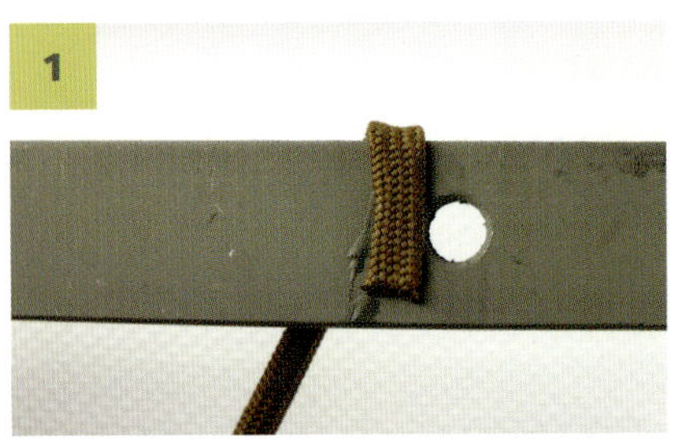

Glue the standing end of the flatline close to the guard on the handle's *omote* side. If you make a flat wrap as underlay, glue the end on the *ura* side.

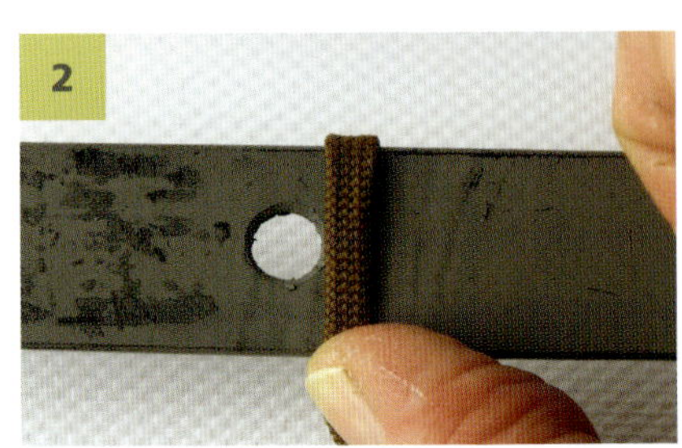

Move the flatline once around the handle to check where the ends have to be glued on.

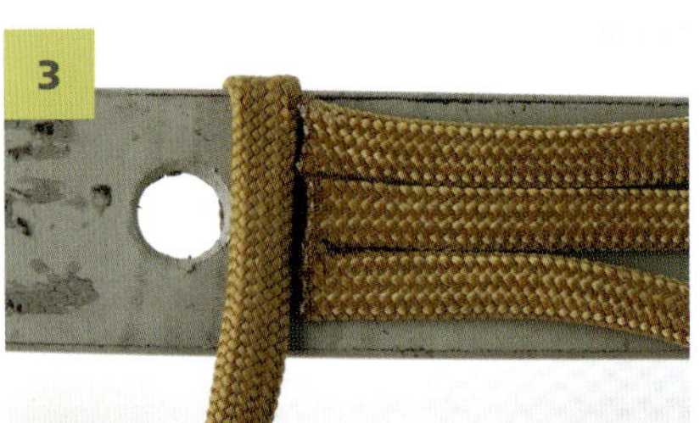

Glue the ends of the weaving cords directly next to the working end on the handle's *ura* side.

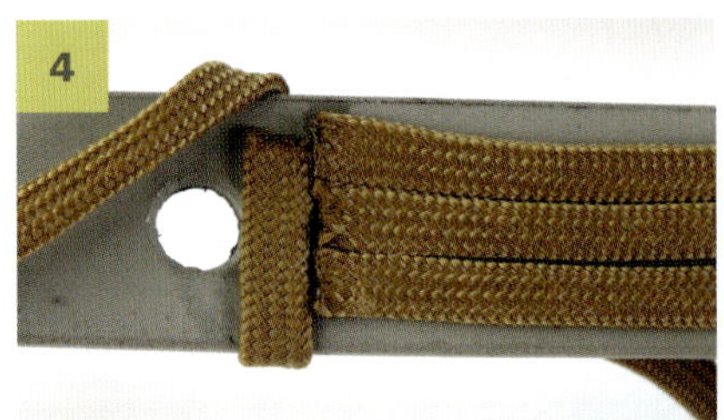

Also glue the ends of the weaving cords on the *omote* side, directly to the beginning of the handle wrap.

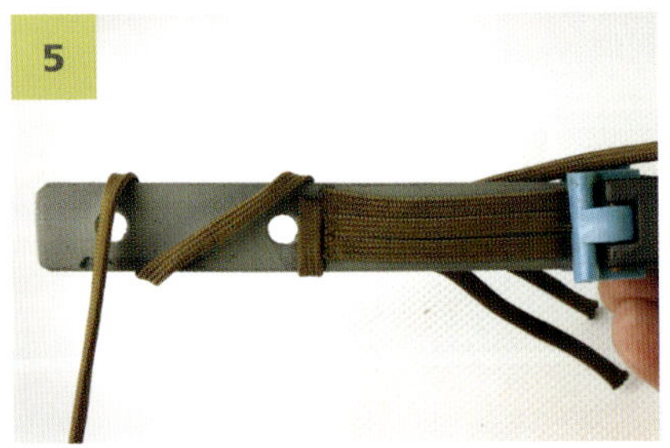

Now everything is in place to start the handle wrap.

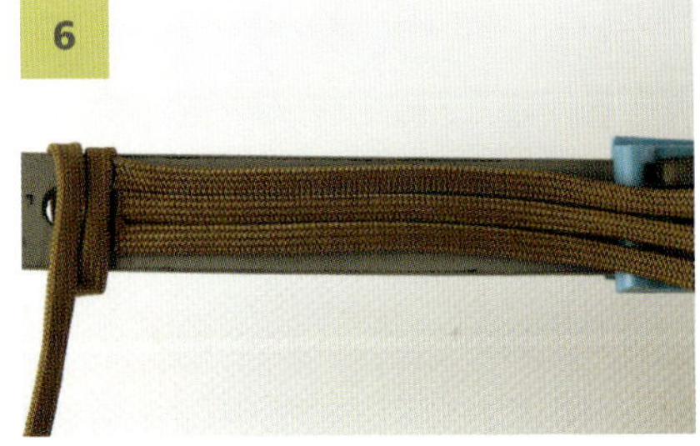

The other side also has everything prepared for the wrap. All cord ends are in position.

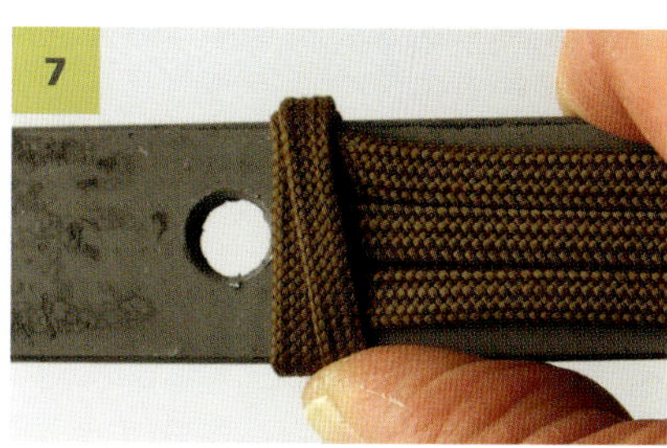

The cord is wrapped twice around the handle and once again on top of itself before we move over to the *ura* side. This is the beginning of the slanted wrap on the backside or *ura* side.

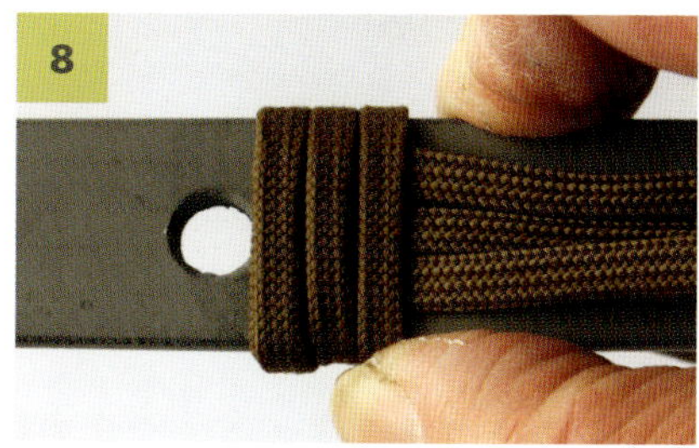

Because we started with a double layer at the guard, the wrap keeps the same thickness when moving over the weaving cords.

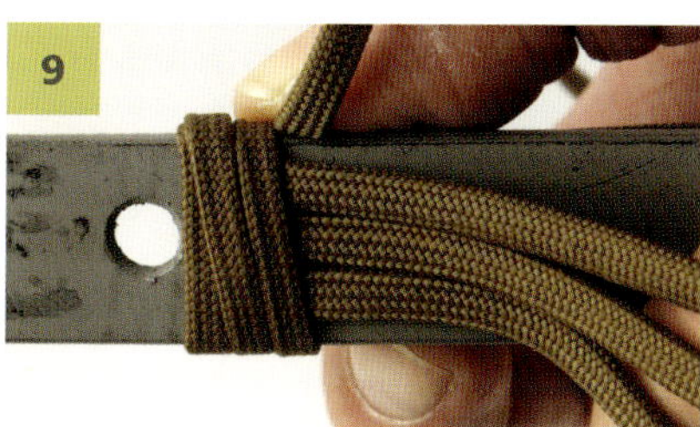

On the *ura* side, the tilted direction of the wrap is distinctly visible.

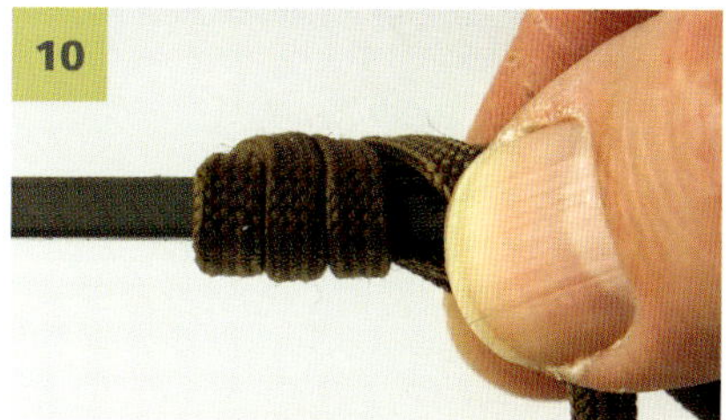

The lateral view of the handle reveals the flat structure and uniform thickness of the wrap.

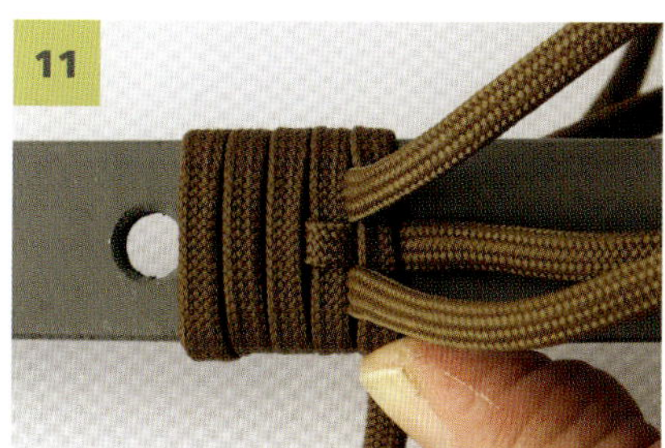

Start weaving with the central end, then with both outer ends, then with the one in the center again, and so forth.

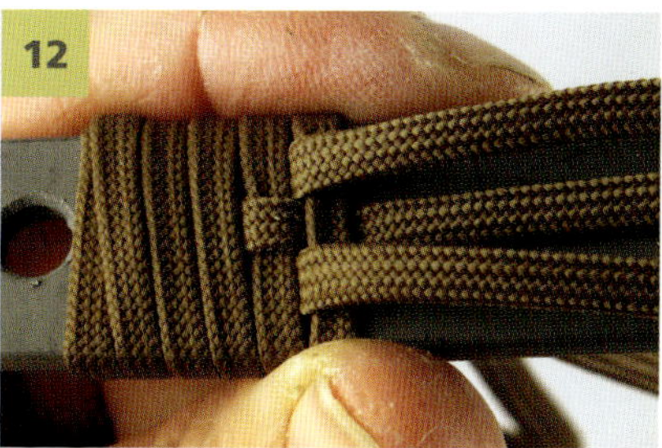

On the *ura* side, the weaving also starts with the fourth turn of the cord.

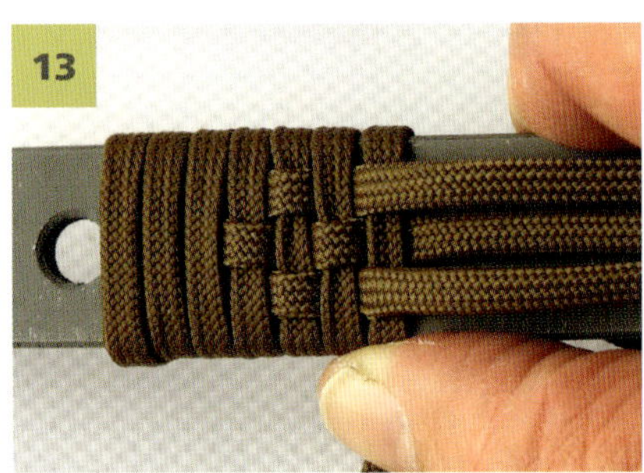

Pull the ends tight with each pass of the working end.

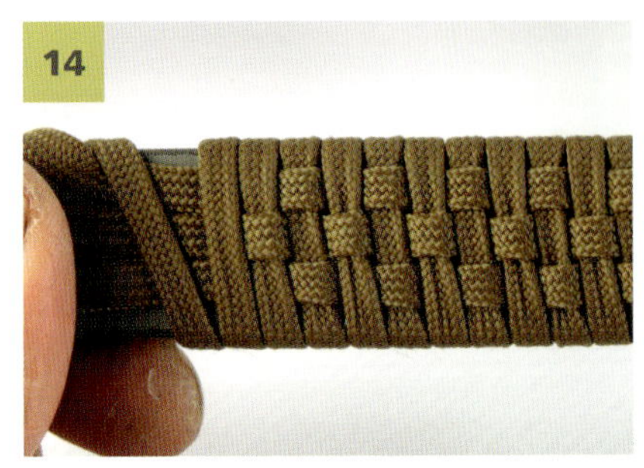

Stop weaving when you are about seven or eight passes away from the end. Make sure you stop with the central end.

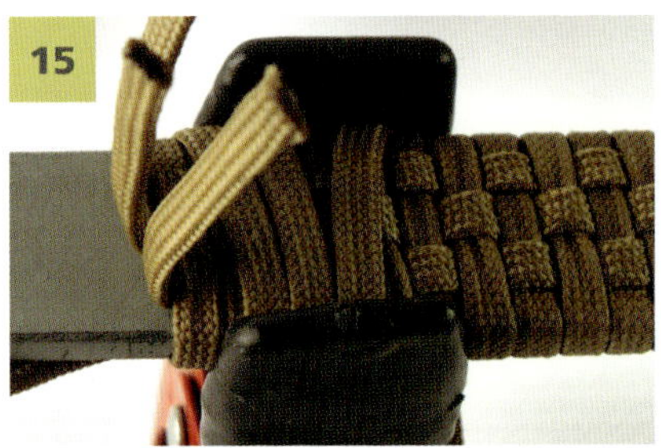

Wrap the working end a few times back over the wrap and place a clamp.

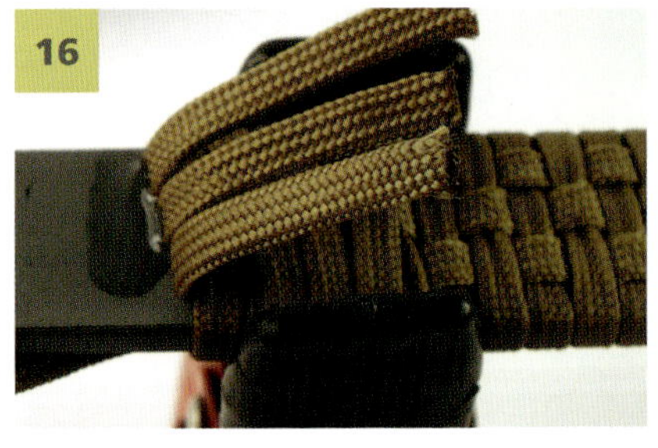

Glue the ends of the weaving cords with a drop of adhesive.

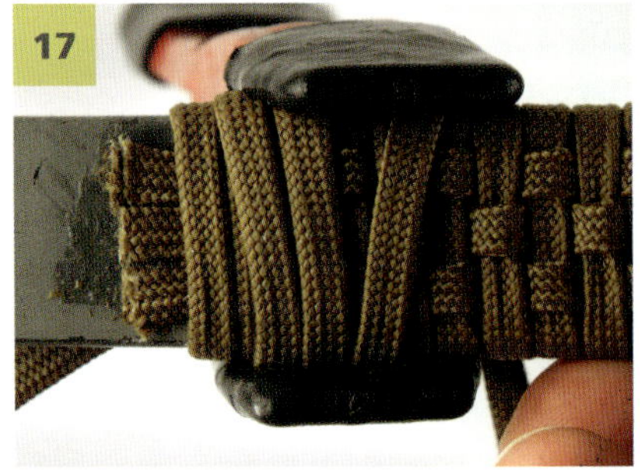

Cut the weaving ends off in such a way that their length is about the same as the width of an empty paracord sleeve.

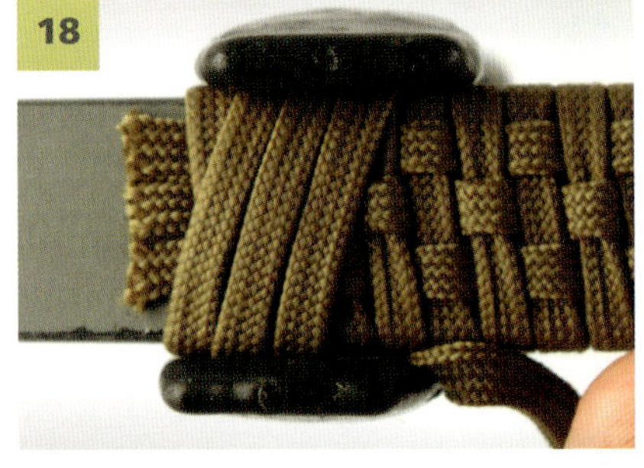

Cut the weaving ends off on the other side of the handle as well, leaving the same length.

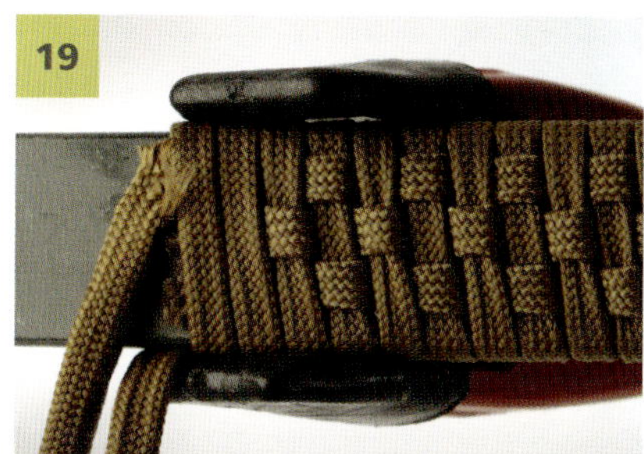

Take a second piece of flatline and cut the end off at an angle. Glue this end to the wrap on the *ura* side as shown here.

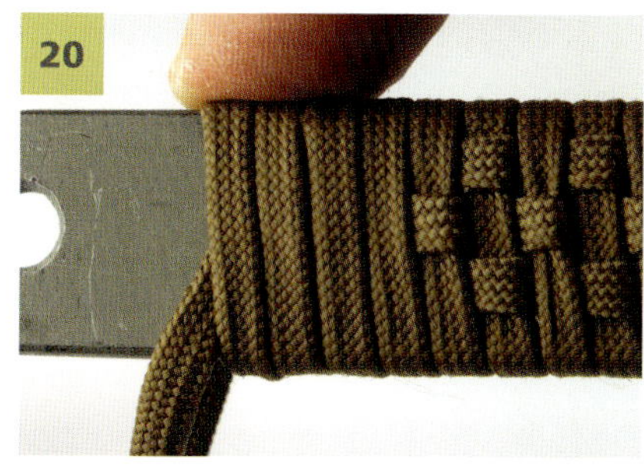

Put two more turns of the cord on top. Now take both working ends to the other side.

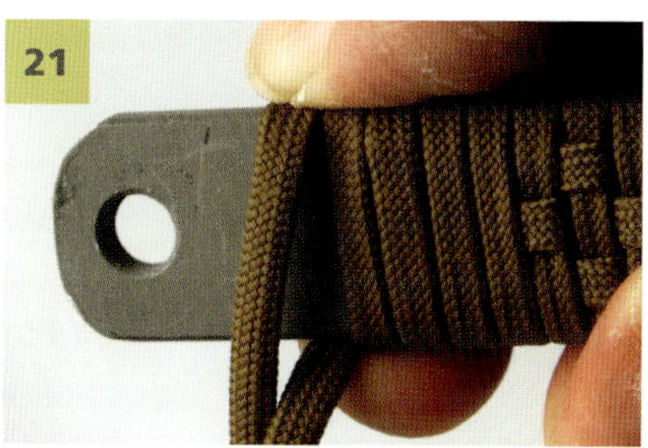

We now have two working ends on the *omote* side to continue with the classic twisted wrap.

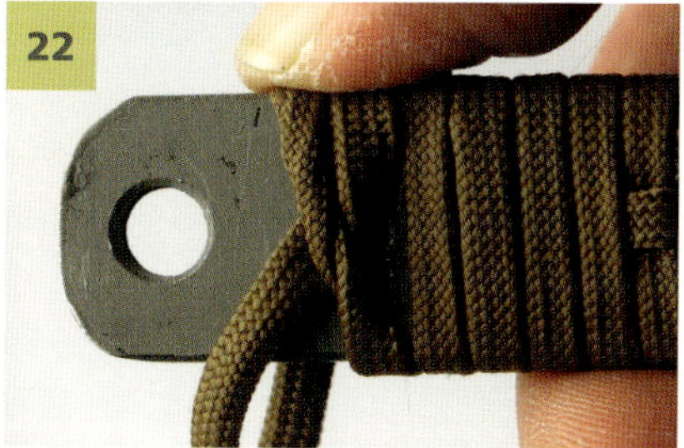

The first twisted crossing on the *omote* side.

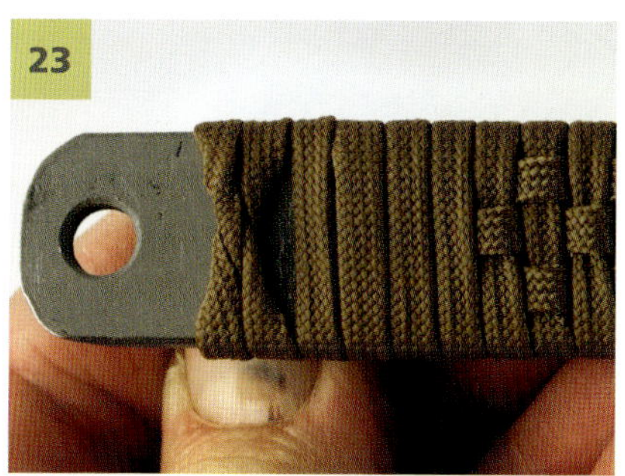

The first crossing is completed.

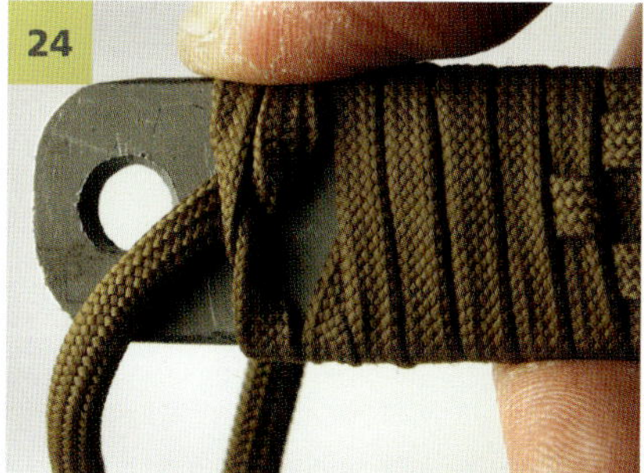

The first crossing on the *ura* side.

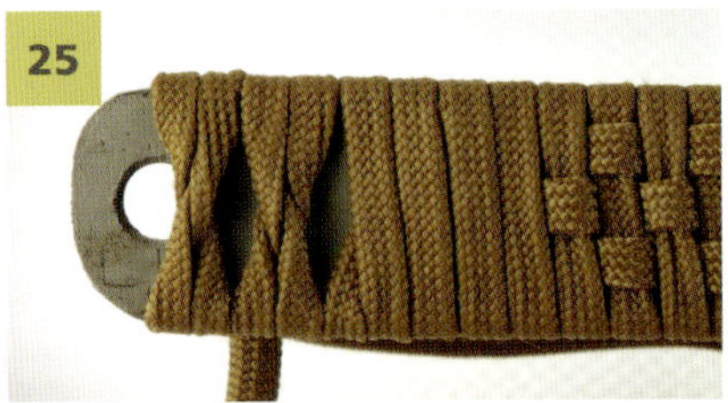

The two opposite crossings on the *ura* side are made.

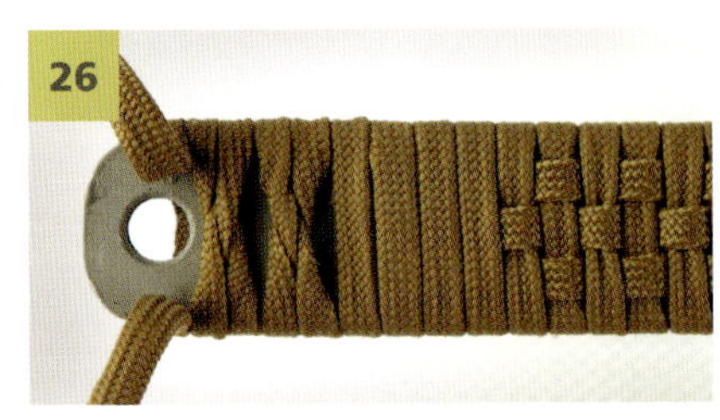

The working ends are glued to both sides of the tang. Now we are ready for the traditional end knots (see 5.2.2 End Knots, p. 60 ff.).

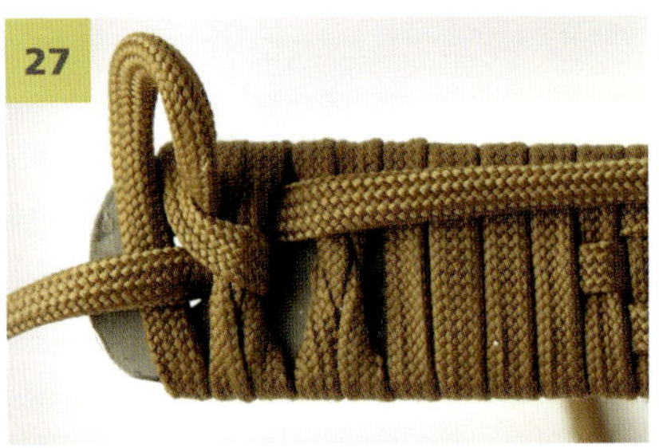

The end knots in progress.

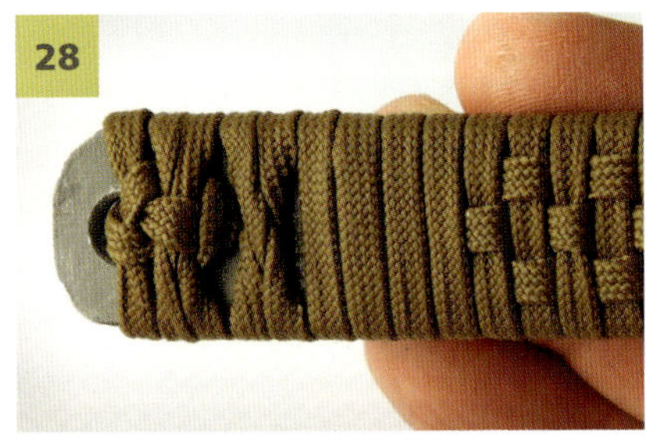

The first knot is finished. Both working ends have been led through the pommel hole on to the other side.

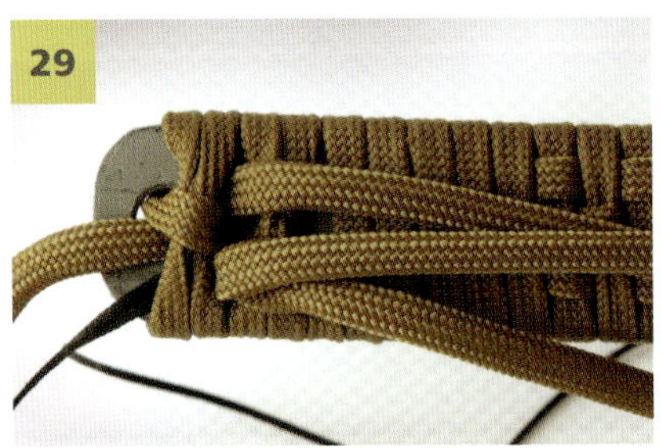

The second knot in progress.

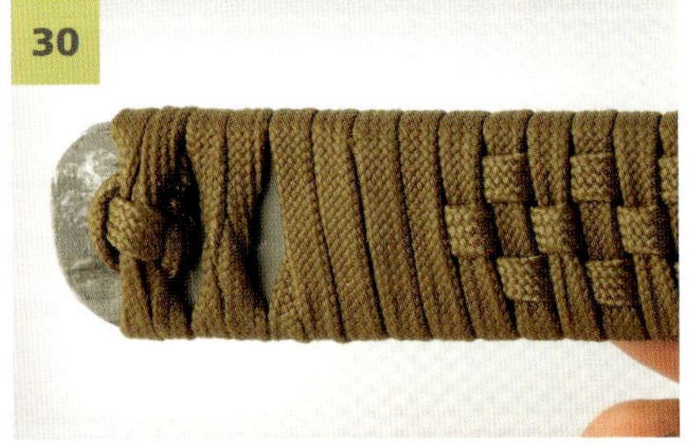

This time we have finished the knots on the *ura* side. The advantage is both working ends are cut off and glued on the handle's backside.

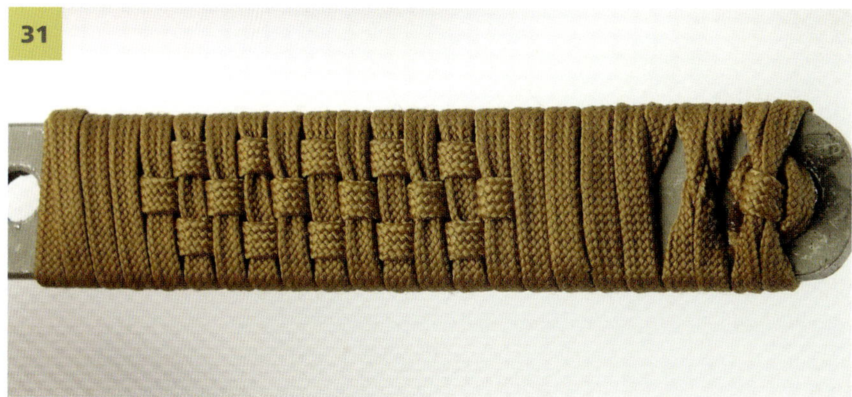

The finished handle wrap on the *ura* side.

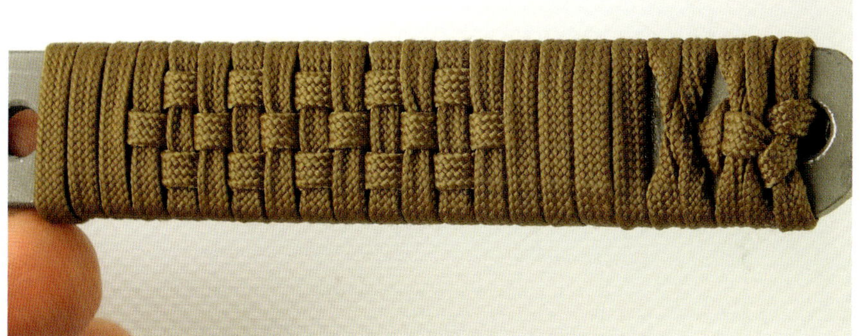

The finished handle wrap on the *omote* side.

Since most modern knife handles wrapped with paracord are relatively short, I left out the traditional start with two twisted crossings on both handle sides. With the traditional way of working, you wrap the handle four times to determine the starting point on the *omote*-side. After two crossings on both sides you cut off the short end and glue it on to the tang. Then you continue with the long working end. The rest of the wrap remains unchanged.

This handle wrap can also be done with the weaving pattern only on the *omote*-side. This is the side you see when the knife is in its sheath or displayed on a stand. In this case the backside is totally flat and thin. In case a *kogatama* (a small additional knife) is used as a desk knife or letter opener, it may be more aesthetic to keep the wrap on the backside as flat as possible.

5.2.6 Braided Crossings from Several Strands

This type of handle wrap is often done with *jabara-ito* silk strands. They are available thinner (about 1.0 mm) or thicker (about 1.5 mm), and are usually sewn together to form pairs. Flatline can replace these double strands. Flatline of paracord type II is about ⅛ in. (3 mm) wide and is acceptable, but a bit thick compared to the originally sewn *jabara-ito*. With smaller bands the pattern can be doubled: two thin bands replace one flatline. The inner strings of paracord often have about a one millimeter diameter and thus open a multitude of possibilities.

To determine the length of the needed paracord, here, too, the handle is wrapped one and a half times. Cut this length of flatline into two equal parts. Melt and mold the ends into fine, flat shapes.

Four Ends of the Same Color

This wrap is a relatively easy weave—or braiding technique—that looks best on wide handles. On slim handles it looks a bit awkward with wide flatline. The handle should be at least 0.787 in. (20 mm) wide in case you work with flatline of type III.

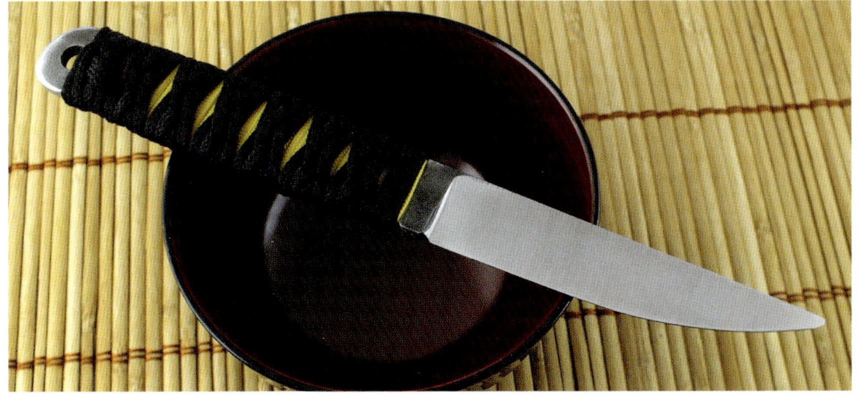

Kaiken with four ends crossing wrap in type II flatline on top of yellow flatline of type III.

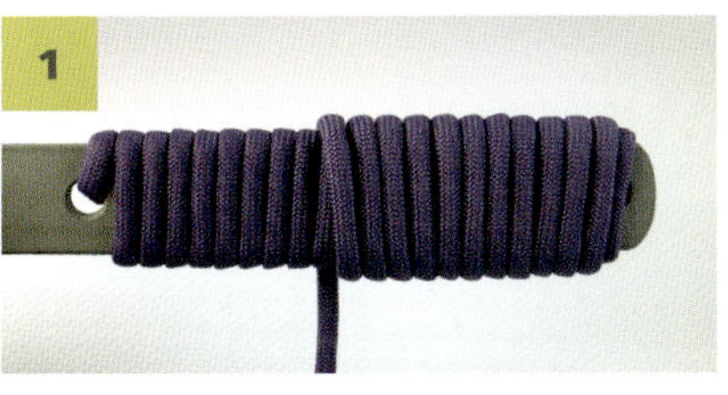

1

Wrap the handle a bit more than one and a half times, then cut off the needed length of cord.

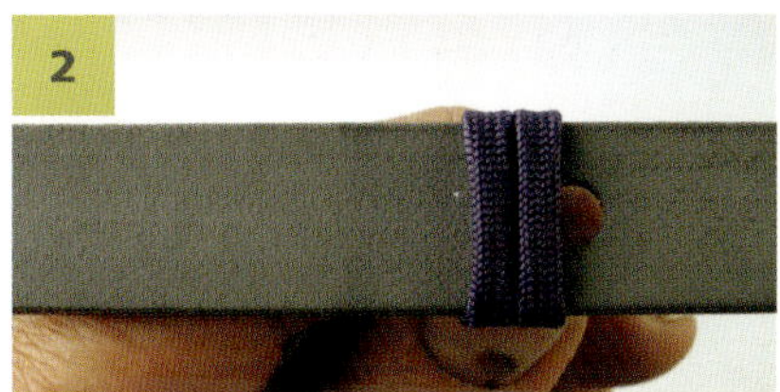

2

Remove the core and center the flatline. Start the handle wrap with the center of the cord on the handle's *omote* side.

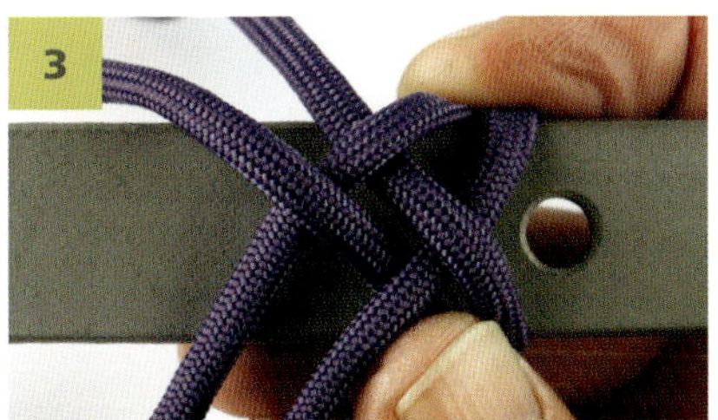

3

Weave the ends on the ura side by leading the first, bottom cord over and under the first and second upper cords. The second, bottom cord goes under and over the upper cords.

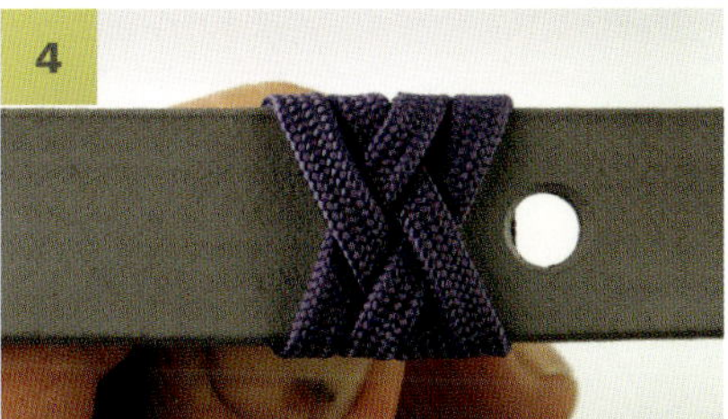

4

Pull all ends tight and make sure all cords move neatly over the handle edges.

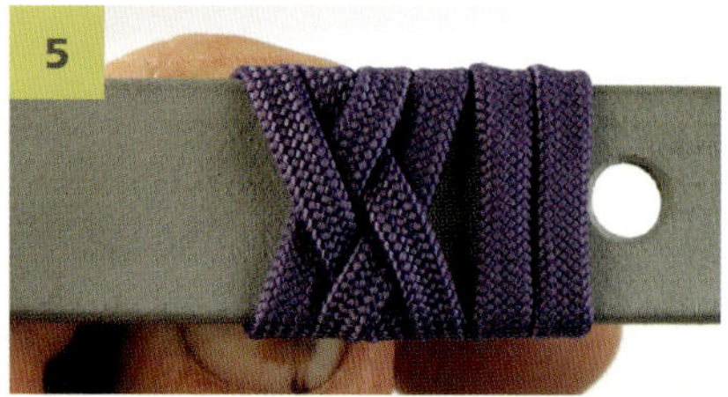

The first weave on the *omote* side.

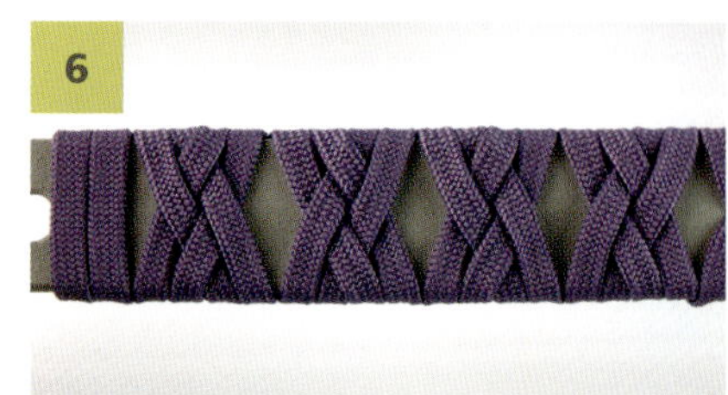

The weaving pattern has reached the end of the *omote* side.

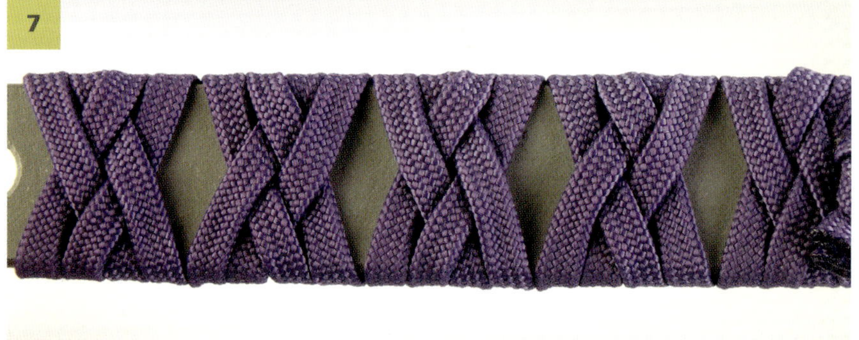

The *ura* side looks like this.

The four-ends braided crossing looks different if it is made from cords of different weights. The smaller the handle the lighter the cord should be to balance the knife.

Four Ends of Two Colors

If you make a four-ends wrap with two colors the pattern becomes asymmetrical; the direction of crossings is alternated. If the direction is not changed, the pattern looks a bit more regular.

To achieve a somewhat more regular appearance of the color structure the start of the handle wrap can be changed. Both cords are crossed at the beginning.

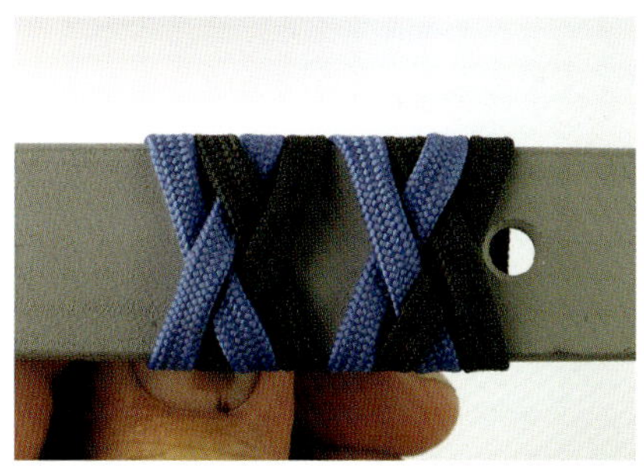

The wrap with four cords and two colors looks asymmetrical. Here the direction of the crossings is alternated.

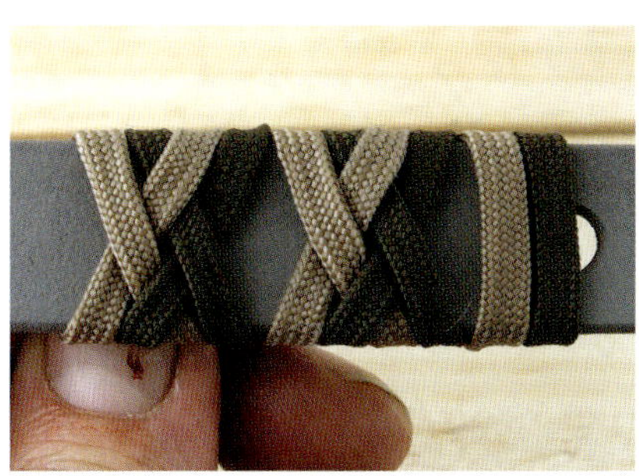

If the direction of crossings is not alternated a kind of diagonally striped pattern is created.

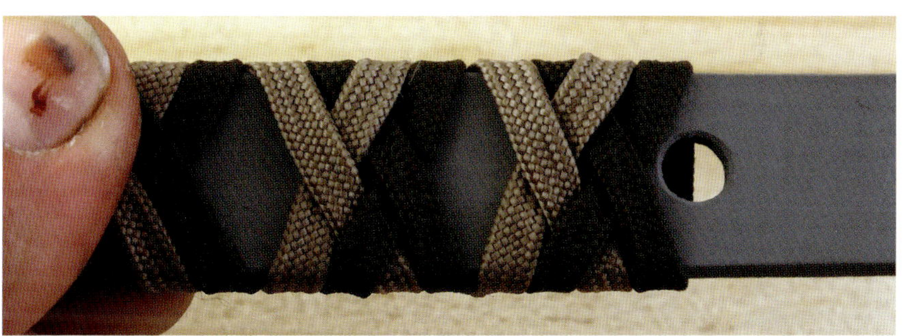

On the *ura* side the entire weaving was done in the same direction.

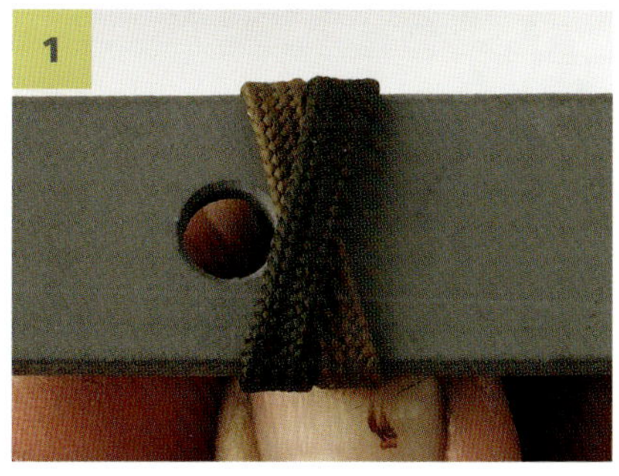

An alternative start of the braid in two colors is to cross both cords at the beginning on the *omote* side.

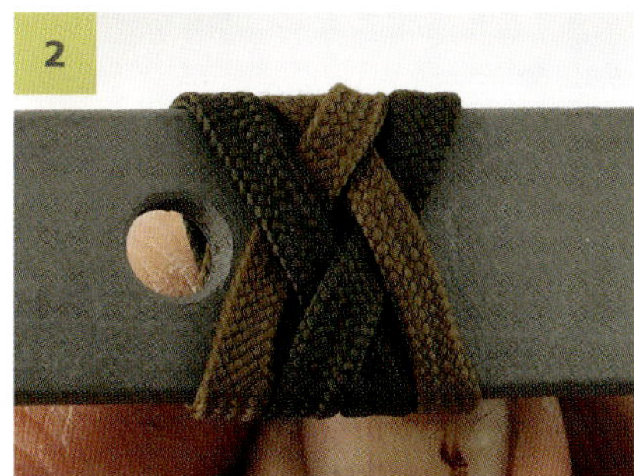

The first braid on the *ura* side.

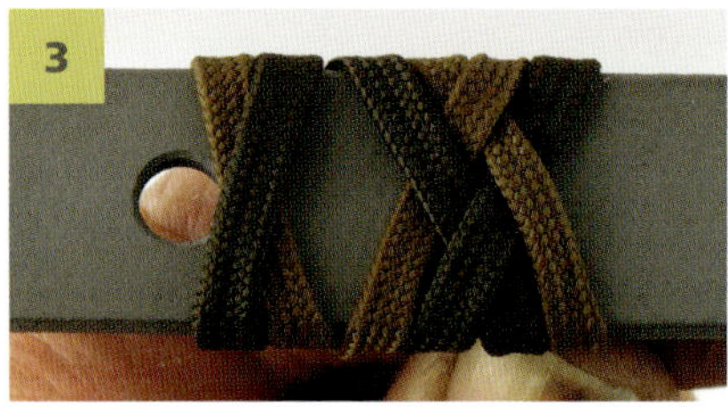

The first braid on the *omote* side is done in the same direction.

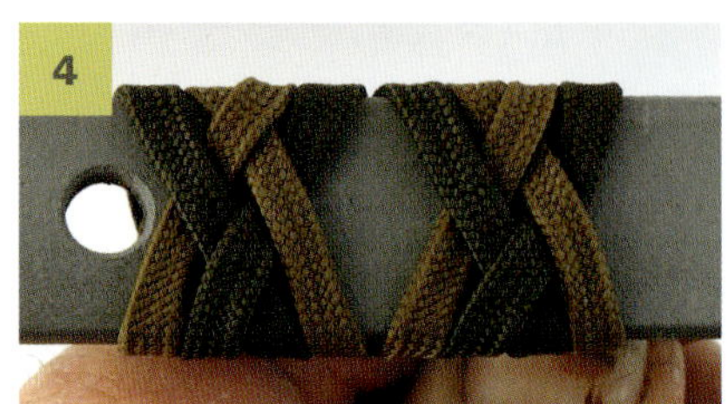

We work in the same direction for the second braid on the *ura* side.

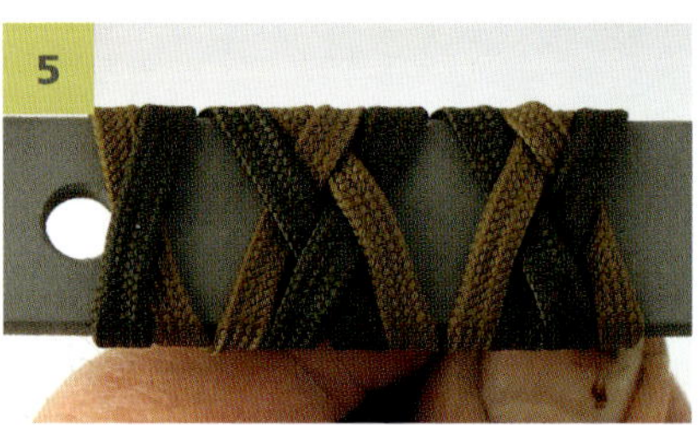

We change the direction on the *omote* side; this way the color structure becomes similar to a zig-zag pattern.

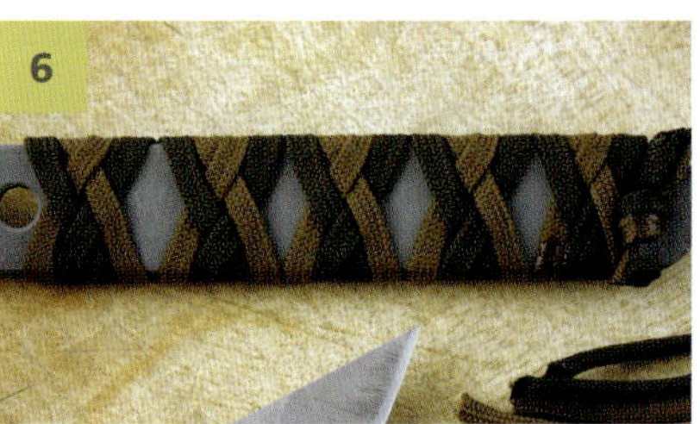

The finished *ura* side with all crossings in the same direction.

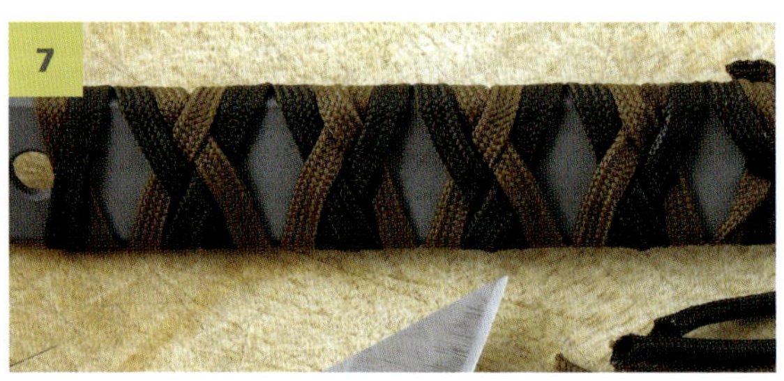

On the *omote* side, the pattern is different because the crossings are done in alternating direction.

While searching for a more uniform appearance I designed another four-ends wrap. It uses four working ends—the same as for the four-ends braided crossing—but actually makes two flat crossings on top of each other, thus the name the "alternative 4 braid."

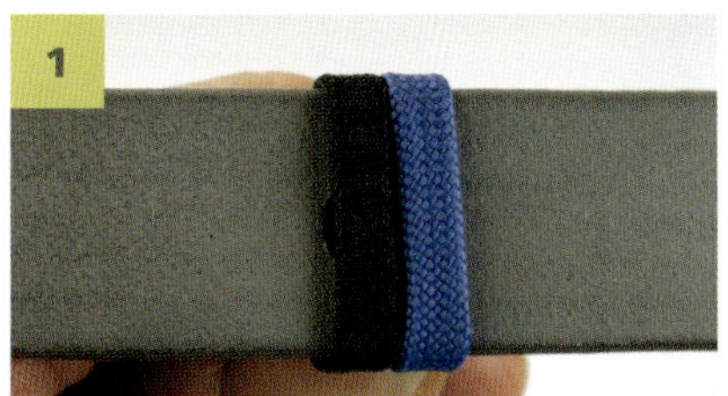

Start with the center of both cords at the guard. The second color—here black—becomes the dominant color on the handle.

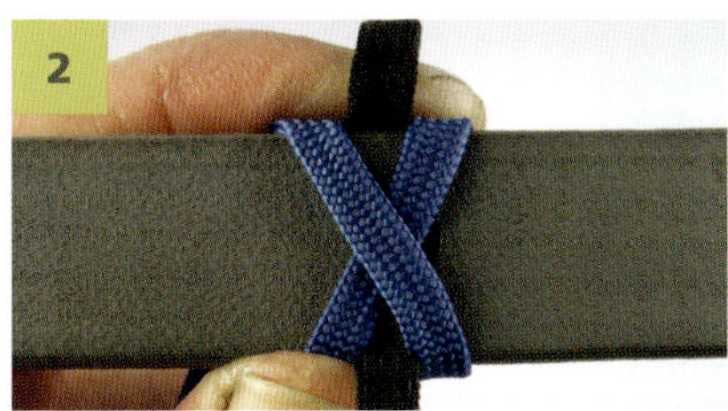

Make the crossings of the first cord ends wide enough so the second cord (black) lies in between. Make sure that tension is kept on all ends of the cords.

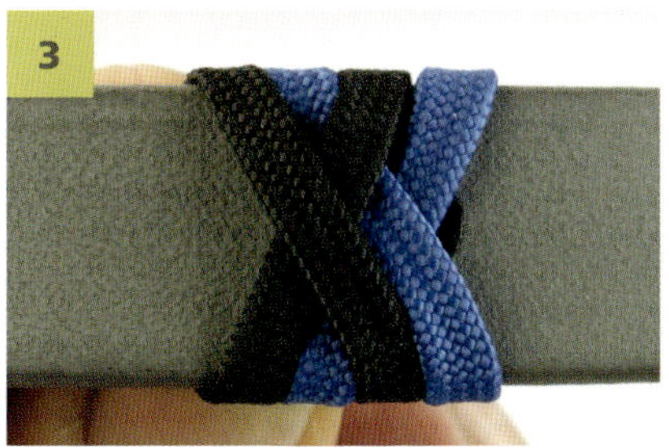

The first double crossing is completed.

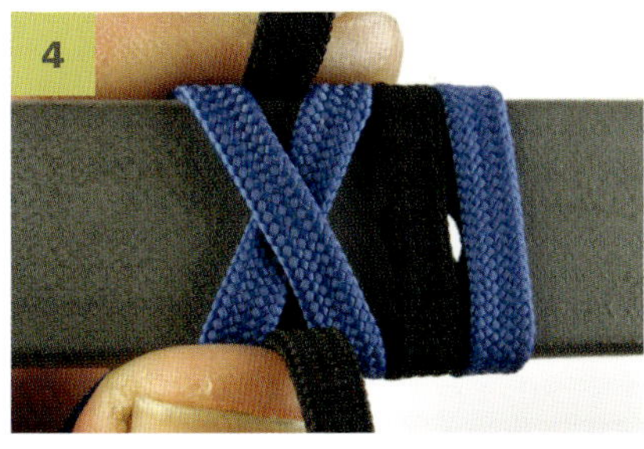

The crossings on the *omote* side are done the same way. The black cord ends cross in the same direction.

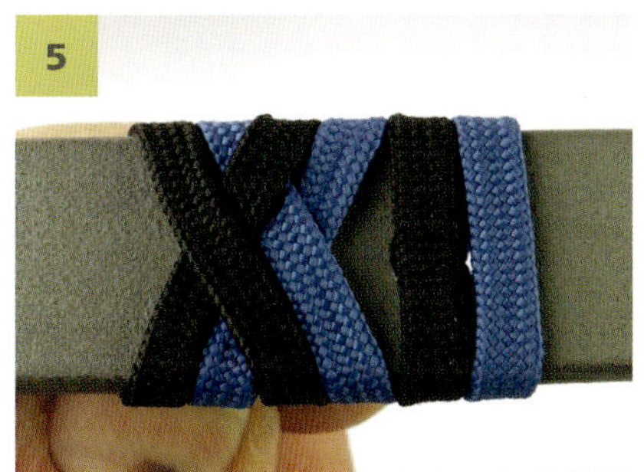

The black cord ends are put over the blue ones.

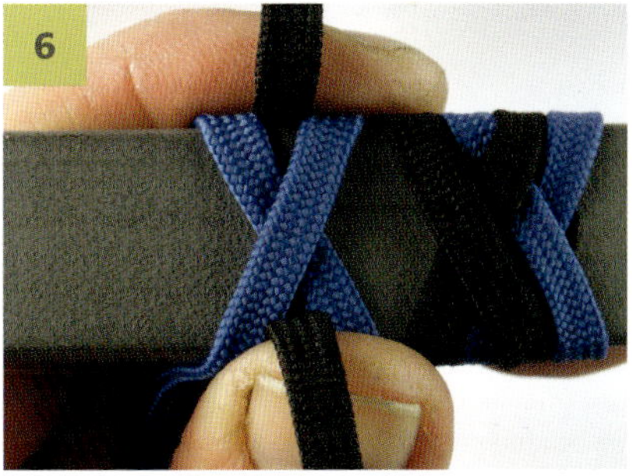

Change the direction to make the second crossing on the *ura* side.

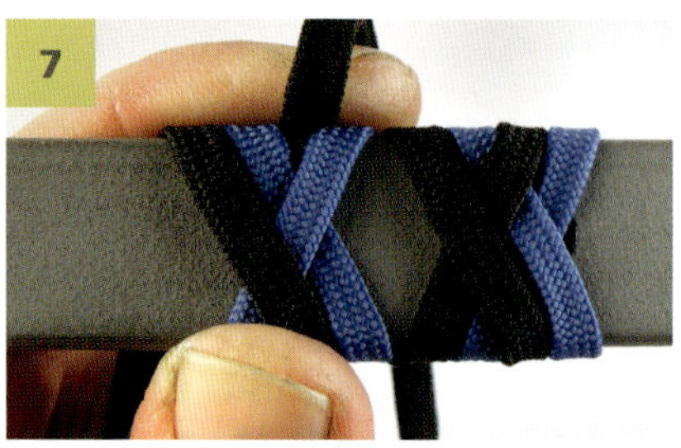

The second pair of cord ends is woven in the same direction as the first pair.

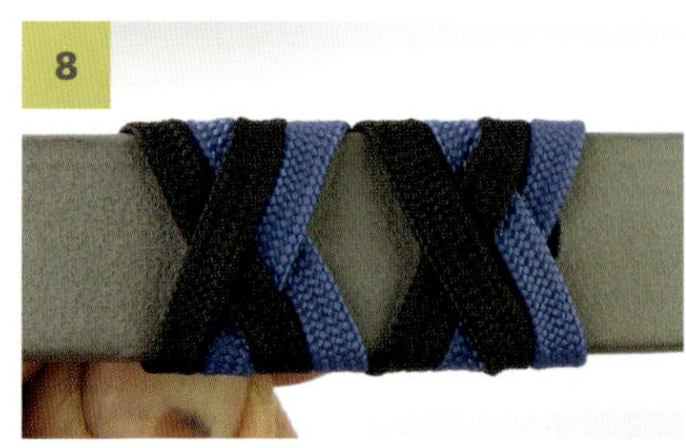

Note the change of direction for the first two crossings on the *ura* side.

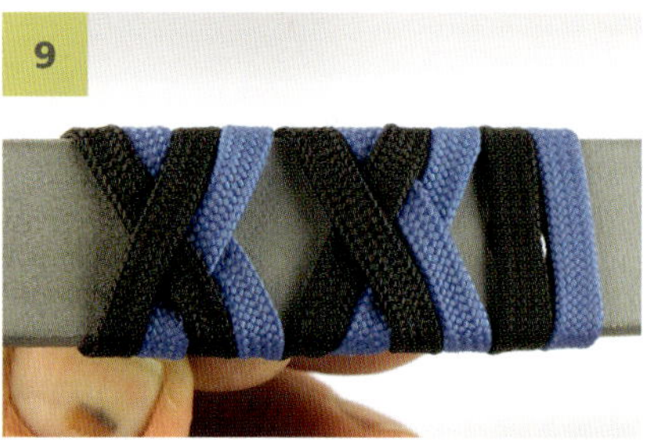

On the *omote* side the wrap slowly takes shape.

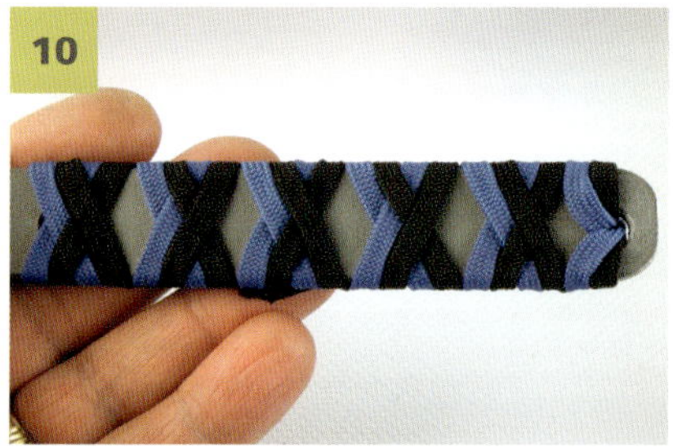

The *ura* side is finished. This handle wrap looks better than the original four-ends wrap with two colors.

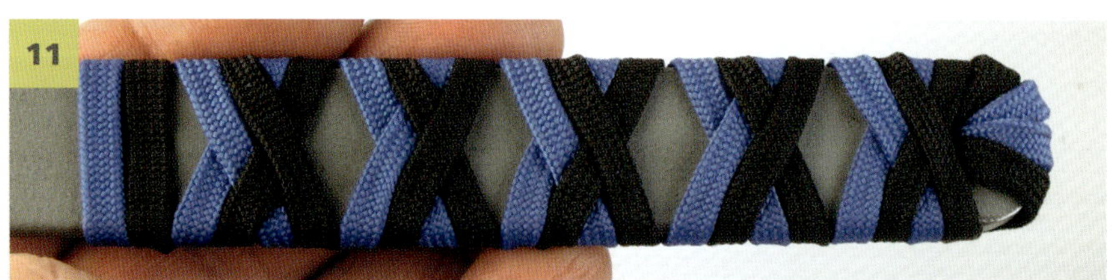

The *omote* side without an end knot.

The handle wrap becomes finer if made with thinner paracord or flatline. A lot of possible variations exist if each flatline of type III is replaced by several cords of type I or type II.

Six Ends

The mesh is done in six steps. In my manual I use two black cords and one silver paracord of type I. The silver cord is put between the two black ones.

The length of the cord is determined by wrapping the handle one and a half times. If the handle is only wrapped with a single cord to determine length simple division by three does not lead to the right result, because a bit more cord is needed for the end knots. But you can also add about 11 ¹³⁄₁₆ in. (thirty centimeters) to every third. This way of weaving is not very difficult and produces a pretty knife.

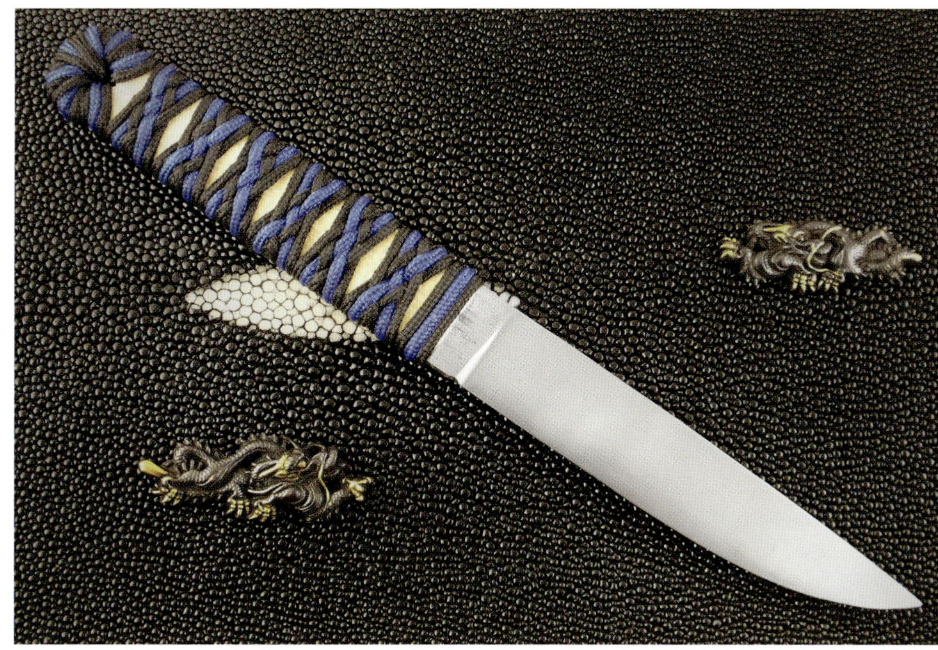

Kaiken with black and blue braided wrap over white ray skin. Here, full paracord of type I was used which still has its core strings.

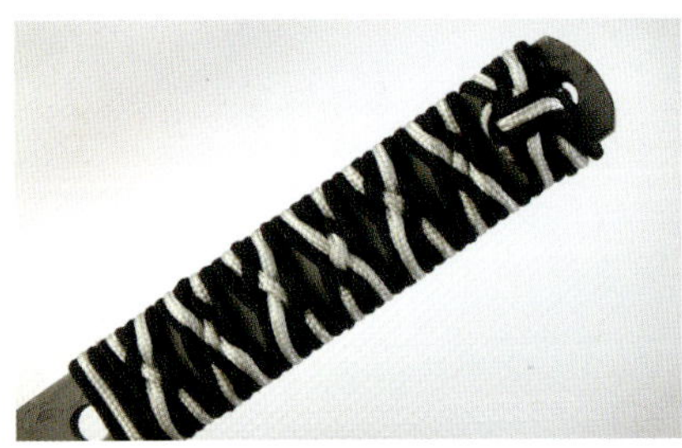

The braided wrap with six ends: two black cords of type I with a silver cord in between.

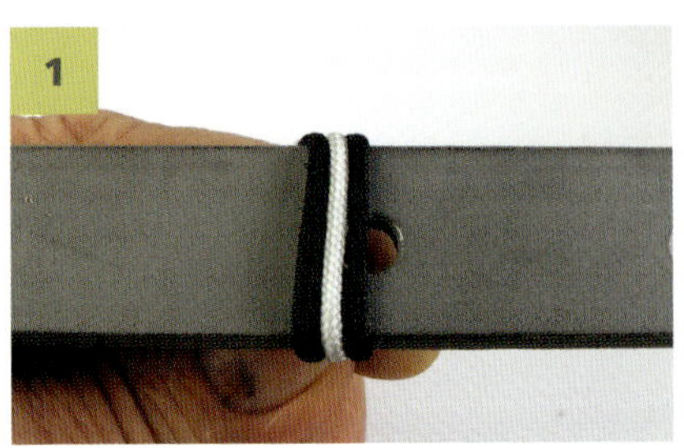

The wrap starts with the center of the three cords on the *omote* side.

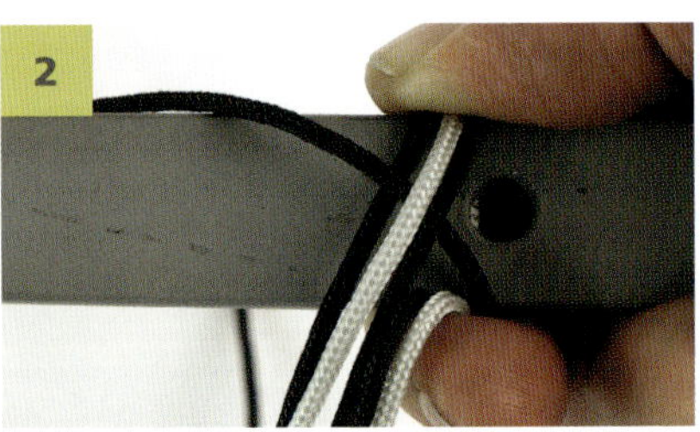

The first of the three lower ends goes upward over the black cord, underneath the silver one, and over the black one again.

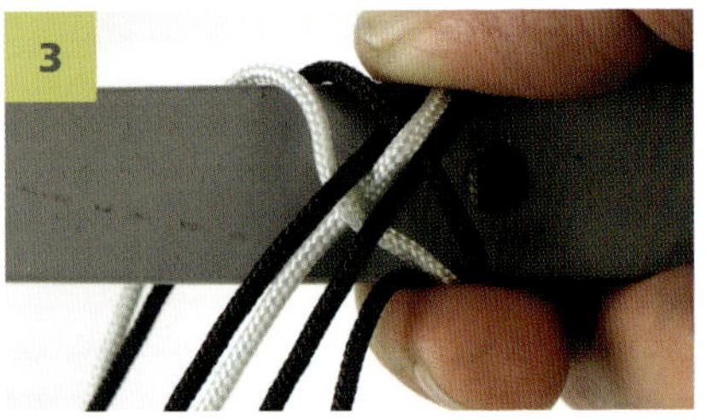

The lower silver cord end goes under, over, and under the other three cords.

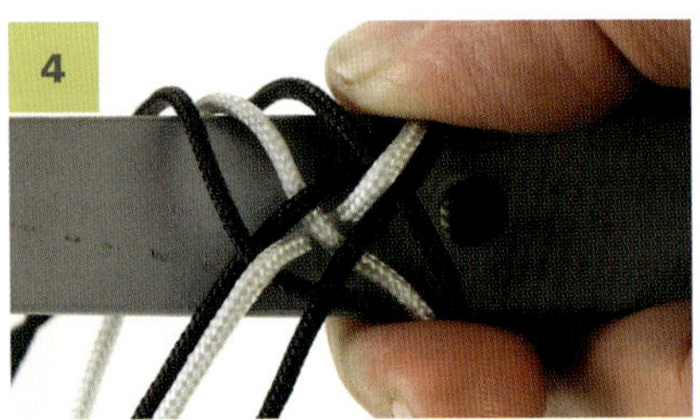

The third cord does the same as the first.

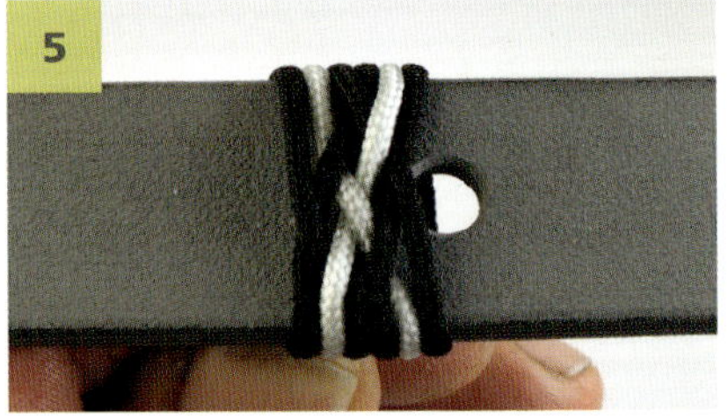

The first crossing is finished. Pull all working ends tight separately to get the weaving pattern right. Press and push the cords into position if necessary to give the pattern its optimal look.

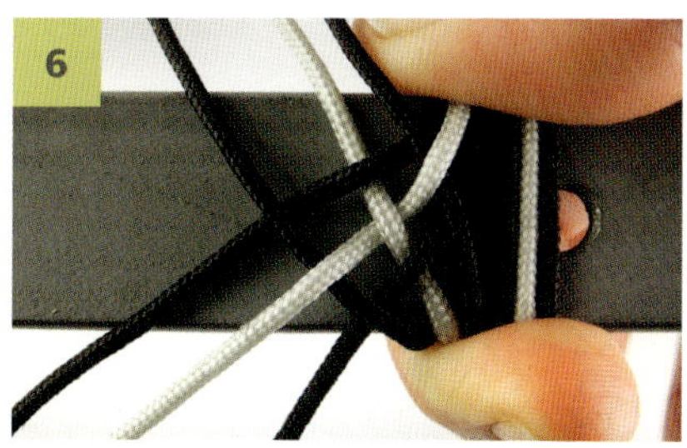

The first round of the weaving pattern on the *omote* side.

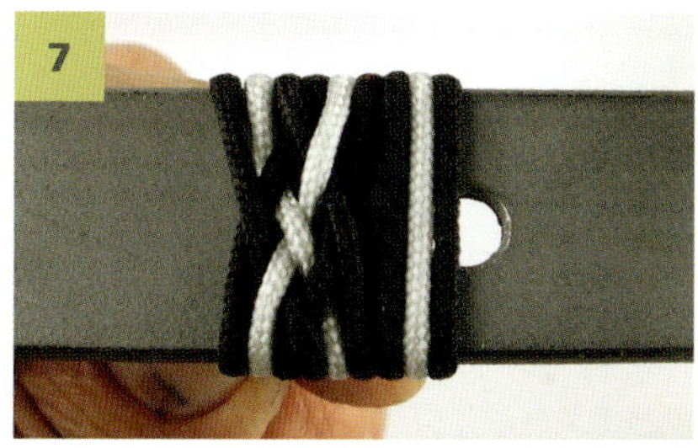

Push everything close together and pull the ends tight.

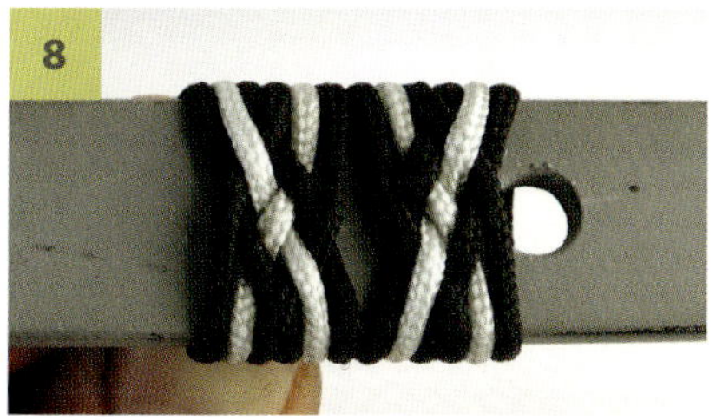

Alternate the weaving direction if desired. For this wrap it is not necessary, but it looks good.

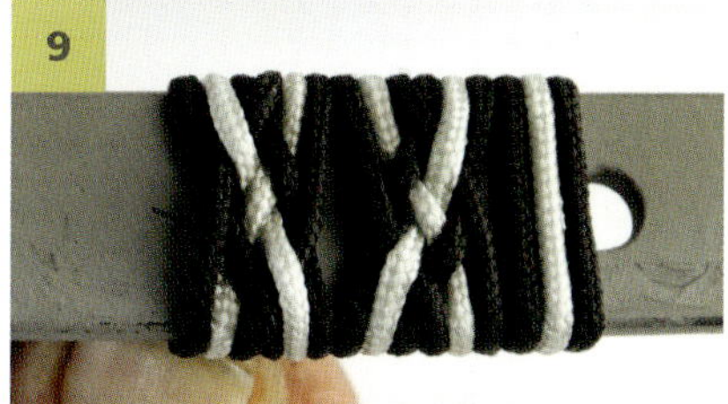

Here the direction of the wrap alternates on the *omote* side, too. Continue pulling the ends tight and press everything close together.

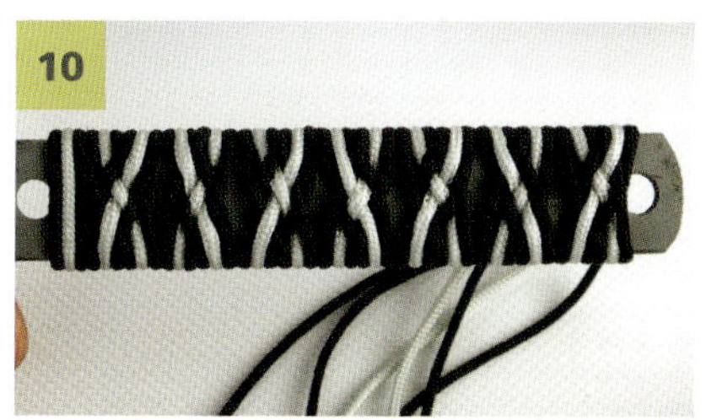

We have reached the end on the *omote* side. The working ends are glued to the sides of the knife tang so we can concentrate on making the end knots.

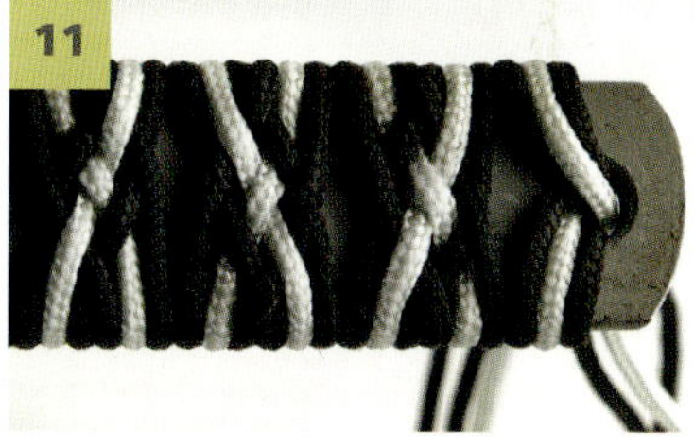

A simple solution for the knots starts with pulling all cord ends through the pommel hole.

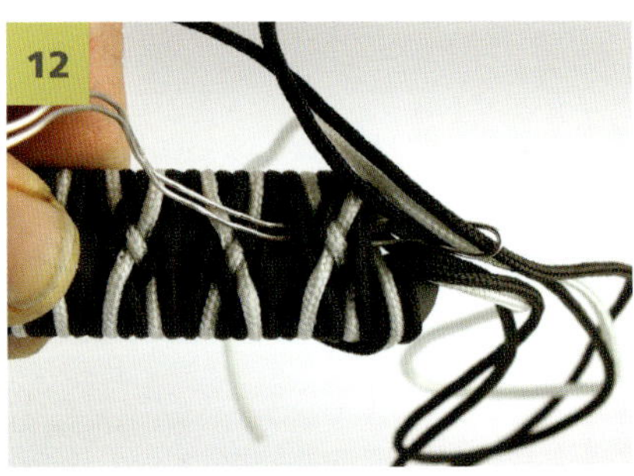

With a bent wire the cords are pulled underneath the last weave.

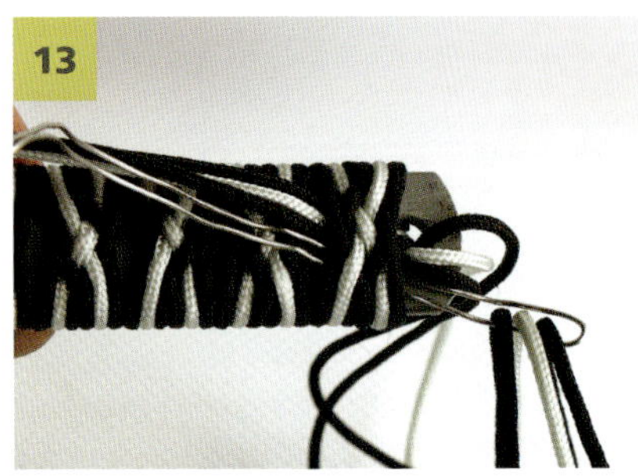

The second set of working ends is also pulled underneath the weave.

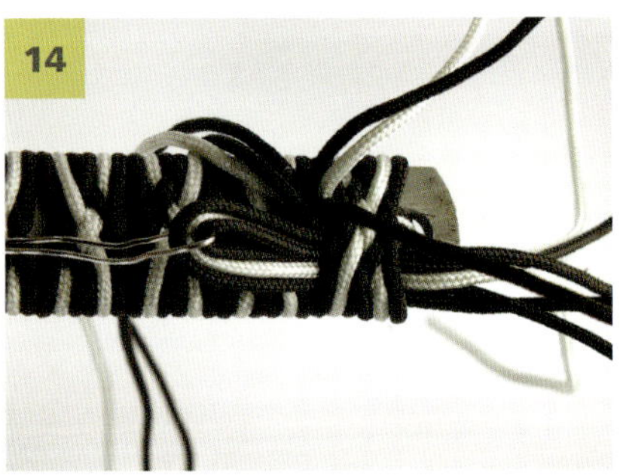

The first set of cord ends goes upward and is pulled underneath the weave again on the right side.

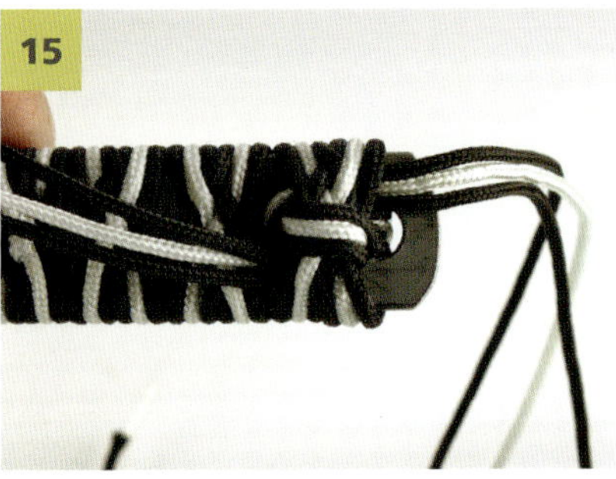

The cord ends which were first led down on the right side have now come up on the left side of the weave.

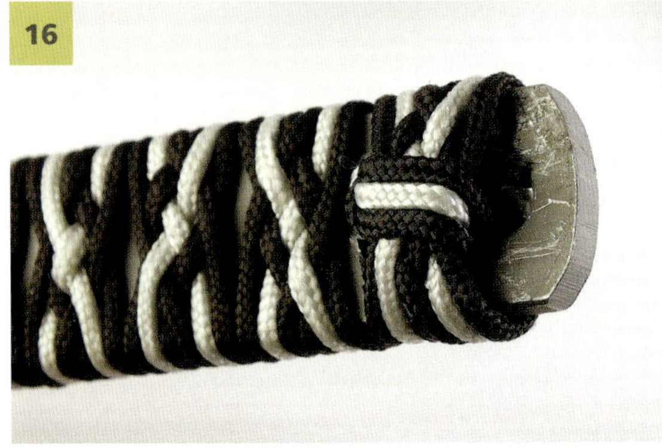

All ends are cut off and can now be trimmed a bit with fine scissors. This knot is only a part of the traditional knot; the bulk of a full end knot would be too much compared to the handle's volume.

5.2.7 Four-Ends-Crossing with Loops

This *tsukamaki* is also done with four ends, but instead of weaving the ends together, two ends will cross each other. With the other ends we will make loops. This example is done with black and golden paracord of type II.

What is special about this kind of handle wrap is that the overall look of the wrap is different for both sides. The colors change their place, and the dominant color of one side is lying underneath the other on the opposite side. Use this as a tip to adjust the position of the cords when starting the handle wrap.

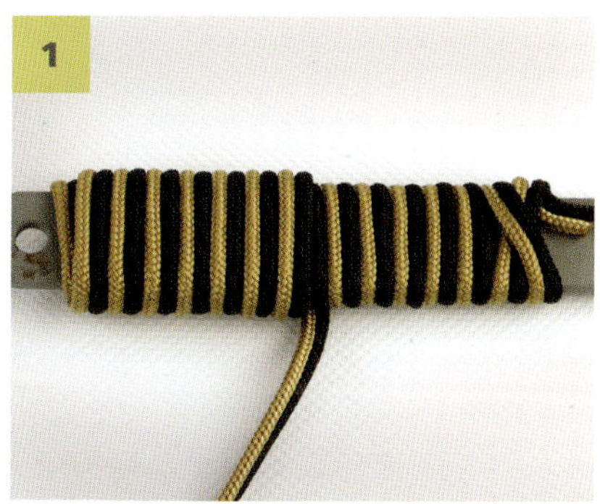

Wrap the handle one and a half times to measure the needed cord length.

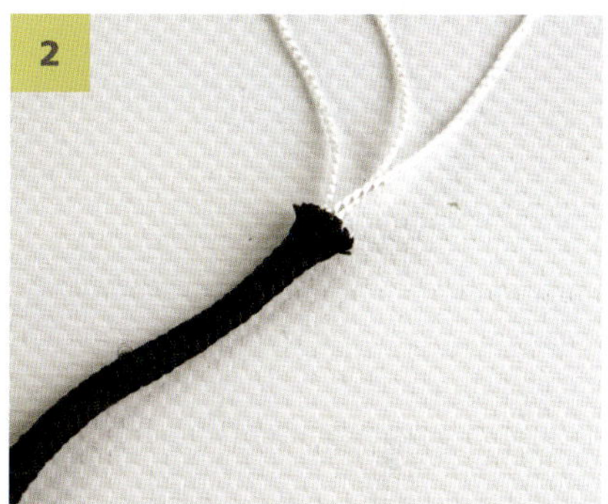

Paracord of type II has three core strings which we remove.

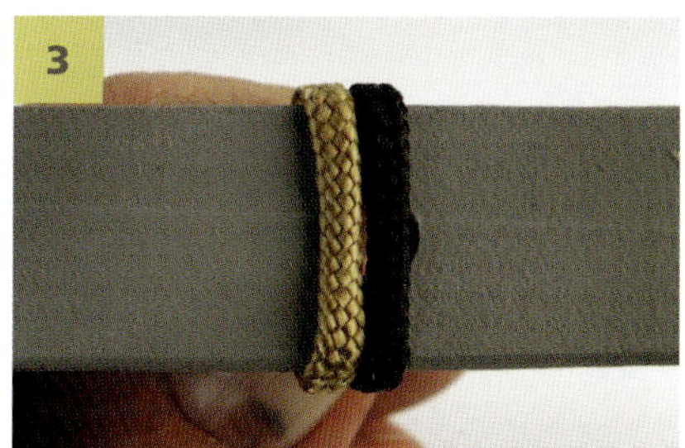

We start with the center of the cords at the guard. I prefer the darker side to be next to the blade.

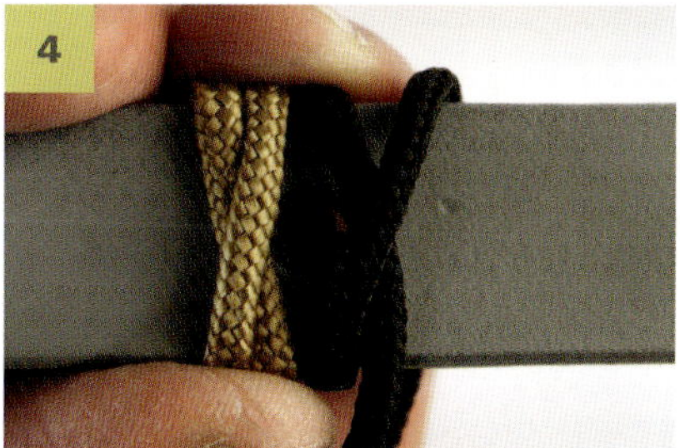

With the black cord ends out of the way on the right side, we cross the golden cord ends.

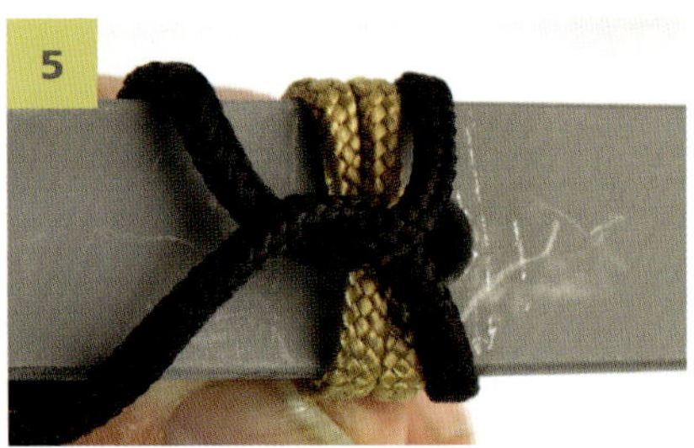

Put the black cord ends over the golden crossing and pull the working ends. Make sure you hold all four ends!

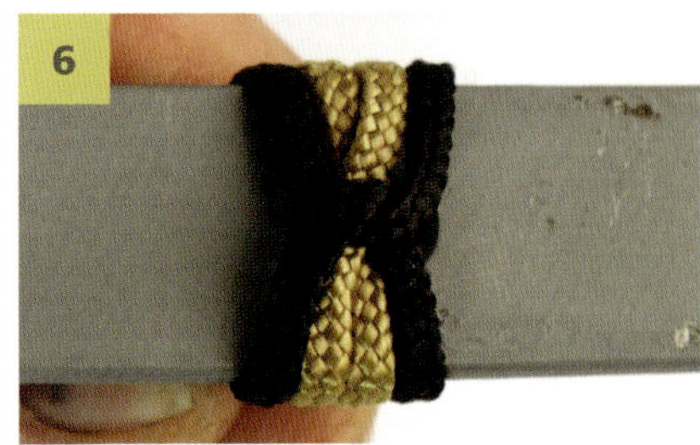

The first crossing is pulled tight.

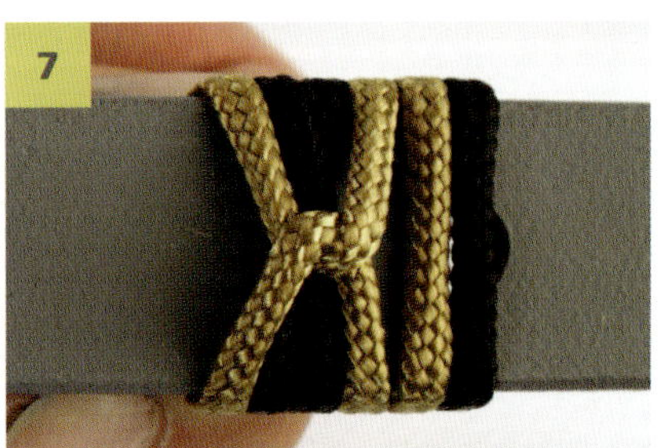

The knife is turned around and the moves are repeated.

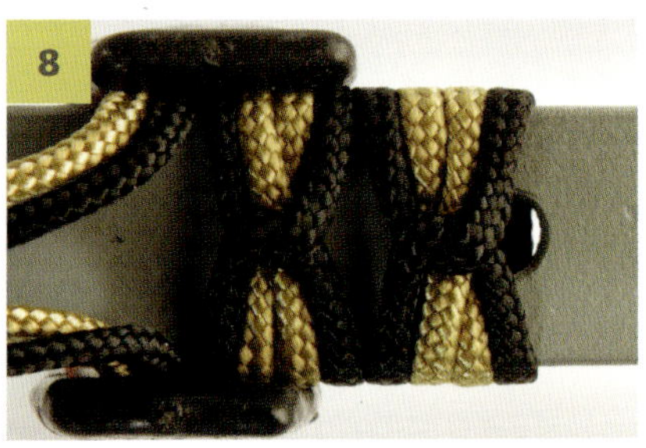

The black cord ends are put over the golden ones and looped through each other.

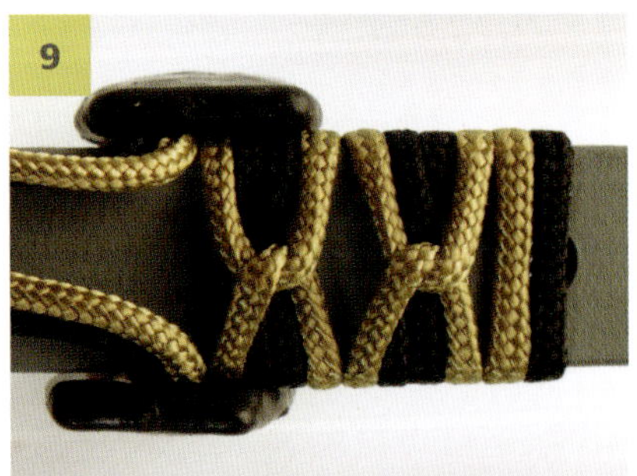

The other side shows the alternating direction of the black crossings.

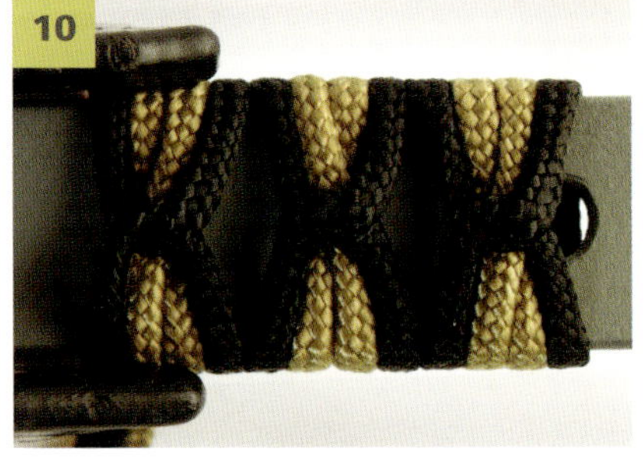

The crossings are repeated, but the golden crossings change direction on this side.

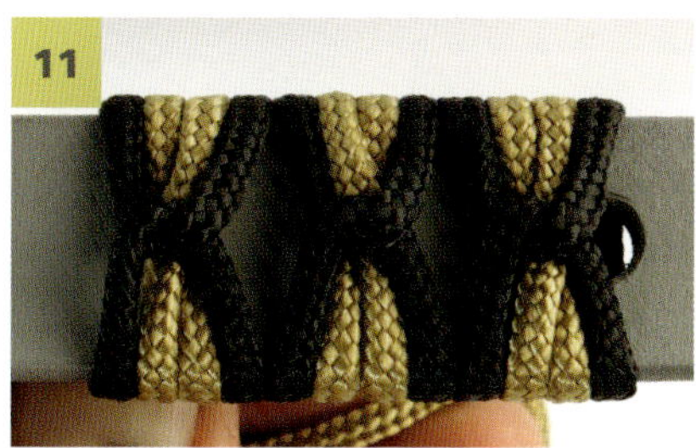

This looks quite nice already!

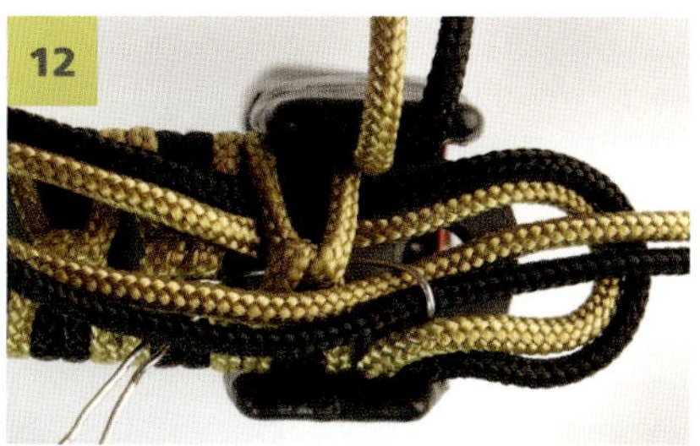

The upper cord ends are also pulled under the crossings with the bent wire.

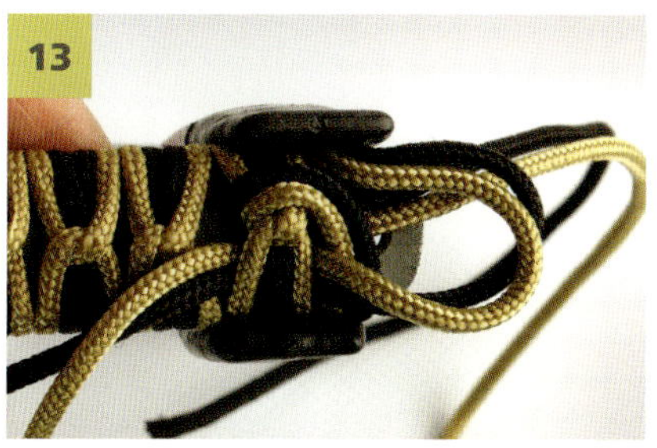

This will become an alternative end knot, because the traditional one would be too thick.

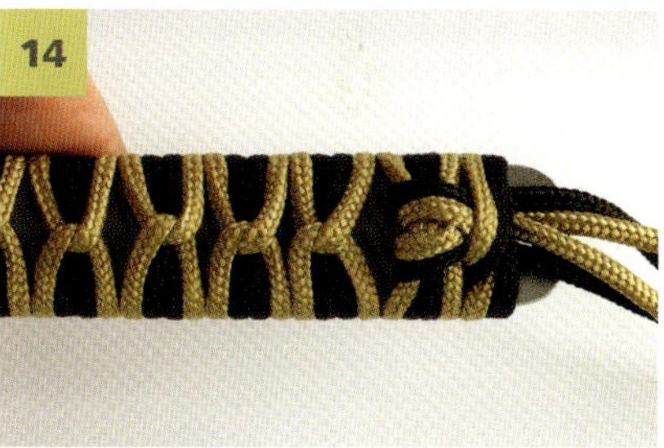

The first alternative knot is finished.

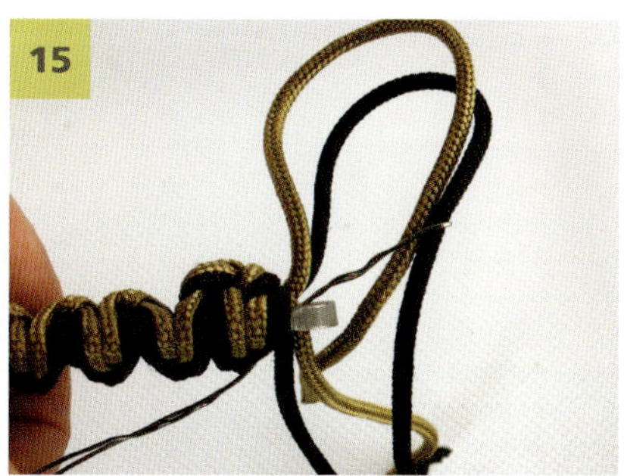

All working ends are pulled through the hole in the tang with the bent wire.

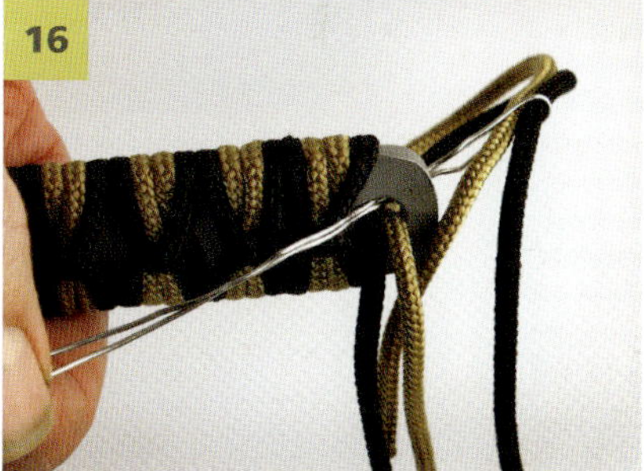

The cords are being pulled through.

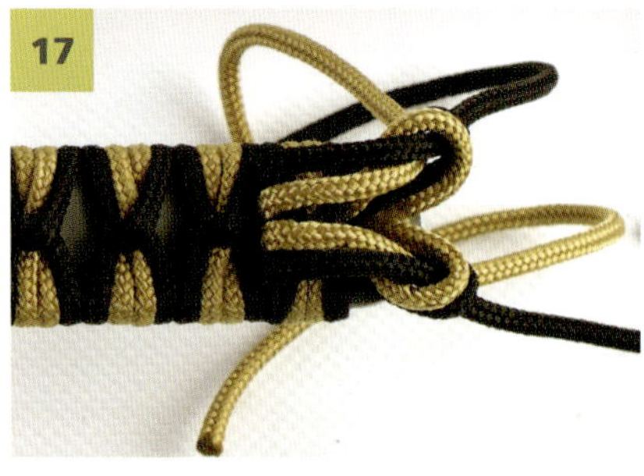

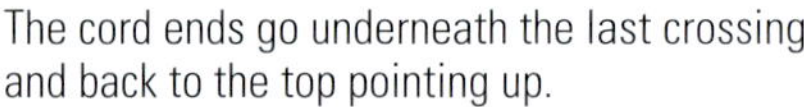

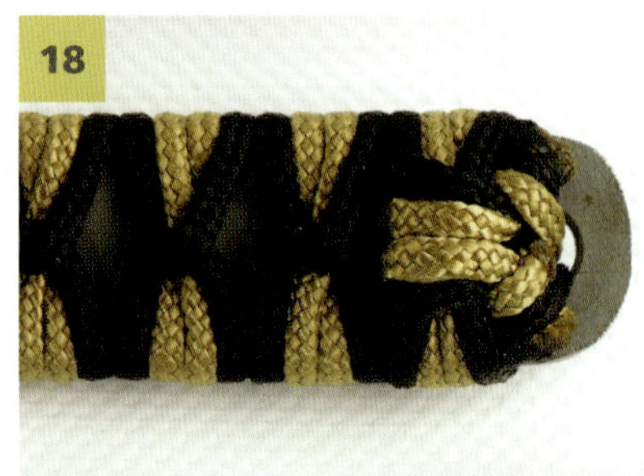

The cord ends go underneath the last crossing and back to the top pointing up.

The ends are trimmed, melted, and shaped.

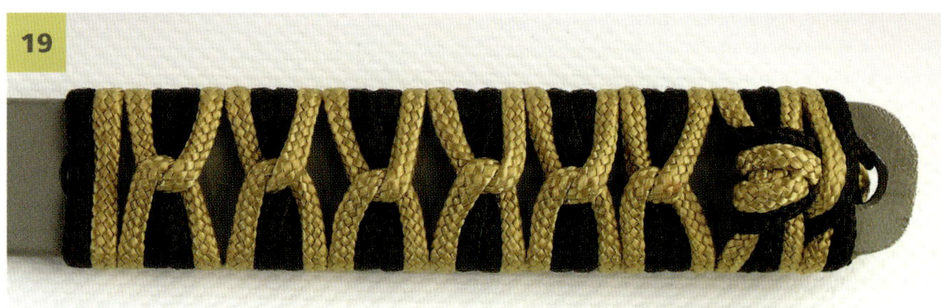

The *omote* side was finished with an alternative *ura* knot. The traditional *ura* knot also would have been too thick.

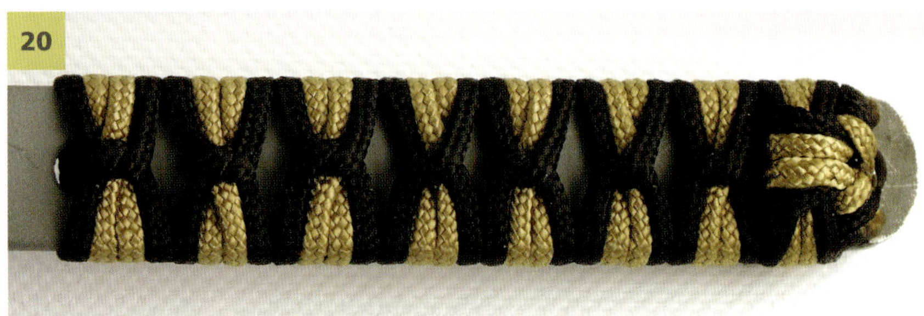

The completed *ura* side with the non-traditional *omote* knot.

5.2.8 Flat Crossing with Four Ends

With this handle wrap the flatlines cross each other. This technique needs clamping, since keeping tension at the ends of the cords is more difficult than with the other wraps. Constant checking of the cord ends is mandatory. It is important to constantly pull all four working ends tight and to keep the crossings close to each other. If you work with two colors, both sides alternate the dominant color.

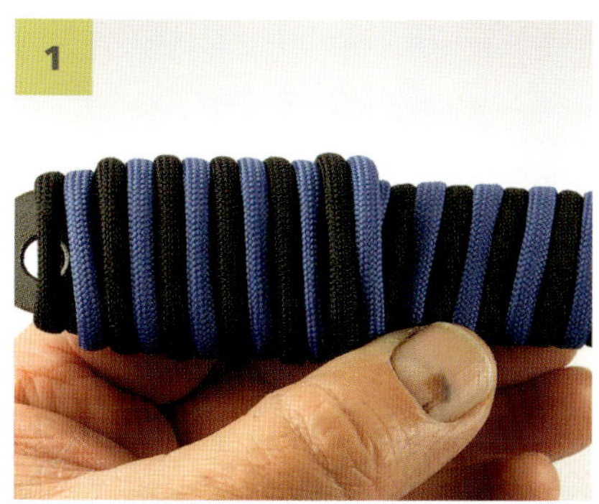

Wrap the handle one and a half times with both cords at the same time before cutting them off.

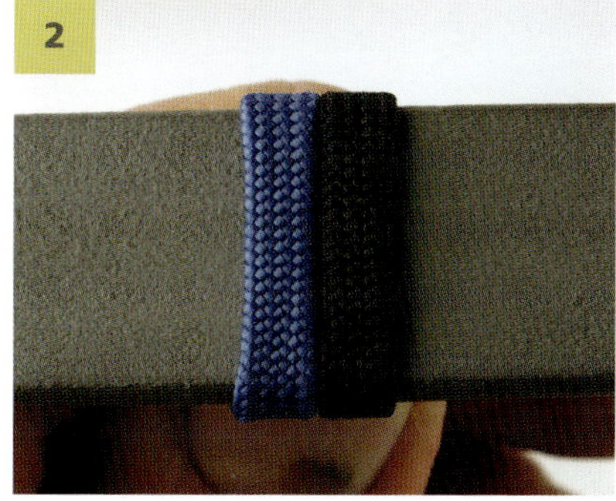

Start the wrap with the center of both flatlines on the *omote* side of the handle. I prefer the darker color to be closest to the blade.

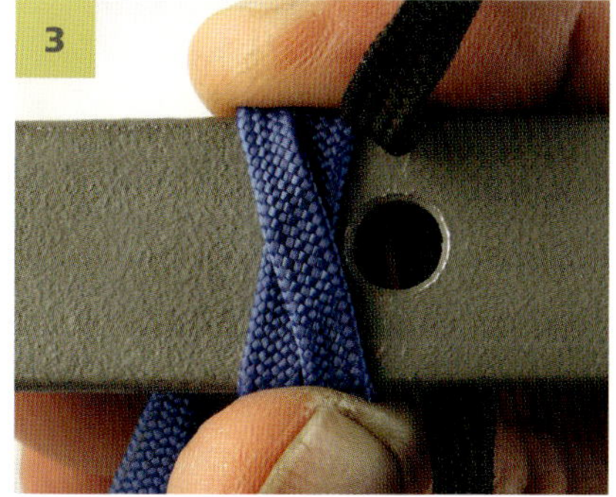

Start with crossing the blue cord ends.

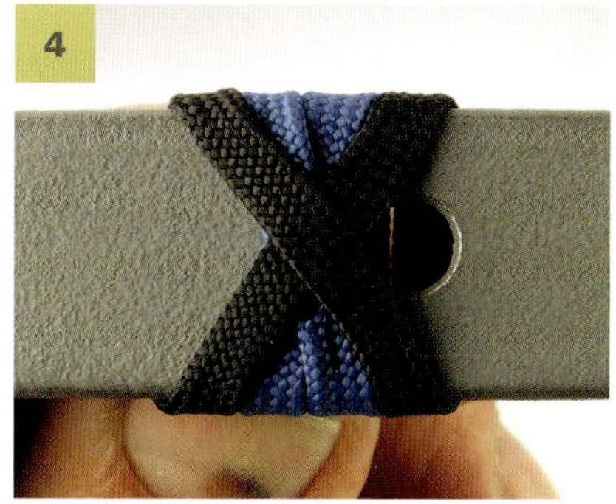

Cross the black cord ends in the same direction on top of the blue ones.

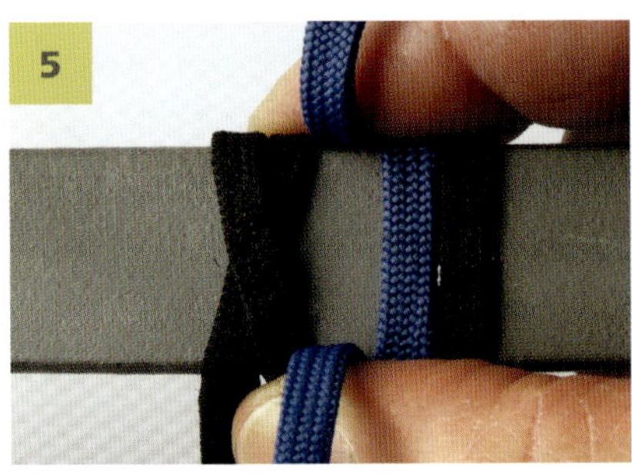

On the *omote* side the crossing is done with the black cord ends first.

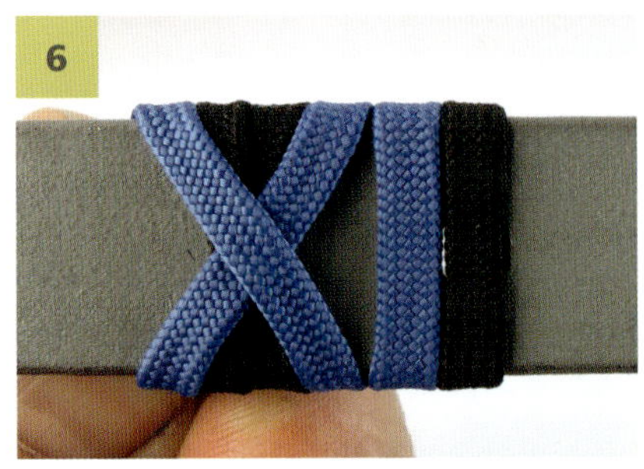

Finish the crossing by putting the blue ends on top of the black ones.

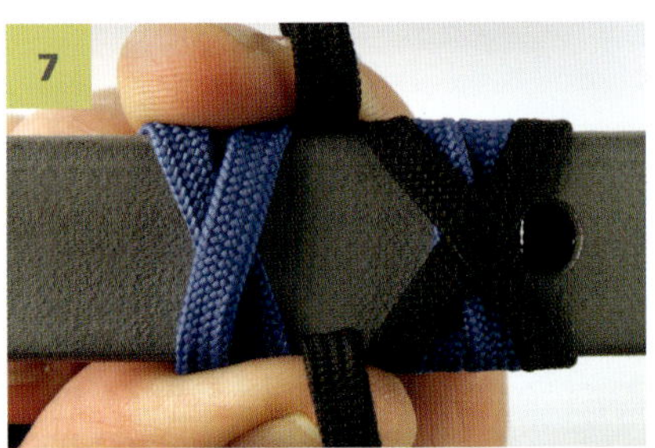

Back on the *ura* side, the blue crossing comes first. The direction of the crossing has changed.

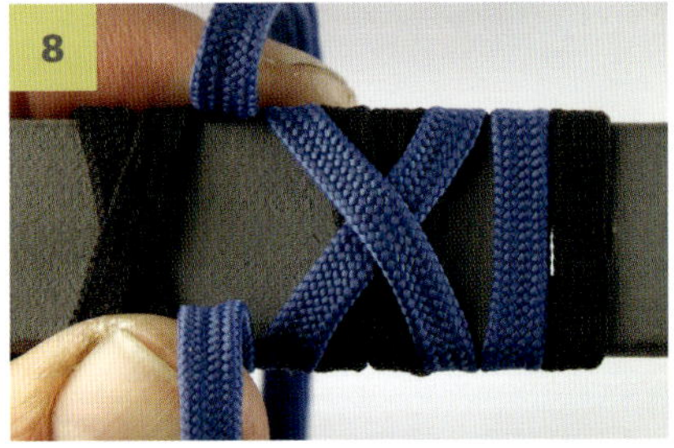

The second crossing has also changed direction, but you do not have to do this.

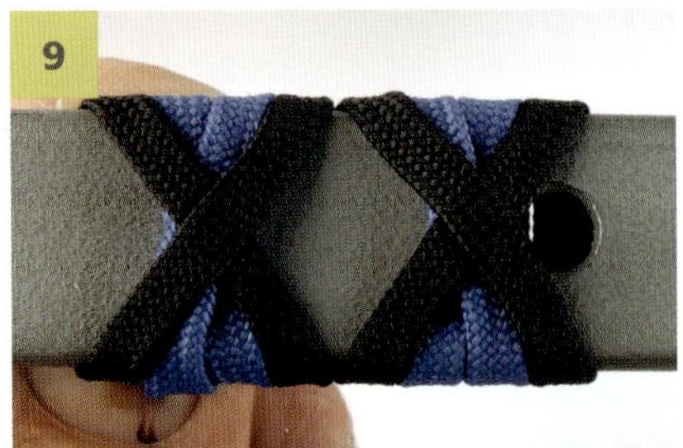

The second crossing still has to be pulled tight.

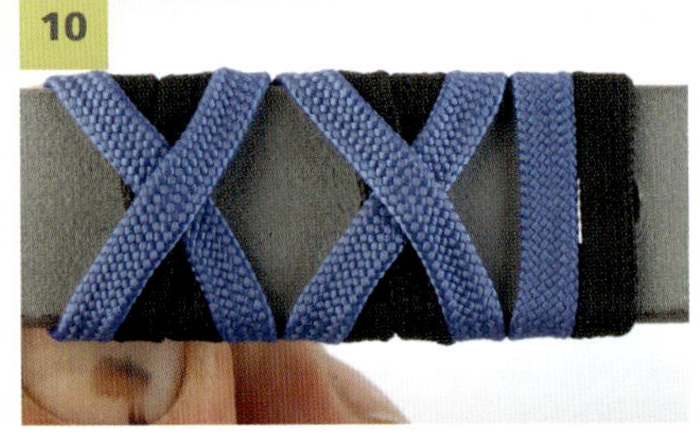

Both directions are shown on the handle's *omote* side. Continue until the end of the tang.

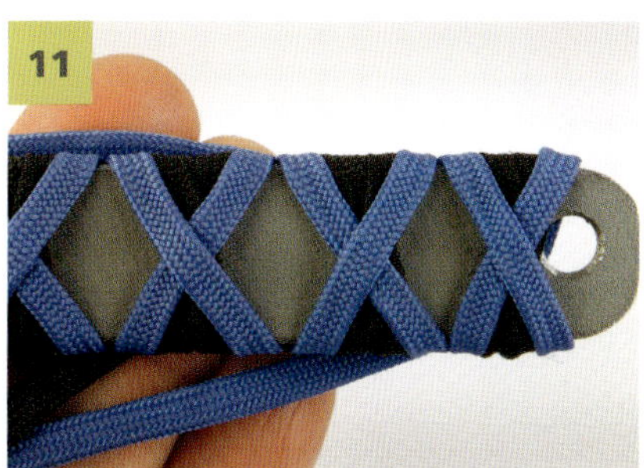

The tang's end is reached.

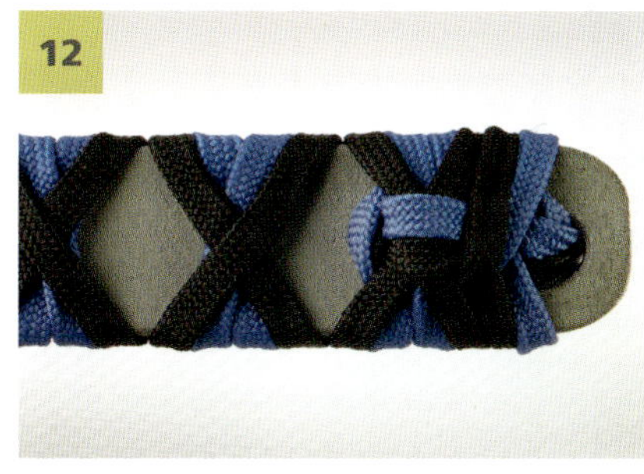

This *ura* knot is based on the traditional version—with the difference that here we work with 2 × 2 flatline.

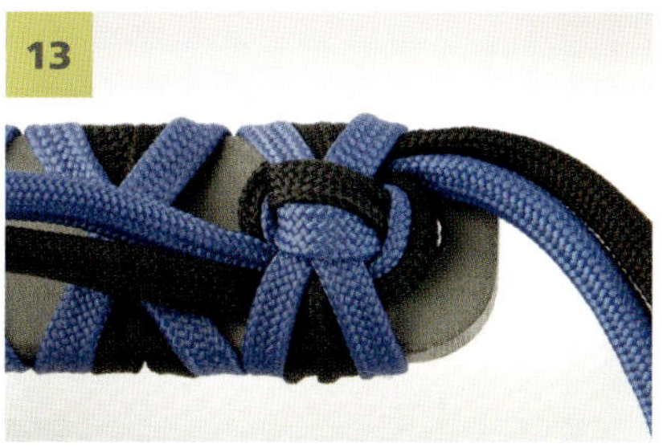

The *omote* knot receives an alternative end so the knot does not become too bulky. The ends are cut off and melted or glued.

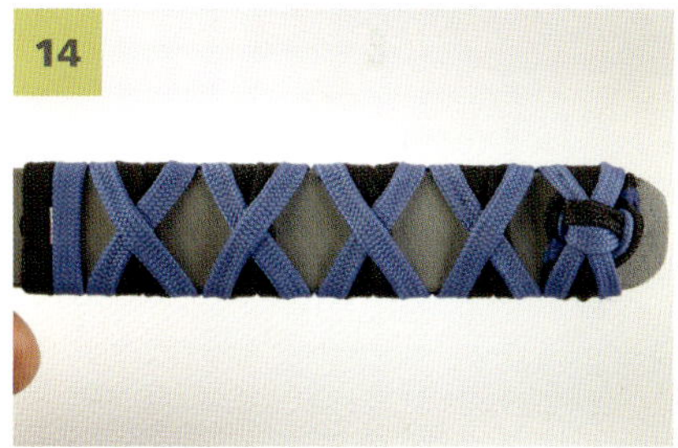

The *omote* side is finished.

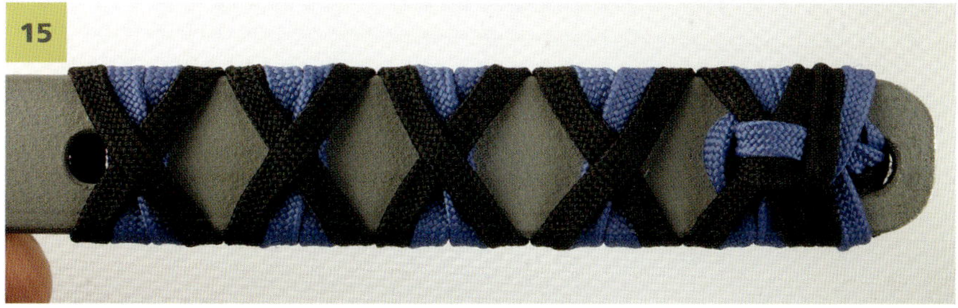

The completed *ura* side.

CHINESE HANDLE WRAPS

6.1 Traditional Chinese Wraps

In 2004, I struggled to find out how the wrap shown next is done. Vince and Grace Evans helped me and taught me the original way to make this wrap. Vince Evans is a highly talented swordsmith and makes museum quality functional reproductions which come as close to the originals as possible.

The version closest to the original handle wrap of Chinese Dao swords is done with a continuous cord or band; flat, woven silk band is best suited for this. Narrow types of flatline excel here. The narrower the handle, the narrower the band or paracord flatline should be.

Pretty handle wraps exist with flatline and with full paracord. I used full paracord of type II and flatline of type III. Handle wraps of paracord flatline come closest to the original Chinese sword wraps.

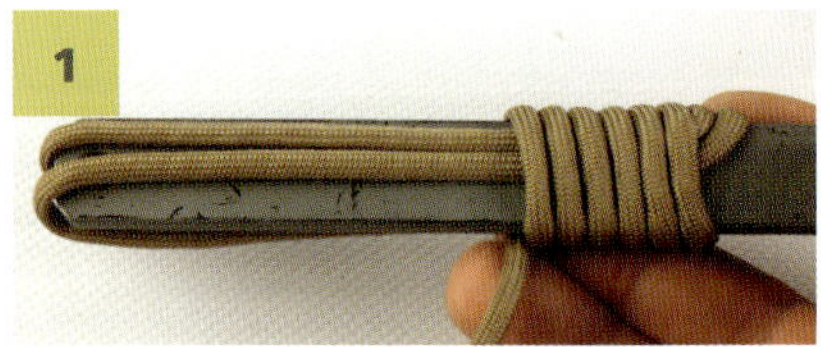

You start the wrap this way to determine the needed cord length.

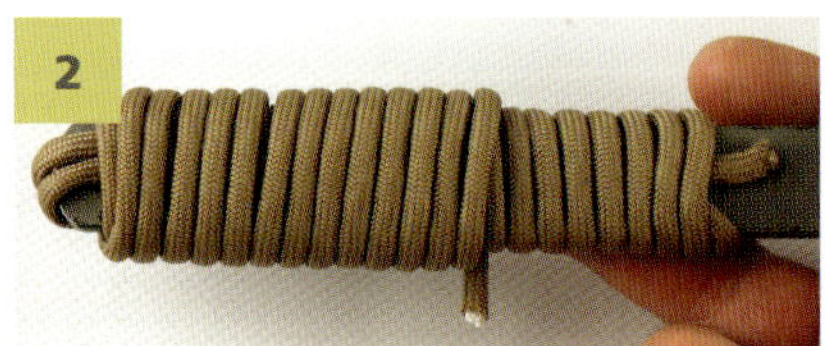

The correct handle length: two loops along the handle's length and one and a half layers around the handle are enough material to end the wrap with a Turk's Head if desired.

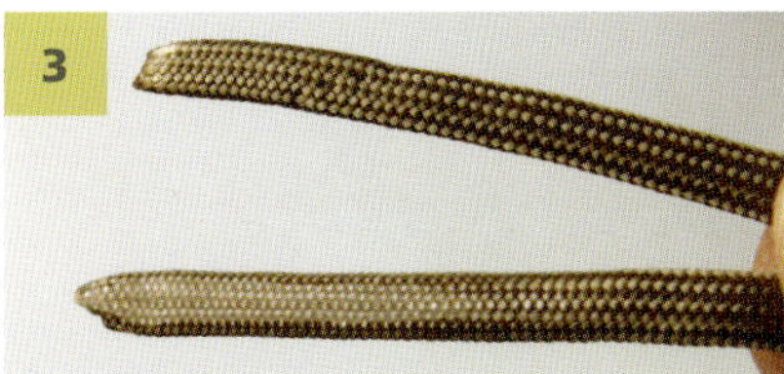

Remove the core of the paracord. The working end gets a stiff tip, the beginning a fine, flat end.

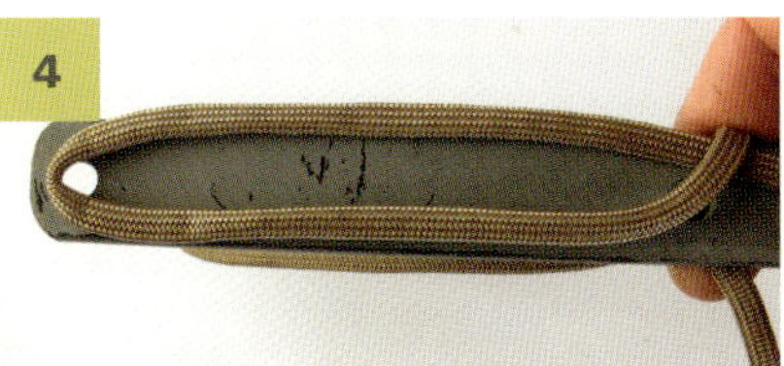

Start with a loop on the backside of the later handle. This side is not visible if the knife is in its sheath.

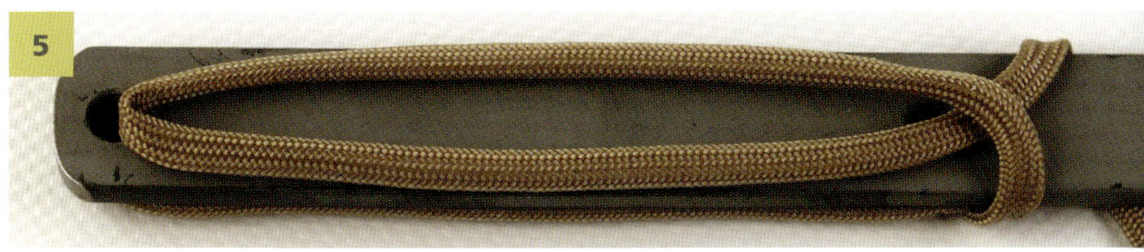

Put the second loop on the front side of the handle.

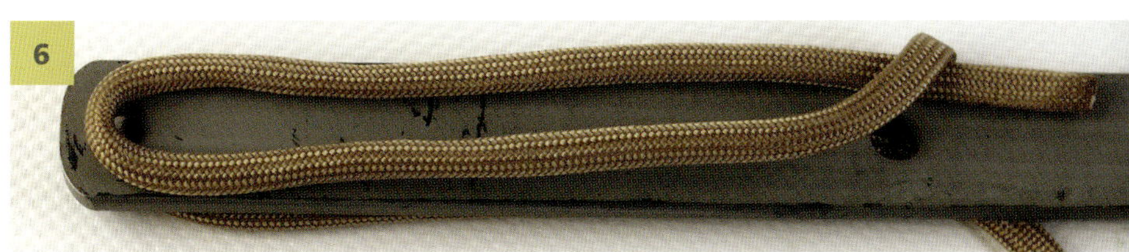

Here once more the loop on the backside. Both loops can be temporarily fixed with an elastic band or adhesive tape until after wrapping has started and everything is kept in place by the wrap.

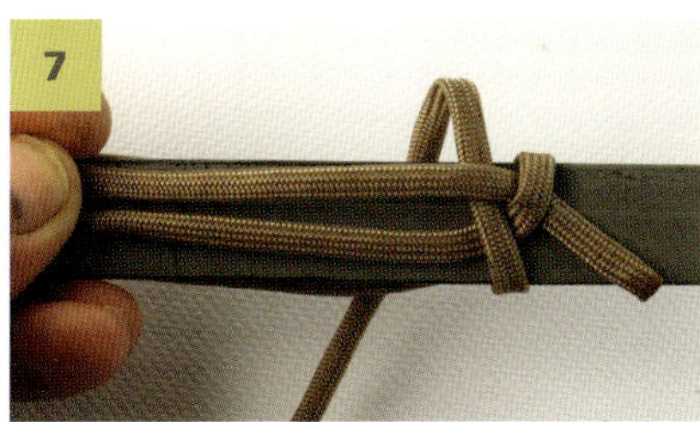

When the loops have been positioned, the working end is led from below through the loop on the handle's backside.

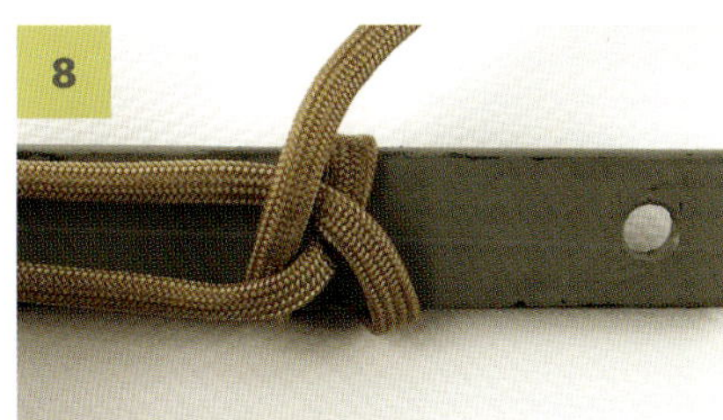

The handle's front side: here, too, the working end is led through the loop.

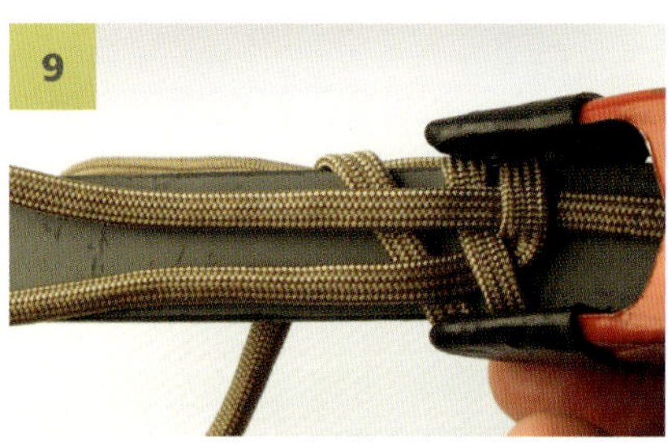

Prior to starting the typical weaving pattern we use a clamp to hold the cord. The first turn on the backside goes under the loop from below.

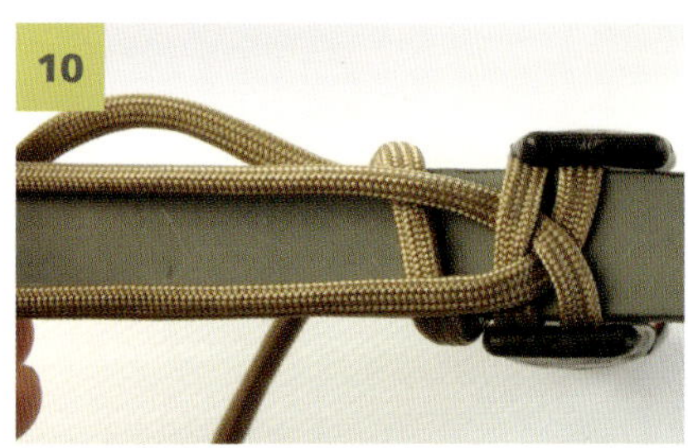

On the front side the cord also runs underneath the loop coming from below.

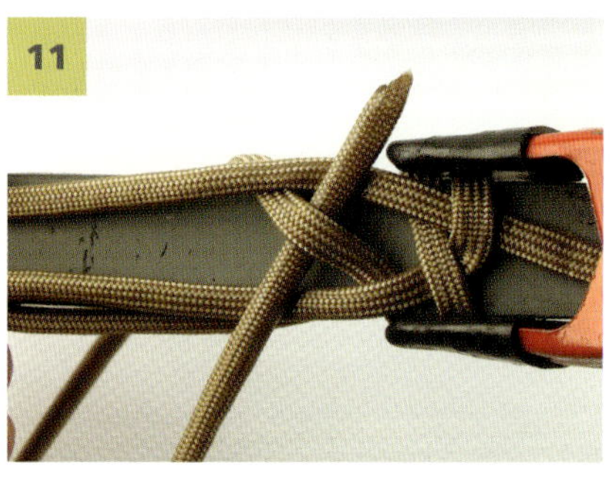

On the backside, the working end now goes over the loop, but takes up the cord in between.

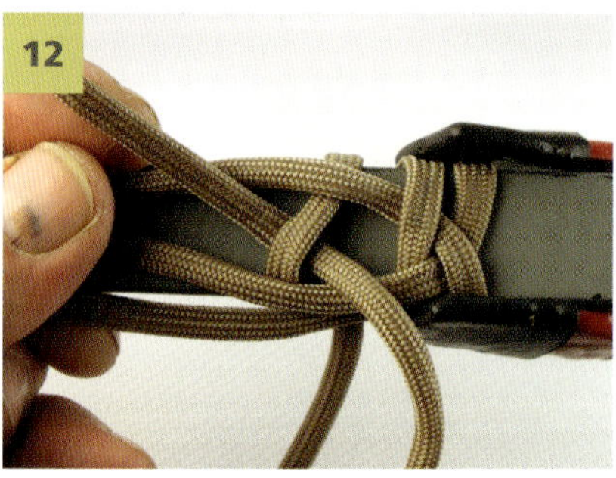

On the front side, the cord also goes on top of the loop and takes up the cord underneath.

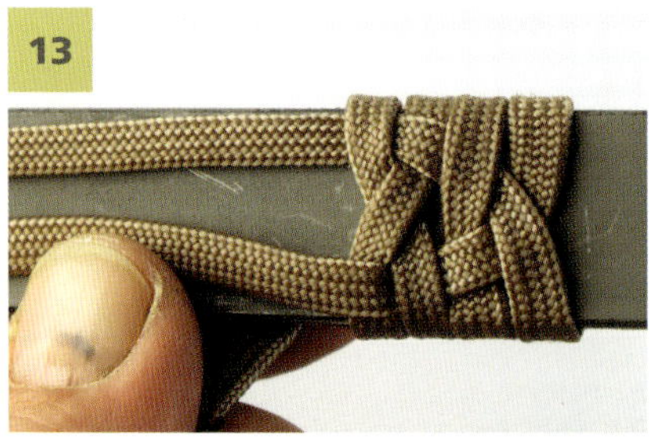

Front view after the first knot: all has already been pulled tight and the length of the loop has been adjusted.

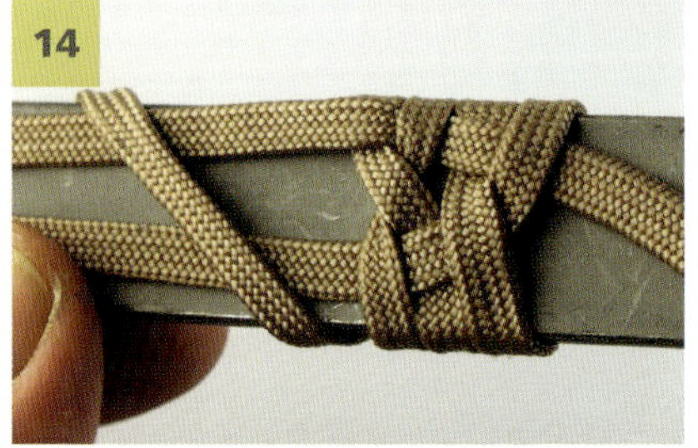

The backside of the first knot: the second weave will start here.

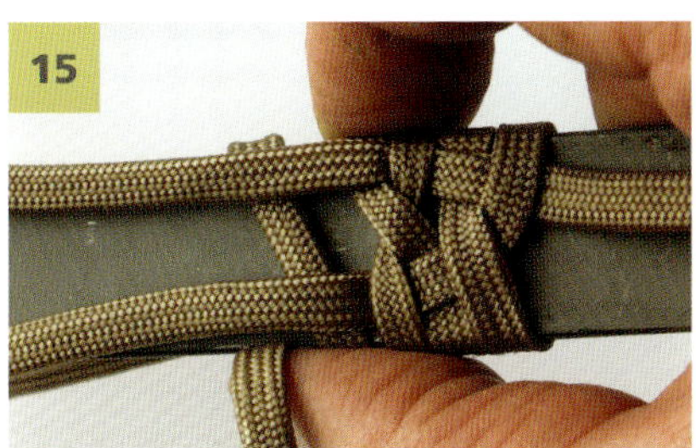

The second weave starts with a tour under the loop on the backside.

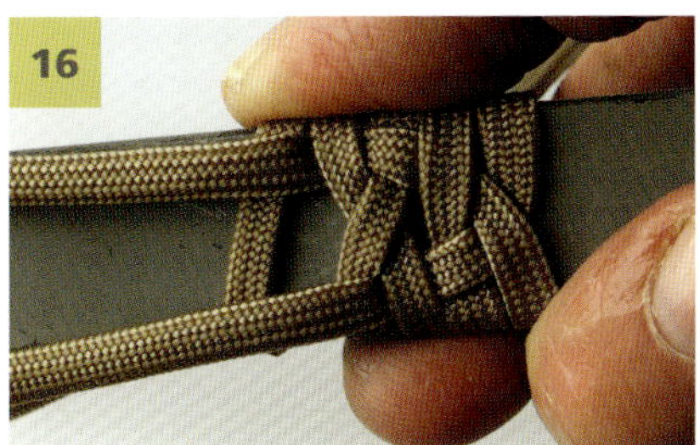

On the front side the cord is also led through under the loop.

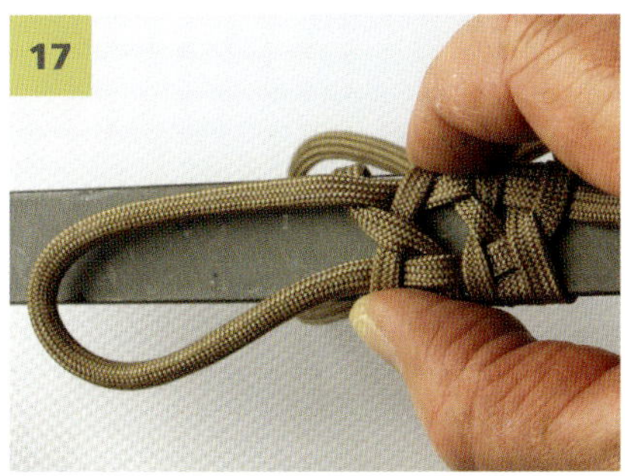

The working end on the backside goes over the loop again and under the cord resting in between.

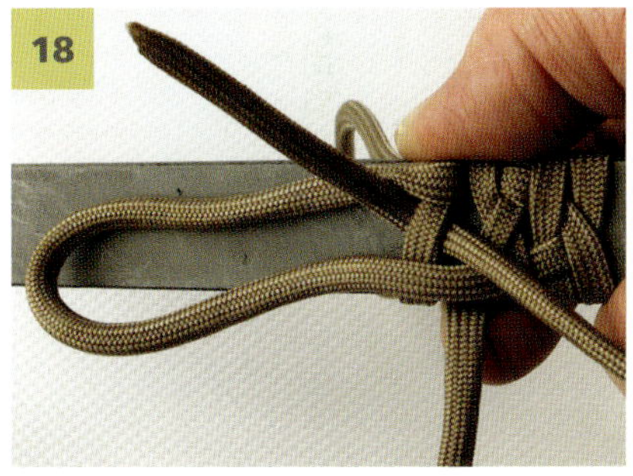

Do the same on the front side, then this weave is also completed.

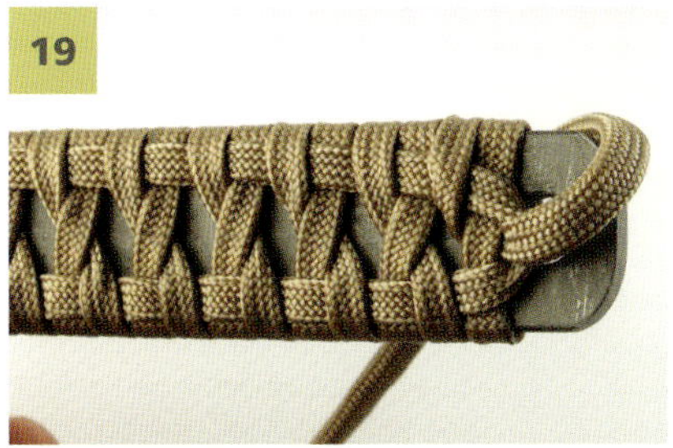

When the end of the handle and loops is reached we can almost imagine the end knot.

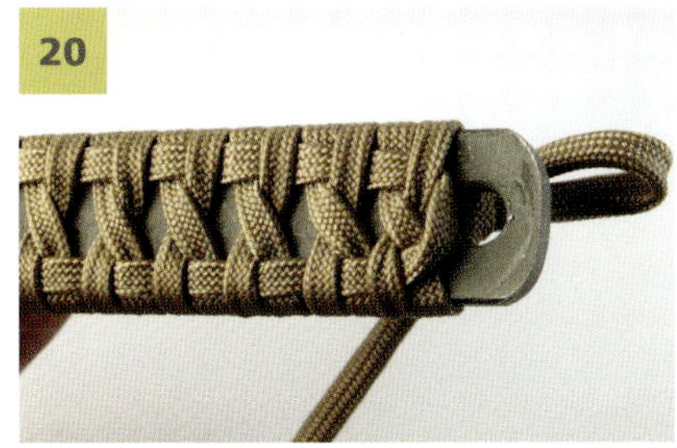

The handle seen from the other side.

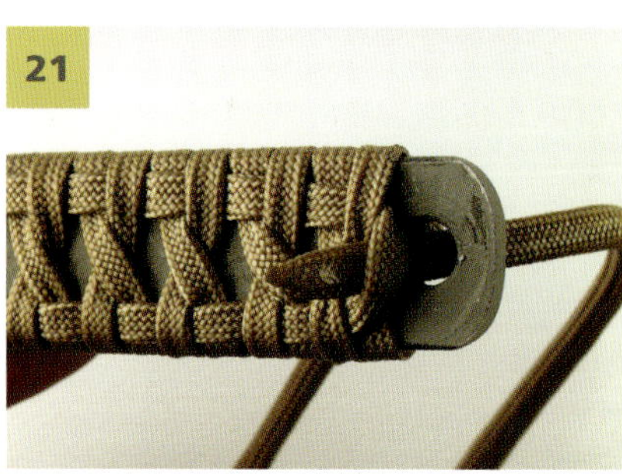

The working end is led through the pommel hole to the other side.

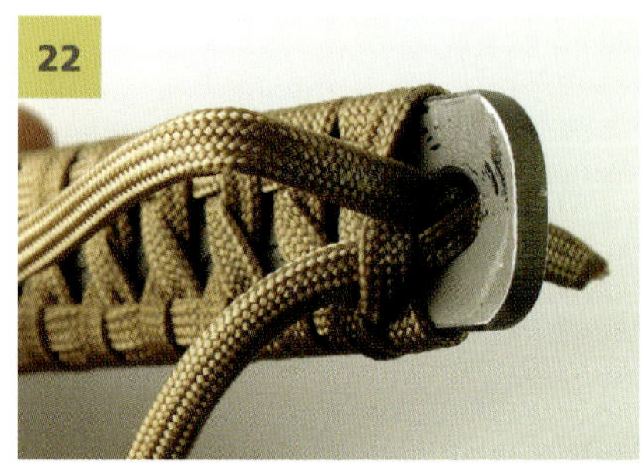

The working end immediately returns through the pommel hole.

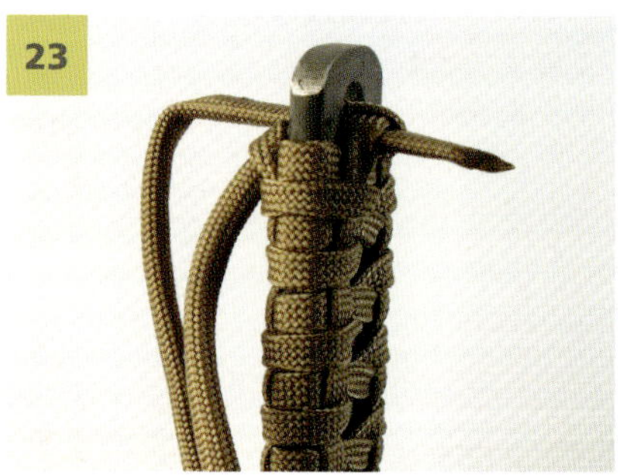

The stiff tip goes through the pommel hole and takes the loop on the other side with it.

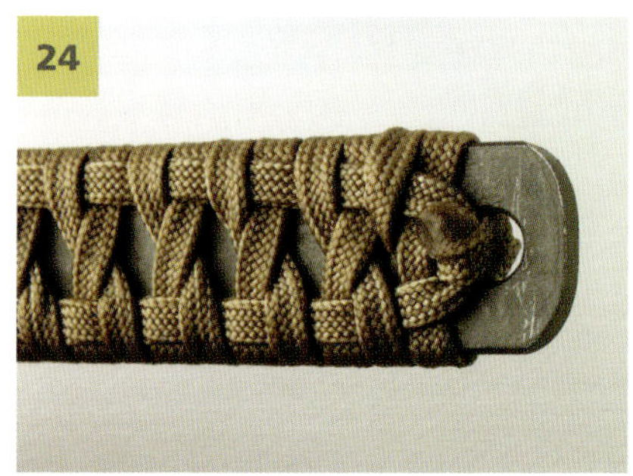

The cord is pulled through. When everything sits neat and tight the cord is trimmed and the end melted.

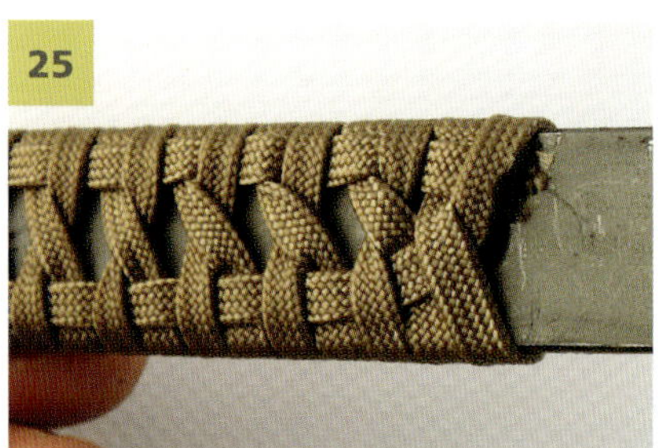

The standing end is also trimmed and melted to prevent unraveling.

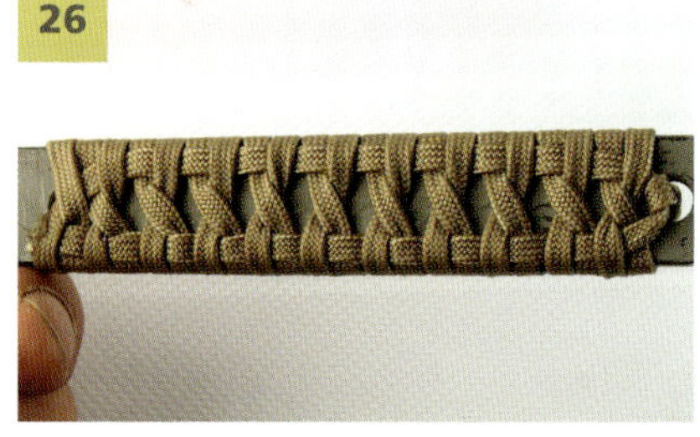

View of the handle's backside. A Turk's Head (see p 112) works miracles if you want to hide the cord's start.

6.2 Alternative Chinese Wraps

6.2.1 Alternative No. 1

The first technique I developed myself, even before I learned the traditional technique used with Dao swords. It looks like a flat diamond wrap with two flatlines woven in on both sides.

For preparation, cut two short cords to a length of a bit more than twice the handle's length. Determine the used length for the wrapping cord by wrapping the handle 1⅓ times. Fold the cord into two halves to determine its center. The cord's center is put down on the handle.

Cross the cord ends on the backside as you do for a flat, Japanese crossing. The first of the two short braiding cords has to rest underneath. Turn the handle around again and start weaving while following instructions. Always hold the cord tight and press the turns of the cord against the previous ones. Pull the weaving ends straight after every crossing.

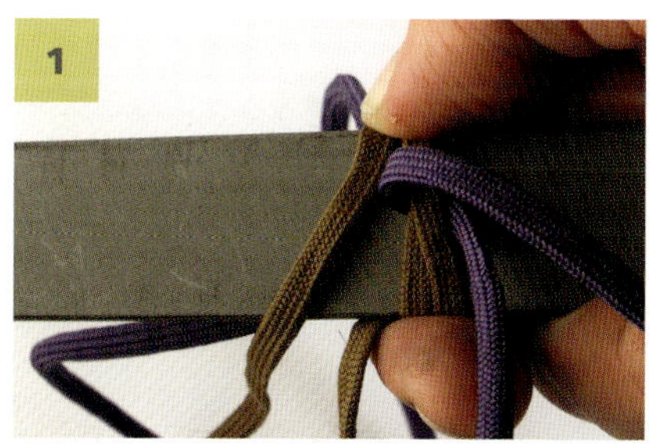

The start of the handle wrap on the backside: the right working end (brown) goes downward.

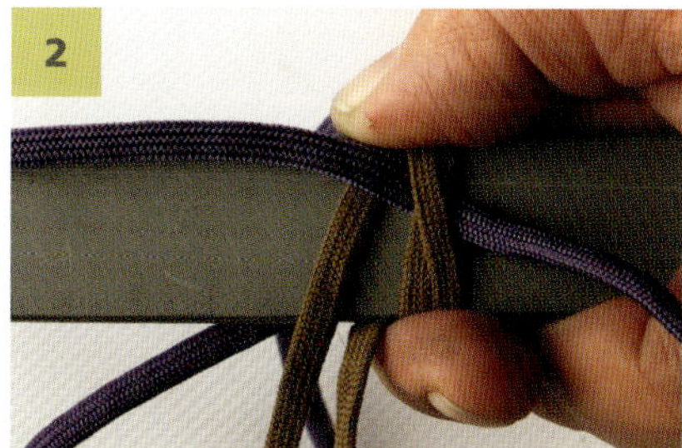

The weaving end (violet) is put over the right working end.

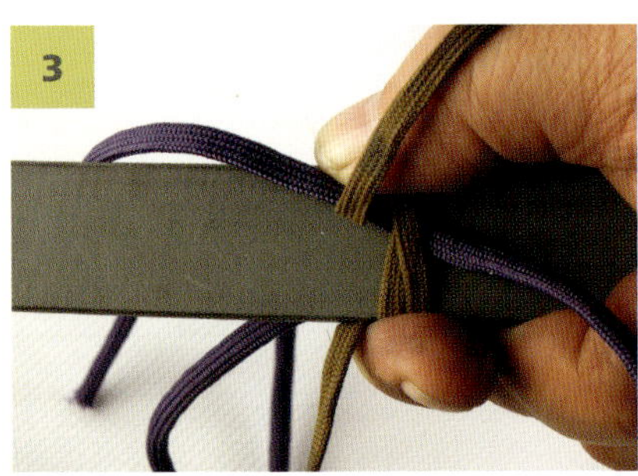

The right working end at first goes up and out of the way.

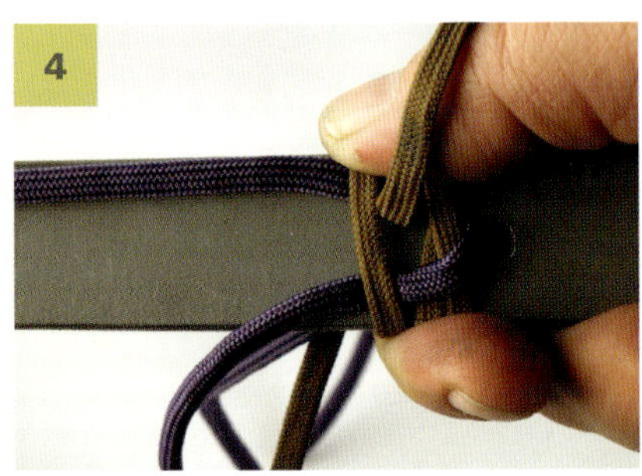

The left working end comes from below and also goes up over the weaving end.

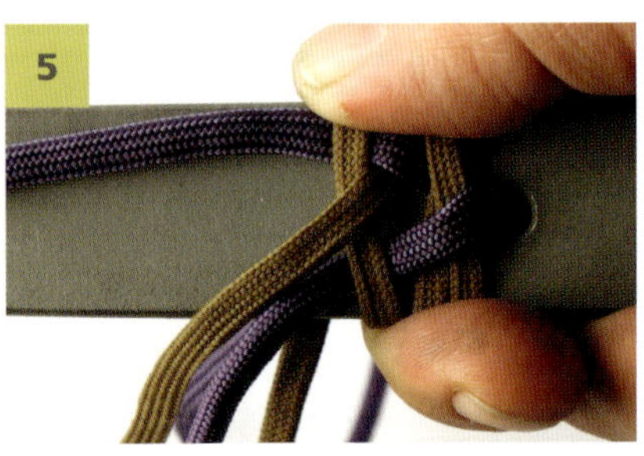

The right working end is put over the left one, but underneath the bottom weaving end.

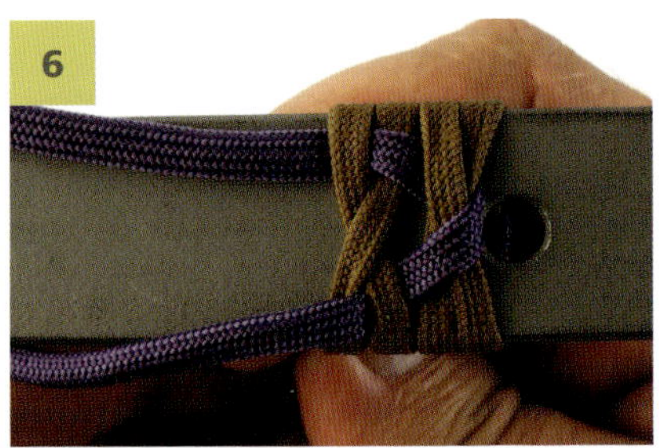

The right working end is led under the bottom weave and pulled tight.

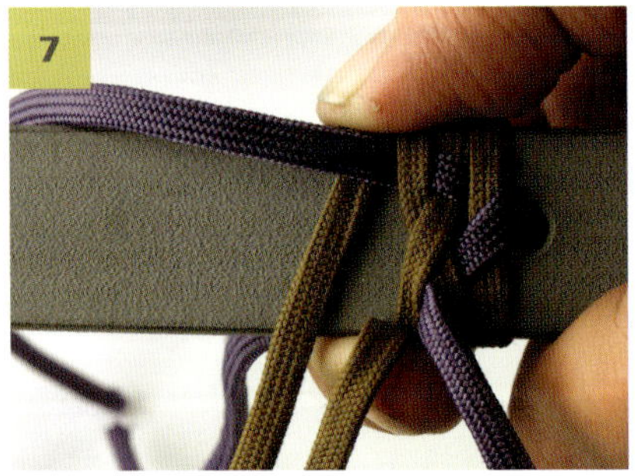

When the handle is turned around, the upper working end goes down.

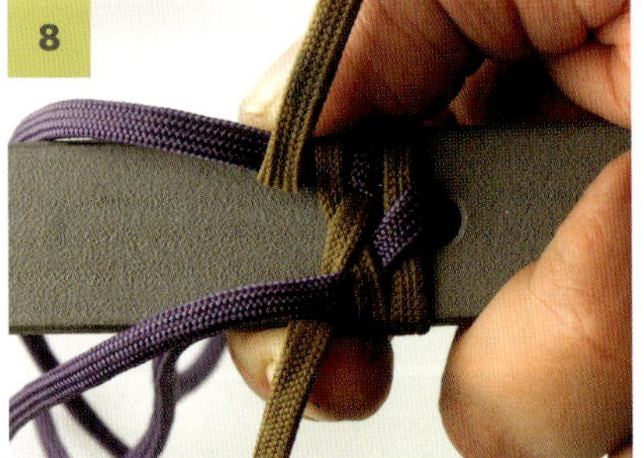

Then it is guided upward and put out of the way. The lower weaving end goes over the other working end.

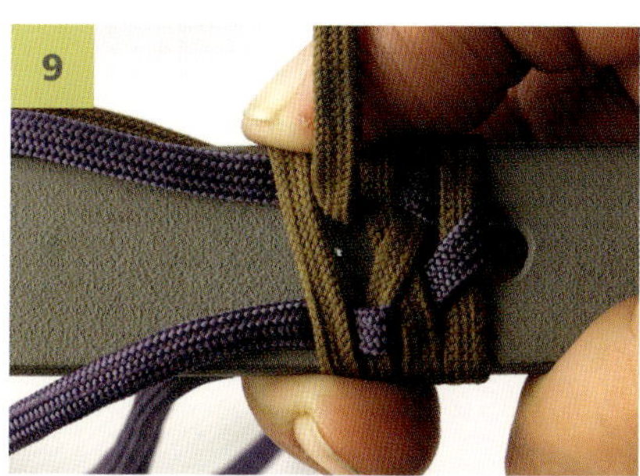

The lower working end now goes up over both weaving ends and over the upper handle edge.

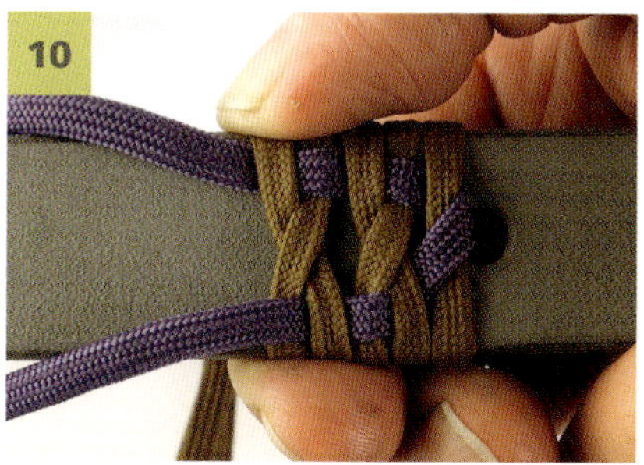

The upper working end goes down and over the other working end, but underneath the weaving end at the bottom.

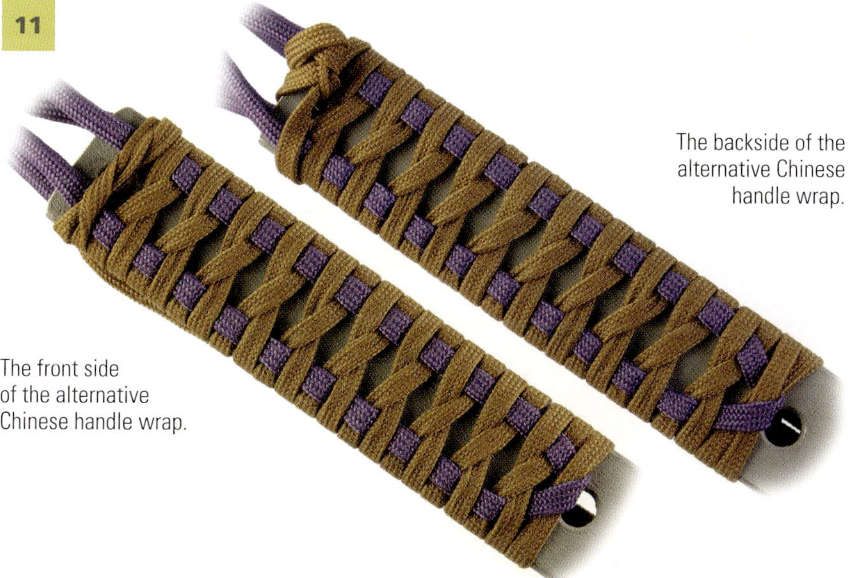

The backside of the alternative Chinese handle wrap.

The front side of the alternative Chinese handle wrap.

At the end you can use a Turk's Head to finish the handle (see next page). In case the knife is shaped like a *puukko*, with a thick pommel and no guard, it is fine if the wrap is done from the blade toward the pommel. You can also make a guard using a Turk's Head Knot.

THE 3 × 5 TURK'S HEAD

For the next handle wrap we need a so-called Turk's Head. The Turk's Head in the 3 × 5 version is the most common of all Turk's Heads. It can be used as a guard or pommel. Since its shape is based on the simple braid with three strands, it is easy to see where the cord has to go during work.

The Turk's Head can be made in two directions: as a right-handed or left-handed knot. The left-handed knot is just a mirror image of the right-handed one.

The Turk's Head is usually knotted in your free hand. For the right-handed version you make the knot on your left hand, holding the working end in your right.

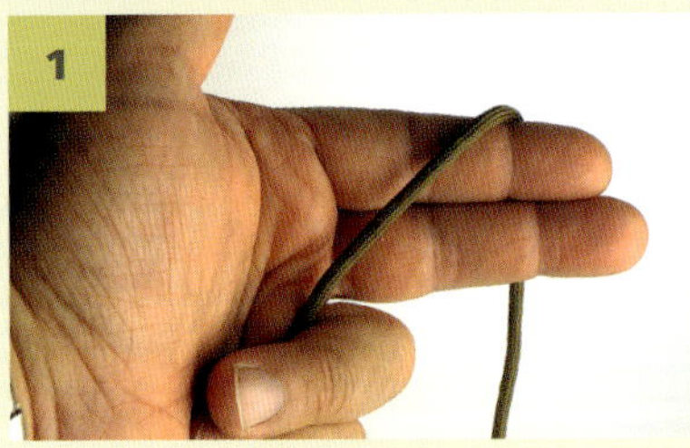

Measure six turns of the cord around your hand. Hold the cord with the working end over your fingertips.

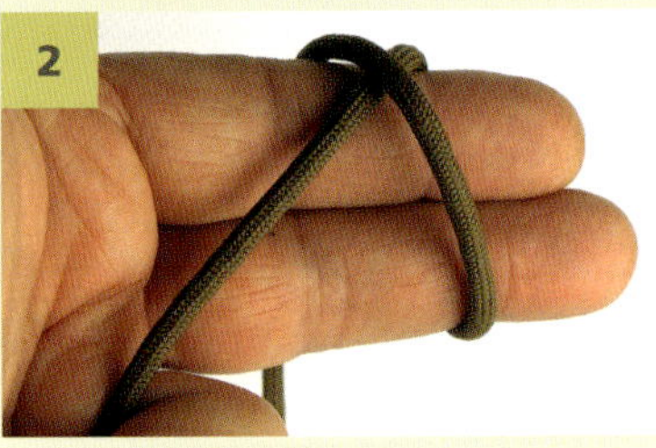

Start the Turk's Head by leading the cord behind your fingers and over the standing end up to the left.

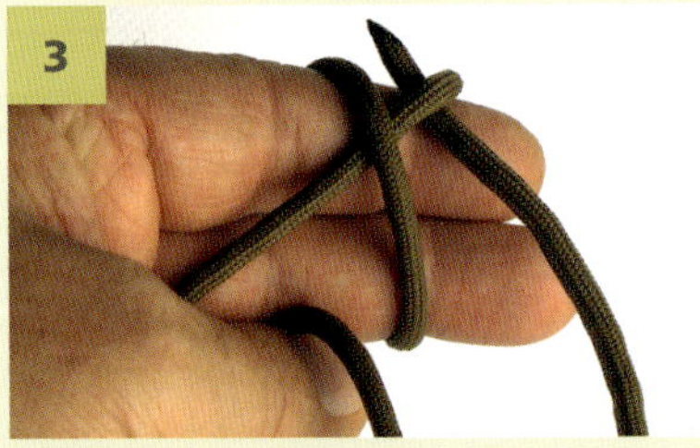

The working end goes downward vertically behind your hand and comes up again on the right side to go up and underneath the upper right piece of cord.

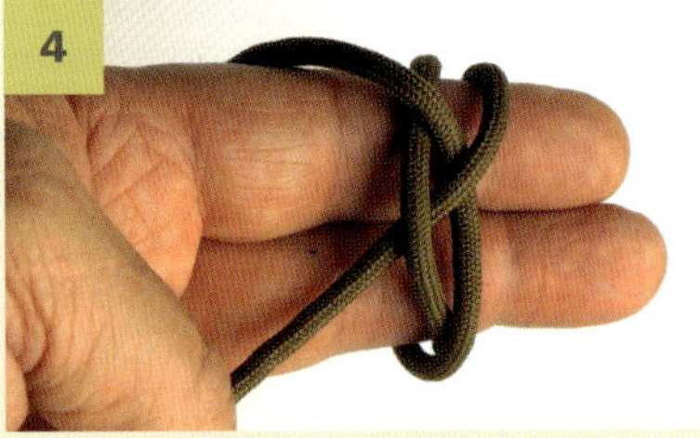

The working end is pulled through completely.

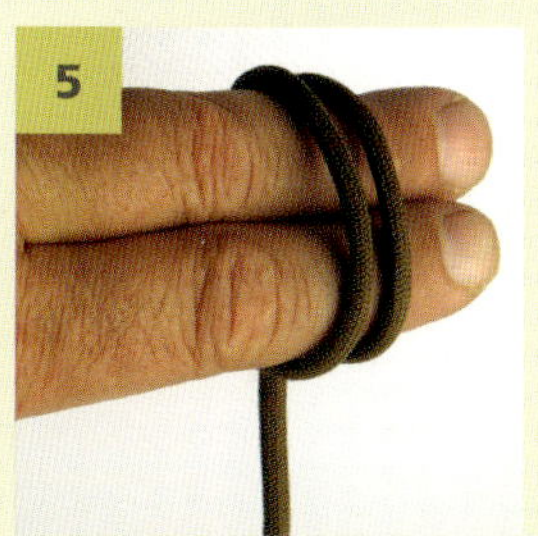

Turn the hand and look at the parallel cords on the backside.

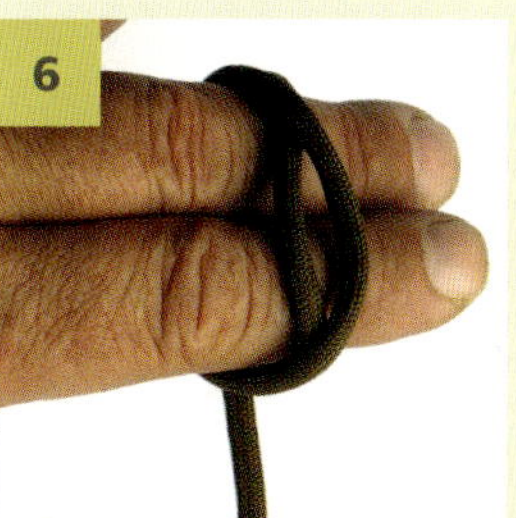

Guide the right cord end to the left under the left one.

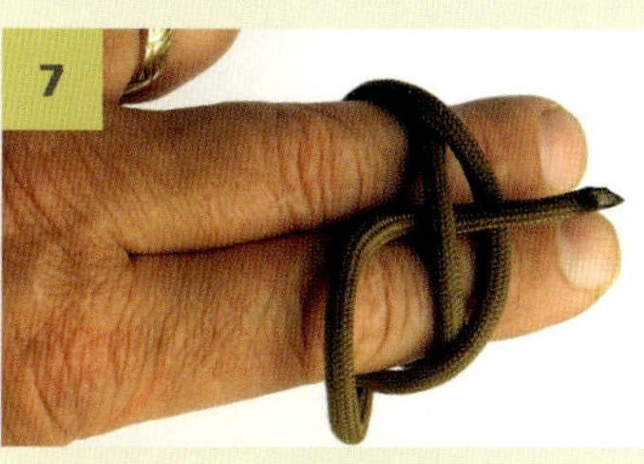

Weave the working end under and over the cords from left to right.

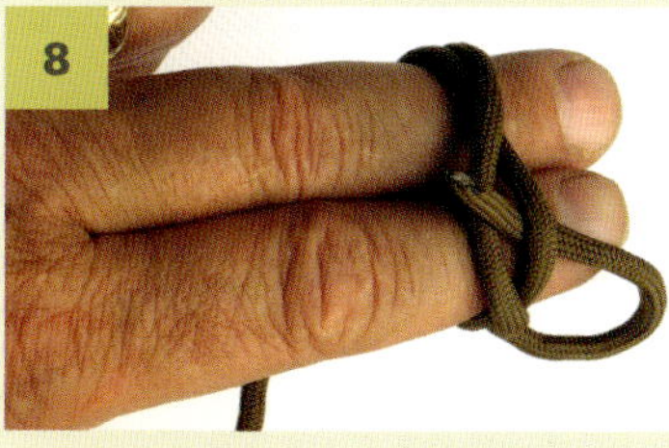

Push the knot on your fingers a bit forward and bring the working end under and over the cords (from right to left).

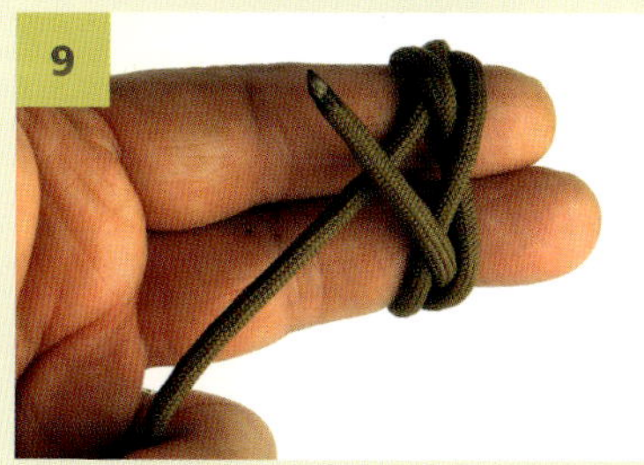

If the knot is turned a bit farther around the finger you can see that the working end has reached the standing end.

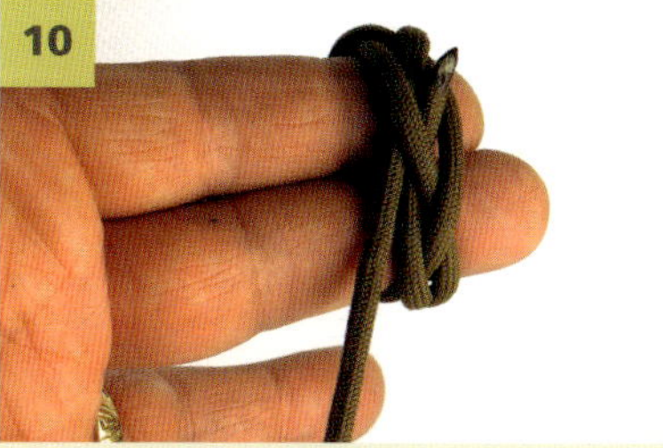

Complete the single Turk's Head by inserting the working end next to the standing end.

Transfer the Turk's Head on to the handle and start with pulling everything tight in reverse order with respect to making the knot.

6.2.2 Alternative No. 2

If you look at the beautiful and clear beginning of the last wrap then it seems practical to wrap in the opposite direction. The pretty start at the pommel looks good and feels good. The end of the wrap can be glued and then covered by a Turk's Head as a guard.

If you start the wrap at the pommel it is more difficult to hold the knife while working in the direction towards yourself. It needs some time to get used to it. If you are used to working from the guard towards the pommel, it is more convenient to turn the knife around as soon as enough of the wrap is done to hold the knife with it.

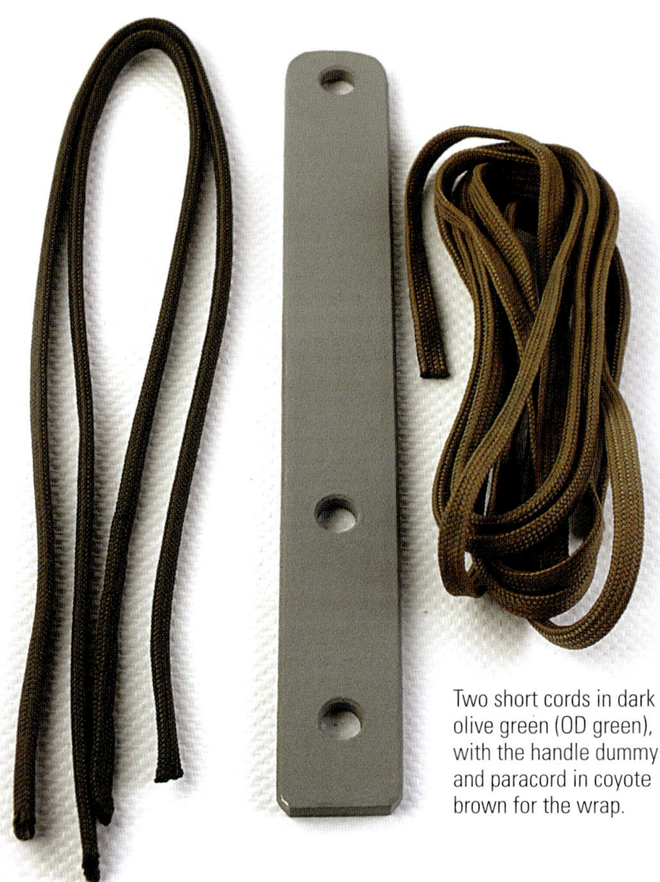

Two short cords in dark olive green (OD green), with the handle dummy and paracord in coyote brown for the wrap.

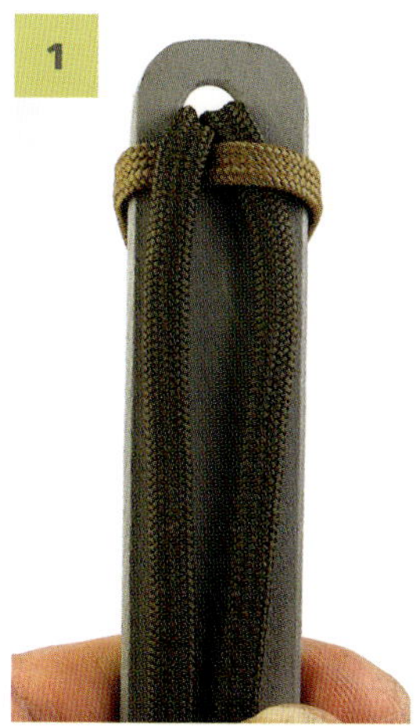

Put the short cords centered through the pommel hole and put the center of the long cord in between.

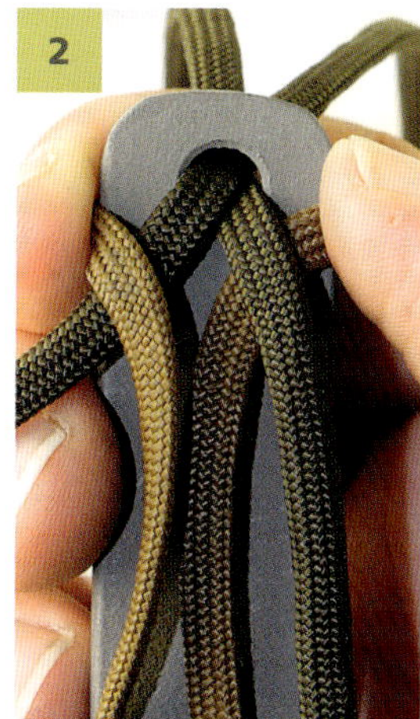

Turn the handle around. Distribute the weaving ends over and under the working ends.

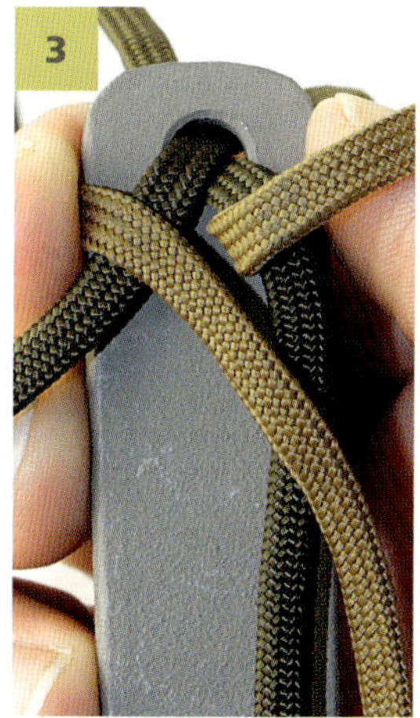

Fold the right working end out of the way and bring the left end over the right weaving end.

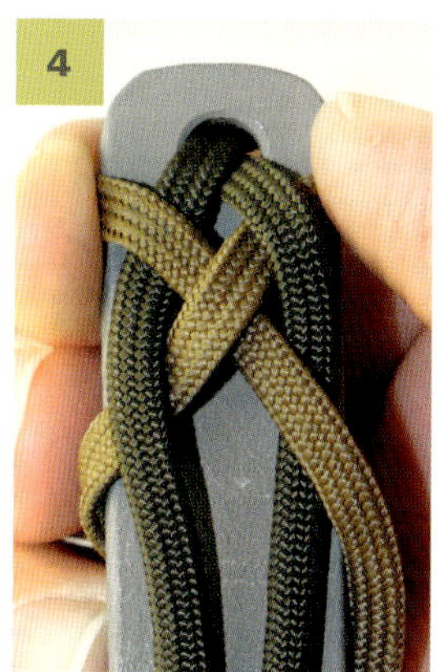

Bring the right working end over the other one and lead it under the left weaving end to the backside.

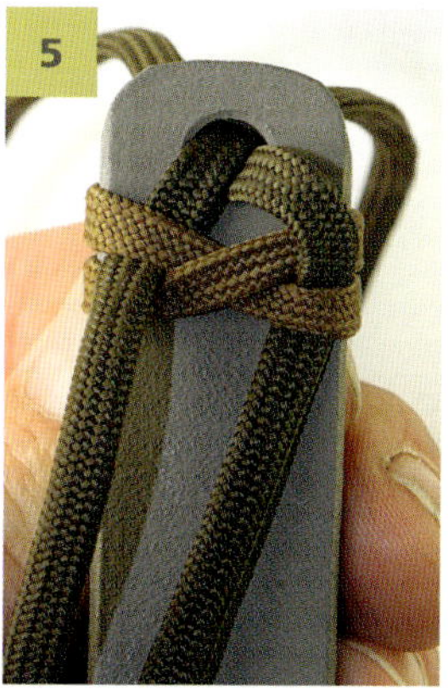

Bring the other working end to the backside as well and pull them both tight.

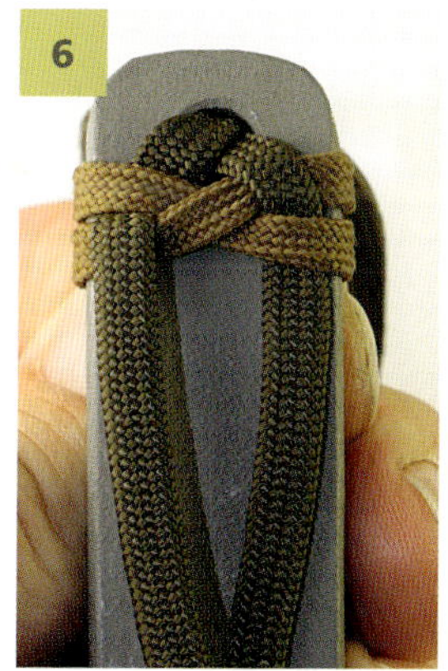

Pull both green weaving ends straight and push everything up in the direction of the hole in the tang.

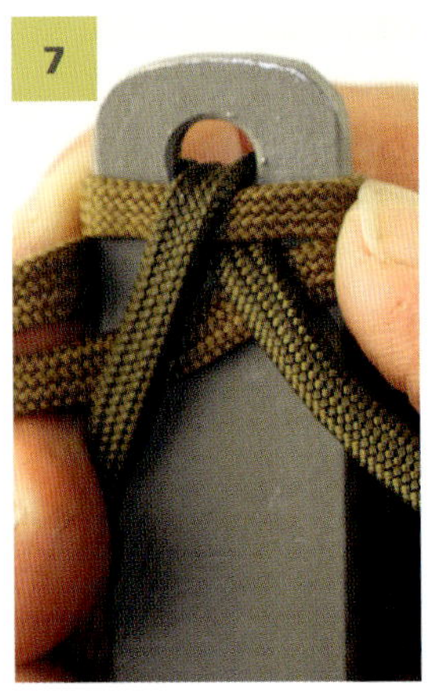

Turn the handle around. The right weaving end lies under the start of the working end, the left weaving end is above.

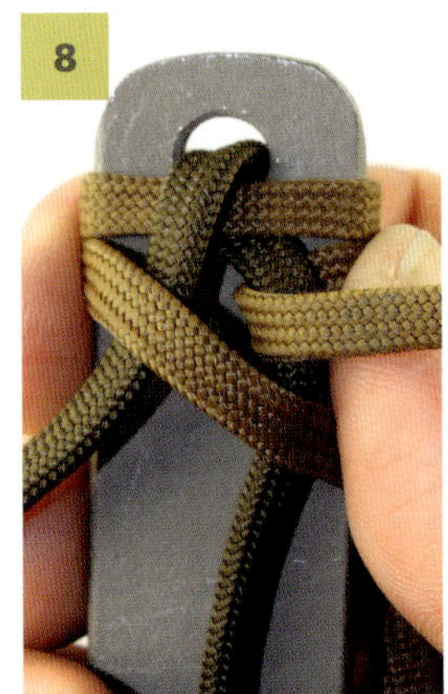

Get the right working end out of the way. Lead the left working end over both weaving ends to the bottom right.

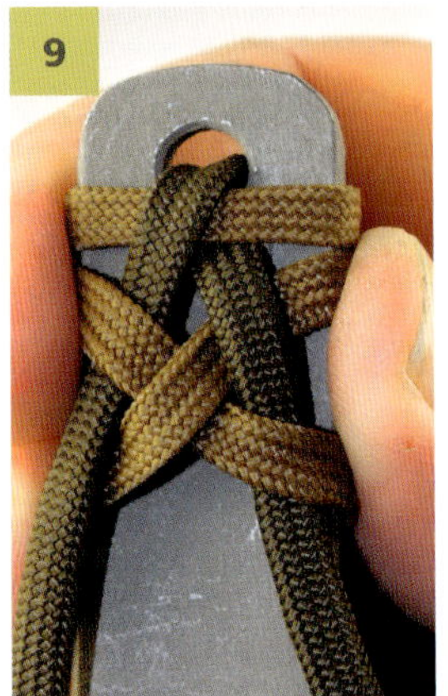

Lead the right working end to the left over the other working end and under the left weaving end.

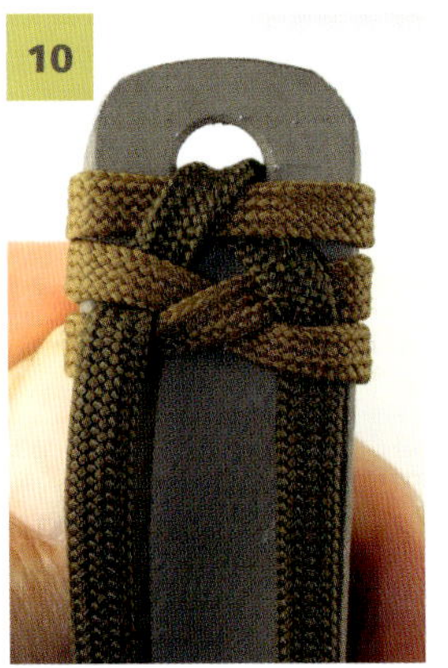

Pull everything tight and close the gaps at the sides.

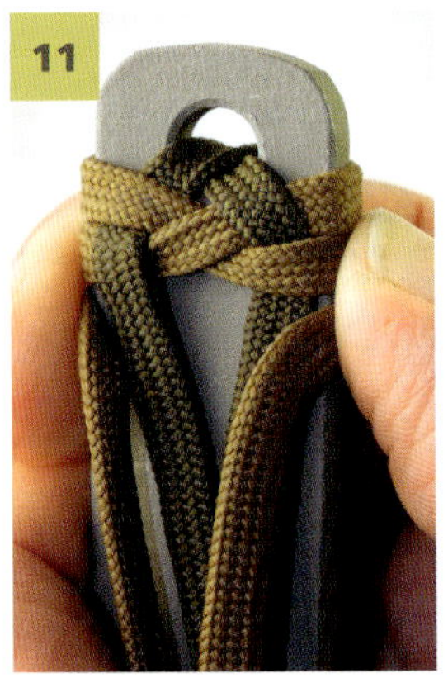

Turn the handle around and continue the wrap.

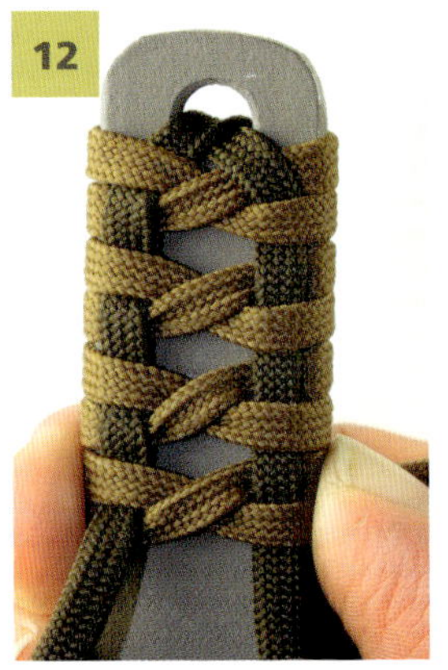

Hold the lines straight. Pull at the weaving ends to make the wrap flatter and to equalize the distances at the sides.

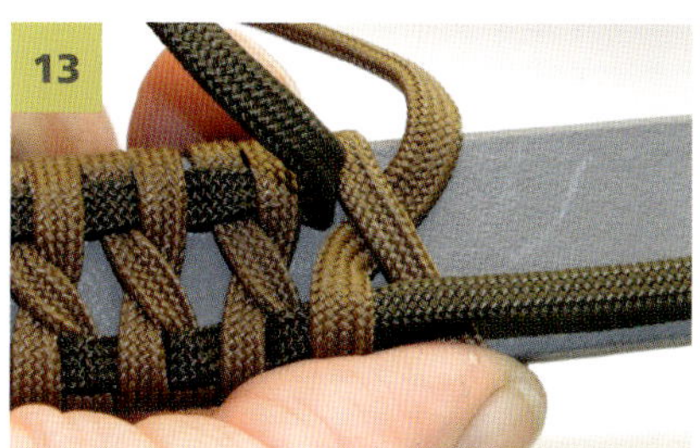

If it is easier for you, you can also turn the knife around after making enough knots and hold the handle at the pommel.

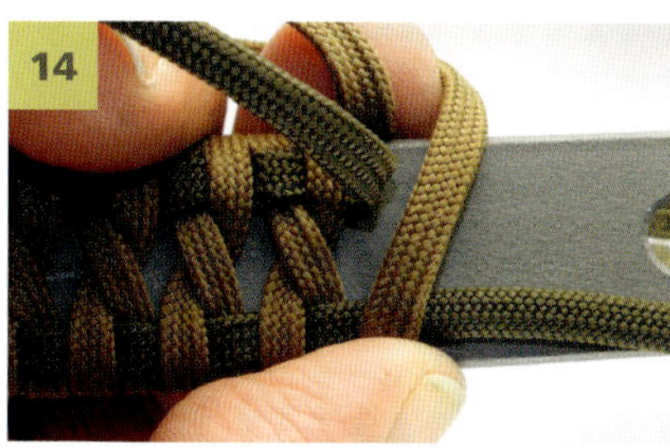

You ought to work away from your body. Fold the ends out of the way and lead the right working end to the left.

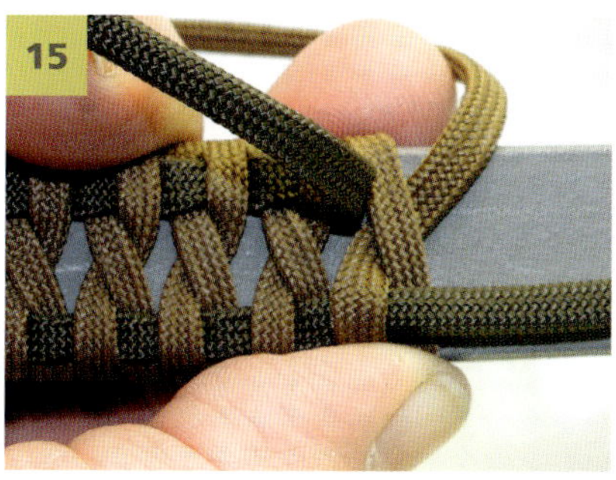

Lead the left working end over the right working end and underneath the right weaving end.

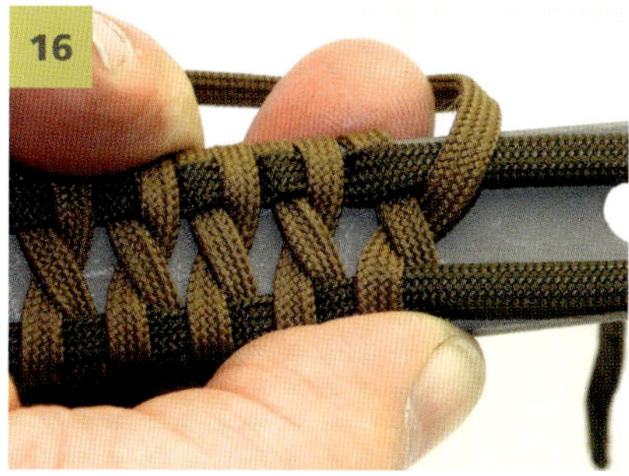

Bring the left weaving end under the working end.

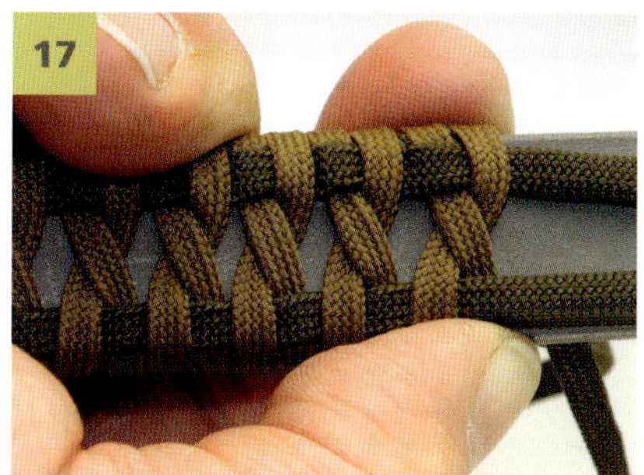

Pull everything tight and straight.

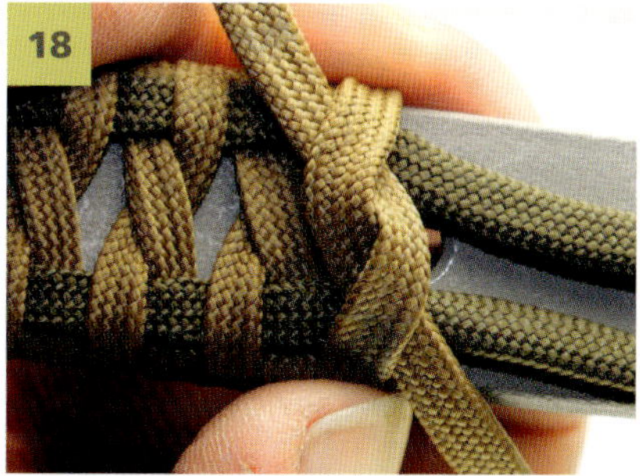

Make an end knot as with the Japanese gunto *tsuka*.

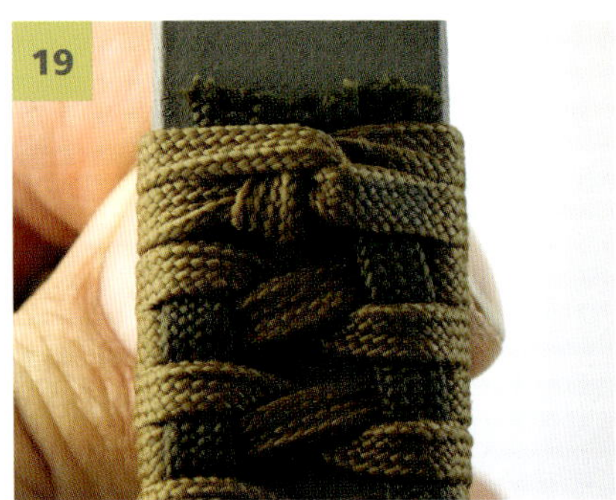

Finish the knot by folding the left ends to the right and the right one on top of them to the left. Cut off the weaving ends. Apply a drop of glue for fixing.

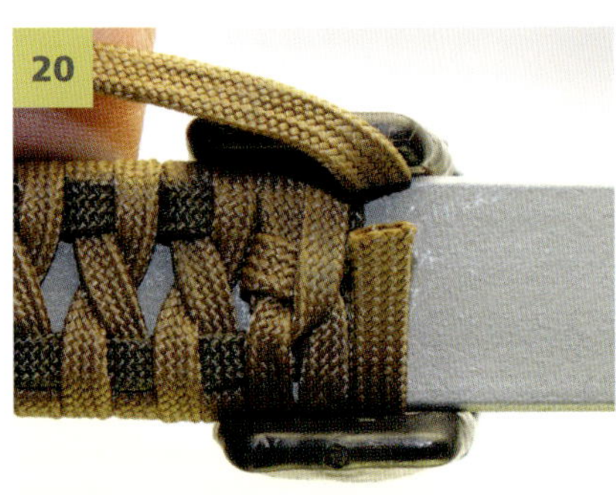

The same knot is also made on the other side. Here a clamp helps to keep everything in position. The right working end is cut off.

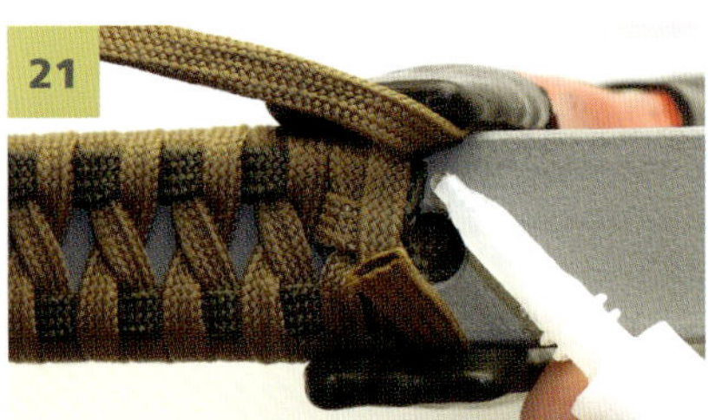

Apply a drop of glue.

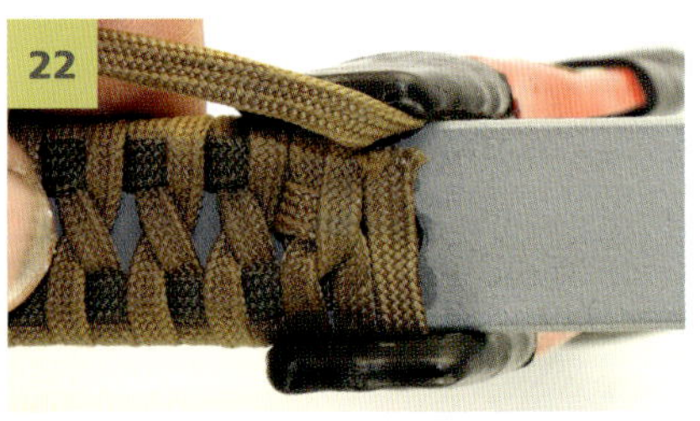

The end is glued in position.

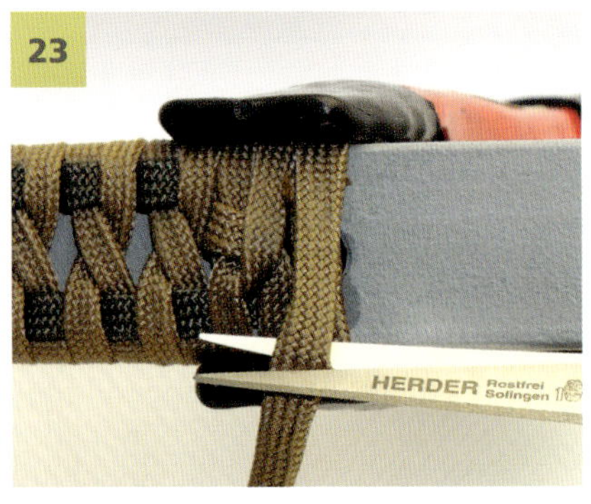

The other end is cut off.

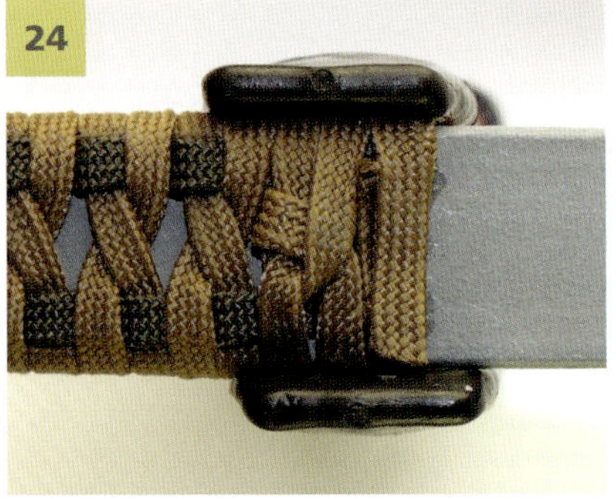

The last end is glued in position.

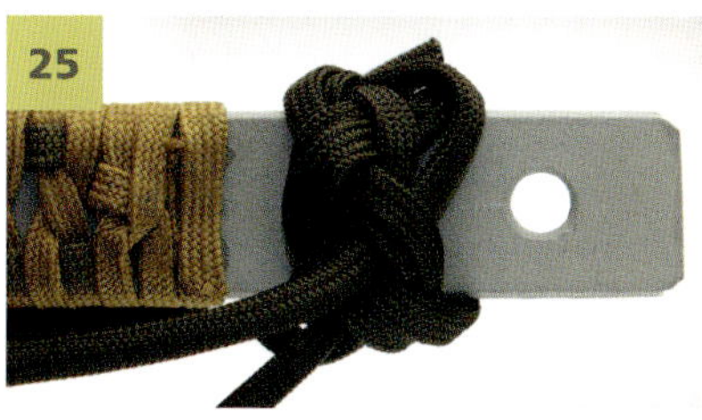

Make a 3 × 5 Turk's Head on your hand and push it over the knife. In this photo the Turk's Head is already partly pulled tight.

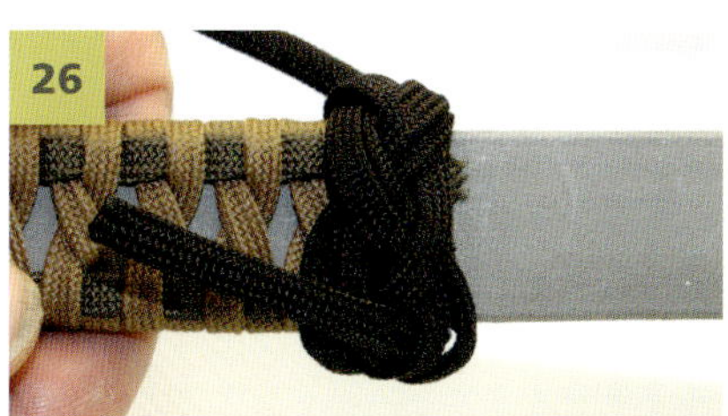

While the knot is pulled tight completely, the flatline cords in the double Turk's Head move on top of each other. In the end this knot has a bit more volume than a single knot.

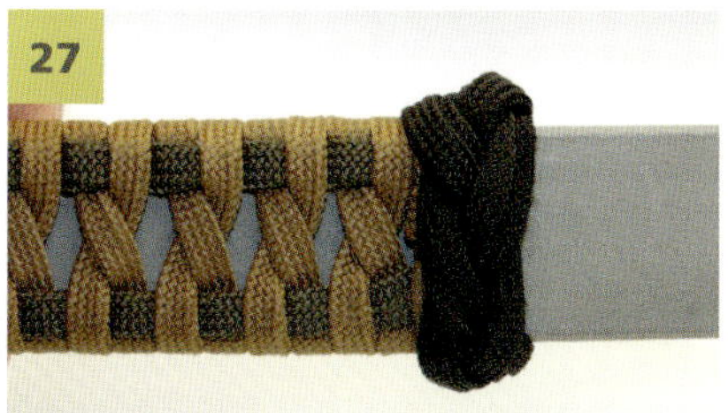

All ends are cut off.

28

The first side of the finished handle.

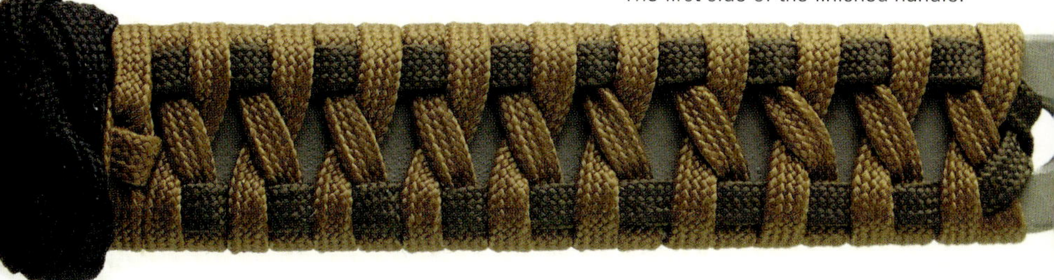

The other side.

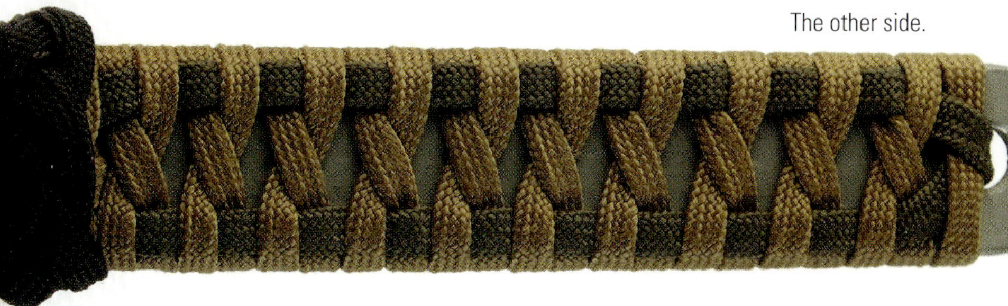

PARADOX HANDLE WRAPS

In 2003, I wrapped knife handles with cotton cord, mainly to impregnate them with resin to make solid handles similar to micarta. While searching for a way to enhance volume while at the same time achieving an aesthetic weaving pattern I worked out this wrapping technique. At the beginning I used two and three millimeter diameter cotton cord. Impregnating the handle hardened them. The resulting handle was also electrically insulating. Sometimes the result was shiny and plastic-like, while the handles at other times were quite rough because of the impregnated cotton fibers standing upright.

Although the handles were never impregnated one hundred percent thoroughly, they could bear a lot of hits before the outer layer was damaged or worn out to such an extent that some more resin was necessary. The whole process was developed further in the following years and the technique is now quite sophisticated. If made with paracord or empty flatline, the knife handle will be much more comfortable than the first generation's hard, impregnated cotton.

7.1 Paradox Flatline Basic Wrap

Wrap the handle two times to determine the necessary length of the cord for work and add some before cutting off the cord. To determine the number of weaving cords, try to maximize an odd number of cords next to each other on the handle. An odd number of cords provides a balanced wrap.

To determine the length of the weaving cords, as a minimum, take 2.5 (to three) times the handle's length. In our example I cut the flatline into ten pieces and melted the ends. In case you make the weaving pattern with full paracord you need at least three times the handle's length.

Super glue is obligatory for this wrap, as the handle wrap is done more easily. You can also do the wrap without super glue, but then you will probably wish you had an additional pair of hands. During the first phase of the wrap, it is very difficult to keep all weaving cords in place. Double-faced adhesive tape, as used for carpeting, is helpful for attaching the cords at the knife tang. The end can be finished with a lot less, or even without any adhesive, if the wrapped handle is immediately finished off with a Turk's Head. The weaving pattern will be finer with flatline paracord than with full cord.

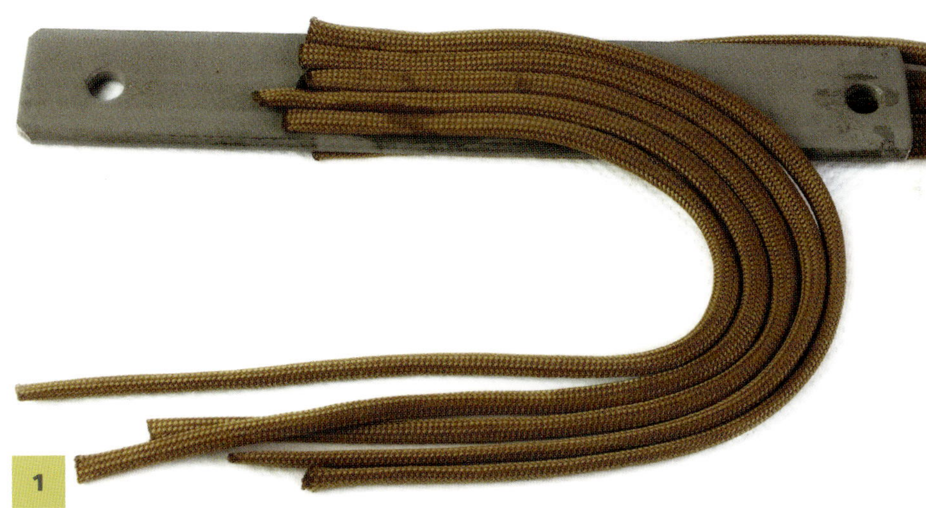

1

The flatline weaving cords are fixed on the knife tang with a line made of super glue. The glue is applied about 0.787 in. (two centimeters) behind the cord ends.

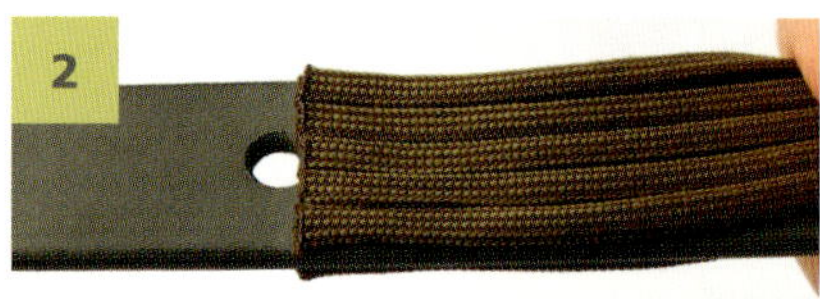

The edges are trimmed, melted, and the cords are glued in position.

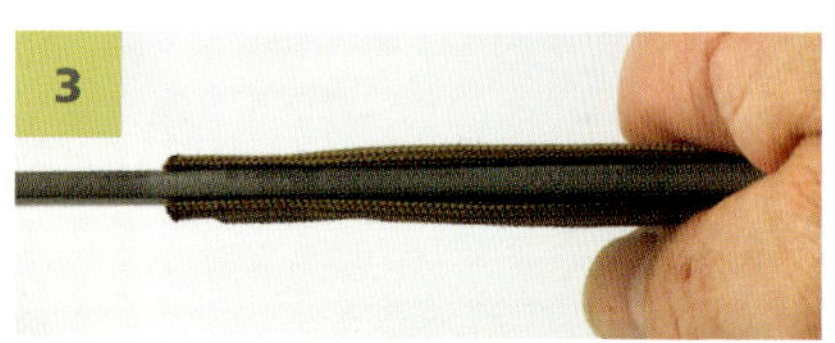

View from the side. The glue line lies about 0.787 in. (two centimeters) behind the front end of the cords, enabling easy trimming of the ends.

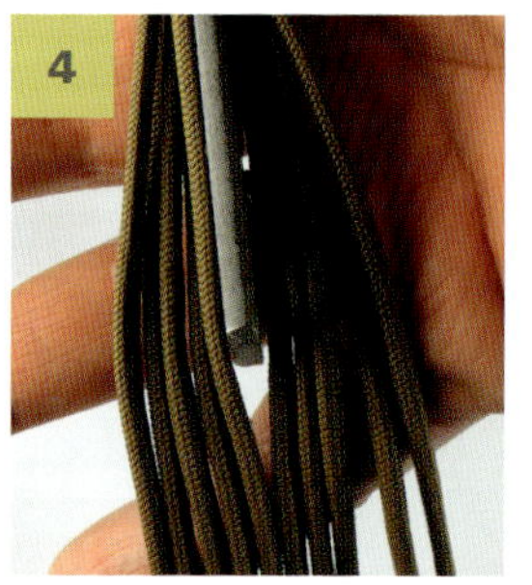

The ten weaving cords are hanging downward freely next to the tang's end.

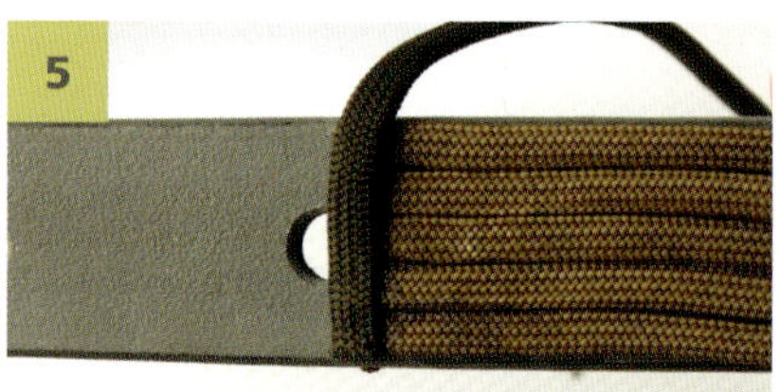

The end of the cord for the wrap is glued to the start of the weaving ends on the tang's backside.

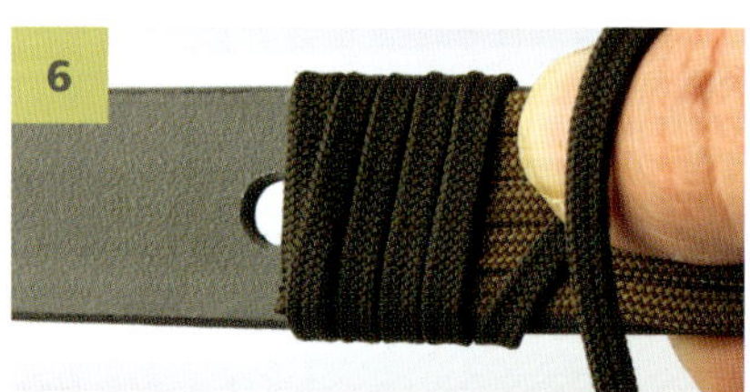

Start by making a full turn around the handle before working forward along the handle.

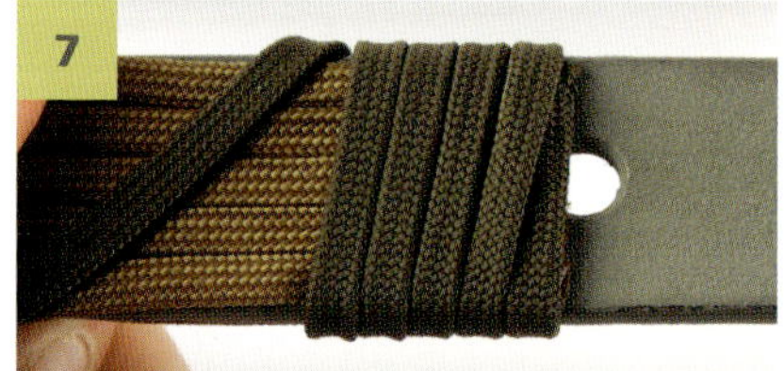

The handle seen from the other side.

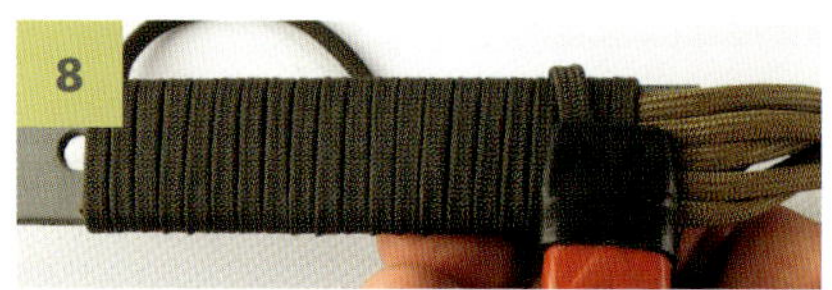

Take a break at the end of the first layer. Clamp the handle tight to keep tension on the cord.

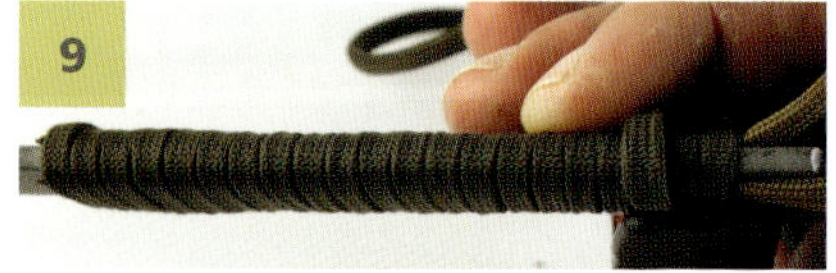

If you look at the handle from the side after finishing the first layer, thickness and structure of the wrap become visible.

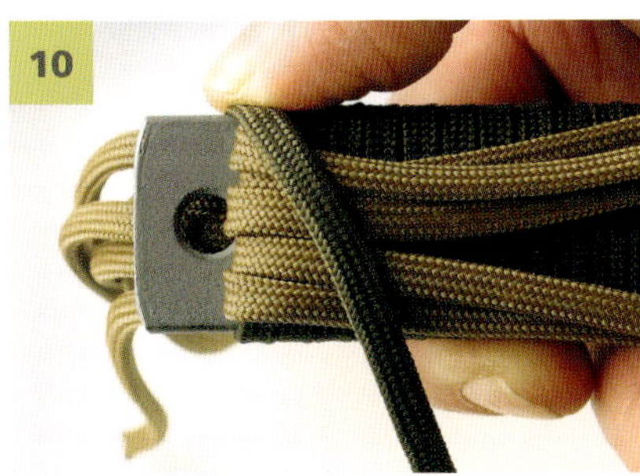

To start weaving, the weaving ends are now folded above the handle wrap in the direction toward the blade.

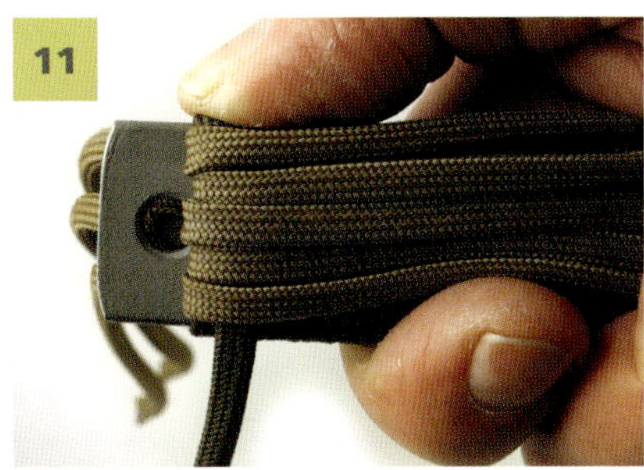

For the first round of the second layer the weaving ends are put over the working cord.

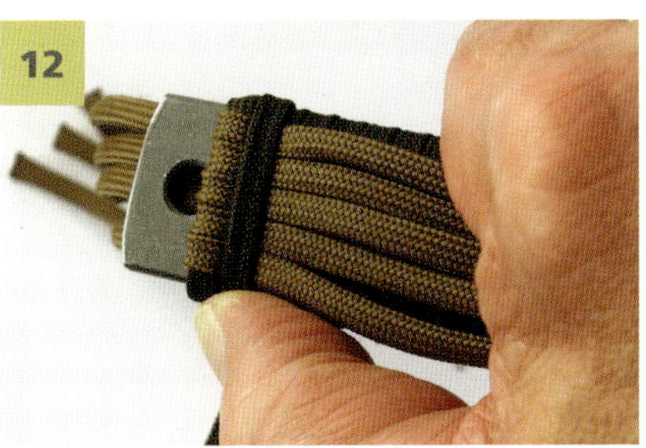

The second turn goes over the weaving cords.

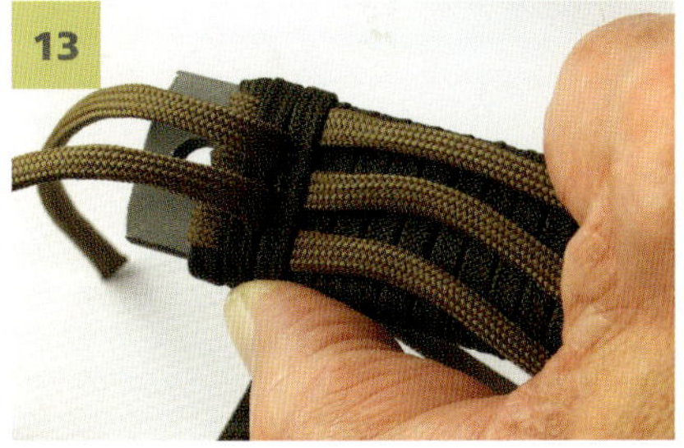

For the third round, the second and fourth weaving cords are folded up in such a way that the working end goes on top of the other cords.

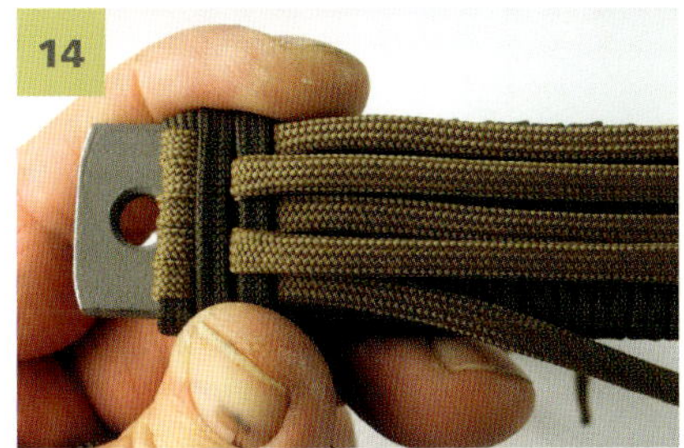

The weaving pattern slowly takes shape.

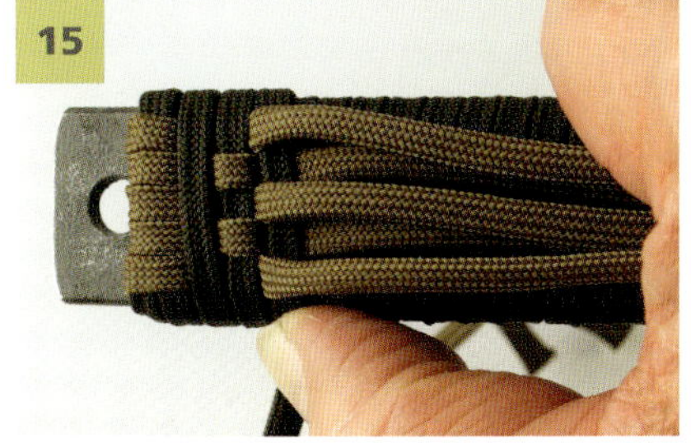

For the next turn the first, third, and fifth weaving ends go over the working end.

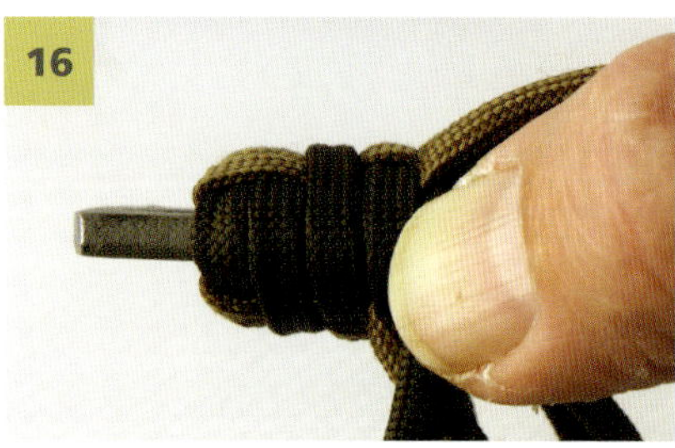

The view from the side shows the pattern and volume.

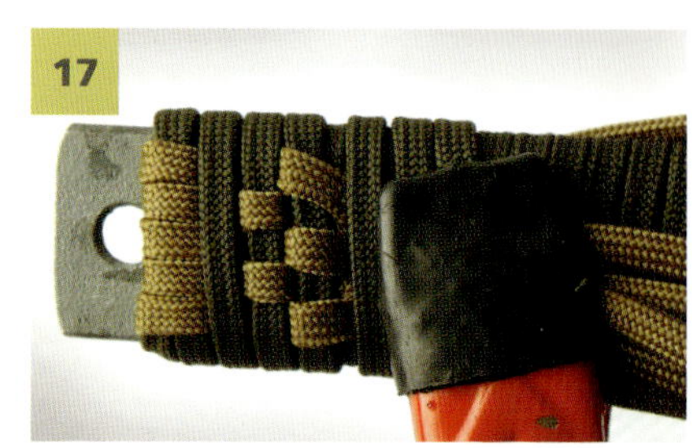

If you need a break, wrap the working cord several times around the handle and clamp everything together.

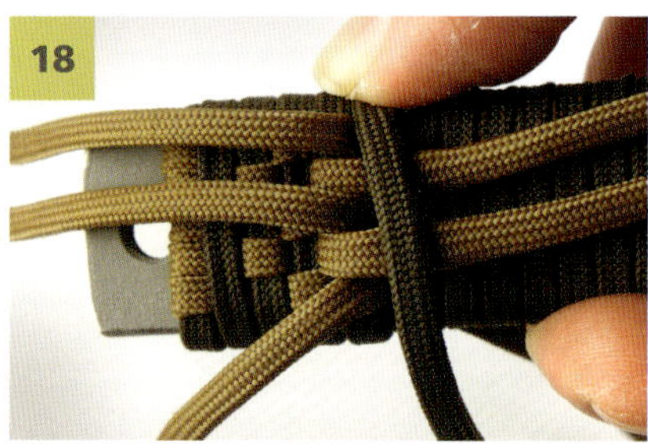

Continue weaving. Make sure all weaving ends are pulled straight and flat each time the working end goes on top of them.

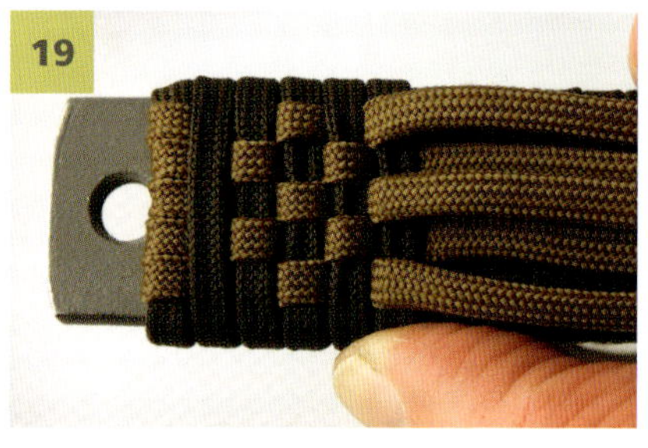

Take care that everything sits tight and straight. Keep tension on the working cord.

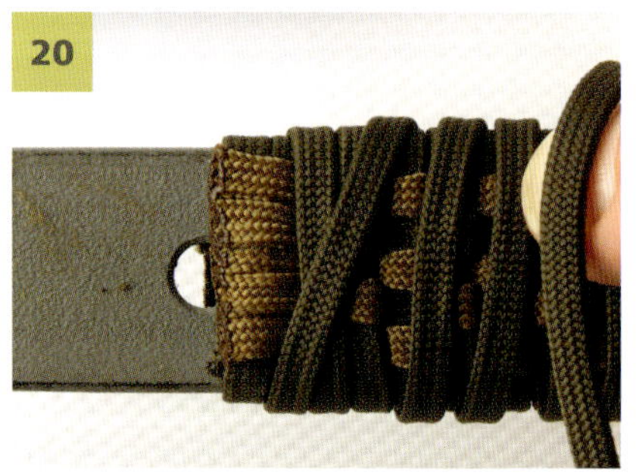

When you have reached the end, wrap the working end a few times around the handle to make holding it more comfortable.

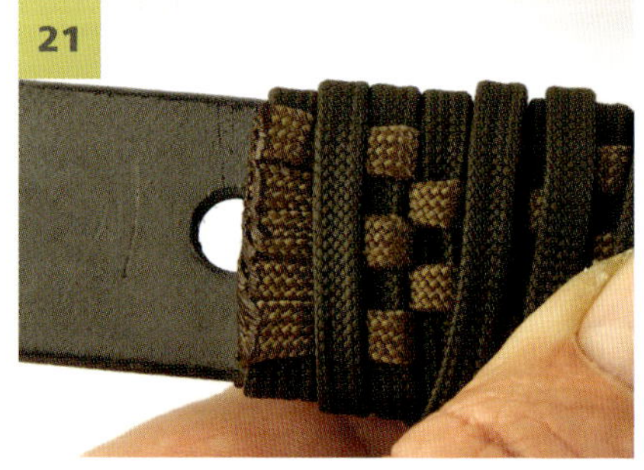

Cut the ends off the weaving cord straight and melt them to prevent unraveling.

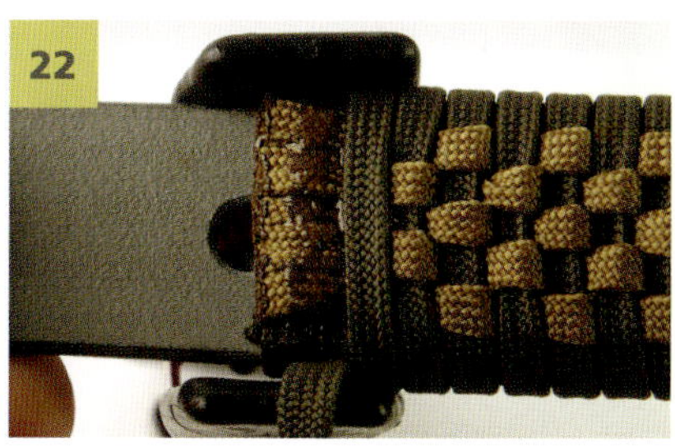

Glue the ends on top of the first layer. Afterward, glue the working end over the ends of the weaving cords.

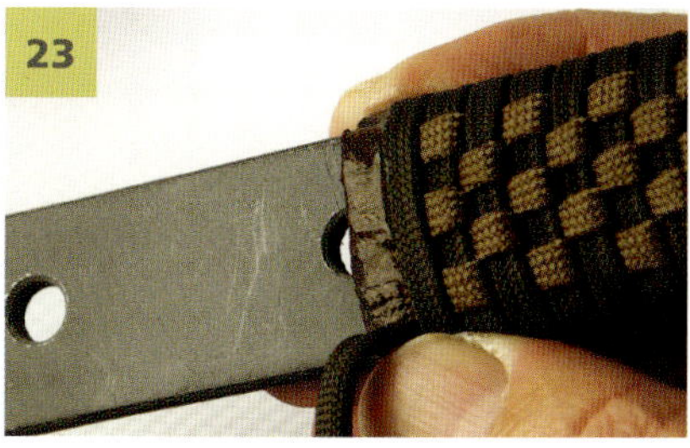

Glue everything the same way on the backside.

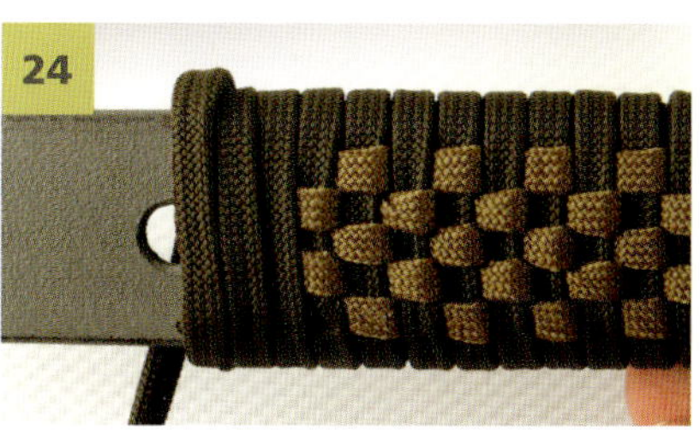

The last round of the working end is glued.

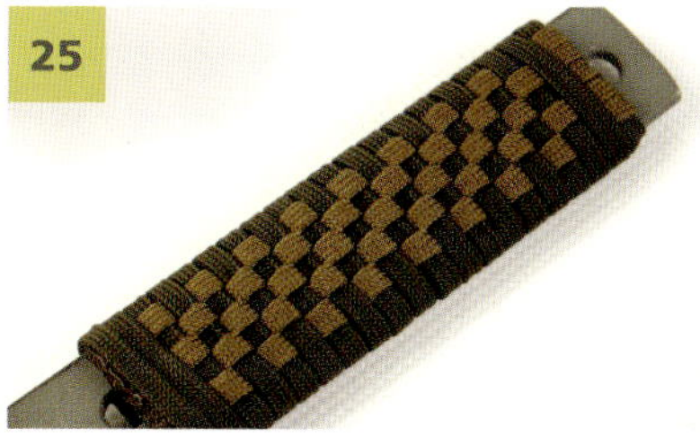

The front side is finished. This handle wrap needs a Turk's Head for completion.

The lateral view of the handle shows the regular pattern and the volume provided by this wrap.

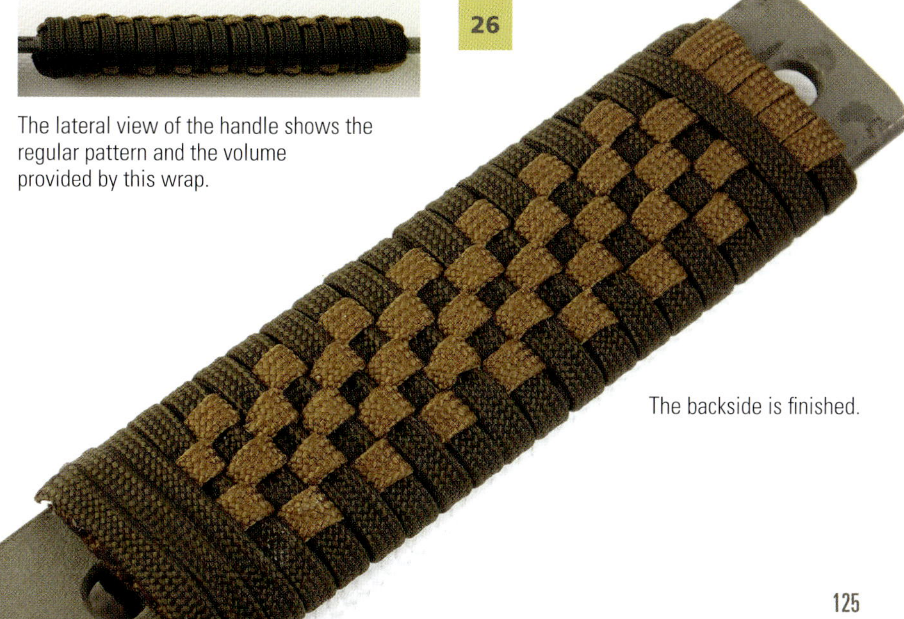

The backside is finished.

7.2 Paradox Wrap from Full Paracord

The technique is the same as for the flatline wrap, but with some specialties, such as extra long weaving cords. The weaving pattern is more open with full paracord compared to the fabric created from flatline, because the weaving cord needs more space between the wrapping cords while it runs above and beneath the cord.

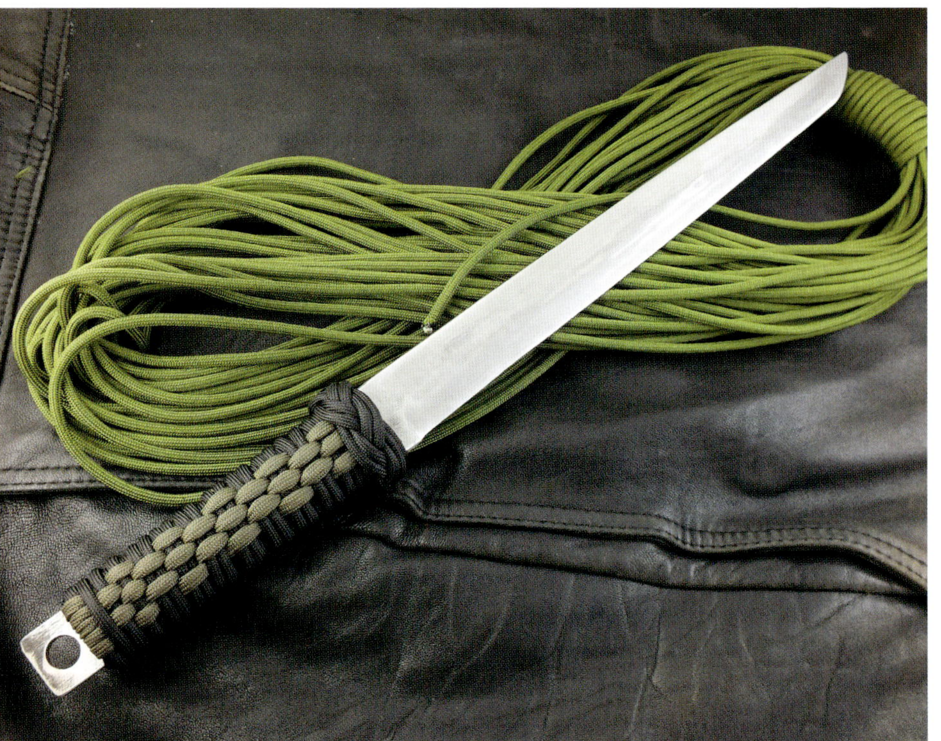

Tanto with paradox wrap of full paracord in black and dark olive green. The Turk's Head was made by continuing the wrapping cord.

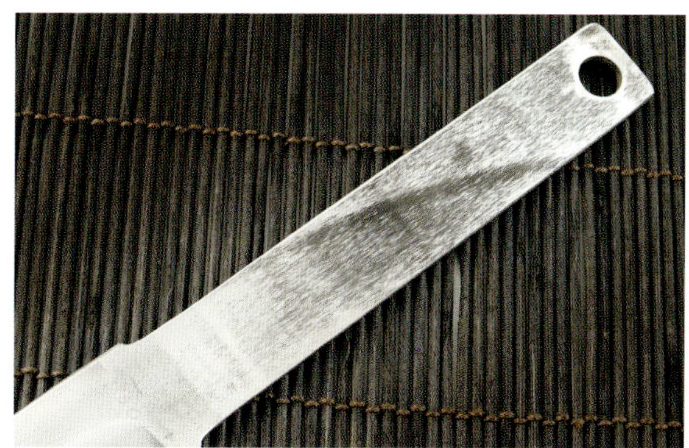

The old handle wrap was removed from this often-used knife. The tang was slightly re-ground for the wrap.

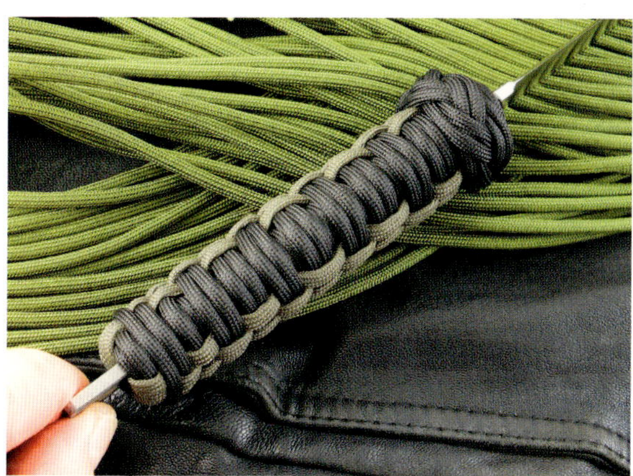

A lateral view of the handle shows the structure. The volume is really neat and fills the hand nicely. Since there is space between the cords on the side the handle does not slip in your hand.

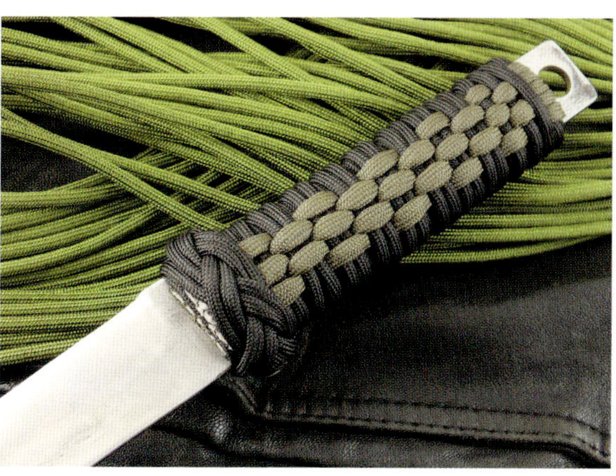

Close-up of the blade side shows the structure and the cut-off ends. If the front end and the Turk's Head are sealed with resin it works perfectly as a guard while the rest of the handle still stays comfortable.

WRAPS WITH FLAT BACKSIDE

In a number of situations it can be useful to have a flat backside and a pretty, decorative wrap on the front side. Different structures on both sides of a knife handle help to orient the knife in the hand without having to look. A flat structure on one side and a more textured structure on the other side tells the user on which side the blade's edge is.

8.1 The Bamboo Wrap

This handle wrap with a flat backside is often used with working knives in Japanese style. The wrap is traditionally made using flat bamboo strips, thus the name. The bamboo strips are replaced by flatline of type III. The backside is usually perfectly flat. The front side has an open structure. Traditional manufacturers put decorative materials such as silk underneath the open structure on the front side; we can use leather (ray skin or other decorative kinds of leather) or paracord.

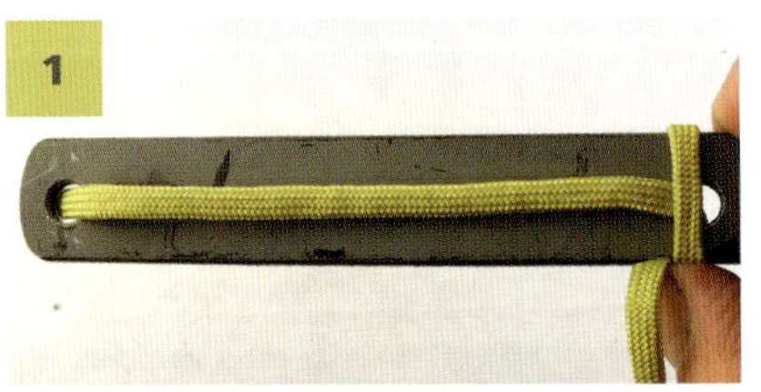

In this example we use the holes. Start with the standing end of the cord next to the pommel hole and pull the working end through the hole next to the blade.

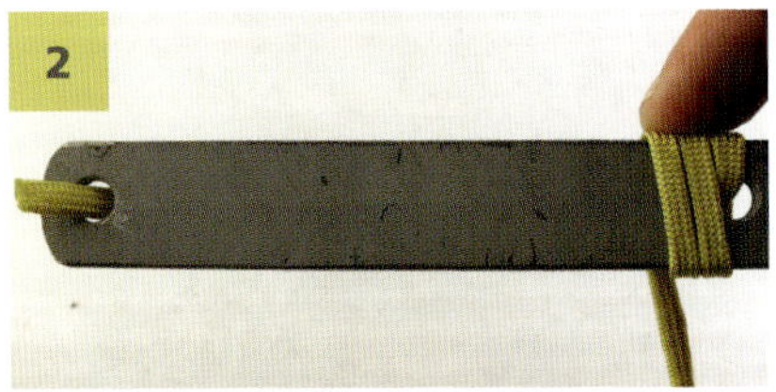

First make two turns around the handle next to the hole at the blade. Hold the cord tight while doing so as usual.

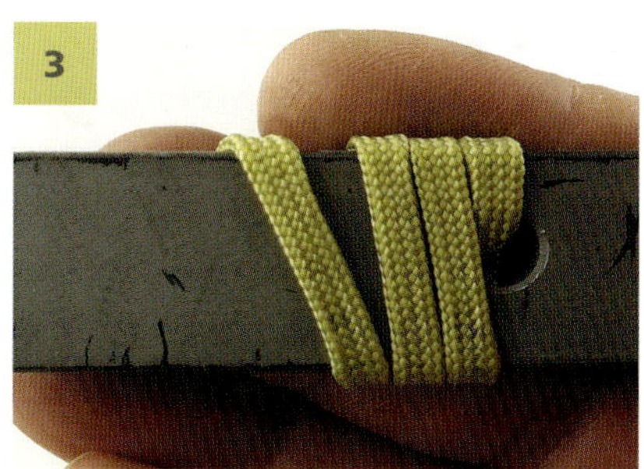

During the third round leave one width of the cord free at the upper edge.

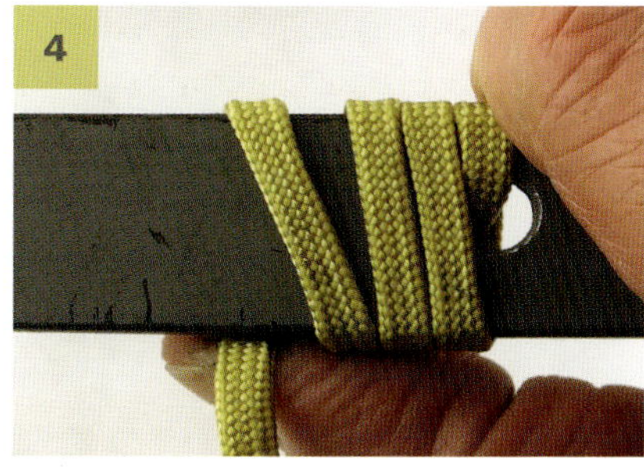

Pull the cord straight down behind the handle. Leave space here as well.

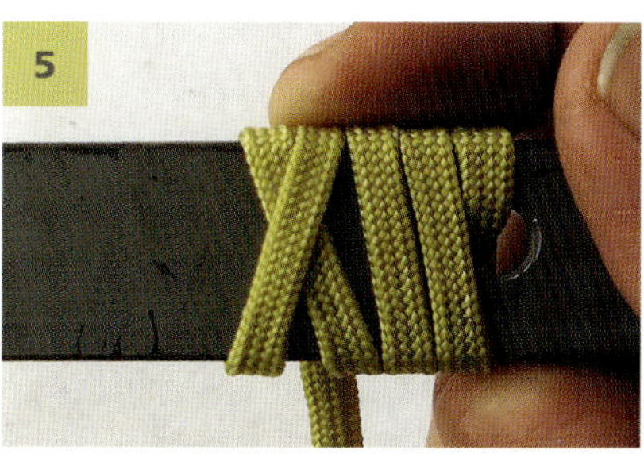

The next round goes up and to the right into the existing space. The working end should come to the front between the two cords at the bottom.

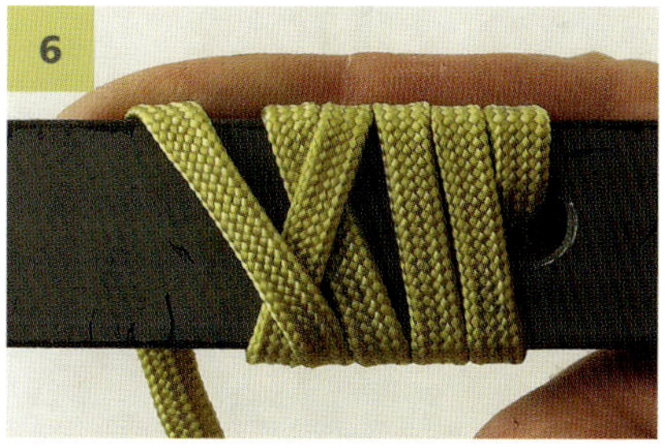

The first weaving pattern is already finished. Start the next one by going to the upper left side and leave space for another cord.

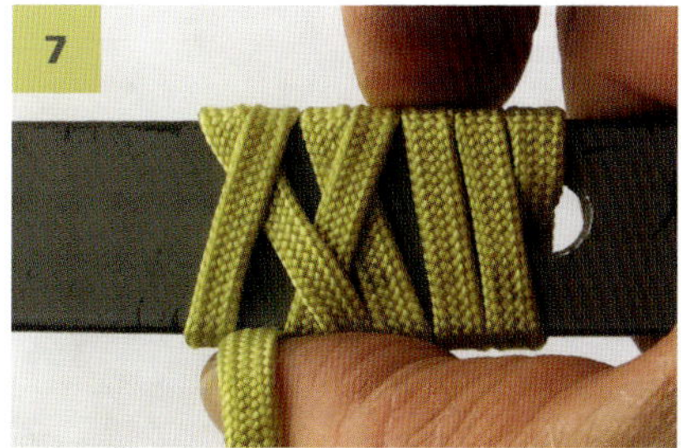

The cord goes down vertically behind the handle and then up toward the left into the free space, then down again.

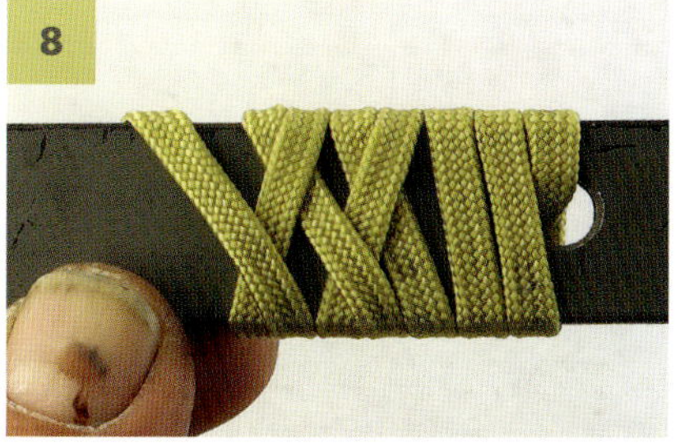

Here the second weave is finished and the third one has been started.

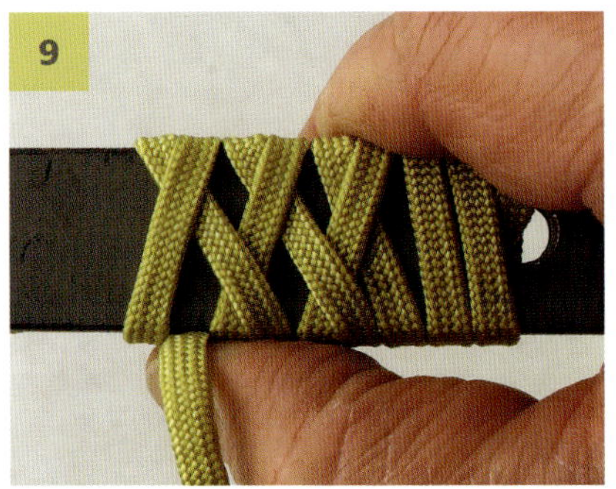

The third weave is already finished.

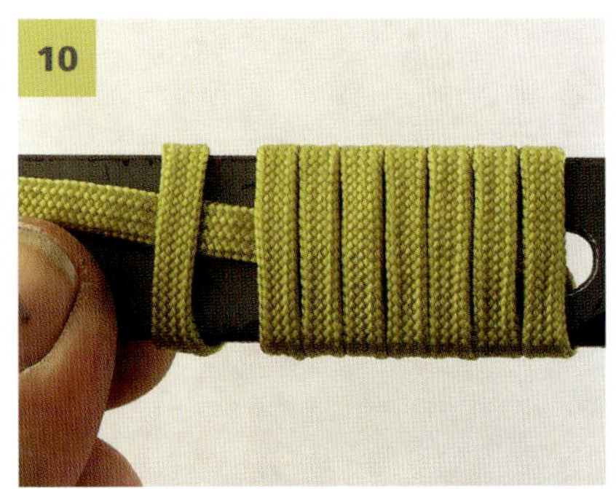

Press the pieces of cord on the backside closer together.

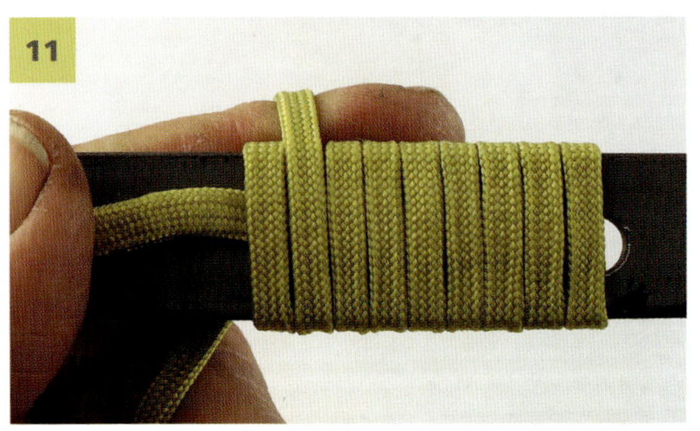

The third weaving pattern ends on the handle's backside.

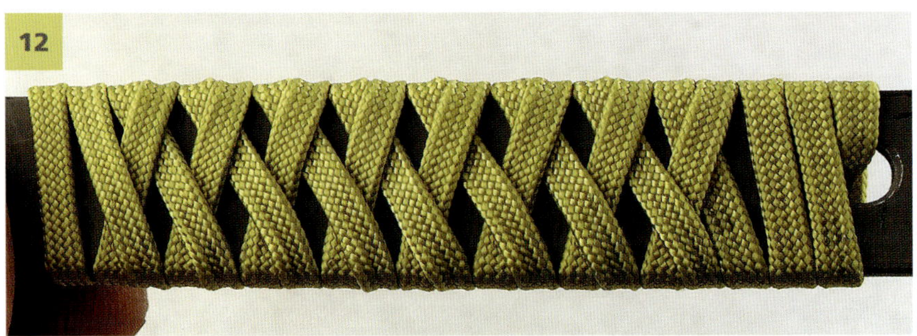

The pommel has almost been reached. A simple wrap is put over the last few widths of the cord.

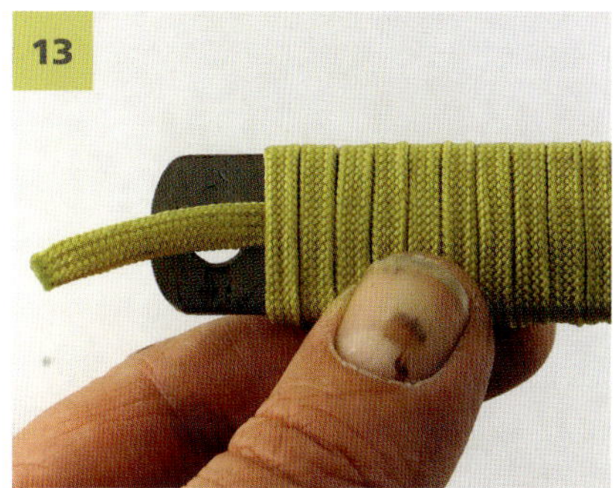

The standing end on the pommel side is now pulled straight.

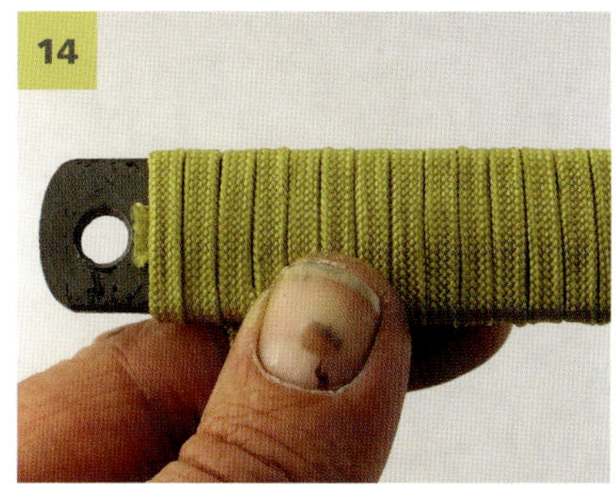

It is cut off and melted slightly with a heated wire or paper clip.

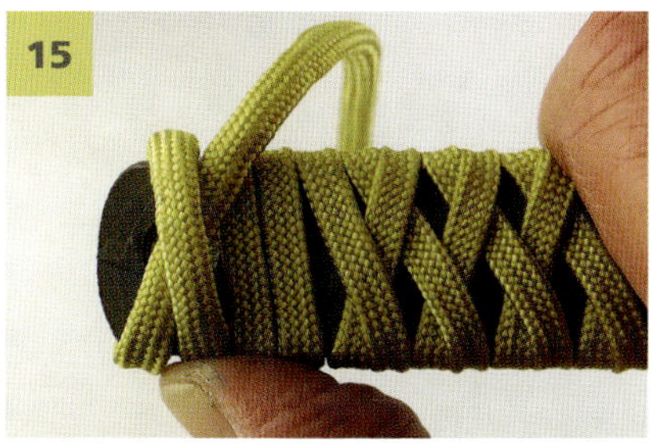

The last turn of the working end goes under the previous one.

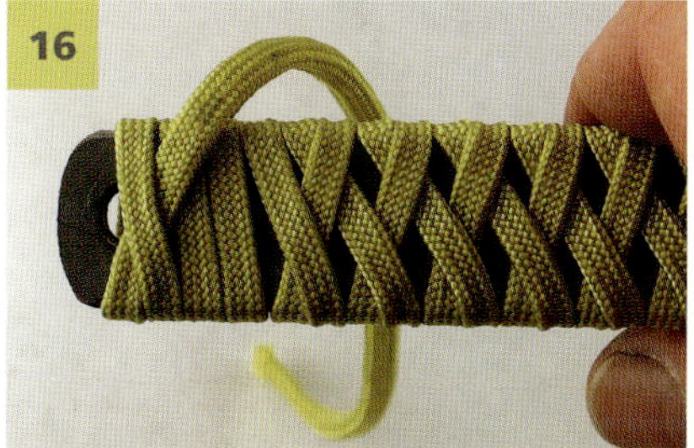

The working end is pulled tight.

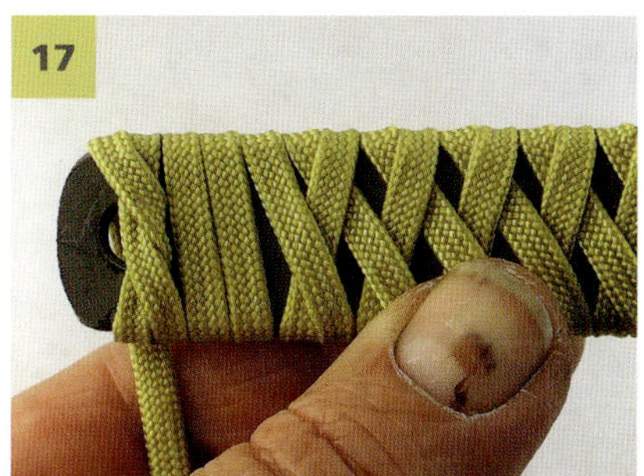

The working end is folded up to the left and led to the other side of the pommel.

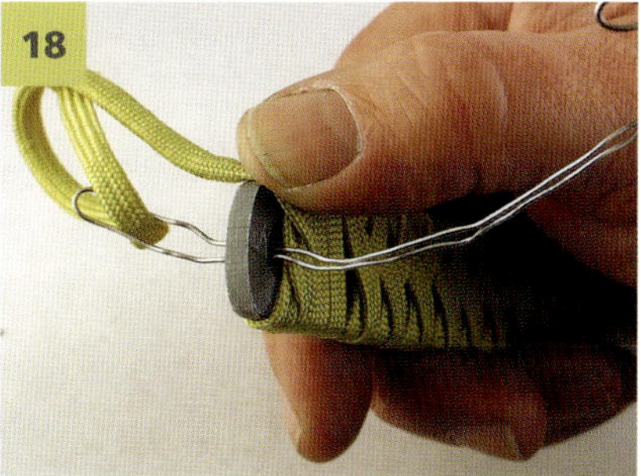

We pull the end through the pommel hole with a bent wire.

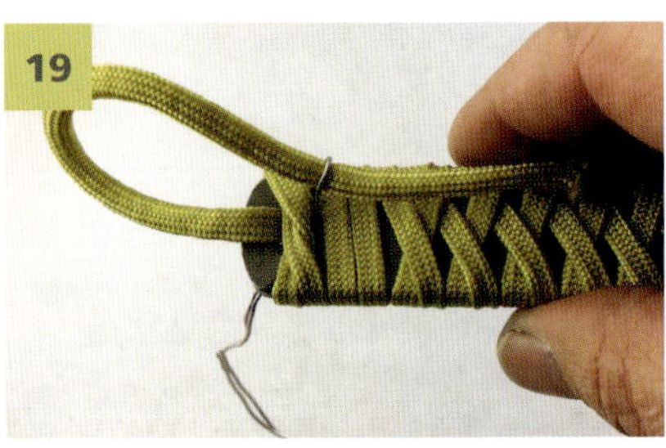

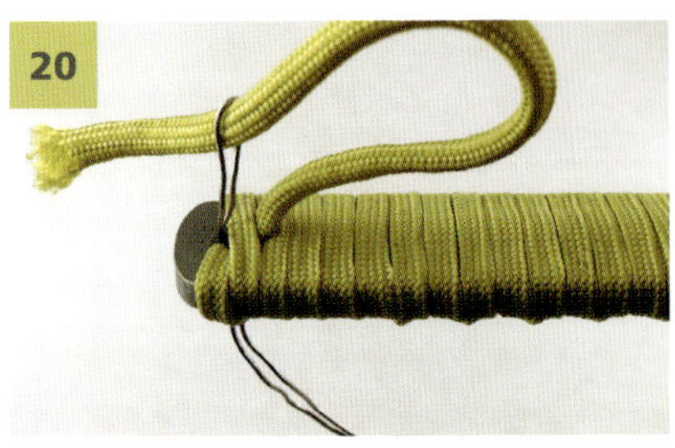

Then the working end is pulled underneath the last crossing with the bent wire and pulled back to the backside.

The backside: with the wire we pull the cord over the last turn back to the front side.

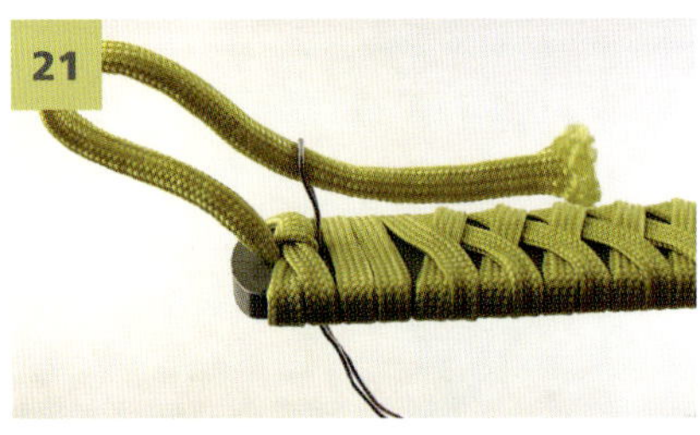

Here the end is led around the wrap for the last time and through the hole toward the backside.

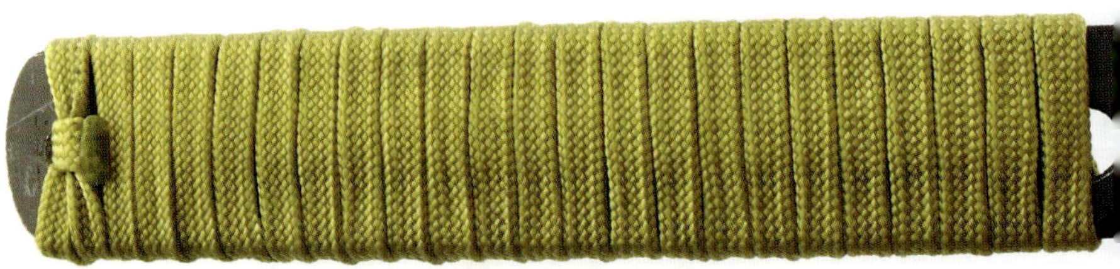

22 The end is cut off and melted. A drop of super glue on the knot provides additional security.

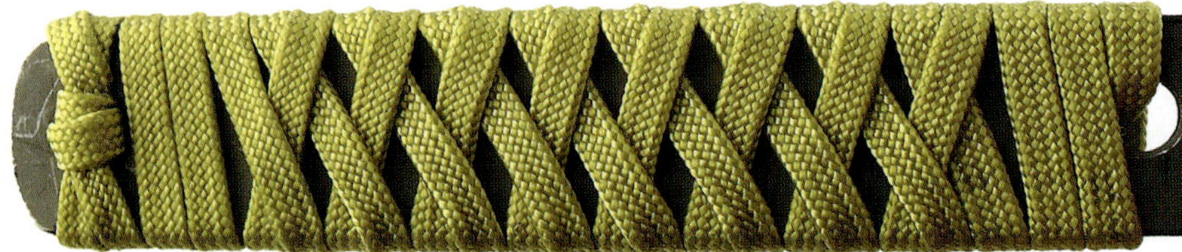

23 The front view of the finished handle displays a neatly balanced handle wrap.

8.2 Bamboo Wrap Type II

In case the knife does not have any holes in the tang there is a second way to make the wrap.

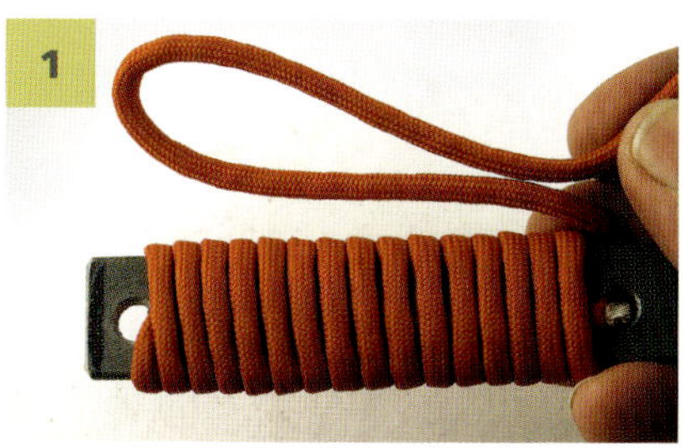

For the bamboo wrap not using holes in the tang we need the length of one wrap around the entire handle and an additional three handle lengths for some more comfort.

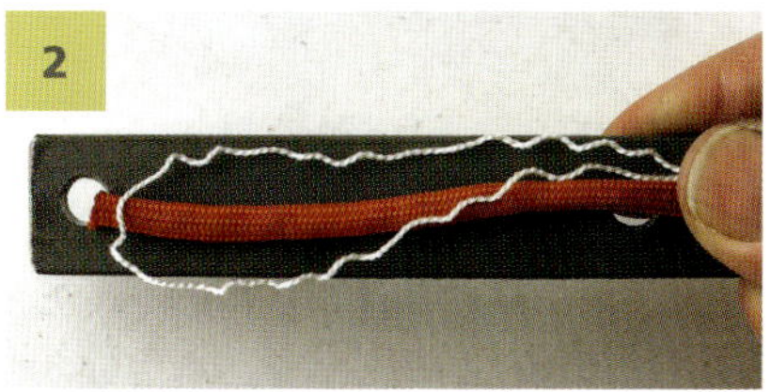

We use a piece of string from the core to pull the end through. Put the standing end of the cord next to the loop and along the handle.

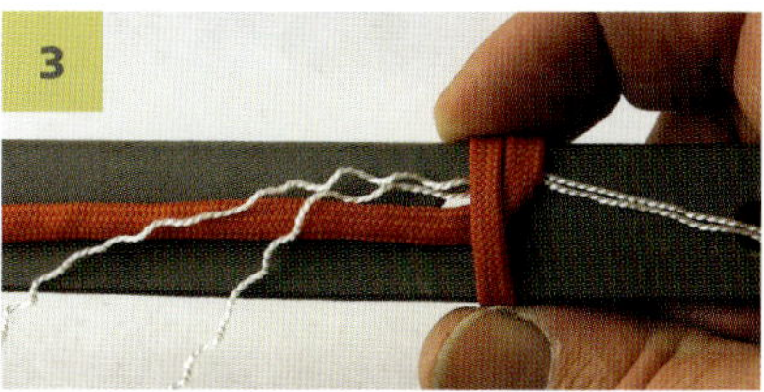

Twist the standing end through ninety degrees and make a full turn up around the tang. We see the backside of the later knife handle.

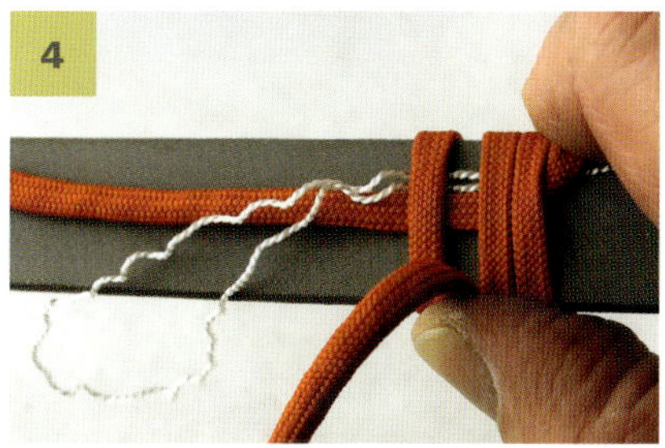

After two rounds the first weave is finished. Hold all cord ends neatly positioned and parallel along the back.

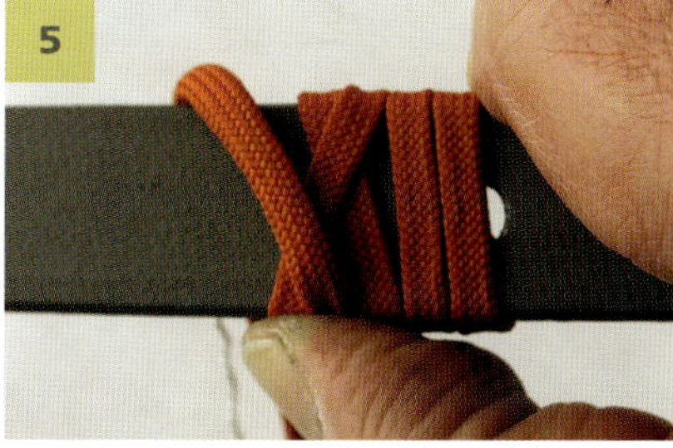

The first weave is finished as soon as we are again on the front side.

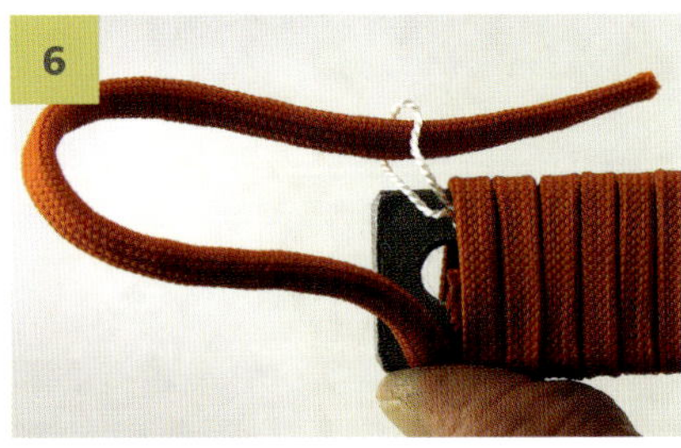

The standing end is cut off at the pommel. The working end goes through the loop of the string to be pulled through underneath the wrap.

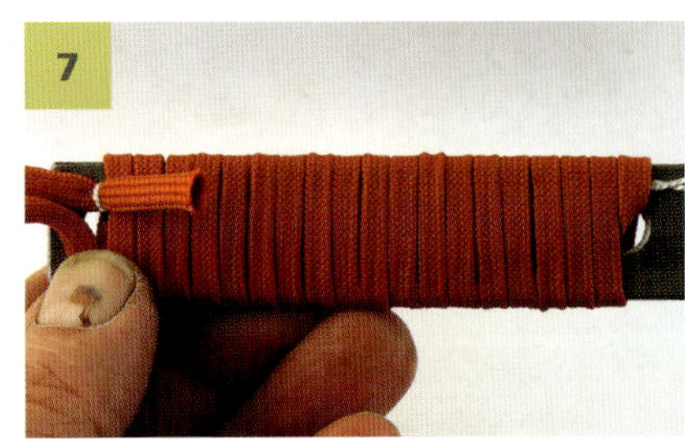

The working end is now completely pulled through under the wrap.

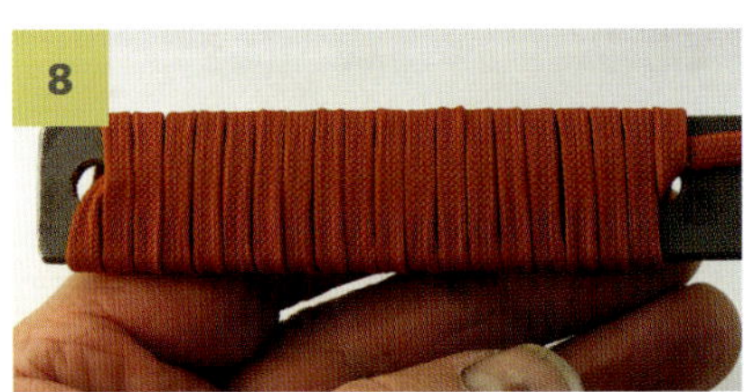

The end is through. The cut-off standing end is covered by the working cord.

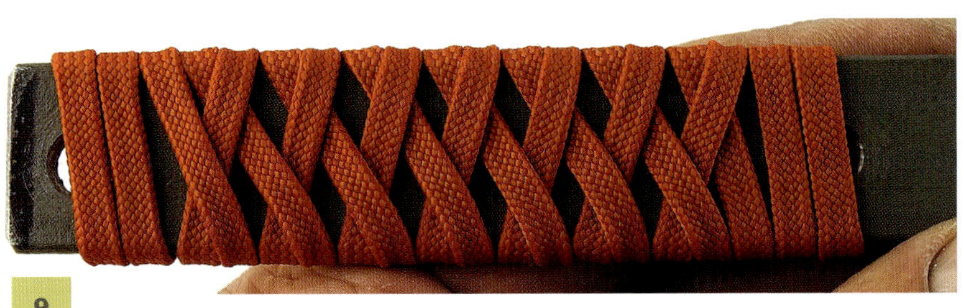

Front view of the handle.

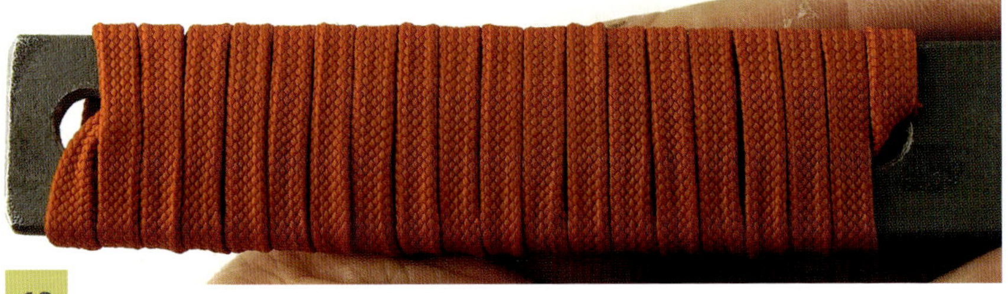

Here the working end has also been cut off.

8.3 Half Wraps

We have seen some wrapping techniques that have a structured pattern on the front as well as the backside. These can be adapted in such a way that they are only woven on the front side.

One example is the Christian *tsukamaki* style. If only the front side receives a weaving pattern then the backside gets an attractive, flat surface. Since the twisted crossings are omitted, the weaving pattern can be continued almost up to the pommel. The end is different from the end of the *tsukamaki* version. Here is an example of the handle wrap with flat backside on a *sgian dubh* blade.

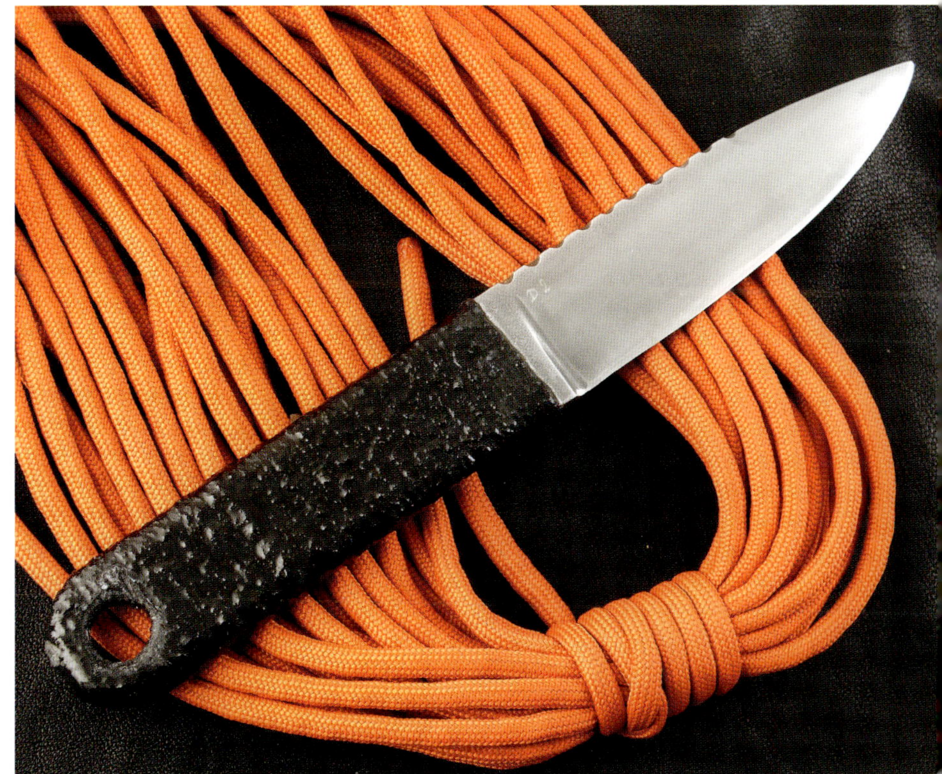

The *sgian dubh* has a basic layer of cotton band impregnated with epoxy resin.

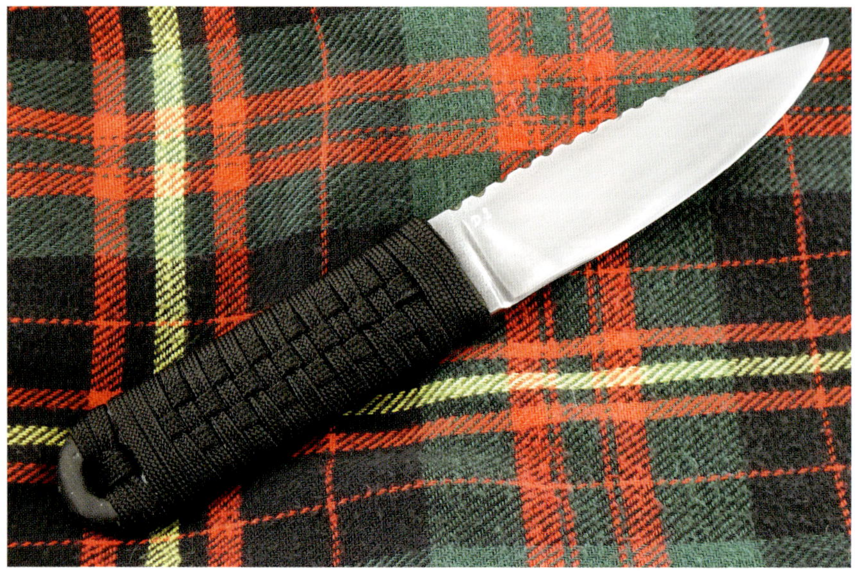

On top of that goes a wrap with a weaving pattern that nicely fits to the knife. The wrap is preserved using impregnated resin.

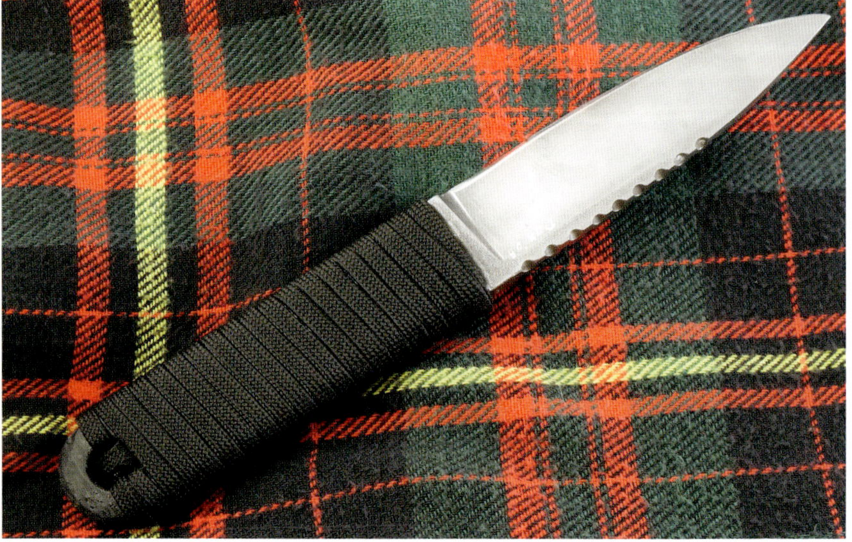

The backside is traditionally wrapped.

8.4 Simple Weaving Pattern with One Weaving End

With the flat wrap, one standing end can be woven into the wrap. Instead of leaving the standing end on the backside and underneath the wrap it is put on the handle's front side and woven into the wrap while working on it. The simple weaving pattern displays a pretty structure with full paracord.

The same wrapping technique with flatline displays a rather closed look and grip feel.

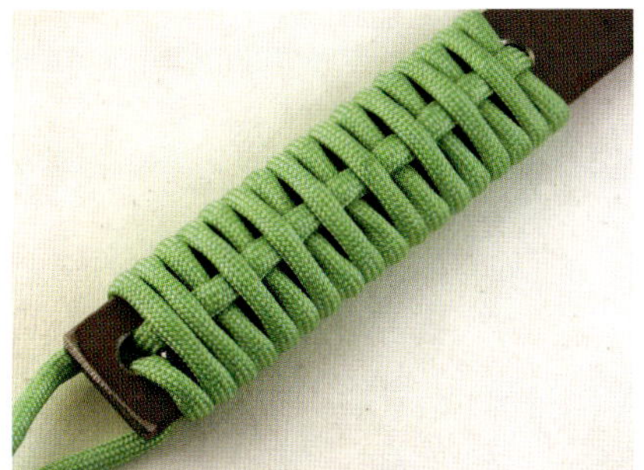

This is a simple wrap with the standing end woven under and over the working end while wrapping the handle.

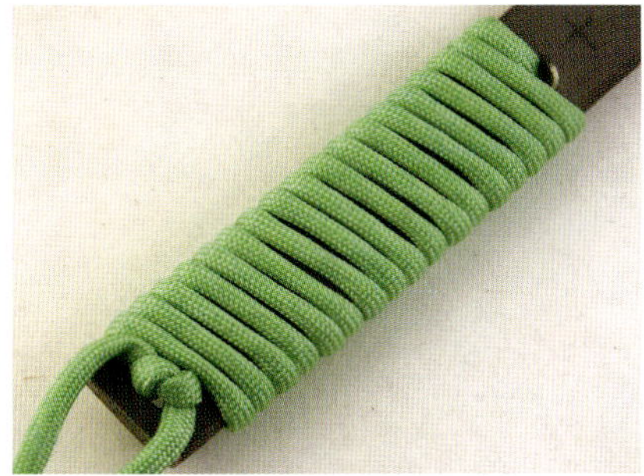

The backside of this wrap rests flat against the handle.

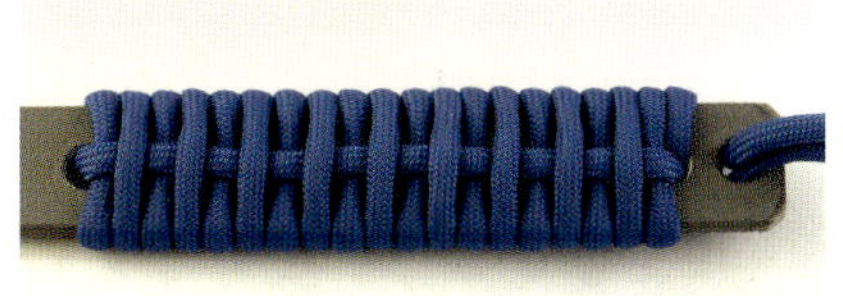

This blue handle wrap has an end knot different from the one used for tactical handle wraps.

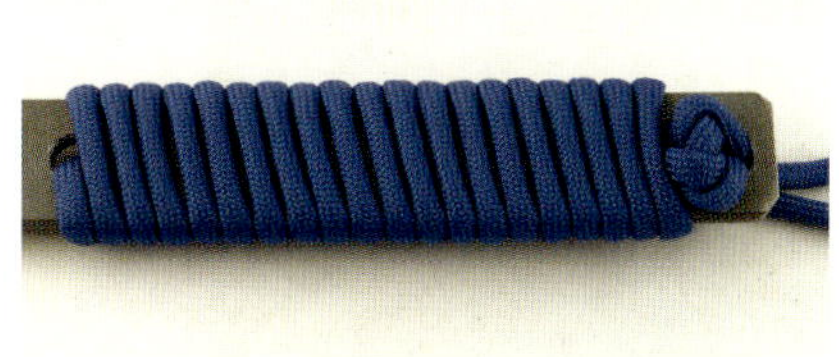

The flat back shows this different end knot.

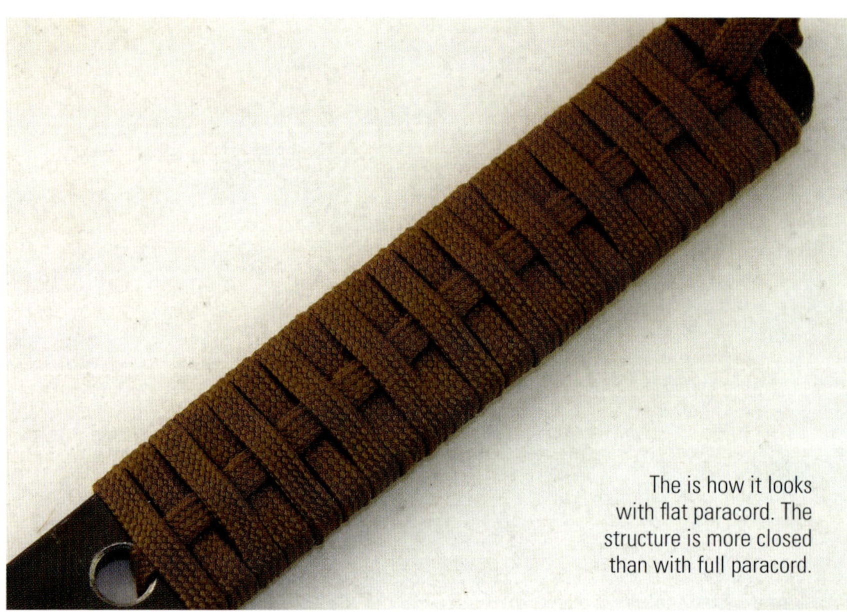

The is how it looks with flat paracord. The structure is more closed than with full paracord.

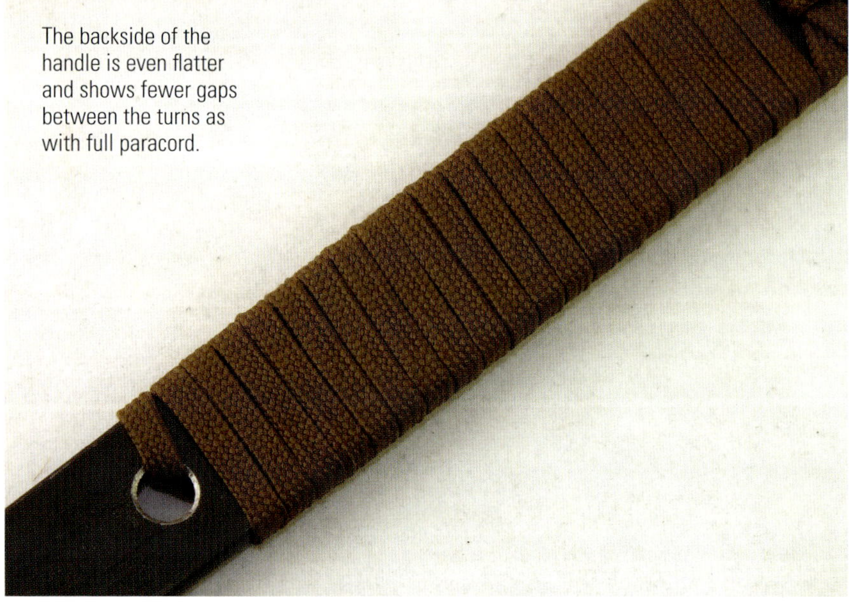

The backside of the handle is even flatter and shows fewer gaps between the turns as with full paracord.

8.5 Handle Wraps with Two Colors

If the cord is doubled and two different color hues are used the result is a nice weaving pattern. The handle wrap is still simple and can be done with little material. For the end knots, the examples in the chapter about tactical handle wraps are well suited.

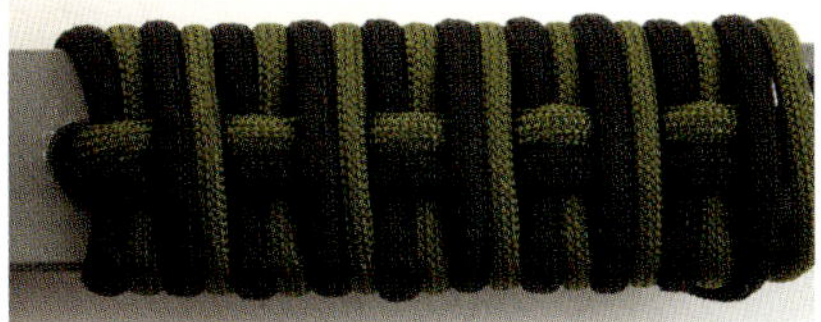

If the handle is wrapped with two cords and both colors are woven simultaneously we achieve this pretty structure.

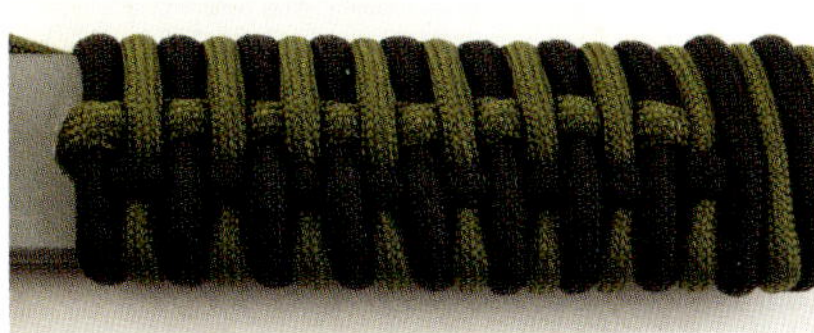

In this example the weaving work is alternated with both cords. This way the resulting pattern looks different.

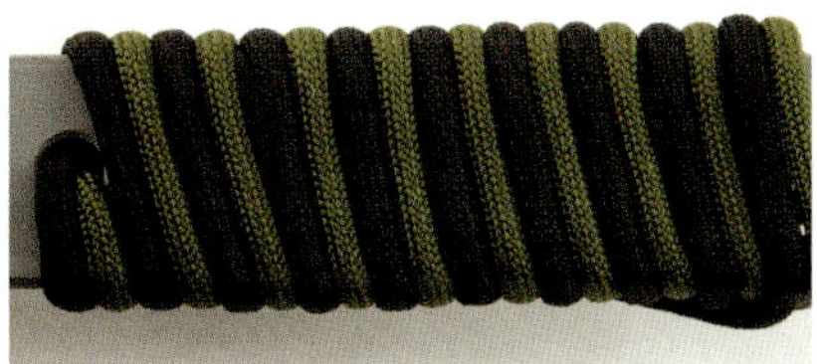

Full paracord:
the backsides of the two
previous handles display
a nice striped pattern.

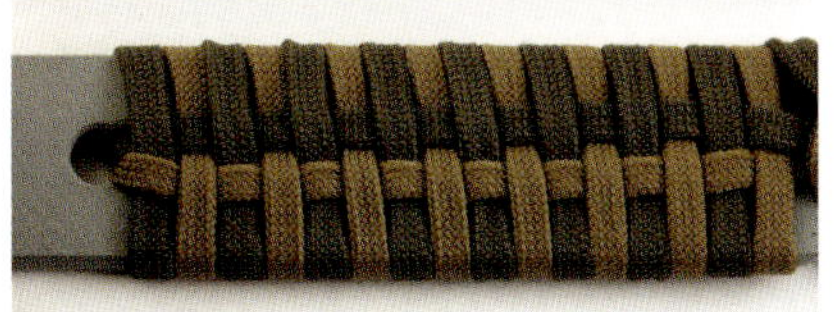

This flat wrap is similar in structure to the second handle wrap of full paracord.

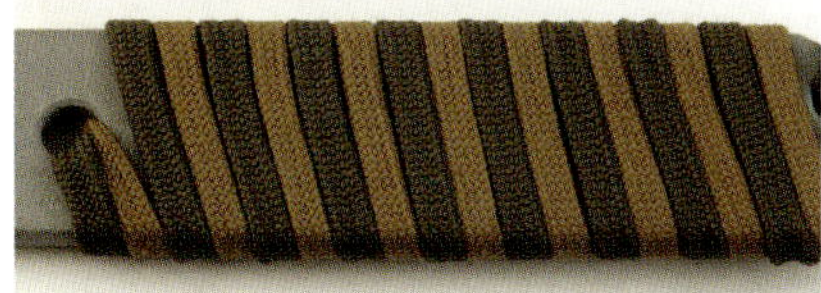

The backside of the flatline wrap shows that the wrap is very thin. An additional layer underneath the wrap can enhance handle volume, while at the same time keeping the structure of the flatline weaving pattern.

8.6 The Triple Weaving Pattern

The simple weaving pattern can be tripled by adding another cord: one loop of flatline keeps the wrapped handle in an appealing oval shape, while the central cord and the wrapping cord stay full paracord. In my example I used black flatline to enhance the visibility of the technique.

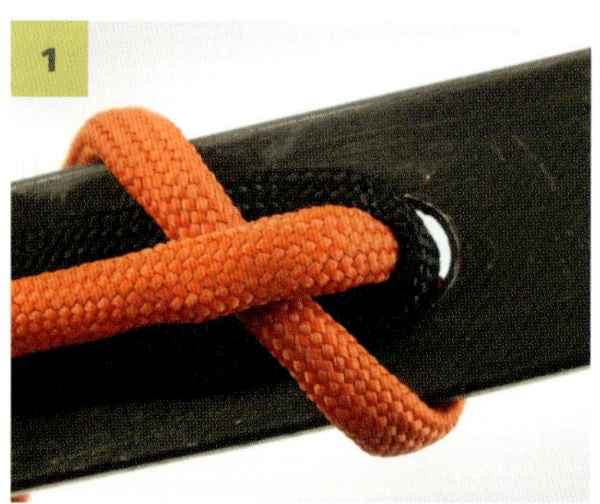

To enhance the simple weaving pattern a bit you can weave one loop of flatline into the structure.

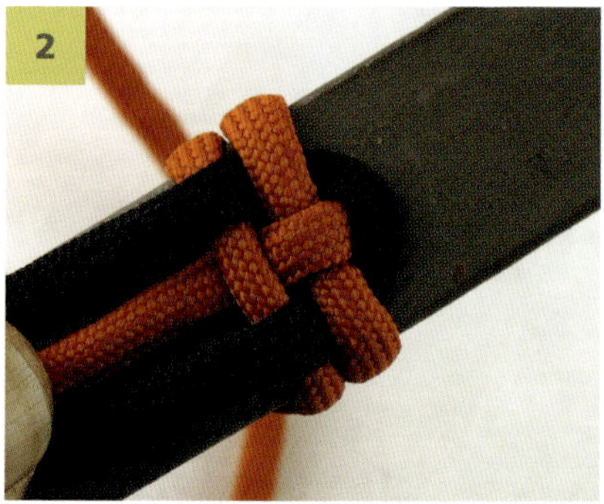

The flatline does the opposite of the full cord during weaving: it goes alternately over and under the cord.

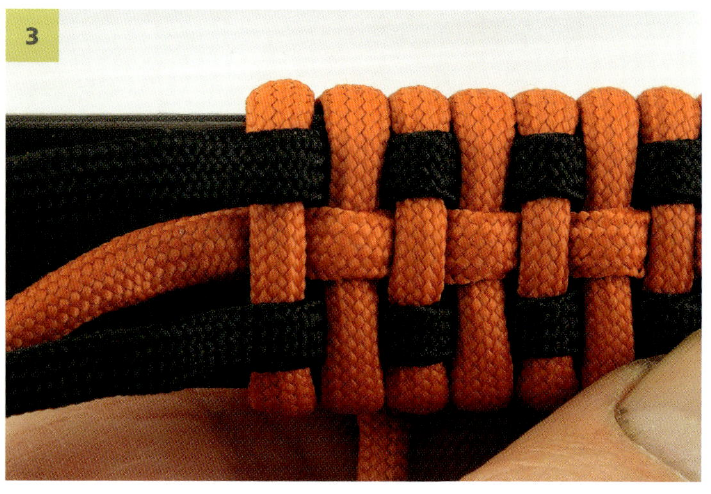

The weaving pattern takes shape.

4

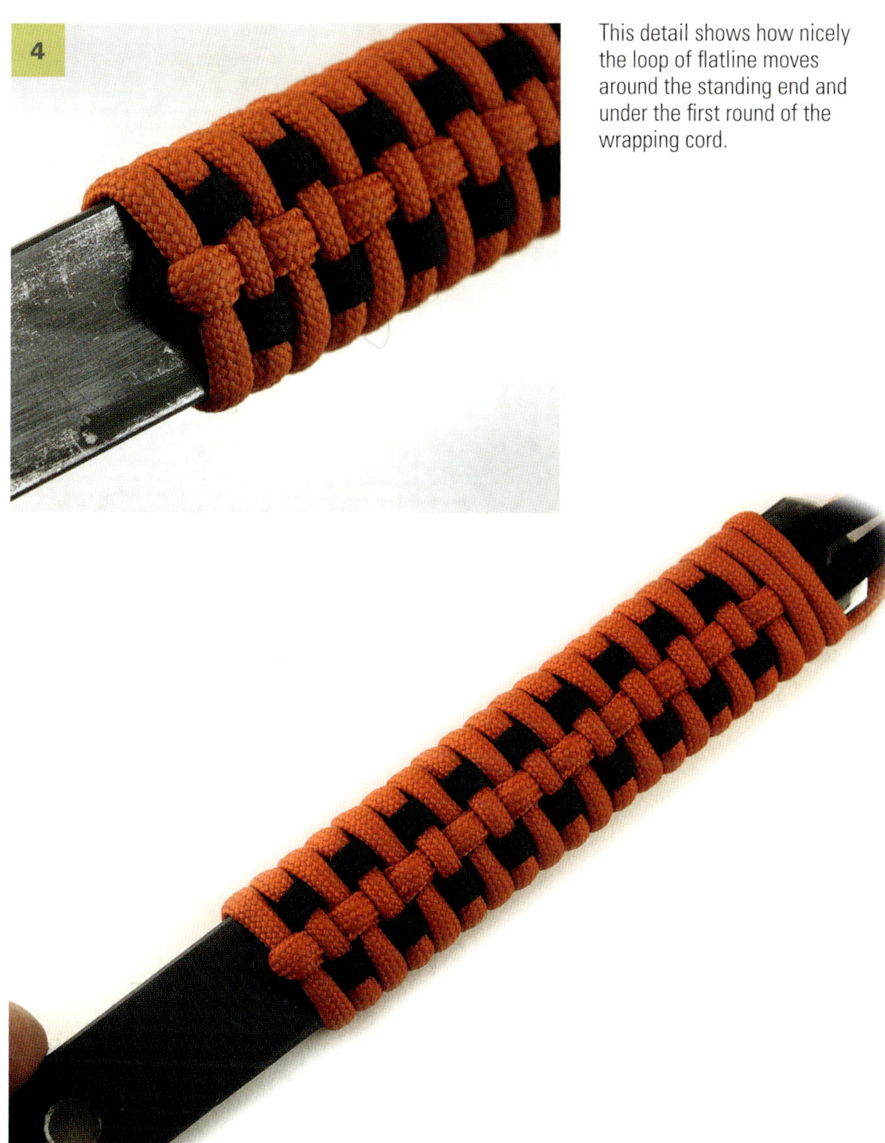

This detail shows how nicely the loop of flatline moves around the standing end and under the first round of the wrapping cord.

The handle wrap is ready to be completed: the flatline still has to be cut off. Knotting the standing cord end and the weaving cord is done in the same way as tactical handle wraps.

8.7 The Double-Faced Triple Weaving Pattern

The triple weaving pattern with flat handle backside can be changed into a full format triple pattern on the front- and backside. If you add two flatline loops to the backside of the wrapped handle we change the handle wrap with flat back into a double-faced triple weaving wrap.

In the example we used green paracord to enhance visibility. For better balance, in practice we would use flatline of the same cord used for the wrap (in this case orange).

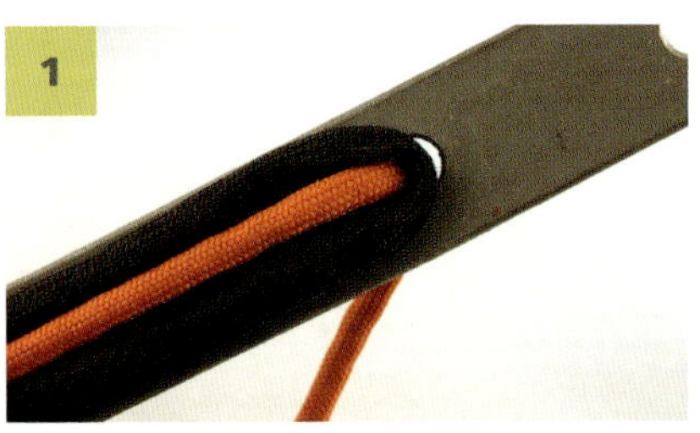

Double-faced triple weaving pattern: on the front side we start the triple weaving pattern in the same way as in chapter 8.6.

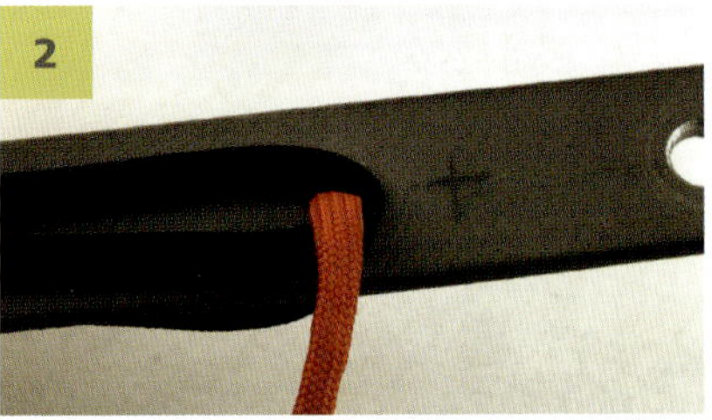

On the backside we also put a flatline loop. At the start of the first round the working end of the cord rests on the handle's backside.

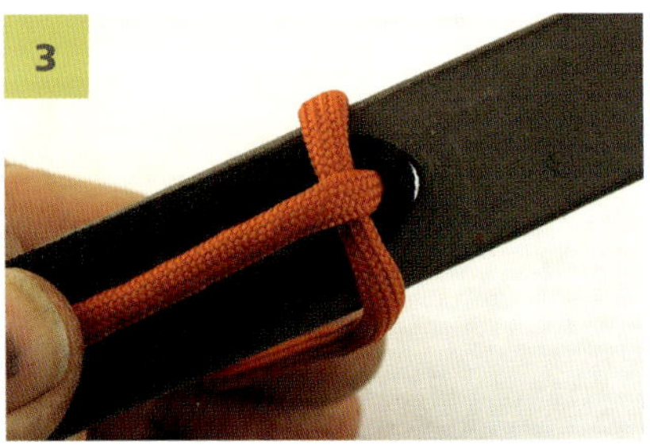

On the front side the working end is led under the standing end and over the flatline loop.

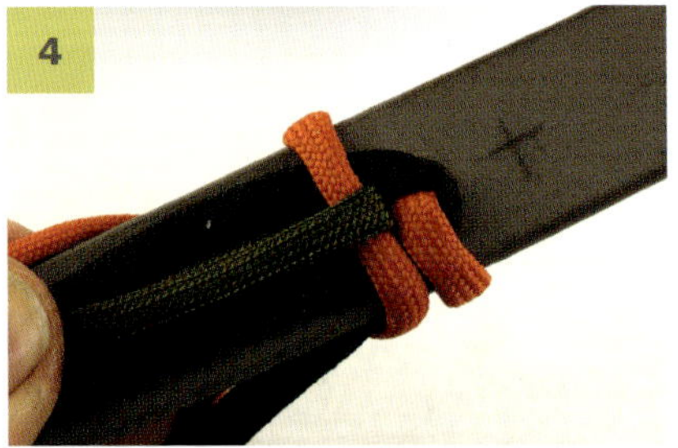

The working cord has passed the backside and a second flatline loop has been added (green).

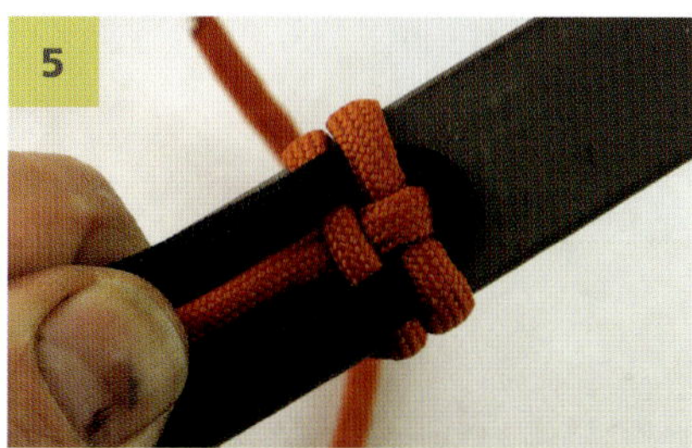

On the handle's front side the wrapping cord has made its second pass over the standing end and under the two black flatlines.

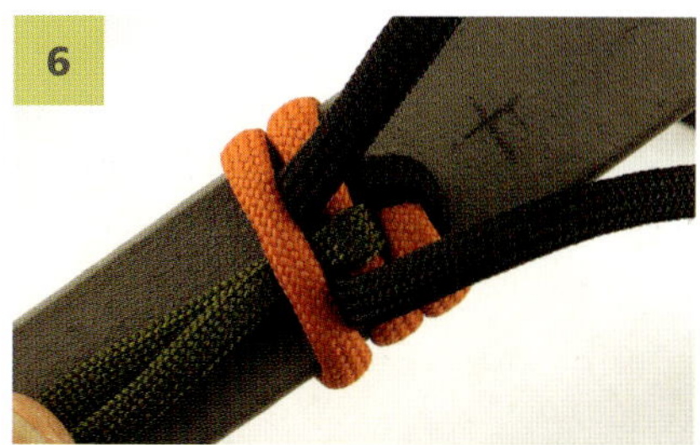

On the backside, both ends of the central flatline go under the working end with the black ends on top. From here on only the upper end of the green flatline is woven in.

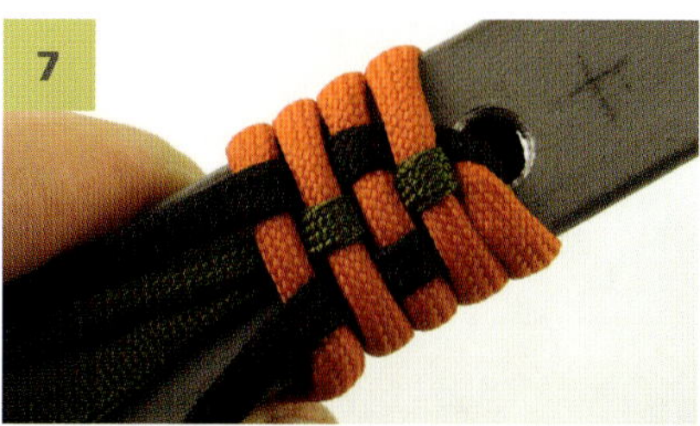

The fourth pass of the cord on the handle's backside.

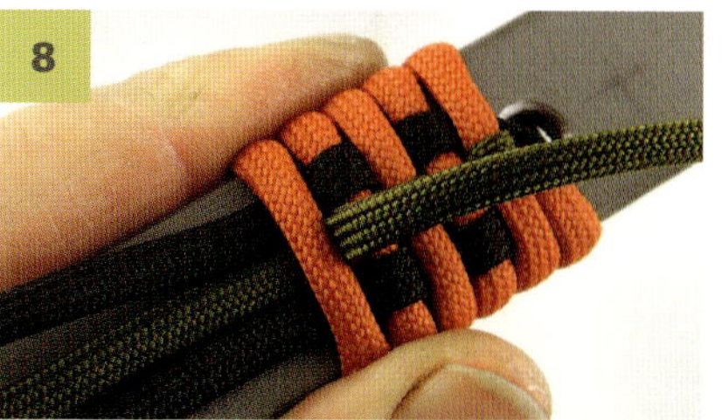

The fifth pass of the wrapping cord. As you can distinctly see, only the upper flatline of the central loop is used for weaving.

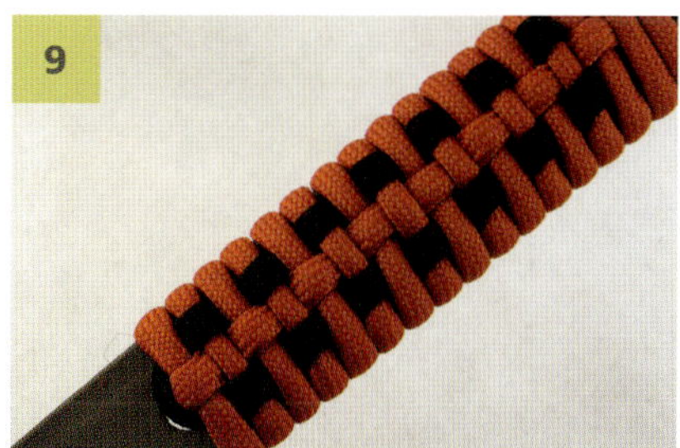

On the front side of the handle the full orange cord can be seen in the center of the weaving pattern.

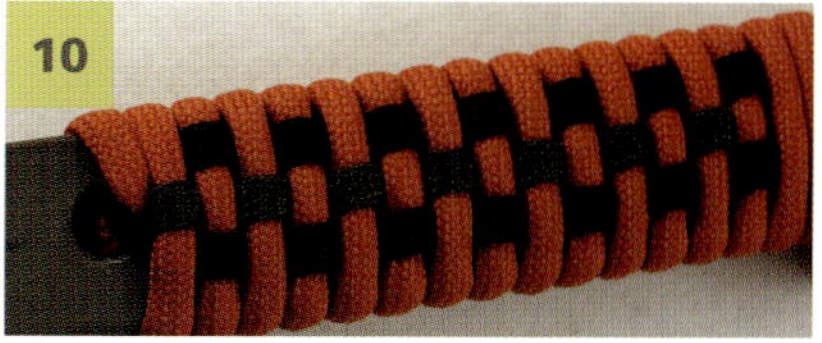

The handle's backside shows the three flat weaving cords. The weaving ends can be trimmed and glued; a Turk's Head can cover the wrap's end. Another solution would be a wrist thong (lanyard).

WRAPS FOR SKELETON HANDLES

9.1 Skeleton Handles with Elongated Opening

If the handle has one or more elongated openings you can simply weave through the holes.

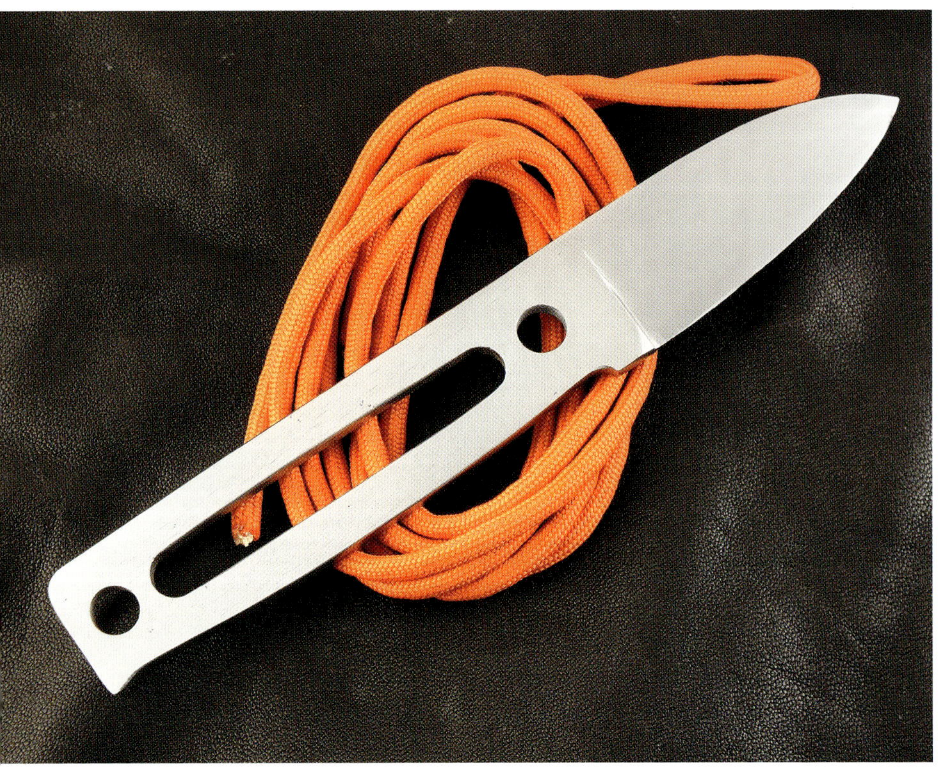

A simple blade with skeleton handle and elongated slot can be wrapped, turning the knife into a comfortable tool.

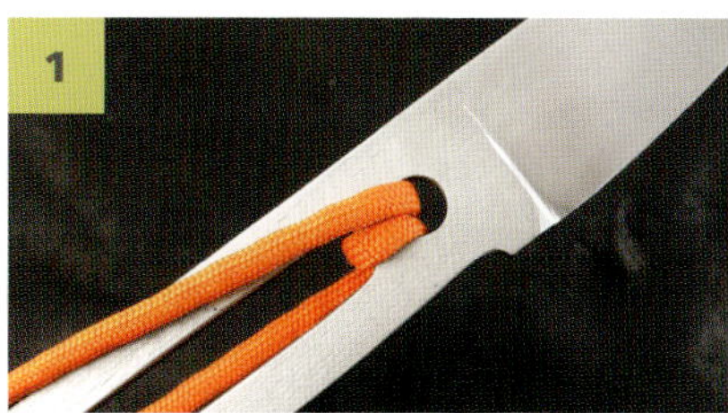

At the beginning, the cord goes two times through the hole and the long slot. The cord's direction is important: it influences the start of the weaving pattern.

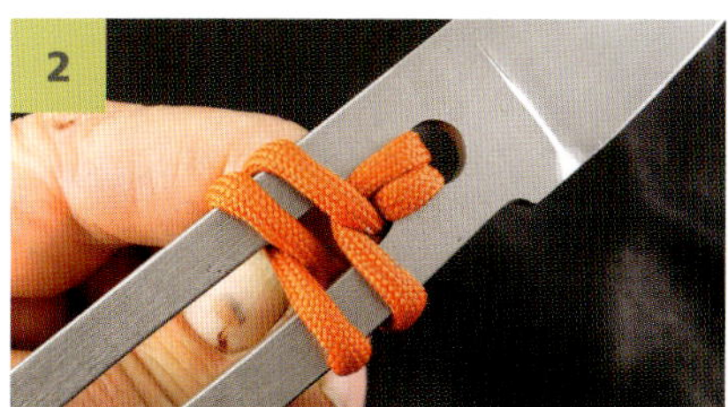

The right working end goes to the left over the other cord, which is led to the right.

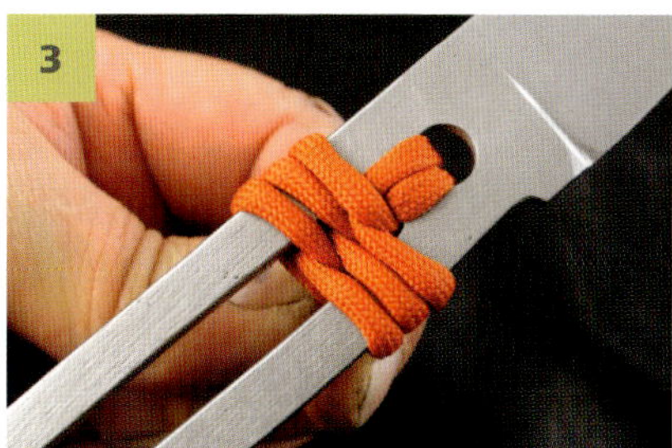

The cord ends are pulled tight and pressed against each other. The herringbone structure of the wrap becomes visible.

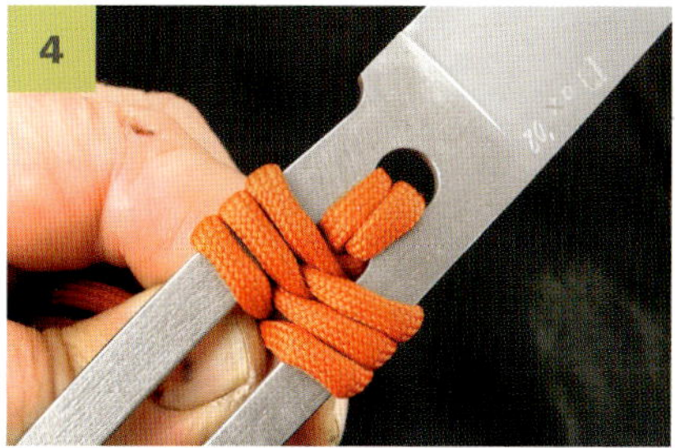

The other side also looks good.

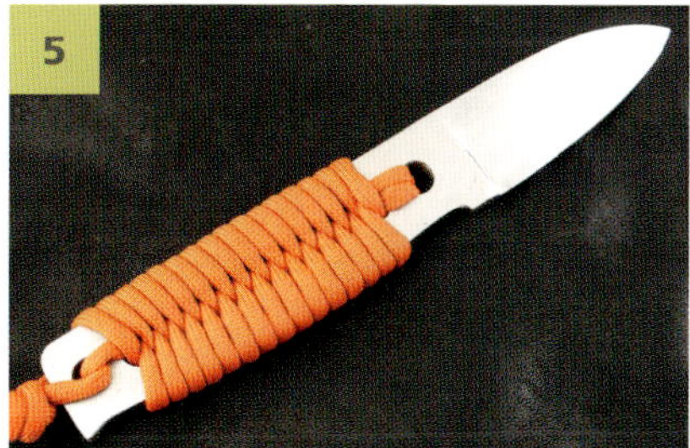

When the handle's end is reached, try to squeeze one more weave through the opening before making the end knot.

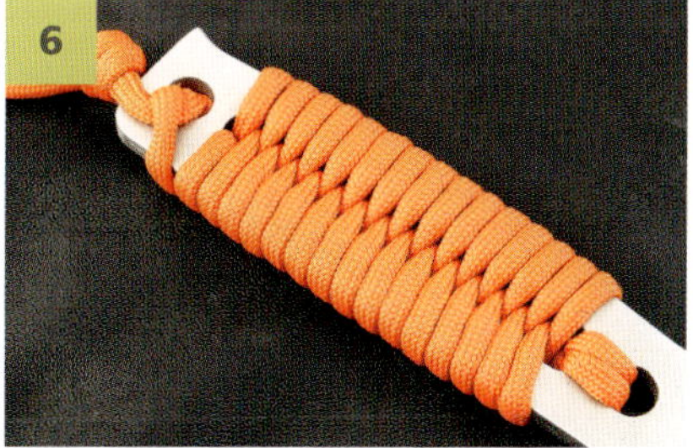

The other side has a perfect and uniform weaving pattern.

THE LANYARD KNOT

The lanyard knot has a woven structure like that of the Turk's Head. It provides a neat way to make a loop suited for various configurations. If a knife has a short handle, a lanyard knot can extend it effectively and enhance handling significantly.

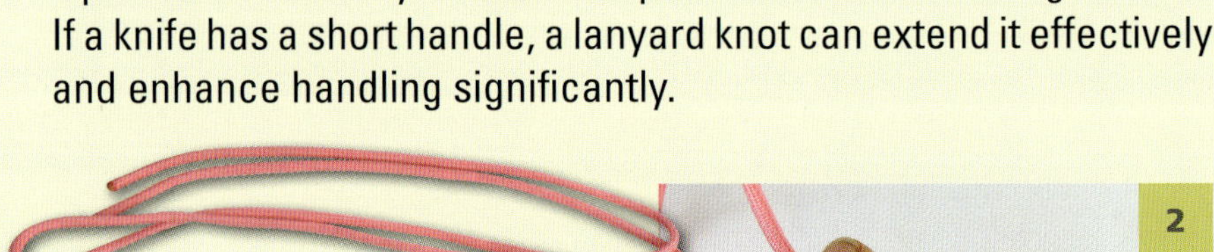

1 Fold the cord in the center.

Take one end. Approach from the upper side of your hand and make a loop with the working end underneath.

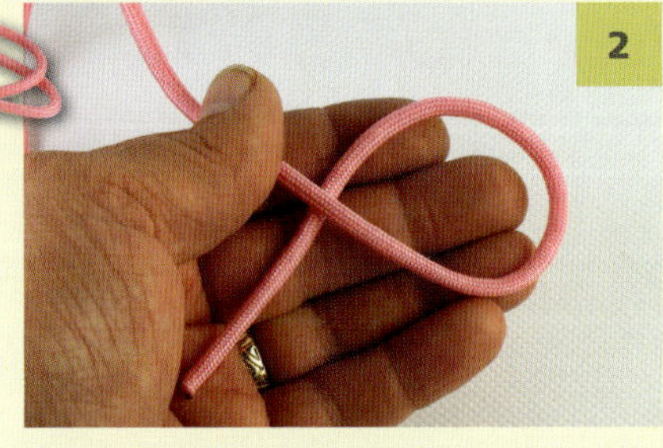

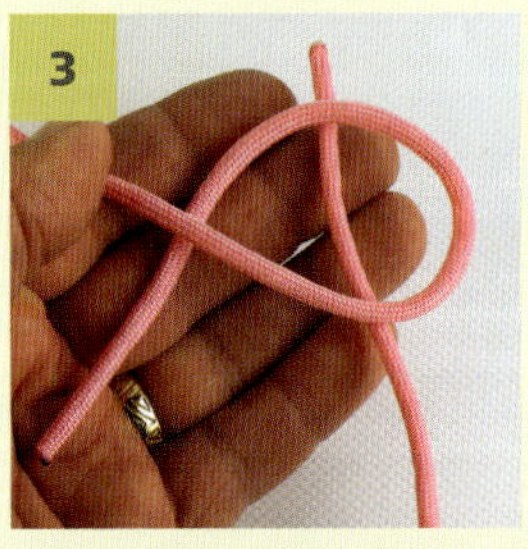

Move the second working end up and under the loop.

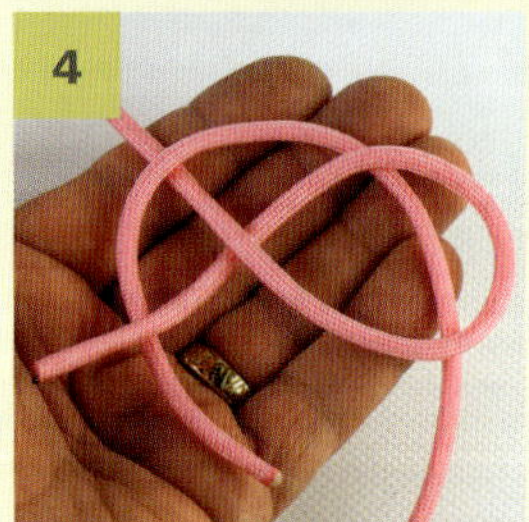

Take the second working end over the cord coming from above and under the first working end.

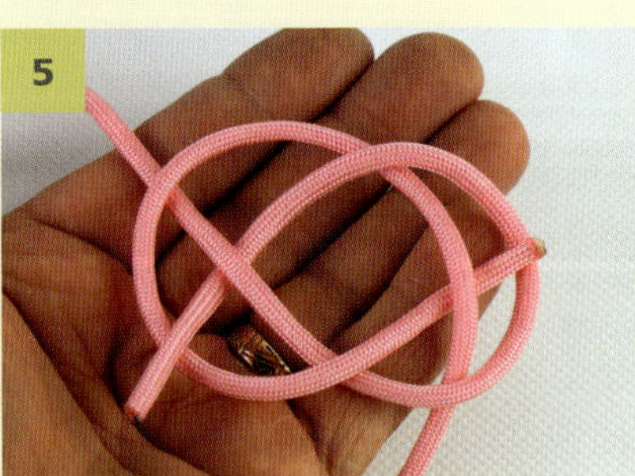

Lead the second working end over the loop, underneath itself, and over the loop on the right side.

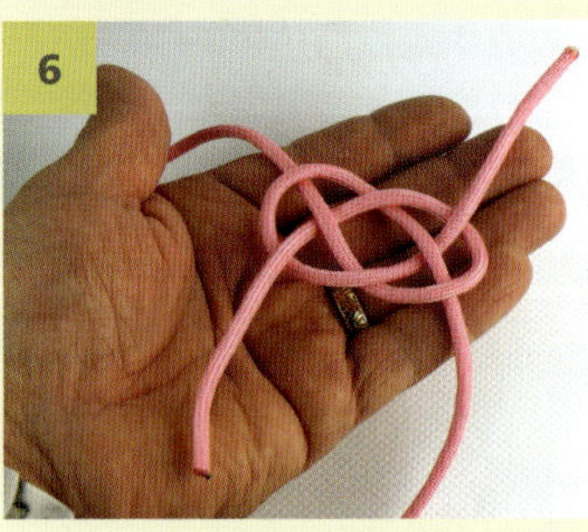

Pull the knot tighter, thereby making the working ends a bit longer.

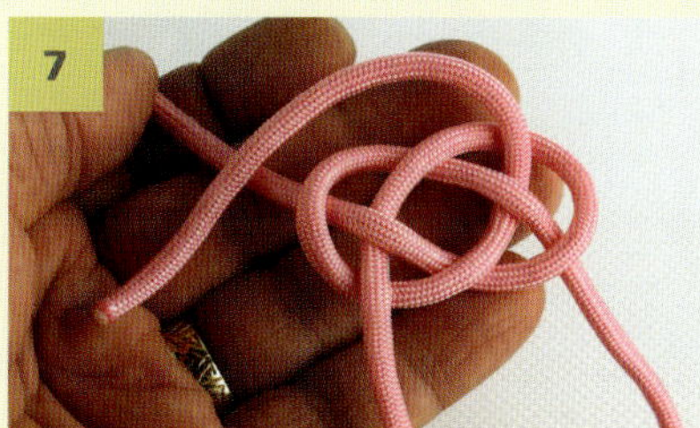

Take the second (upper) working end to the left above the cord.

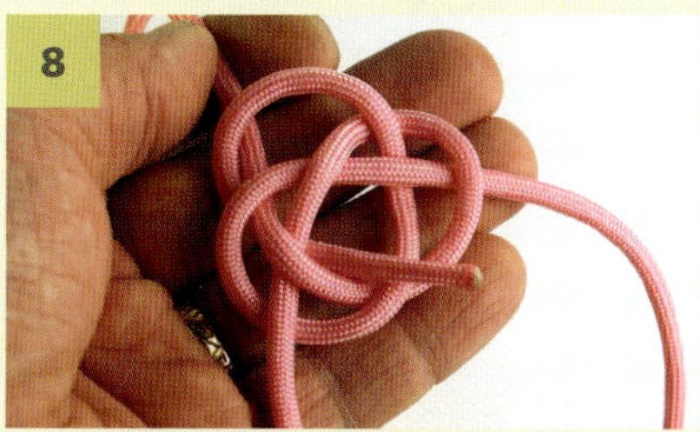

Lead the working end from above through the center of the knot.

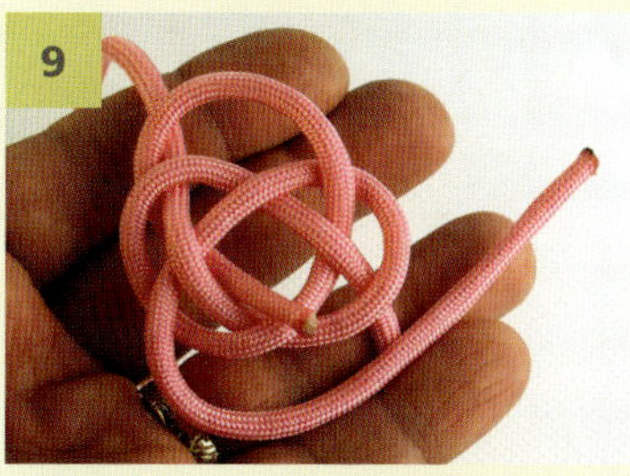

Take the other working end to the left and over the cord going down.

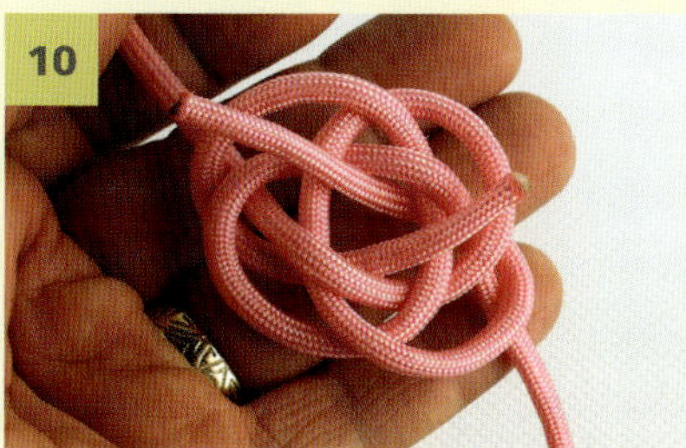

Then the working end goes down underneath the knot and up through the center.

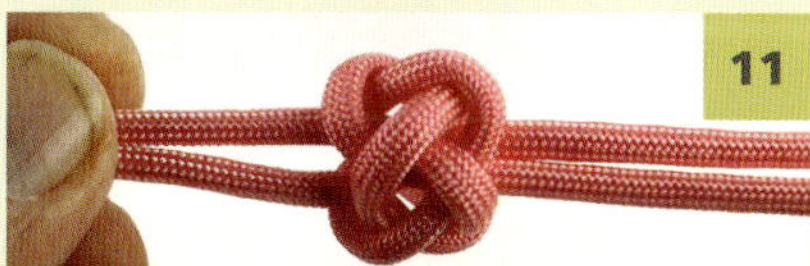

Pull at the knot with the loop on the left side and the working ends on the right.

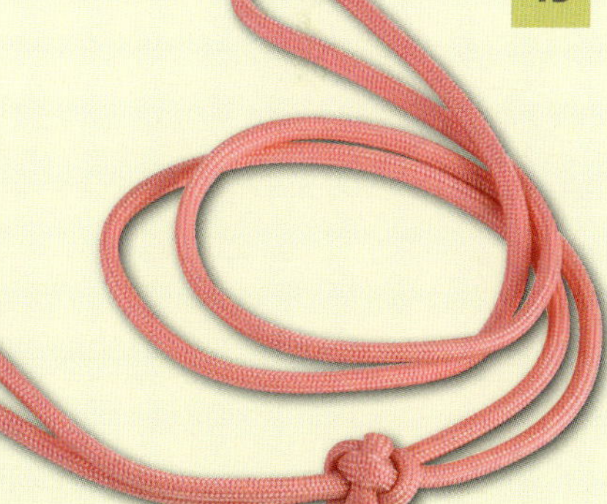

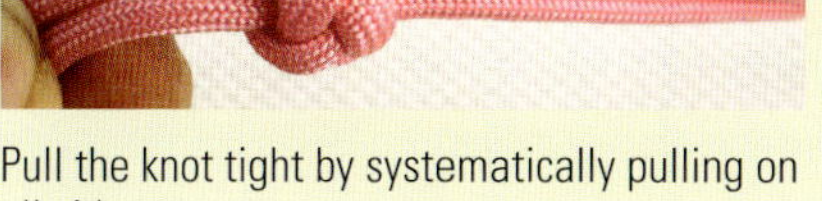

Pull the knot tight by systematically pulling on all sides.

The lanyard knot is finished.

9.2 Skeleton Handles with Round Holes

Skeleton handles with a larger number of holes can also be provided with functional handle wraps. If the knife has a very short handle less than 3 $^{15}/_{16}$ in. (ten centimeters) long, a lanyard knot can enhance the feel of the grip by creating a flexible elongation of the handle.

We equipped two similar knives with a simple but very stable handle wrap. The broader of the knives is 3.2 mm thick and receives a thin wrap of paracord in two colors. The second knife has a slimmer handle; the steel is only 2.2 mm thick. We provide a bit more volume for it by placing a full loop underneath the wrap.

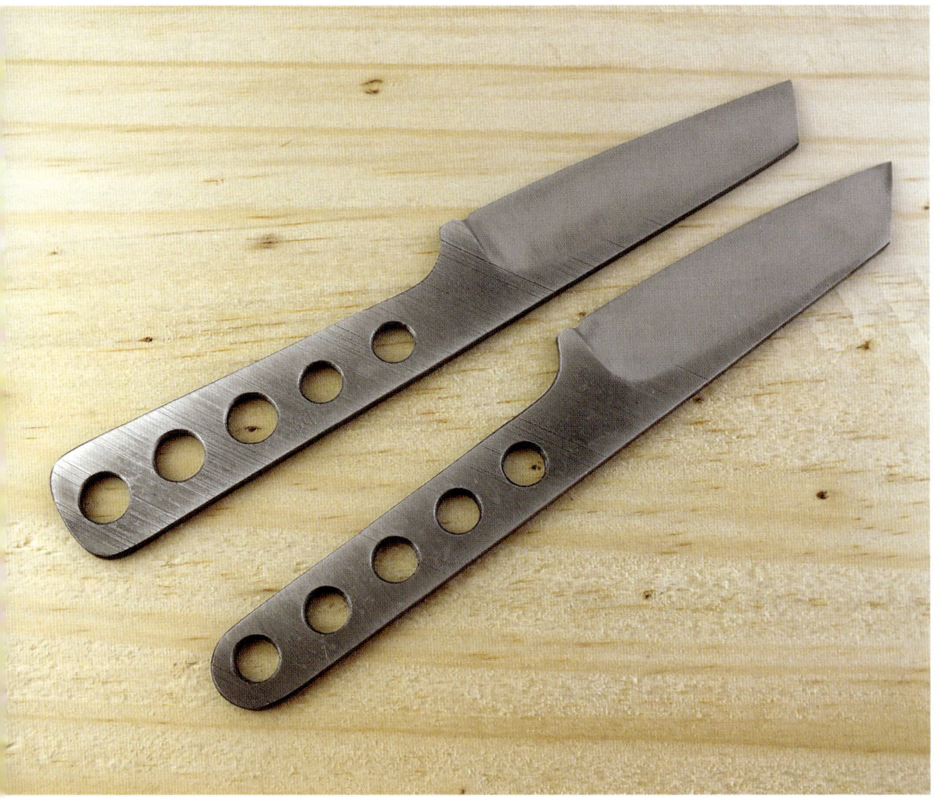

Two similar neck knives with skeleton handles are ready to receive a wrap. Both are D2 steel hardened to 60 HRC.

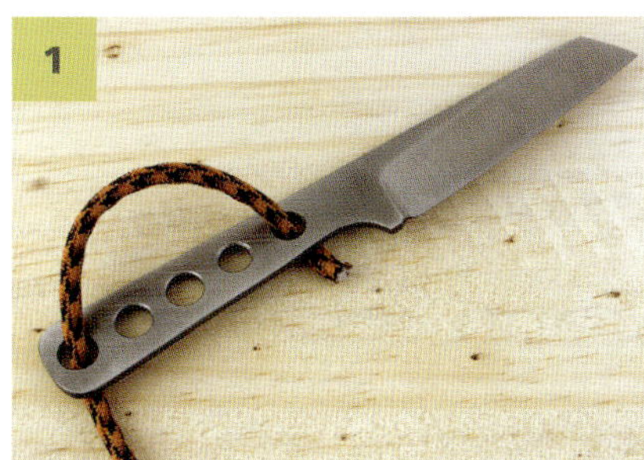

The cord is pulled through the pommel hole and the first hole.

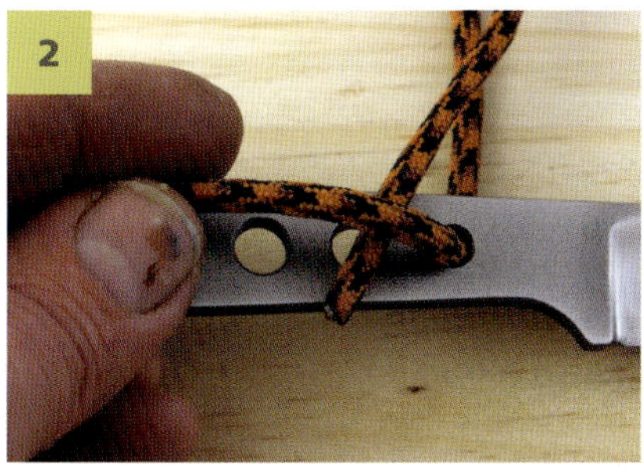

The cord goes through the first hole and comes back to the front and under itself via the backside.

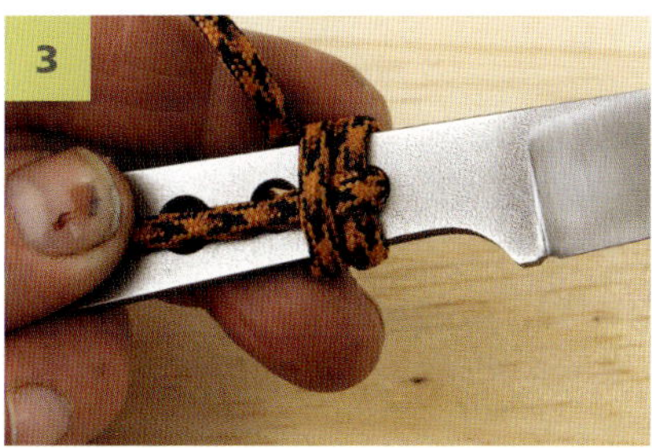

The second round now goes over the cord's standing end. It continues this way for the remaining rounds.

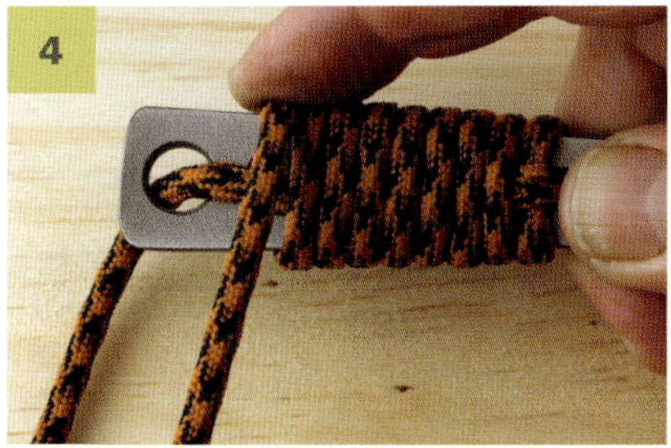

When second to last hole is reached the working end has to be pulled through.

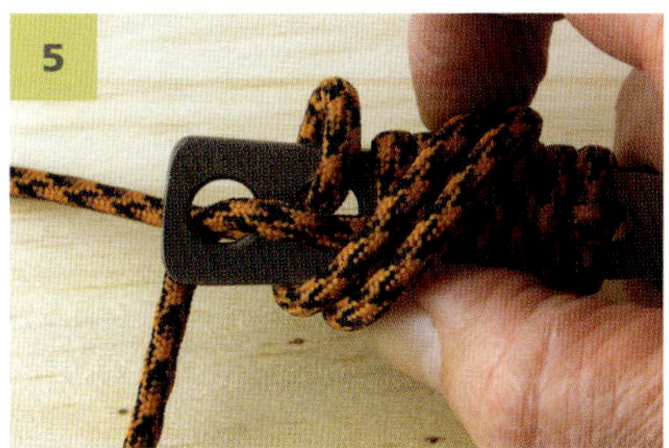

Loosen two or three turns to make space so the working end can be led from below through the second to last hole.

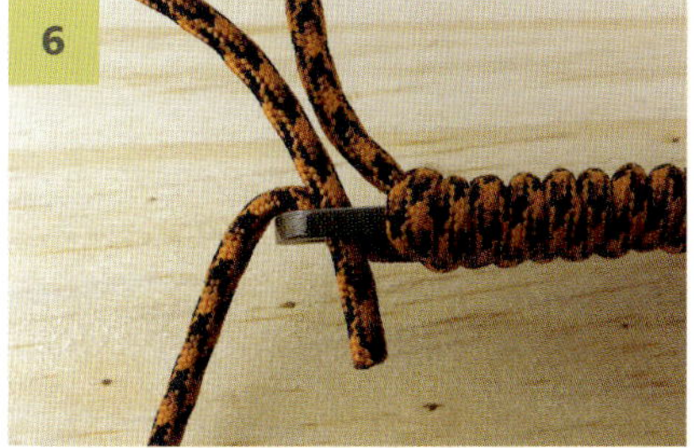

After the cord has been guided through the second to last hole, you pull the loosened turns tight again prior to leading the working end through the pommel hole.

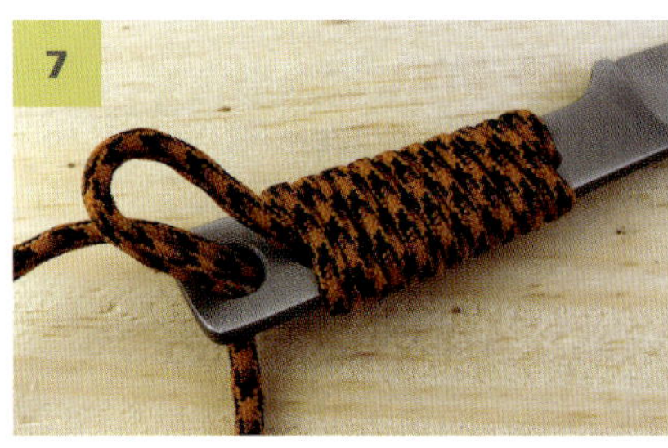

Pull all loose turns tight individually and lead the working end through the pommel hole.

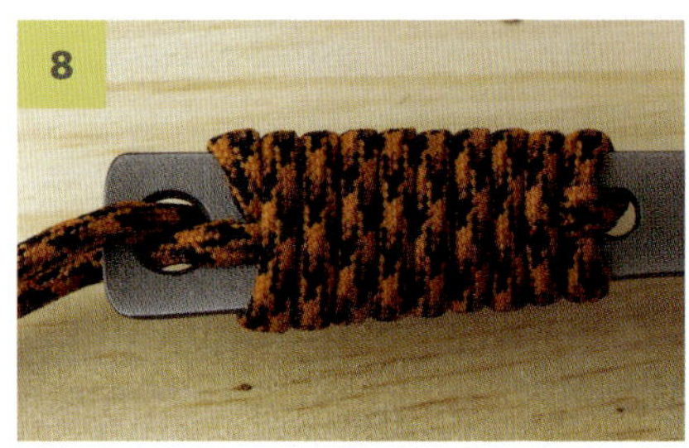

All parts of the cord are pulled tight and straight. The working and standing ends are on opposite sides of the handle.

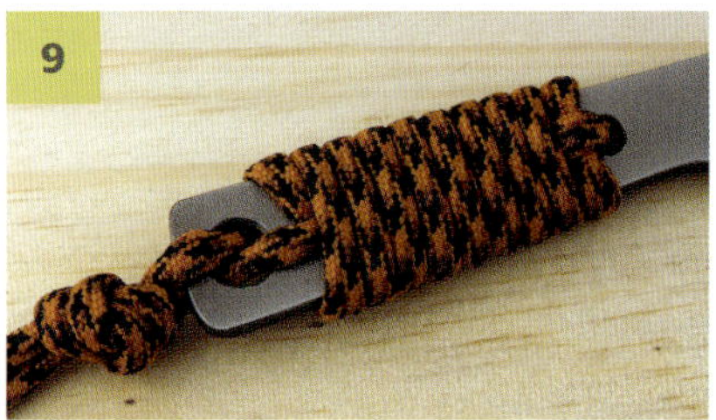

An overhand knot may be sufficient for completion, but . . .

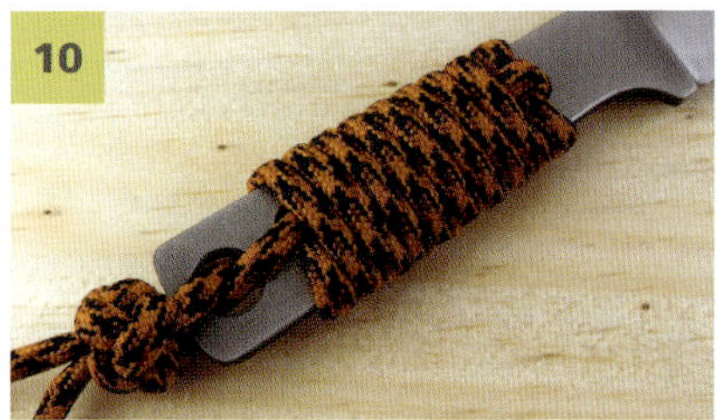

. . . a lanyard knot is so much nicer and effectively extends the handle by 0.7874 in. (two centimeters).

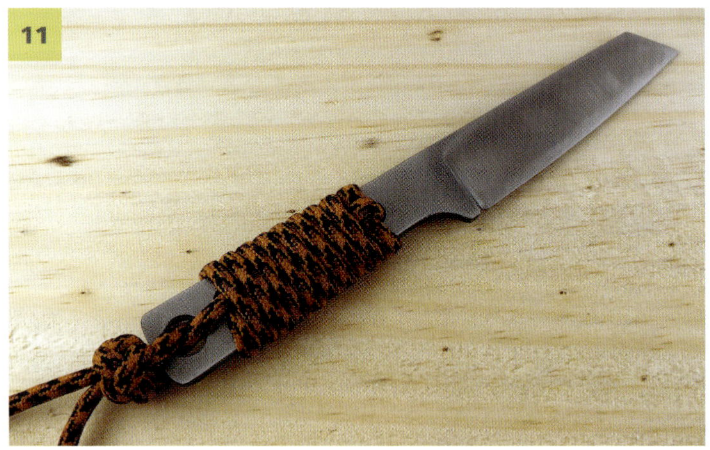

Our Neck Knife is finished.

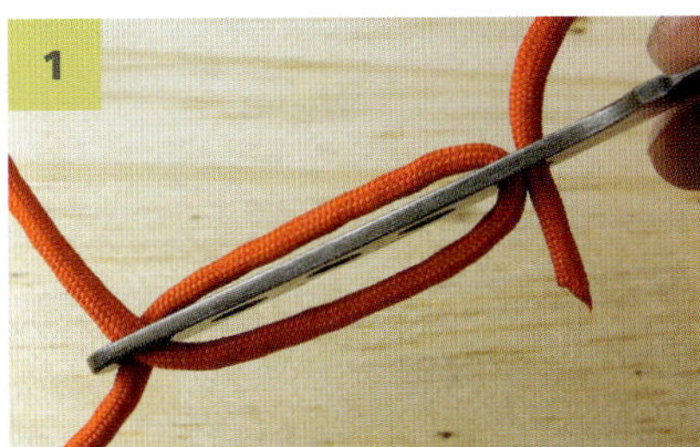

For the slimmer knife, the working end goes two times each through the pommel hole and the front hole.

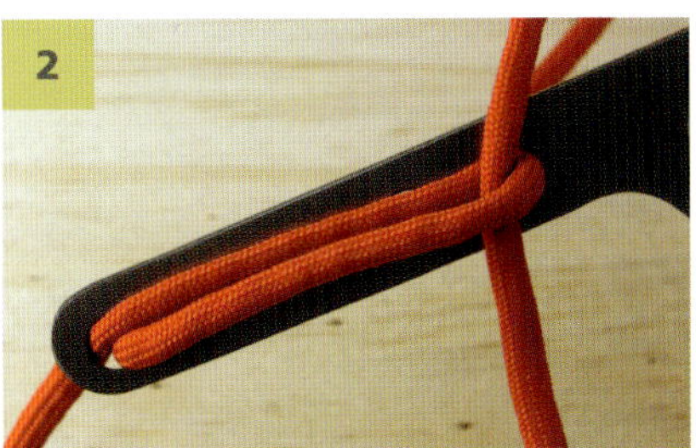

The working end goes back to the other side and is led between the two strands already in position.

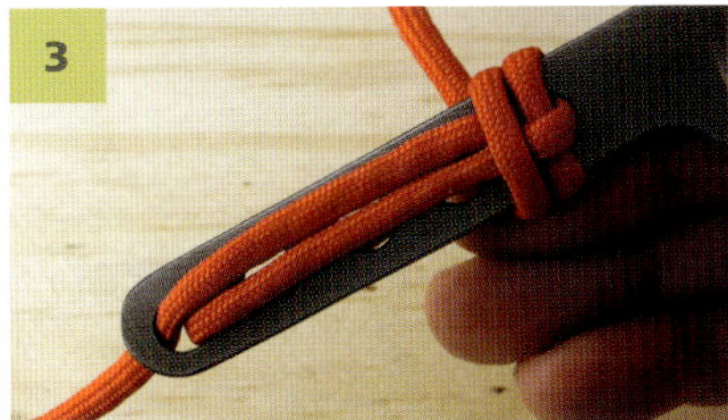

In the second round the cord goes over both strands. This is also the case for all following turns.

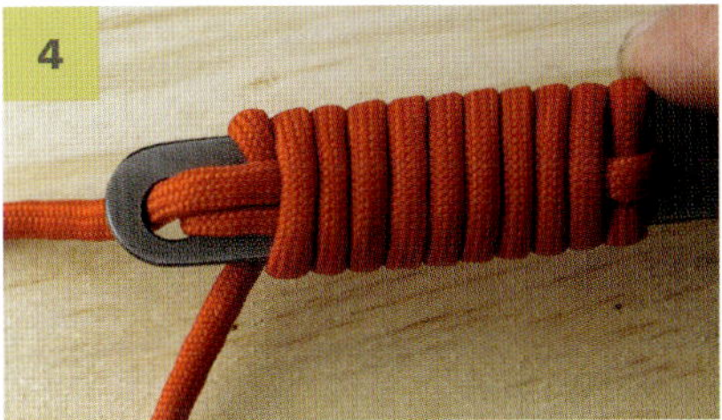

The loops ought to be tight, and the turns uniform.

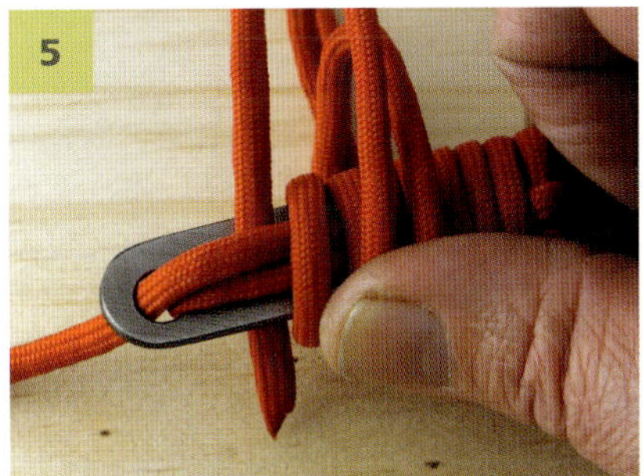

When you reach the second to last hole loosen a few turns to make space for guiding the working end through the hole.

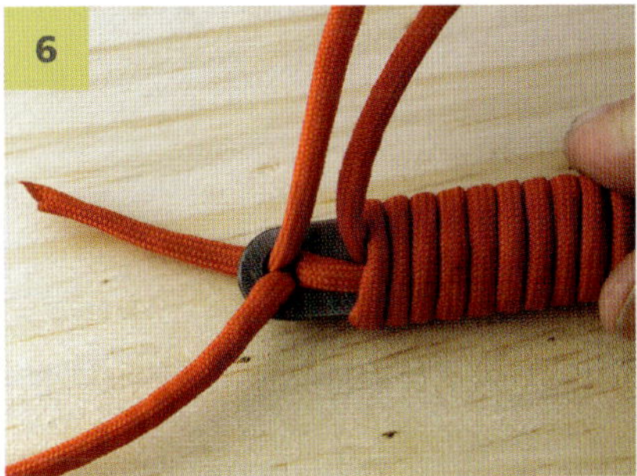

After pulling the turns tight again, the working end goes through the pommel hole—opposite to the standing end.

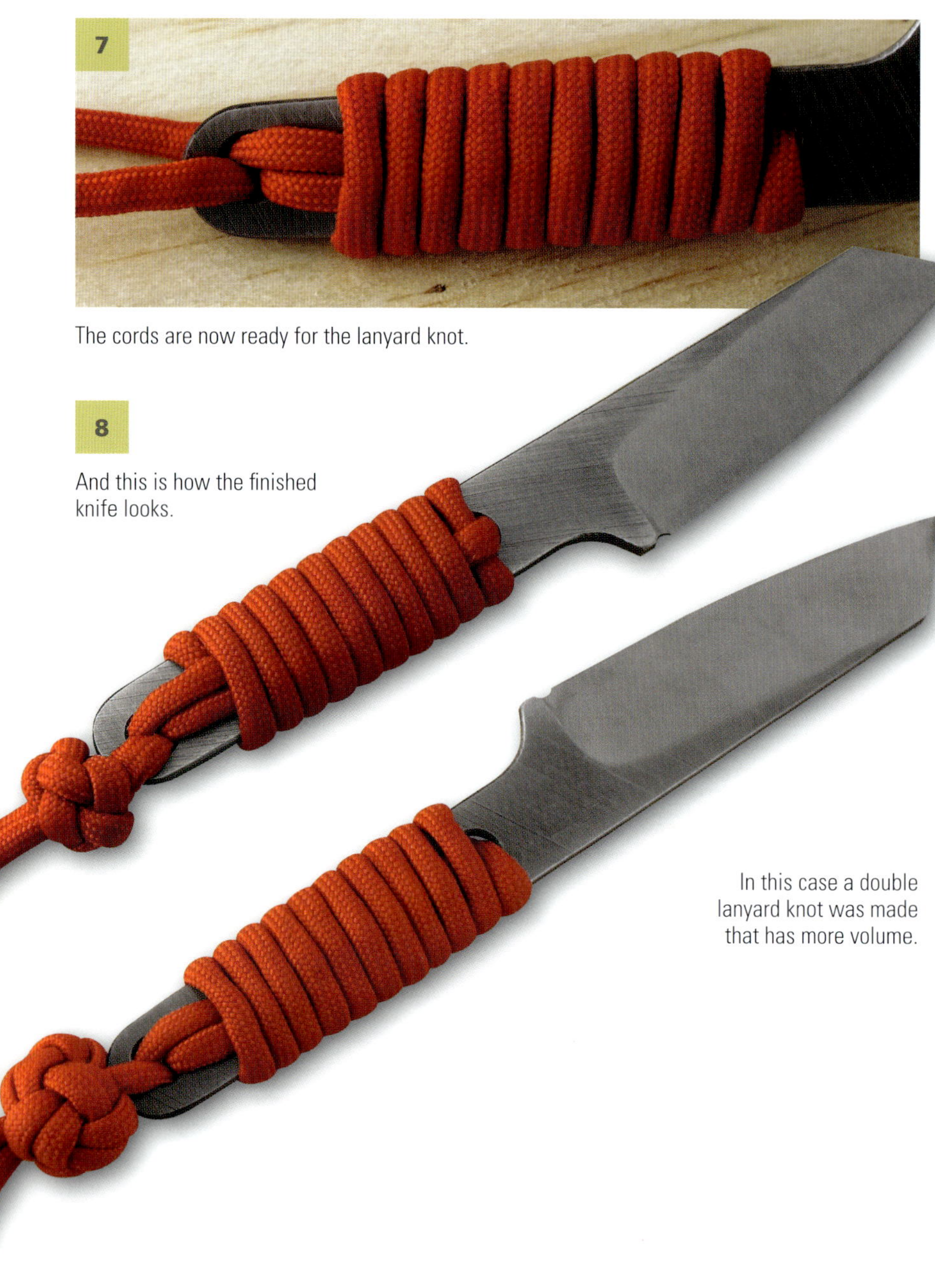

7

The cords are now ready for the lanyard knot.

8

And this is how the finished knife looks.

In this case a double lanyard knot was made that has more volume.

SEALING THE HANDLE WRAP

Japanese *tsukamaki* artists and *koshirae* makers used resin and lacquers to seal handles, wooden parts of handles, and sword sheaths. They used sensitive products such as paper band to create certain types of *ito*. Lacquer stabilizes and protects the handle wrap. We use different resins to stabilize handle wrap: resins with one component as well as some two components.

10.1 Materials

Some knifemakers use wood hardeners. These are products based on acrylic which are used to repair dry, rotten wood. These products penetrate deeply into rotten wood. Often they harden overnight. If a paracord wrap is soaked it hardens the same way as wood.

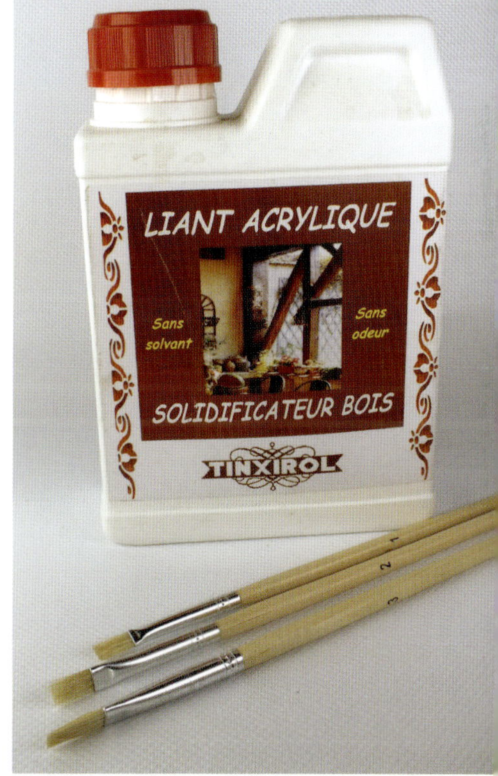

Wood hardener based on acrylic is one of the possibilities for hardening the wrap on a knife handle.

10.1.2 Polyurethane Resin

One-component polyurethane resin can also be used. Two main groups exist: polyurethanes which are marketed as resin or lacquer and polyurethane glues. I prefer working with UV stabilized, crystal clear polyurethane resins. Yellowing due to aging is minimal. If we stabilize handles which have been dyed very dark or are wrapped in black, honey-colored resin looks equally good. For our purposes glues have several disadvantages: they are viscous and do not penetrate as well into the cord, and most polyurethane glues are amber or honey-colored and yellow considerably.

The creation of bubbles can be very pronounced with some products. This happens if too much resin is used. Polyurethane reacts with the moisture in the air to harden. If the cord or wrap are really saturated bubbles are created which do not always burst, and small craters appear in the plastic-like surface after the resin has hardened.

The lifetime of an open polyurethane container is quite restricted. Each time the container is opened a bit of air and moisture gets inside. This moisture reacts with the resin's surface and reduces its shelf life.

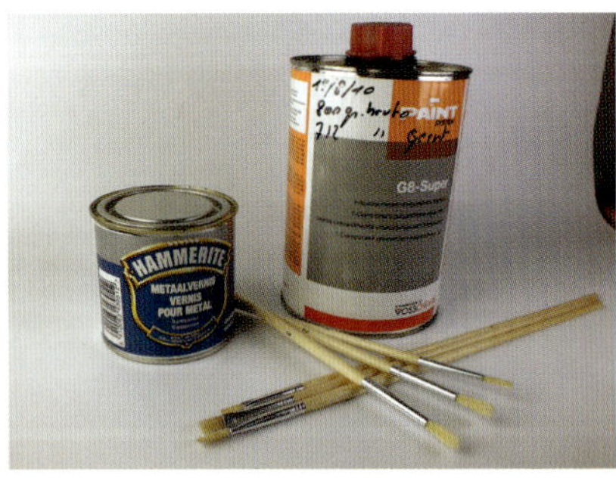

The bigger can contains clear polyurethane resin, while the small can has metal varnish for protecting a knife tang against corrosion.

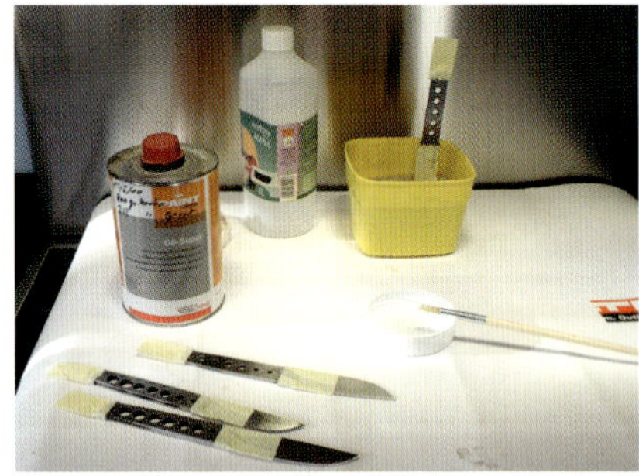

Working with resins underneath the range hood in the kitchen; the hood provides necessary ventilation. Polyurethane resin is used for sealing the handle wrap.

10.1.3 Laminating Resins

Laminating resins are my favorite. These resins were especially developed for the construction of laminates from glass fiber, carbon fiber, and Kevlar. They are always two-component systems. There are polyester systems and epoxy systems.

Polyester resin: Polyester resin is part of the polyester repair sets for cars and is also offered separately in specialized shops. Its lifetime is limited. The mixing ratio quite often is 50-to-1, which is very difficult to create in small amounts. Polyester resin works very well on dark paracord.

Two-component epoxy systems: Two-component epoxy systems are available in a wide variety of types. Resins with low viscosity are best suited for our kind of application. The more fluid the mixed resin is the better it soaks into the paracord.

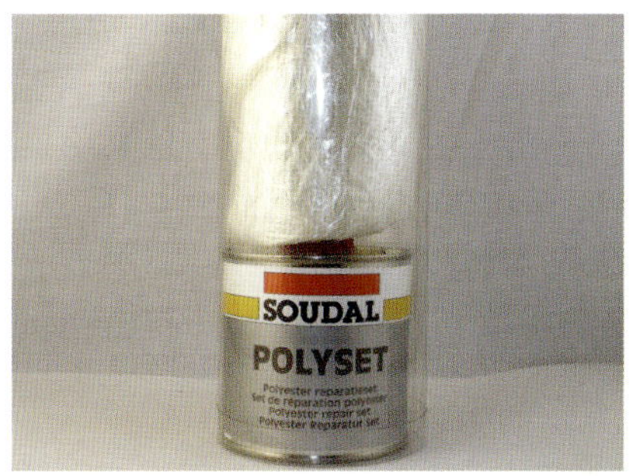

Polyester resin in a car repair set. If you still have one of these sets left test the resin prior to use.

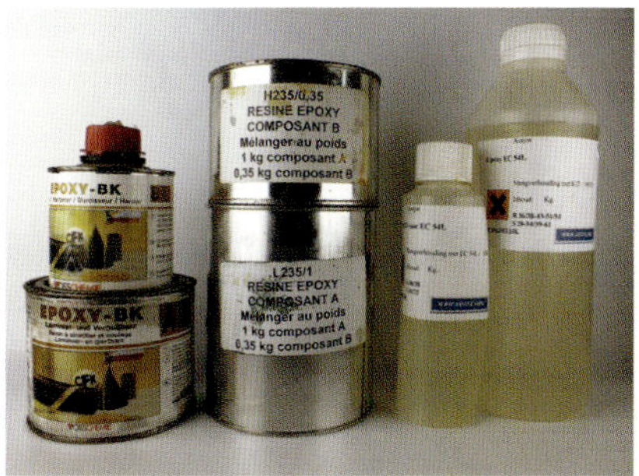

For the systems in the image the mixture ratios are 100:20, 100:35, and 100:60.

Epoxy systems with natural color quite often have a clear resin component and an amber-colored hardener. The resulting synthetic resin ranges from honey- to amber-colored and was not designed for preventing further yellowing. In contrast, UV stabilized crystal clear epoxy systems have transparent resins and hardeners.

NECESSARY TOOLS

- For safety: latex or disposable gloves with high protective factor
- protective goggles
- paintbrush, not too wide
- rag (as lint-free as possible) and acetone (needed to wipe off spills and to remove surplus resin from impregnated windings)
- crepe paper (used to protect the knife and to avoid resinous fingerprints on the blade)
- small syringes (for dosing amounts)
- a small, solvent-proof bowl (to mix the two-component systems; you can also use the lid of glass jars or blister packages)
- wooden popsicle sticks (for stirring the resin)

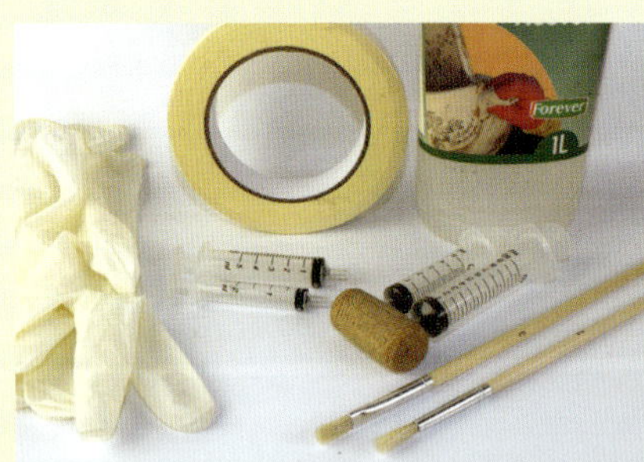

The essential tools for working with resin: syringes for two-component systems, disposable gloves (of latex, butylene, or nitrile), crepe paper and acetone, and paintbrush and rag.

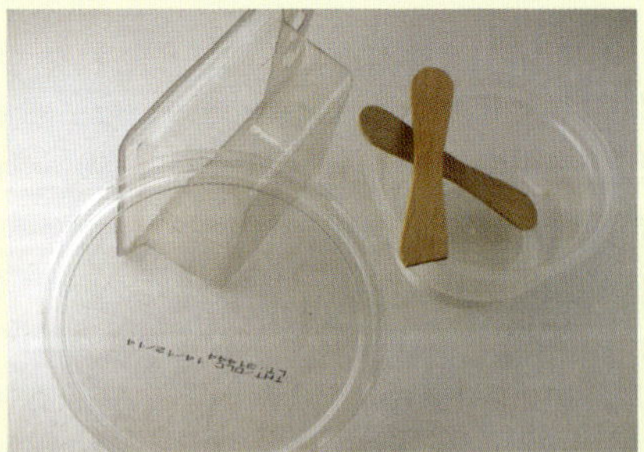

I use blister packages for mixing two-component resins and glues. Popsicle sticks, often with the end cut off, are handy mixers.

Different epoxy systems require different mixing ratios. I use systems with a resin/hardener ratio between 100:20 and 100:60. These mixing ratios are no problem even with the small amounts necessary for knife handles.

Epoxy systems have a much longer lifetime than polyester. I tested and used resins which were several years old by impregnating a test cord or shoelace and giving it enough time to cure. If the test object hardens for twenty-four to forty-eight hours and breaks afterward, the resin is still good. If the object bends after two days then either the resin is no longer good or the mixing ratio is wrong.

For impregnating an average knife handle only 0.34 fl.oz. (10 ml) of resin are needed. Even with kitchen scales having an accuracy of one gram it is difficult to weigh these small amounts correctly. I use small syringes to measure exact amounts of resin and hardener.

10.2 Technique

If all knife parts—with the exception of the handle wrap—are protected by tape we can start impregnating. Make sure the tape adheres to the steel to prevent any seepage.

Hold the knife in your hand at the blade and apply small amounts of resin with a paintbrush. Distribute the resin and allow it to soak the handle wrap. When the cord has absorbed all the resin apply some more. Proceed systematically and return to the already soaked area. Turn the knife around regularly to see whether drops are forming. Distribute surplus resin over the areas which are not saturated or remove the surplus resin with a lint-free cloth.

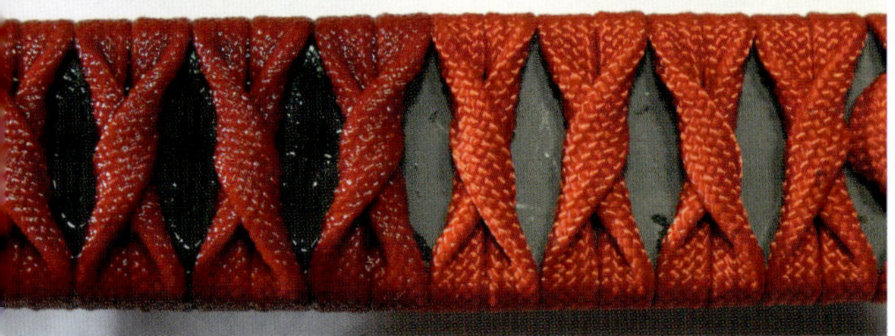

The wrap is halfway impregnated. In this example the diamonds are covered, too, as would be an underlay or flatline. Note the difference in colors.

If you impregnate a handle wrap over ray skin it is best to avoid any resin on the ray skin. If the knife has a layer of cord underneath the upper wrapping it is a good idea to impregnate both layers.

If no more resin is absorbed by the handle wrap, surplus has to be removed with a lint-free rag. Dabbing works fine. Remove the surplus resin from the shiny areas.

If the epoxy resin has not been absorbed well enough a hairdryer may help. The resin should be heated up to about 158°F (70°C). This makes the resin more fluid and the air stream blows it into the smallest gaps of the handle wrap. This technique is especially useful in case you try to completely impregnate a heavy handle wrap. Protect the area behind your working surface because epoxy drops may be blown away from the handle.

If the resin is dry but not completely cured, the adhesive tape can be removed. Now the dry but still soft resin which has seeped underneath the tape can still be removed with a wooden or plastic spatula without scratching the blade. Soft varnish spots, fingerprints, and glue residue from the tape are removed with acetone. Afterward hang up the knife or put it in a sandbox to allow the resin to dry completely.

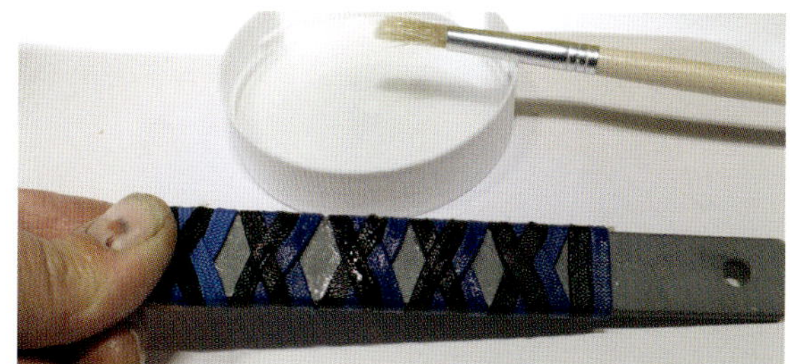

Do not apply too much if you want to impregnate a handle wrap, otherwise the result has a plastic appearance and is shiny wherever too much resin was applied.

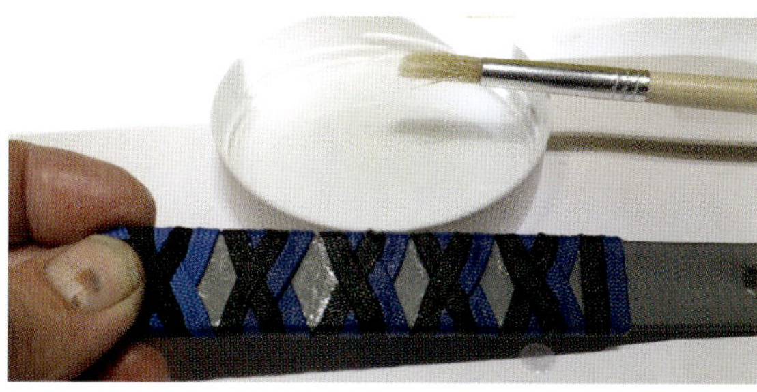

Here the surplus resin was dabbed off the impregnated wrap with a lint-free cloth.

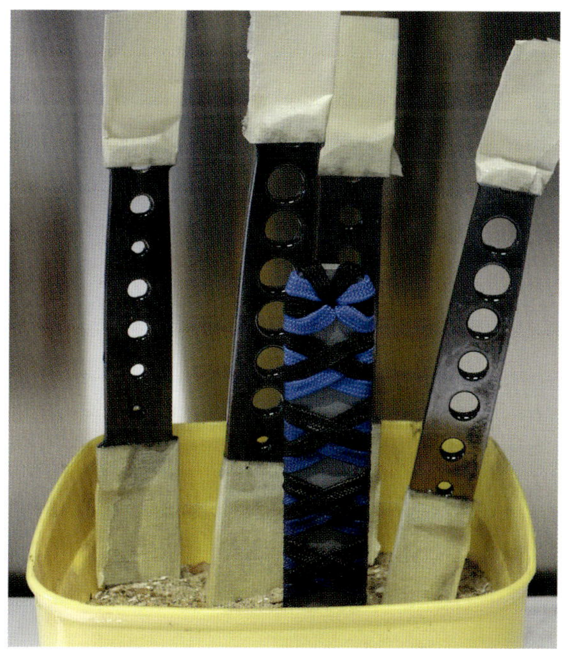

A box with sand is a useful holder for drying.

BIBLIOGRAPHY

These books are standard volumes in the world of knots and ropes:

Ashley, Clifford W. *The Ashley Book of Knots.* New York: Doubleday, 1944.

Buck, Thomas L. *The Art of Tsukamaki.* Charleston Lloyd & Tutle Publishing, Ltd., 2011.

More books delivering insight into the fascinating world of Japanese swords:

Kapp, Leon. *The Craft of the Japanese Sword.* Tokyo: Kodansha International, 1987.

Sinclair, Clive. *Samurai Swords, A Collector's Guide to Japanese Swords.* New York: Chartwell Books Inc., 2009.

Victor, Harris. *Cutting Edge, Japanese Swords in the British Museum.* Boston: Tuttle Publishing, 2004.